13009690

W9-BTI-706

ECONOMICS JOURNALS AND SERIALS

Recent Titles in
Annotated Bibliographies of Serials: A Subject Approach
Series Editor: Norman Frankel

Library and Information Science Journals and Serials: An Analytical Guide
Mary Ann Bowman, Compiler

Philosophy Journals and Serials: An Analytical Guide
Douglas H. Ruben, Compiler

Dentistry Journals and Serials: An Analytical Guide
Aletha A. Kowitz, Compiler

Agricultural and Animal Science Journals and Serials: An Analytical Guide
Richard D. Jensen, Connie Lamb, and Nathan M. Smith, Compilers

Financial Journals and Serials: An Analytical Guide to Accounting, Banking,
Finance, Insurance, and Investment Periodicals
William Fisher, Compiler

ECONOMICS JOURNALS AND SERIALS

An Analytical Guide

Compiled by
Beatrice Sichel
and Werner Sichel

Annotated Bibliographies of Serials: A Subject Approach, Number 5

Greenwood Press
New York • Westport, Connecticut • London

Library of Congress Cataloging-in-Publication Data

Sichel, Beatrice.
  Economics journals and serials.

  (Annotated bibliographies of serials, ISSN 0748-5190 ;
no. 5)
  Includes indexes.
  1. Economics—Periodicals—Bibliography.
2. Economics—Periodicals—Indexes. I. Sichel, Werner.
II. Title. III. Series.
Z7164.E2S49   1986 [HB1]   016.33'005   85-31697
ISBN 0-313-23810-3 (lib. bdg. : alk. paper)

Library of Congress Catalog Card Number: 85-31697
ISBN: 0-313-23810-3
ISSN: 0748-5190

First published in 1986

Greenwood Press, Inc.
88 Post Road West, Westport, Connecticut 06881

Printed in the United States of America

HB
l
SH9
1986

The paper used in this book complies with the
Permanent Paper Standard issued by the National
Information Standards Organization (Z39.48-1984).

10 9 8 7 6 5 4 3 2 1

Contents

Series Foreword

The effects of the "information explosion" have been pronounced in the area of serial publishing. Encouraged by the availability of wordprocessing and computer printing, masses of material have been flowing from the presses. Many of the new journals and serials have proved to be ephemeral, ceasing publication as a result of financial difficulties, mergers, or loss of interest by the editorial staff. However, a large number of useful new publications remain, augmenting older titles, which have undergone important editorial changes. On-line bibliographic databases and electronic publishing have also affected the direction of serial publishing. Despite modern technology, as the amount and type of material in most disciplines have proliferated, subscription prices for serials have been maintaining a steady upward trend while library budgets generally have been declining.

The intent of the ANNOTATED BIBLIOGRAPHIES OF SERIALS: A SUBJECT APPROACH series is to make the task of serial selection and use more systematic through identifying, collecting, annotating, and indexing currently published English-language serials in the major fields of knowledge: social, natural, and applied sciences; humanities; medicine; and business. The scope of the series is worldwide. Serials cited are from the many countries where English is a primary or important language, notably the United States, Canada, the United Kingdom, Ireland, Australia, New Zealand, South Africa, Nigeria, India, Pakistan, and Israel. It is worth noting that journals of international importance from areas of the world where the national language is not widely understood outside the country are often published wholly or in part in English.

Each series volume provides comprehensive coverage of the English-language serials in one subject area with extensively annotated entries for each serial. Titles are included if their primary focus is on the discipline of the particular volume. Many fields overlap, and it is sometimes difficult to decide where the dividing line should be. Occasionally, the same serial will appear in more than one volume, with the annotation pointing to its applicability to the subject area in question. The comprehensiveness of coverage and informative annotations, both exceeding that of other guides to serial literature, will aid librarians in deciding whether a particular title is appropriate for their collections and aid scholars in determining whether the title will be useful for their research.

For the purposes of this series, "serial" is applied to periodicals having a frequency of issue of at least one per year. This includes

journals, publications of professional associations, magazines, selected
newsletters, almanacs, and conference proceedings. Newsletters are
included only if they publish significant articles or have unique
features. The newsletter literature is voluminous, and in many
disciplines would provide enough material for a separate volume. The
same can be said for government documents. Only the most important
government publications are included in these series volumes.

The serial entries are culled from extensive searches of manual and
computerized information sources. Basic indexing and abstracting
services, thorough searches of the most important resource collections,
contacts with library associations and other professional associations
in the pertinent disciplines, all have been utilized by the volume
authors. Wherever possible, volume authors have personally examined
representative issues of each serial and have acquired information
directly from publishers.

Frontmatter contains introductory material, including a "How to Use
this Book" section, a table of abbreviations, and directories of
microform and reprint companies and/or databases as appropriate.
Abbreviations or acronyms for indexes, abstracts, and databases may be
included in the table of abbreviations or, if an extensive list, may be
given in one or more separate tables. Depending on the subject matter,
some volumes are divided into chapters according to classified sub-
disciplines, while others are arranged in one unclassified sequence.
Entries are alphabetical by title. Most volumes will include a geographical index, an index of publishers, and a subject index or classified title index. Depending on the organization of the volume, an
alphabetical title index may be added.

It is hoped that the information provided by ANNOTATED
BIBLIOGRAPHIES OF SERIALS will facilitate access to and help strengthen
bibliographic control of the rapidly growing body of serial titles.

Norman Frankel
Series Editor

Preface

Beatrice Sichel is an academic librarian and Werner Sichel is an academic economist. Our marriage may not have been made in heaven, but for the purpose of writing this book we complemented each other perfectly.

From the beginning, our goal has been to write a reference book that will serve the needs of both librarians and economists. We cater to acquisitions librarians who have to make many difficult choices in a large number of diverse subject areas. We also attend to the requirements of professional economists and persons in allied fields who attempt to maximize their research efficiency. In addition, we recognize that researchers often face the dilemma of selecting the most appropriate journal for publication of their articles. We hope that this volume contributes towards easing all of these tasks.

In recent years, the literature of economics has proliferated as has the literature of other disciplines. It has become increasingly difficult for both economists and librarians to remain informed about the expanding list of serial literature. An additional problem, also not unique to economics, is that the subject has no clearly marked boundaries and is frequently intertwined with other disciplines. Economics is an integral part of business fields such as finance, marketing, and management as well as of political science, sociology, anthropology, history and law. Its substantial use of quantitative methods often obscures the line between it and mathematics, statistics, engineering, and operations research. The serial literature runs the gamut between highly sophisticated theoretical articles aimed at select groups of professional economists and "how to" discussions for the general public. We have attempted to be comprehensive and yet to exclude the large number of serials that primarily focus on a discipline other than economics. Many value judgments had to be made. We examined close to 700 titles out of which we chose 450.

Our selection process consisted of compiling a list of titles gathered from Ulrich's International Periodical Titles, the Journal of Economic Literature, the Social Sciences Index, and the Public Affairs Information Service Bulletin. Questionnaires and requests for sample copies were sent to the editor or publisher of each publication. The majority responded and provided useful information. In addition, we personally examined the titles available in the current periodical collections of Green Library at Stanford University, the Jackson Business Library at Stanford University, the Main Library at University of California at Berkeley, and the Social Sciences Library at the

University of California at Berkeley. In most instances, we also examined the issues of several prior years in order to get a more accurate picture of the scope of the periodical.

Most of the serial titles in this volume are published more than once a year, very few annuals have been included. Most of the titles are published by commercial publishing houses or university presses. We have, however, included a few of the most important U.S. government publications, international organization publications, and newsletters containing information of interest to a wider audience than their own membership. Several entries were selected on the basis of their value as sources of important economic data.

The bibliography consists of an alphabetical listing of titles with an annotation that is both descriptive and evaluative. Each serial entry is arranged in a three part format. The first part supplies concise bibliographic details about the publication. The second part provides a narrative covering scope of content, editorial objectives, authority of contributors, technical level, and when applicable, a comparison to related publications. The final part describes the format of the publication and includes its organization, feature sections, the number of articles, and any special features that we considered might be of particular interest to readers.

We have, to the greatest extent possible, followed the Anglo-American Cataloguing Rules, 2nd ed., in determining the correct title for each entry. Therefore, in most cases the subtitle has not been used to identify the entry, but has been introduced later in the annotation. In the few instances in which the title seemed ambiguous, the subtitle has been included as part of the title.

The bibliography is followed by a brief chapter made up of the major English-language abstracts and indexes that cover the discipline of economics. Each title is fully annotated in the same way as are the entries in the body of the bibliography.

At the end of the book you will find three indexes--a Geographical Index, an Index of Publishers, and a Classified Title Index. The latter classifies titles according to the American Economic Association classification schedule. We used a two tier system of primary subject heading and secondary subject heading. If a serial was devoted to a narrow speciality, it was assigned a secondary subject heading. If a title covered more than one secondary subject field within the same primary field, it was assigned the primary subject heading. Titles that deal with a wide range of topics or that overlap two primary fields were assigned two subject headings and are found under both of them.

It is a pleasure to acknowledge the help we have received in writing this book and preparing it for publication. Our initial thanks go to the editor of this series, Norman Frankel, who invited us to undertake this project and who helped guide it through its several stages. Additional guidance was provided by Marilyn Brownstein, Acquisitions Editor at Greenwood Press, to whom we are also grateful.

Our work on the book began and later was completed at Western Michigan University. However, the major portion of the research and writing was done at Stanford University during a sabbatical year for both of us. Werner Sichel was a Visiting Scholar at the Hoover Institution, Stanford University which generously supported our effort. We wish to thank our colleagues at the Hoover Insitution and especially its director, W. Glenn Campbell and its head of the Domestic Studies Program, Thomas G. Moore. The libraries at Stanford University and to a lesser degree at the University of California, Berkeley became our second home. We have never worked in better library settings or with more cooperative and competent librarians. We wish to single out the staff at Jackson Library, the Business School Library at Stanford University, as those who put up with us and aided us most.

We are grateful for the expert secretarial and typing services provided by Audrey Carlson, Christina Freeman and Linda Sigel at the Hoover Institution and Bonnie Guminski and Becky Ryder at Western Michigan University. Finally, we thank Scott Bassage at the Hoover Institution and Mark Liberacki at Western Michigan University for providing us with invaluable computer assistance.

Beatrice Sichel
Werner Sichel

How to Use this Book

The titles in this book are arranged alphabetically. A geographical index, index of publishers, and classified list of titles provide alternate access.

Each entry has two main parts. The first part lists bibliographic information about the title, while the second is an annotation describing its contents and format.

Part one of the entry includes the following information:

1. An entry number.

2. **NAME:** As it appears on the cover or title page.

3. **DATE FOUNDED:** As provided by the publisher, listed in reference works, or printed in the first volume.

4. **TITLE CHANGE:** Previous titles are listed where relevant, along with date changed when information was provided.

5. **FREQUENCY:** How often the title is published.

6. **PRICE:** Subscription price as provided by publisher or found in reference works, and in currency so listed.

7. **PUBLISHER:** Name and address as provided or found in reference works.

8. **EDITOR:** Name as provided or found in reference works.

9. **ILLUSTRATIONS:** Descriptor used only if title contains illustrations.

10. **INDEX:** Descriptor used only if title has an index.

11. **ADVERTISEMENTS:** Descriptor used only if title contains advertisements.

12. **CIRCULATION:** As provided by publisher or found in reference works.

13. **MANUSCRIPT SELECTION:** How materials are selected for publication.
                               Descriptor used only if information was
                               provided by publisher.

14. **MICROFORMS:** Descriptor used only if available. Abbreviation for
                     vendor listed.*

15. **REPRINTS:** Descriptor used only if available. Abbreviation for
                   vendor listed.*

16. **BOOK REVIEWS:** Descriptor used only if title contains book
                       reviews.

17. **SPECIAL ISSUES:** Descriptor used only if special issues are
                         published.

18. **INDEXED/ABSTRACTED:** Descriptor used only if title is indexed or
                             abstracted. Abbreviations listed for
                             indexes and abstracts.**

19. **DATABASE:** Descriptor used only if title is available on-line.
                   Abbreviations listed for databases.***

20. **TARGET AUDIENCE:** As evaluated by the authors.****

21. **SAMPLE ISSUES:** Descriptor used if sample issues available free to
                        libraries and/or individuals.

*   See Directory of Microform and Reprint Publishers

**   See Table of Abstracts and Indexes

***   See Table of Databases

**** See Table of Abbreviations

Table of Abbreviations

Currency

DFL	Dutch Florin
FIM	Finnish Markka
₤	British Pound
NOK	Norwegian Krone
R	Rand
SEK	Swedish Krona
SFr	Swiss Franc

Frequency of Publication

a	annual
bw	biweekly (every two weeks)
ir	irregular
m	monthly
q	quarterly
sm	semimonthly (twice per month)
w	weekly
2/yr	two issues per year
3/yr	three issues per year
5/yr	five issues per year
6/yr	six issues per year

Target Audience

AC	Academic
GP	General Public
SP	Specialist

Table of Abstracts and Indexes

Table of Databases

ABI	ABI Inform
ACCTIND	ACCOUNTANT'S INDEX
AGRICOLA	AGRICOLA
AGRIS	Agrindex
AMERH	AMERICA: HISTORY AND LIFE
BIOAG	BIOLOGICAL AND AGRICULTURAL INDEX
BIOSIS	BIOSIS PREVIEWS
CAB AB	CAB ABSTRACTS (Commonwealth Agricultural Bureaux Abstracts)
CAS	CHEMICAL ABSTRACTS SERVICE FILES
CBI	CBI (Canadian Business Index)
COMPENDEX	COMPENDEX (Computerized Engineering Index)
ECONAB	FOREIGN TRADE AND ECONOMICS ABSTRACTS
ECONLIT	ECONOMIC LITERATURE INDEX
EMBASE	EMBASE (Exerpta Medica's Abstracting Journals)
HISTAB	HISTORICAL ABSTRACTS
INSPEC	Information Service - Physics, Electrical & Electronics, and Computer & Control Abstracts
LABORDOC	LABORDOC (International Labour Documentation)
LEXIS	LEXIS
LRI	LEGAL RESOURCE INDEX
MATHFILE	MATHFILE
MC	MANAGEMENT CONTENTS
MEDLINE	MEDLINE
NEXIS	NEXIS
PAIS INT	PAIS INTERNATIONAL
PF	PREDICASTS FILES
PSYAB	PSYCHOLOGICAL ABSTRACTS
SOCAB	SOCIOLOGICAL ABSTRACTS
SSI	SOCIAL SCIENCE INDEX

Directory of Microform and Reprint Publishers

BHW   Bell and Howell
Old Mansfield Road
Wooster, OH 44691

DATCO   Data Courier, Inc.
620 South Fifth
Louisville, Kentucky

DAW   Dawson's Back Issues
Folkestone, Kent
CT19 SEE England

ELSEV   Elsevier Sequoia S. A.
P.O. Box 851
CH-1001 Lausanne 1, Switzerland

EPML   E. P. Microform, Ltd.
East Ardsley, Wakefield
West Yorkshire WF3 2AT England

HJM   Harold J. Mason, Inc.
P.O. Box 32363
Phoenix, AZ 85064

INFOII   Infordata International Inc.
175 East Delaware Place, Suite 4602
Chicago, Illinois 606111

ISI   Institute for Scientific Information
3501 Market Street
University City Science Center
Philadelphia, PA 19104

JOHNSON Johnson Reprint Co.
111 Fifth Ave.
New York, NY 10003

JPG   James P. Gains
          University of South Carolina
          College of Business Administration
          Columbia, SC 29208

KR   Kraus Reprint Co.
          Route 100
          Millwood, NY 10546

KRC   Kolossos Rapid Copy
          310 East Washington Street
          Ann Arbor, MI 48104

KTO   K.T.O. Microform
          Route 100
          Millwood, NY 10546

MAR   Maruzen Co., Ltd.
          P.O. Box 5050
          Tokyo International 100-31 Japan

MIC   Micromedia Ltd.
          P.O. Box 502, Station S
          Toronto, Ontario M5J 2L7 Canada

MIM   MIM Microforms International Marketing Co.
          Mawell House, Fairview Park
          Elmsford, NY 10523

NTIS   National Technical Information Service
          5285 Port Royal Road
          Springfield, VA 22161

OPEC   OPEC Secretariat
          Obere Donaustrasse 93
          A-1020 Vienna, Austria

RESREP   Researchco Reprints
          1865 Trinagar
          Delhi -110 035, India

ROTH   Fred B. Rothman
          10368 West Centennial Road
          Littleton, CO 80127

SZ   Swets & Zeitlinger
          Backsets Department
          Heereweg, 347 B
          Lisse, The Netherlands

UMI   University Microfilms International
          300 N. Zeeb Road
          Ann Arbor, MI 48106

UML   University Microfilm Ltd.
           St. John's Road, Tylers Green
           High Wycombe, Bucks HP10 8HR England

UTP   University of Toronto Press
           Periodicals Department
           5201 Dufferin Street
           Downsview, Ontario M3H 5T8 Canada

WMI   World Microfilms, Ltd.
           62 Queens Grove
           London NW8 6ER England

WSH   William S. Hein & Co.
           1285 Main Street
           Buffalo, NY   14209

ECONOMICS JOURNALS AND SERIALS

Bibliography

001.   ABA Banking Journal. DATE FOUNDED: 1908. TITLE CHANGES: Banking;
Journal of the American Bankers Association. (1934-1979), Journal of the
American Bankers Association. (1908-1934). FREQUENCY: m. PRICE: $20/yr.
PUBLISHER: American Bankers Assoc., Simmons-Boardman Publishing Corp.,
P.O. Box 530, Bristol, Connecticut 06010. EDITOR: Lyman B. Coddington.
ILLUSTRATIONS. INDEX. ADVERTISEMENTS. CIRCULATION: 42,000. MANUSCRIPT
SELECTION: Editor. REPRINTS: 1,000 or more, production manager. BOOK
REVIEWS. SPECIAL ISSUES. INDEXED/ABSTRACTED: ABA BankLit, AcctInd, BPI,
BPIA, PAIS. DATABASES: ACCTIND, MC, PAIS INT. TARGET AUDIENCE: SP.
SAMPLE COPIES: Libraries and Individuals.

The ABA Banking Journal is published by the foremost association of
American bankers primarily for the benefit of its members. It offers
practical information to keep its members well-informed about current
banking practices in the United States. Coverage extends to every aspect
of banking and may focus on topics such as education, employees, the
federal reserve system, interest rates, marketing, mortgages, bank
technology and public relations. There are occasional "Special Reports"
which carry four to six articles focused on such topics as productivity
in banking, regional banking trends, or international banking. The
articles are non-technical in nature and do not employ mathematical or
statistical methodologies. They do include data as required. The
articles are written by staff editors, academics, business consultants,
and bank executives.
    A typical issue contains ten to twelve articles, usually two to five
pages in length. Regular features include pending legislation, government regulations, employee relations, investments, regional reports,
banking operations, a newsletter on workshops and publications, and a
calendar of meetings and conferences. Some issues include a "Books for
Bankers" section that contains a few brief unsigned book reviews. There
is an annual index divided into subject, author, and names mentioned in
the articles.

002.   Abstracts of Bulgarian Scientific Literature, Economics and Law.
DATE FOUNDED: 1971. FREQUENCY: q. PUBLISHER: Bulgarian Academy of
Sciences, Scientific Information Center, 1 "7 Noemvri" St., Sofia,
Bulgaria. EDITOR: D. Bradistilov. INDEX. MANUSCRIPT SELECTION: Board of
Editors. TARGET AUDIENCE: AC, SP.

Abstracts of Bulgarian Scientific Literature, Economics and Law is published in its entirety in Russian, the Economics section in English, and the Law section in French. It contains abstracts of articles that originally appeared in Bulgarian. The economic abstracts are classified on a subject basis in fourteen categories: "Political Economy of Socialism...", "Social-Economic Development of ... Bulgaria", "National Economy Planning...", "Management of the National Economy", "Industrial Economy", "Rural Economy", "Transport Economy", "Labour ...", "Home Trade, Prices...", "Economic Integration...with Capitalist and Developing Countries", "Finances and Credit", "Statistics and Accounting", "Political Economy of Contemporary Capitalism and Economic Theories", and "Economy of the Developing Countries".

Each issue contains from seventy-five to ninety-five economic abstracts. Each individual abstract is from one-half to about a page in length. Most are signed, but no affiliation of the abstracts is provided. Some are noted as having been prepared by the author.

003.   Abstracts of Hungarian Economic Literature. DATE FOUNDED: 1971. FREQUENCY: 6/yr. PRICE: $42/yr. PUBLISHER: Hungarian Scientific Council for World Economy, Scientific Information Service, H-1531 Budapest, P.O.B. 36, Hungary. EDITOR: Tamas Felvinczi. INDEX. CIRCULATION: 1,000. MANUSCRIPT SELECTION: Editors. TARGET AUDIENCE: AC,SP.

Abstracts of Hungarian Economic Literature contains English abstracts of selected books and articles on economics and related topics originally written by Hungarian authors. Abstracts are arranged according to subject specialization. Twenty-five categories such as "General Economics", "International Economics", and "Manpower, Labour, and Population" are used. The abstracts are sufficiently long and complete to enable the reader to attain a good understanding of the main ideas and information conveyed in each work.

Each issue is from 225 to 350 pages in length making the average volume about 1,800 pages. Each issue contains from 90 to 140 individual abstracts or in excess of 700 per volume. The average length of an abstract is about two and one-half pages with the range being from one and one-half to seven pages. Each issue begins with a table of contents which makes reference to the abstract number assigned to each book or article abstracted in that issue. Each issue contains an "Index of Authors", a "Geographical Index", and an "Index of Periodicals" for that issue and the last number of each volume offers a cumulative summary index of these three indexes plus the table of contents.

004.   The ACES Bulletin. DATE FOUNDED: 1958. TITLE CHANGES: The ASTE Bulletin (1958-1971). FREQUENCY: q. PRICE: $25/yr. institutions, $10/yr. personal. PUBLISHER: Association for Comparative Economic Studies, Arizona State University, Department of Economics, Tempe, Arizona 85287. EDITOR: Josef C. Brada. INDEX. CIRCULATION: 500. MANUSCRIPT SELECTION: Editor and Referees. MICROFORMS: KR. REPRINTS: Authors. BOOK REVIEWS. INDEXED/ABSTRACTED: InEcA, JEL, PAIS. DATABASES: ECONLIT, PAIS INT. TARGET AUDIENCE: AC,SP. SAMPLE COPIES: Libraries.

The ACES Bulletin is a publication of a professional association of economists whose interests focus on the comparison of planned versus market economies. It includes analytical studies of aspects of the

economies of specific socialist countries. Studies also compare the
economic performance of specific socialist and capitalist countries.
Examples of the former type include articles dealing with sales taxes
and price subsidies in Poland, product quality in the Soviet Union, the
Hungarian clothing industry, and Soviet agriculture. Examples of the
latter type include articles on topics such as wheat yields in socialist
and capitalist systems, distribution of income under capitalism and
market socialism, and economic fluctuations under market and planned
economies. The articles are scholarly in nature and have extensive
references. Most of them are descriptive in style. The authors are
predominantly academic economists affiliated with American universities.
Other contributors include European academics, researchers with UN
agencies or U.S. government agencies, and researchers from Socialist
countries. The ACES Bulletin covers the same subject areas as the
Journal of Comparative Economics but is less technical.
    A typical issue includes four or five full-length articles. Two or
three signed book reviews appear in some issues.

005.   Across the Board; the Conference Board Magazine. DATE FOUNDED:
1939. TITLE CHANGES: Conference Board Record (1939-1976). FREQUENCY:
11/yr. PRICE: $30/yr. PUBLISHER: The Conference Board, Inc., 845 Third
Ave., New York, New York. 10022. EDITOR: Howard H. Muson. ILLUSTRATIONS.
INDEX. ADVERTISEMENTS. CIRCULATION: 40,000. MANUSCRIPT SELECTION:
Editors. REPRINTS: Publisher. BOOK REVIEWS. INDEXED/ABSTRACTED: BPI,
BPIA, DPD, KeyEcS, PAIS, Pred, WorkRelAbstr. DATABASES: ABI, ECONAB, MC,
PAIS INT, PF. TARGET AUDIENCE: GP,SP. SAMPLE COPIES: Libraries and
Individuals.

Across the Board; the Conference Board magazine is a publication aimed
at informing the business community about current trends in business,
economics, domestic and foreign policy, social issues, technology, and
intellectual controversies. According to the magazine's own survey,
almost eighty percent of its readership is composed of high-level
business executives. Recent issues have included articles that deal with
U.S. antitrust laws, advertising, labor relations, and modern economic
thought. The magazine reflects the current trend of multinational
business ventures by including articles about industries and economic
conditions in countries around the world. The articles are non-technical
in nature and understandable to non-economists. Data are included but no
quantitative methodologies are employed. The articles are written by
staff writers, economists, attorneys, and business experts.
    A typical issue contains seven articles, each from five to nine pages
in length, a "Commentary" section which offers opinions on how new
trends may impact on business, and a section containing one or two
signed book reviews of three to four pages each.

006.   Acta Oeconomica. DATE FOUNDED: 1966. TITLE CHANGES: Acta Oeconomica; Academiae Scientiarum Hungaricae (1966-1970). FREQUENCY: 8/yr.
PRICE: $80/yr. PUBLISHER: Akademiai Kiado, H-1051 Budapest, Alkotmany U.
21. Hungary. EDITOR: Tamas Foldi. INDEX. ADVERTISEMENTS. CIRCULATION:
1,000. MANUSCRIPT SELECTION: Editor and Referees. REPRINTS: Authors or
Library of the Institute of Economics of the Hungarian Academy of

Sciences. BOOK REVIEWS. INDEXED/ABSTRACTED: InEcA, IntBibE, JEL, PAIS, WAERSA. DATABASES: CAB AB, ECONLIT, PAIS INT. TARGET AUDIENCE: AC, SP. SAMPLE COPIES: Libraries and Individuals.

Acta Oeconomica, published by the Hungarian Academy of Sciences, provides a forum for presenting Hungarian economic thought to foreign audiences and occasionally offers an exchange of ideas by invited economists from other countries. The articles deal with economic development strategies in Hungary, economic planning in Hungary, production planning in Hungary, planning in other centrally planned economies, international economic cooperation, and East–West trade. Most of the articles are expository in nature with tables of data, but occasionally a theoretical article using mathematical modelling or statistical analysis is included. The authors are predominantly Hungarian economists employed as academics or government planners.

A typical issue contains seven to twelve articles, each ranging from ten to twenty pages in length. Occasional short reviews and comments on already published works are included. Most issues have three to five signed book reviews ranging from two to five pages in length and a "Books Received" section. The latter are predominantly Hungarian with an occasional English language title dealing with Eastern European economies. Articles in recent volumes are in English with abstracts in Russian.

007.   The AEI Economist. DATE FOUNDED: 1977. FREQUENCY: m. PRICE: $24/yr. PUBLISHER: American Enterprise Institute for Public Policy Research, 1150 17th St. N.W. Washington, D.C. 20036. EDITORS: Herbert Stein, A. Willis Robertson. INDEX. CIRCULATION: 9,000. MANUSCRIPT SELECTION: Editors. REPRINTS: Publisher. INDEXED/ABSTRACTED: PAIS, Pred. DATABASES: PAIS INT, PF. TARGET AUDIENCE: AC, GP, SP. SAMPLE COPIES: Libraries and Individuals.

The AEI Economist is "intended to clarify current issues of economic policy in an objective manner". Not all economists would agree that the AEI's fairly conservative outlook is entirely objective, but most would characterize this publication as one that offers interesting and responsible viewpoints on current economic policy issues. Representative commentaries from recent issues are Herbert Stein's "Reflections on Foreign Economic Policy" and Arthur L. Broida's "Why the Inflation Outlook is Worrisome". Occasionally a research article pertaining to a current economic policy issue such as John W. Kendrick's "Productivity and Cost Prospects for 1984-1985" is included. From time to time this periodical will reproduce an important report such as the February 1984 "Policy Statement by the Committee to Fight Inflation". Most articles and reports are non-technical and can be understood by non-economists. They are devoid of mathematical and statistical methodologies. The AEI Economist is edited and in large part written by Herbert Stein, former member of the President's Council of Economic Advisers and Senior Fellow of the American Enterprise Institute and A. Willis Robertson, Professor of Economics at the University of Virginia.

Each issue is only from eight to twelve pages in length and features a single article that takes up most of the space. Notices of books published by AEI are included.

008.   Africa; an International Business, Economic and Political
Monthly. DATE FOUNDED: 1971. FREQUENCY: m. PRICE: Ŀ15/yr. PUBLISHER:
Africa Journal Ltd; London, Kirkman House, 54a Tottenham Court Road,
London WIP OBT, England. EDITOR: Okey Nwankwo. ILLUSTRATIONS. ADVERTISE-
MENTS. MANUSCRIPT SELECTION: Editor. BOOK REVIEWS. SPECIAL ISSUES.
INDEXED/ABSTRACTED: IntBibE, SSI, WAERSA. DATABASES: CAB AB. TARGET
AUDIENCE: GP.

Africa; an International Business, Economic, and Political Monthly is a
magazine, equivalent to Time or Newsweek in the United States, that
covers events in African countries. The main focus of this magazine is
current economic and political events of Africa. A typical issue
includes articles dealing with world-wide current events influencing
African nations, political events of Africa, blacks living outside of
Africa (in the U.S. and in the Caribbean), black artists, and a section
on business and economics. In recent issues the latter has included
articles on topics such as price changes for palm oil, implications of a
World Bank report, agricultural economics in Tanzania, Nigeria's
problems with the International Monetary Fund, tobacco production, and
West African banking concerns. Articles are non-technical and written in
an narrative style. The authors are staff journalists and no information
regarding their training or level of expertise is provided.
     Each issue contains a large number of short articles. Photographs
accompany articles. Most issues provide a list of currency exchange
rates between African countries and England, the U.S., France, and West
Germany. Recent issues have included a column, "African Miscellany" that
reports on specific business projects in various African countries.
Several brief signed book reviews appear in each issue.

009.   Africa Development/Afrique et Developpement. DATE FOUNDED: 1976.
FREQUENCY: q. PRICE $35/yr. institutions, $30/yr. personal. PUBLISHER:
Council for the Development of Economic and Social Research in Africa,
B.P. 3304, Dakar,Senegal. EDITOR: Abdalla S. Brijra. INDEX. MANUSCRIPT
SELECTION: Editor. BOOK REVIEWS. INDEXED/ABSTRACTED: WAERSA. DATABASES:
CAB AB. TARGET AUDIENCE: AC,SP.

Africa Development/Afrique et Developpement is published by a research
institute supported by a number of African governments and some private
foundations outside of Africa. This publication emphasizes articles
dealing with economic development in Africa but also includes a few
articles that focus on social or political concerns of African countries. Most of the articles are expository in nature but a few contain a
statistical analysis of their research findings. The authors are
academics at universities in Nigeria, Ghana, Libya, Senegal, and Zaire.
Occasionally, contributions are made by African specialists associated
with universities or research institutes outside of Africa.
     A typical issue includes six articles ranging in length from twelve
to twenty-six pages. Articles are published in French or English but
more than half of them appear in English. Some issues include a "Documents" section which publishes reports and recommendations issued by
international organizations such as the World Bank or African organizations such as the Organization of African Unity. Occasionally, one or
two lengthy signed book reviews are included. Many issues have a section
named "Focus on Research and Training Institutes" that reports on a

specific research institute in an African country and describes its organization objectives, and current research projects. A list of "Books Received" appears in each issue.

010.   African Economic History. DATE FOUNDED: 1976. FREQUENCY: a. PRICE: $10/yr. institutions, $15/yr. personal. PUBLISHER: African Studies Program, University of Wisconsin - Madison, 1454 Van Hise, 1220 Linden Dr., Madison, Wisconsin 53706. EDITORS: Margaret Jean Hay, Allan Isaacman, Paul Lovejoy. ILLUSTRATIONS. ADVERTISEMENTS. CIRCULATION: 500. MANUSCRIPT SELECTION: Editors and Referees. REPRINTS: Publisher. BOOK REVIEWS. SPECIAL ISSUES. TARGET AUDIENCE: AC, SP.

African Economic History is a publication that offers historical research studies on the African economy. It "focuses on recent economic change in Africa as well as the colonial and pre-colonial economic history of the continent." Articles deal with a variety of topics in economic history including colonial economic policies, the labor system in specific African countries, development of European plantations in Africa, histories of specific firms, cotton cultivation in Chad, and salt trade in the Sahara region in the middle ages. The articles are scholarly in nature with extensive footnotes. Quantitative methodologies are not employed. The authors and the members of the editorial board are academics from universities all over the world.
    A typical issue contains six or seven articles, each ranging from ten to thirty pages in length. Some articles are based on theses or presentations made at conferences. Articles appear in French or English although the predominant language of the journal is English. Most issues contain an extensive book review section. The section presents as many as twenty-five signed reviews, each two to four pages in length. Occasionally, an entire issue is devoted to a single topic under the guidance of a guest editor such as the 1983 issue on "Business Empires in Equatorial Africa".

Afrique et Developpement. see Africa Development/Afrique et Developpement.

011.   Agricultural Economics Research. DATE FOUNDED: 1949. FREQUENCY: q. PRICE: $8.50/yr. PUBLISHER: United States Department of Agriculture, Economic Research Service, GHI Bldg., 500 12th St., S.W. Washington, D.C. 20250. EDITORS: Judith Latham, Gerald Schluter. ILLUSTRATIONS. CIRCULATION: 2,500. MANUSCRIPT SELECTION: Editors and Referees. MICRO-FORMS: CIS, InfoII. REPRINTS: Editors. BOOK REVIEWS. INDEXED/ABSTRACTED: BioAb, BioAg, ChemAb, InEcA, IntBibE, JEL, PAIS, WAERSA. DATABASES: BIOAG, BIOSIS, CAB AB, CAS, ECONLIT, PAIS INT. TARGET AUDIENCE: AC,SP. SAMPLE COPIES: Libraries and Individuals.

Agricultural Economics Research is a government publication which focuses on research topics in agricultural economics. Specifically, this journal publishes articles "(1) reporting results of economic research supported by U.S.D.A., (2) describing new methods or critically evaluating old methods still in use, and (3) describing new or expanded areas of research or statistics." Most of the papers report on empirical studies conducted with U.S. data. The articles are of a scholarly nature and frequently use mathematics and statistics in their discussion. The writers are staff economists with the Economic Research Service, the Statistical Reporting Service, or academics reporting on U.S.D.A. supported research projects. This journal is entirely different from the Economic Research Service's Agricultural Outlook which offers facts and figures and a general agricultural economic forecast, but not the scholarly research articles found in Agricultural Economics Research.

A typical issue begins with "In this Issue" a section in which the editor provides an introduction to the articles. It is followed by three to five research articles that average about ten pages each, two to three carefully prepared signed book reviews, and up to three research reviews which are "shorter, sometimes less rigorous pieces with the same subject areas as the major articles."

012.   Agricultural Outlook. DATE FOUNDED: 1975. MERGER: Demand and Price Situation (1950-1975) and Farm Income Situation (1966-1975). FREQUENCY: 11/yr. PRICE: $31/yr. PUBLISHER: United States Department of Agriculture, Economic Research Service, GHI Bldg., 500 12th St., S.W., Washington D.C. 20250. EDITOR: W. Keith Scearce. ILLUSTRATIONS. INDEX. ADVERTISEMENTS. CIRCULATION: 7,000. MANUSCRIPT SELECTION: Editor. MICROFORMS: NTIS. REPRINTS: NTIS. SPECIAL ISSUES. INDEXED/ABSTRACTED: Pred, WAERSA. DATABASES: CAB AB, PF. TARGET AUDIENCE: SP. SAMPLE COPIES: Libraries and Individuals.

Agricultural Outlook is a government publication that provides information on the economic outlook and current situation for the food and fiber industries of both the U.S. and other countries. This title primarily supplies data on agricultural economics and is of interest to agribusiness managers, researchers, commodity traders, and financial institution officers. The articles are descriptive in style and incorporate charts, graphs, and tables of data. Although they are not signed, they are written by staff writers with backgrounds in economics. Agricultural Outlook supplies the facts and figures which are frequently utilized by writers for the scholarly and research-oriented Agricultural Economics Research, a publication by the same agency.

Each issue follows a set format. The first part presents articles distributed among four sections -- 1) "Agricultural Economy" dealing with acreage and prices of various commodities, 2) "World Agriculture and Trade" dealing with production and prices of various commodities on the world market, 3) "Farm Income Update" and 4) "General Economy." These articles vary from three to ten pages in length. The second part contains data for statistical indicators such as farm income, farm prices, livestock production, crop production, general economic data, and world agricultural production. Many issues include a two to four page "Special Report" discussing an aspect of world agriculture and its implication for U.S. agriculture.

013.   Akron Business and Economic Review. DATE FOUNDED: 1970. TITLE CHANGES: University of Akron Business Review, (Spring, 1970-Winter, 1970). FREQUENCY:q. PRICE: $6/yr. PUBLISHER: University of Akron, Bureau of Business Research, 302 E. Buchtel Ave., Akron, Ohio 44325. EDITOR: J. Daniel Williams. INDEX. CIRCULATION: 2,000. MANUSCRIPT SELECTION: Editorial Review Board. MICROFORMS: UMI. REPRINTS: Publisher. INDEXED/

ABSTRACTED: AcctInd, BPIA, PAIS, WorkRelAbstr. DATABASES: ABI, ACCTIND, MC, PAIS INT. TARGET AUDIENCE: AC,SP. SAMPLE COPIES: Libraries and Individuals.

The Akron Business and Economics Review is a business school publication that aims to serve as a forum for contemporary problems and applied research in the fields of business and economics. Emphasis is placed on business practices and research methodology. It is not parochial in coverage which sets it apart from the majority of business school publications. Most articles focus on problems and issues in economics, accounting, finance, insurance, management, and marketing. Recent issues have included several articles dealing with government regulation of industry. Occasionally this journal publishes a philosophically based economics article such as "Some Implications of Talmudic Business Ethics" and "Two Views of the Future of the Entrepreneur." Articles vary as to technical content. Some are written in a narrative style while others employ mathematical and statistical methodologies. The authors are predominantly academics in departments of economics and business, but occasionally an article is written by a qualified professional not in academe. Compared to other business school publications, its scope and level most resembles St. John's University's Review of Business.

A typical issue contains from six to ten articles averaging about nine pages in length. A brief summary of each article appears at the beginning of each issue.

014.   Alaska Review of Social and Economic Conditions. DATE FOUNDED: 1964. TITLE CHANGES: Alaska Review of Business and Economic Conditions (1964-1977). FREQUENCY: q. PRICE: Free. PUBLISHER: University of Alaska, Institute of Social and Economic Research, 707A St., Suite 206, Anchorage, Alaska 99501. EDITOR: Ronald Crowe. ILUSTRATIONS. CIRCULATION: 2,200. MANUSCRIPT SELECTION: Editor. INDEXED/ABSTRACTED: PAIS. DATABASES: PAIS INT. TARGET AUDIENCE: GP. SAMPLE COPIES: Libraries and Individuals.

Alaska Review of Social and Economic Conditions is the publication of an interdisciplinary social science research institute. It focuses on the state of Alaska as it is "intended to provide information on the State's social and economic conditions to the general public and to government officials, businessmen, civic leaders, research institutions and other interested agencies." Recent issues have dealt with the following topics: "Effects of Oil Revenues on State Aid to Local Governments in Alaska", "The Struggle for an Alaska Gas Pipeline: What Went Wrong?", "Alaska's Economy Since Statehood...", "Use in Alaska of North Slope Natural Gas", "Sustainable Spending Levels from Alaska State Revenues", "The Demand for Labor in Alaska", "Federal Revenues and Spending in Alaska", "Changes in the Well-being of Alaska Natives...", and "Prices and Incomes - Alaska and the U.S. ...". Articles are sufficiently non-technical for non-economists to understand. They are expository in style but typically include a great deal of data which are presented in tables and charts. The authors are predominantly academic economists and research associates with the Institute. Occasionally an economist with a consulting firm makes a contribution.

Each issue is from fifteen to forty pages in length which is entirely taken up by a single article.

015.   American Business Law Journal. DATE FOUNDED: 1963. FREQUENCY: q.
PRICE: $12/yr. PUBLISHER: Western Newspaper Publishing Co., 537 East
Ohio St., Indianapolis, Indiana 46204. EDITOR: Art Wolfe. INDEX.
ADVERTISEMENTS. CIRCULATION: 1,900. MANUSCRIPT SELECTION: Editors.
REPRINTS: Authors. BOOK REVIEWS. INDEXED/ABSTRACTED: AcctInd, BPI, BPIA,
ILP. DATABASES:ACCTIND, MC. TARGET AUDIENCE: AC. SAMPLE COPIES: Li-
braries.

The American Business Law Journal is the official publication of the
American Business Law Association, a professional association of
academics trained in business, economics and law who teach in the field
of business law outside of law schools. This journal does not advocate a
particular viewpoint and is aimed primarily at a readership interested
in commercial and corporate law. Most articles analyze and offer
interpretations of important legal decisions. Economists and economics
students would be particularly interested in the many articles pertaining to labor and antitrust law. Articles are analytical in nature and
written in a narrative style. The authors are predominantly academics
who teach either business law or economics. Most hold law degrees.
Occasionally practicing attorneys also make contributions.
    A typical issue includes an editorial dealing with Association
concerns or legal viewpoints, three articles averaging about thirty
pages in length, and two or three comments of ten to twenty pages each
that deal with specific legal decisions. Approximately half of the
issues include a book review section containing one to four signed
reviews.

016.   American Demographics. DATE FOUNDED: 1979. FREQUENCY: m. PRICE:
$48/yr. PUBLISHER: Peter Francese, American Demographics, Inc., P.O. Box
68, Ithaca, New York 14850. EDITOR: Cheryl Russell. ILLUSTRATIONS.
INDEX. ADVERTISEMENTS. CIRCULATION: 7,500. MANUSCRIPT SELECTION: Editor.
MICROFORMS: UMI. REPRINTS: Publisher. BOOK REVIEWS. INDEXED/ABSTRACTED:
BPI, BPIA, PAIS, Pred. DATABASES: MC, PAIS INT, PF. TARGET AUDIENCE: GP.
SP. SAMPLE COPIES: Libraries and Individuals.

American Demographics is a publication of Dow Jones and Company, Inc. It
is aimed at market researchers and government planners as well as a
general audience. It analyzes census data and describes demographic
trends in lay terms. Population statistics are turned into information
that non-statisticians can use. Some titles of representative articles
appearing in recent issues are "The Growing Gap Between Blacks",
"Occupational Winners and Losers", and "The New Census Bureau Projections". The authors include research analysts, business and government
demographers, academics, and members of the editorial staff.
    Each issue includes two to four feature articles which average about
five pages in length. In addition, each issue contains six to eight
shorter articles distributed among various departments such as "Demographic Forecasts" - a forecast of a particular segment of the population, "Close Up" - an analysis of the population of a state or region,
"Micro-computing" - a report on software programs geared towards
demographic studies, and "Demogaffes" - a humorous essay about events
occuring 100 or 200 years ago. From one to three signed book reviews
appear in each issue. The December issue features the "Special Research

Section." This section provides a geographic ranking of variables such
as family type, income, housing, education, and other data valuable to
business firms. All information is taken from the U.S. Census Data.

017.   American Economic Review. DATE FOUNDED: 1911. FREQUENCY: q.
PRICE: $100/yr. institutions (includes sub. to JEL), personal: with
membership. PUBLISHER: American Economic Association, 1313 21st Ave.
South, Nashville, Tennessee 37212. EDITOR: Robert Clower. ILLUSTRATIONS.
INDEX. ADVERTISEMENTS. CIRCULATION: 25,000. MANUSCRIPT SELECTION:
Referees and Board of Editors. MICROFORMS: KTO, UMI. REPRINTS: Authors.
SPECIAL ISSUES: Papers and Proceedings of Annual Meeting, May. INDEXED/
ABSTRACTED: AcctInd, BPI, BPIA, InEcA, IntBibE, JEL, KeyEcS, PAIS, SSI,
WAERSA, WorkRelAbstr. DATABASES: ACCTIND, CAB AB, ECONAB, ECONLIT, PAIS
INT, SSI. TARGET AUDIENCE: AC,SP.

The American Economic Review, the most prestigious journal in the field
of economics, is published by the American Economic Association which is
the primary organization of professional economists. Coverage extends to
all areas of the field of economics. Microeconomic problems have been
addresssed somewhat more often than macroeconomic problems. Papers
normally follow the format of an introduction which presents a hypothesis, a formal presentation of a model (usually in mathematical form), a
presentation describing the empirical data and providing the test
results, and conclusions. Most articles are technical in nature and
employ modern quantitative methodologies. The authors are professional
economists from academic institutions, government agencies, and research
institutes. The majority are American, but contributions are also made
by European, Canadian, Israeli, and Australian economists.
    A typical issue contains about fifteen articles, each ranging from
ten to twenty pages in length and a section of "shorter papers" containing ten to fifteen articles ranging from two to ten pages in length.
Comments from readers dealing with papers in previous issues are
included. A "notes" section announces future conferences and career
changes of members. The December issue lists Doctoral Degrees (with
dissertation titles) conferred during the previous academic year.

018.   The American Economist. DATE FOUNDED: 1958. FREQUENCY: 2/yr.
PRICE: $12/yr. institutions, $8/yr. personal. PUBLISHER: Omicron Delta
Epsilon, Department of Economics, P.O. Drawer AS, University of Alabama,
University, Alabama 35486. EDITOR: Michael Szenberg. ILLUSTRATIONS.
INDEX. ADVERTISEMENTS. CIRCULATION: 9,000. MANUSCRIPT SELECTION:
Referees. MICROFORMS: UMI. BOOK REVIEWS. INDEXED/ABSTRACTED: BPI, InEcA,
IntBibE, JEL, WorkRelAbstr. DATABASES: ECONLIT. TARGET AUDIENCE: AC,SP.

The American Economist is a journal published by an international
student honor society in economics. It covers a full range of areas in
economics, both in microeconomics and macroeconomics. Generally the
articles are quite theoretical in nature and present mathematical
models, use statistical analysis, and provide empirical evidence for
support. Representative topics include economic tools for pollution
control, economic incentives for safety regulations, the relationship of
corporate accounting strategy to market structure, and profit maximiza-
tion of regulated firms. The authors are predominantly academics with
occasional contributions from graduate students.

A typical issue includes ten to fifteen articles averaging six pages in length. Some issues also contain brief notes, comments on previously published articles, and authors' replies. A book review section contains from two to six fairly substantial signed reviews. This journal offers some special features not found in other titles. Course reading lists in various areas of economics, obtained from professors at prestigious universities, appear occasionally. A recently added section is "Life Philosophy" - the credo of prominent economists. The Fall 1983 issue includes "the life philosophy of Paul Samuelson". The Chapter Roll of the Society, along with the name of each faculty advisor, appears in the Spring issue.

019.   American Journal of Agricultural Economics. DATE FOUNDED: 1919. TITLE CHANGES: Journal of Farm Economics (1919-1967). FREQUENCY: 5/yr. PRICE: $35/yr. institutions, $25/yr. personal. PUBLISHER: Heffernan Press, 35 New St., Worcester, Massachusetts 01604. EDITORS: Gordon C. Rausser, Richard E. Just. ILLUSTRATIONS. INDEX. ADVERTISEMENTS. CIRCULA-TION: 7,000. MANUSCRIPT SELECTION: Editors and Referees. REPRINTS: AAEA Business Office, Dept. of Economics, Iowa State University, Ames, IA 50011. BOOK REVIEWS. INDEXED/ABSTRACTED: BPI, BPIA, InEcA, IntBibE, JEL, WAERSA. DATABASES: CAB AB, ECONLIT, MC. TARGET AUDIENCE: AC,SP.

American Journal of Agricultural Economics is the official journal of the American Agricultural Economics Association, the national profes-sional organization of agricultural economists. The purpose of the Journal is to "provide a forum for creative and scholarly work in agricultural economics." Articles concentrate on the economics of agriculture, natural resources, and rural development. The primary focus is on the U.S., but occasionally articles deal with agriculture in other countries. Representative topics include the relationship between land and commodity prices, the relationship between farm size and community development, rangeland management, and international trade in agricul-tural commodities. All articles are research papers and present theoret-ical models and supporting data. Most of the authors are economists affiliated with American universities or researchers with Federal government agencies. It is similar in subject coverage and technical level to the Northeastern Journal of Agricultural and Resource Economics but has a broader geographic scope.
    A typical issue contains a dozen articles, each about ten pages in length. A dozen shorter "notes", each about five pages in length, present discussions on methodological points or comments on previously published papers. Each issue also includes ten signed book reviews. The December issue consists of the proceedings from the annual meeting of the American Agricultural Economics Association. Announcements of the recipients of AAEA fellowship awards and reports on other Association business also appears in that issue.

020.   American Journal of Economics and Sociology. DATE FOUNDED: 1941. FREQUENCY: q. PRICE: $10/yr. PUBLISHER: The Journal, 5 East 44th St., New York, New York 10017. EDITOR: Will Lissner. ILLUSTRATIONS. INDEX. CIRCULATION: 2,500. MANUSCRIPT SELECTION: Editor. MICROFORMS: BHW, KR, UMI. INDEXED/ABSTRACTED: InEcA, IntBibE, JEL, KeyEcS, PAIS, PsyAb,

SocAb, SSI, WAERSA, WorkRelAbstr. DATABASES: CAB AB, ECONAB, ECONLIT, PAIS INT, PSYAB, SOCAB, SSI. TARGET AUDIENCE: AC. SAMPLE COPIES: Libraries and Individuals.

The American Journal of Economics and Sociology is published with grants from the Francis Neilson Fund and the Robert Schalkenbach Foundation. The Journal's stated goal is to serve as a forum for "constructive synthesis in the social sciences" and to publish the results of inter-disciplinary research in the solution of basic problems of democratic capitalism. It is the opinion of the editorial board that "economic, social, and political problems can be solved through the application of scientific method and philosophical inquiry." This title focuses on social reform in a broad sense. Although articles concentrate on economics, the areas of history, geography, political science, sociol-ogy, anthropology, and philosophy are included. Economics articles often focus on development and tax issues. The viewpoints of Thorstein Veblen and Henry George are frequently featured. Articles often reflect institutionalist economic thought and present viewpoints that are unconventional and outside the mainstream of contemporary economics. Most articles are expository in style but occasionally a paper utilizes a mathematical model. Authors are predominantly academics, but some are employed by government agencies or research institutes.

A typical issue includes nine articles, averaging twelve pages in length. Interspersed among the full length articles are short notes encompassing a variety of items such as announcments of new reference books, excerpts from research reports and speeches, news about li-braries, annotations of new books, and biographical sketches.

Analyse de Politiques. see Canadian Public Policy/Analyse de Politiques.

021.   The Annals of Regional Science. DATE FOUNDED: 1967. FREQUENCY: 3/yr. PRICE: $22/yr. PUBLISHER: Western Washington University, Dept. of Economics, Bellingham, Washington 98225. EDITOR: Michael K. Mischaikow. ILLUSTRATIONS. INDEX. CIRCULATION: 1,300. MANUSCRIPT SELECTION: Editor and Referees. BOOK REVIEWS. INDEXED/ABSTRACTED: PAIS. DATABASES: PAIS INT. TARGET AUDIENCE: AC, SP.

The Annals of Regional Science, subtitled a Journal of Urban, Regional, and Environmental Research and Policy, is a scholarly journal aimed at offering the reader "the results of recent research ranging over resource management, location of economic activities, regional and urban planning, transportation, and environment quality." Annals is guided by an international editorial committee and publishes research studies conducted in countries all over the world, although studies conducted in the U.S. predominate. Most of the articles are applied research studies, but occasionally a theoretical paper is included. Some representative topics in recent issues are residential location behavior in Seoul, settlement patterns in U.S. rural areas, and analysis of freight charges in the U.S. Articles are usually quite quantitative in nature and make substantial use of mathematics and statistics. The authors, predomi-nantly American economists, are affiliated with academic institutions or federal government agencies. The Annals of Regional Science offers more applied research than the Journal of Regional Science which emphasizes theoretical studies.

A typical issue includes five to seven articles, ranging from ten to twenty pages in length. Some issues have a "Communications" section which includes shorter comments and replies to comments. Each issue contains an extensive book review section. The twenty-five to thirty signed reviews cover books dealing with a broad range of subjects.

022.   The Antitrust Bulletin. DATE FOUNDED: 1955. FREQUENCY: q. PRICE: $60/yr. institutions, $30/yr. personal. PUBLISHER: Federal Legal Publications, Inc., 157 Chambers St., New York, New York 10007. EDITOR: William J. Curran III. INDEX. ADVERTISEMENTS. CIRCULATION: 2,000. MANUSCRIPT SELECTION: Editor-in-Chief. MICROFORMS: UMI. REPRINTS: Publisher. BOOK REVIEWS. SPECIAL ISSUES. INDEXED/ABSTRACTED: BPIA, CLI, ILP, InEcA, IntBibE, JEL, PAIS. DATABASES: ECONLIT, MC, PAIS INT. TARGET AUDIENCE: AC,SP.

The Antitrust Bulletin is a leading journal in the antitrust law – industrial organization field. The subtitle displayed on the cover, "The Journal of American and Foreign Antitrust and Trade Regulation" accurately describes the scope of the articles which deal with legal decisions, their interpretations, their implementation, and their policy implications. Most articles are expository in style and can be understood by readers having minimum proficiency in mathematical and econometric methodology. The authors are practicing attorneys, industrial organization economists and professors of law. The Antitrust Bulletin is similar in scope of coverage to the Antitrust Law and Economics Review.
    A typical issue contains six articles, each from twenty to fifty pages in length. They are arranged in three categories -- Domestic Antitrust, Foreign Antitrust, and Economics. Occasional issues are devoted to a particular topic and may include texts of official documents along with statements made by authorities in the U.S. Department of Justice or the Federal Trade Commission. A special issue may also be devoted to publishing the proceedings of a major antitrust conference. For example, the Spring 1984 issue contains the papers and discussions presented at the Tenth Anniversary meeting of the Economic Policy Office of the Antitrust Division of the U.S. Department of Justice. Two signed book reviews appear in most issues.

023.   Antitrust Law and Economics Review. DATE FOUNDED: 1967. MERGER: Antitrust and Macroeconomics Review (1978). FREQUENCY: q. PRICE: $67.50/yr. PUBLISHER: ALER, Inc., Beach P.O. Box 3532, Vero Beach, Florida 32960. EDITOR: Charles E. Mueller. ILLUSTRATIONS. MANUSCRIPT SELECTION: Editor. BOOK REVIEWS. INDEXED/ABSTRACTED: BPI, BPIA, ILP, PAIS. DATABASES: MC, PAIS, INT. TARGET AUDIENCE: AC,SP.

The Antitrust Law and Economics Review is a "public interest" journal that deals with policy issues in the antitrust/industrial organization area of economics. It sees its mission as an "intellectual brokerage operation" with the supply side being industrial organization economists and the demand side being the policymaking - legal fraternity made up of judges, lawyers, Congressmen, and agency officials plus their advisers. Representative topics covered in this journal are merger policy, predatory pricing practices, the use of retail price maintenance, entry barriers, economic concentration, product differentiation, and the relationship between oligopoly and inflation. Articles deal with

technical concepts in a narrative form. Articles include data but avoid
mathematics and statistical methodologies. In this regard this journal
deviates greatly from most others in the field such as the Review of
industrial Organization, the Journal of Industrial Economics and the
Journal of Law and Economics. It most resembles the Antitrust Bulletin.
The authors are predominantly academic economists (including those
temporarily with the antitrust agencies); the rest being lawyers or
social scientists with extensive economics backgrounds.

Each issue begins with a six to eight page editorial discussing a
specific antitrust or industrial organization topic. Most issues contain
about five articles which range from ten to forty pages in length. A few
issues include a "Who's Who in Antitrust Economics" which consists of
biographical sketches of economists in the field. These and other issues
sometimes feature lengthy interviews with such economists.

024.   Applied Economics. DATE FOUNDED: 1969. FREQUENCY: 6/yr. PRICE:
$102/yr. PUBLISHER: Chapman and Hall, 11 New Fetter Lane, London, EC4P
4EE, England. EDITOR: Maurice Peston. INDEX. ADVERTISEMENTS. CIRCULA-
TION: 1,000. MANUSCRIPT SELECTION: Editor and Referees. INDEXED/
ABSTRACTED: BPIA, InEcA, IntBibE, JEL, WAERSA. DATABASES: CAB AB,
ECONLIT, MC. TARGET AUDIENCE: AC, SP. SAMPLE COPIES: Libraries.

Applied Economics is a British journal of high repute. Its primary
purpose "is to encourage the application of economic analysis to
specific problems in both the private and the public sector." It aims at
fostering quantitative studies "the results of which promise to be of
use in the practical field and help to bring economic theory nearer the
realities of life." The articles address a broad range of problems and
are both microeconomic and macroeconomic in nature. They emphasize
economic conditions in the U.K., the U.S., or British Commonwealth
countries, but recent issues included articles examining problems in
such countries as Taiwan, Italy, and Belgium. Representative topics
include portfolio behavior of pension funds in the U.S., fiscal policy
in the U.K., the market for teachers in British Columbia, and a comparative analysis of political approaches to smoking control. The articles
are scholarly research studies employing fairly sophisticated mathematical, statistical or operations research techniques. Each article
typically presents a model which is applied to a particular problem.
Conclusions are drawn on the basis of the empirical results obtained.
Most of the authors are professional economists affiliated with universities in the U.K., the U.S., or British Commonwealth Countries.

Each issue contains from ten to twelve full length articles. These
range in length from five to twenty pages.

025.   The Arbitration Journal. DATE FOUNDED: 1937. TITLE CHANGES: The
Arbitration Journal (New Series) (1946-). FREQUENCY: q. PRICE: $30/yr.
PUBLISHER: American Arbitration Association, 140 West 51st St., New
York, New York 10020. EDITOR: Charlotte Gold. ILLUSTRATIONS. INDEX.
MANUSCRIPT SELECTION: Editor. BOOK REVIEWS. INDEXED/ABSTRACTED: BPI,
BPIA, ILP, PAIS, WorkRelAbstr. DATABASES: MC, PAIS INT. TARGET AUDIENCE:
SP.

The Arbitration Journal is the official publication of an association of
professional arbitrators, lawyers, and industrial relations experts. The

Association promotes the belief that dispute resolution can be accomplished better by arbitration than through litigation in the courts. The journal offers articles dealing with arbitration of labor-management disputes, family disputes, public sector employee disputes, and patent disputes. Other articles report on the use of medical evidence in labor disputes, strike misconduct cases, and religious practice grievances. Arbitration decisions made in foreign countries are included occasionally. The articles are discriptive in nature and may be illustrated with photographs. The authors are lawyers, labor arbitrators, or professors of business, economics, or industrial relations.

A typical issue includes six to eight articles, each five to ten pages in length. Regular features are an "Editorial" by the president of the Association, an "Opinion Page" of short commentaries by professional arbitrators, a "Review of Court Decisions" section covering recent cases and "Letters to the Editor". Four or five signed book reviews appear in each issue. A selected list of recent acquisitions by the Association's library is included at the back of each issue.

026.   AREUEA Journal. DATE FOUNDED: 1973. TITLE CHANGES: American Real Estate and Urban Economics Association Journal (1973-1977). FREQUENCY: q. PRICE: $30/yr. PUBLISHER: American Real Estate and Urban Economics Association, P.O. Box 39114, Washington D.C. 20016. EDITORS: James B. Kau, C.F. Sirmans. ILLUSTRATIONS. INDEX. ADVERTISEMENTS. CIRCULATION: 1,000. MANUSCRIPT SELECTION: Editorial Review Board and selected reviewers. MICROFORMS: UMI. REPRINTS: JPG. SPECIAL ISSUES. INDEXED/ABSTRACTED: BPI, InEcA, JEL, SSI. DATABASES: ABI, ECONLIT, SSI. TARGET AUDIENCE: AC,SP. SAMPLE COPIES: Libraries and Individuals.

The AREUEA Journal, subtitled Journal of the American Real Estate and Urban Economics Association, focuses on "research and scholarly studies of current and emerging real estate and urban issues." Its intent is "to facilitate communications among members of the academic research community and practicing professionals ...and to provide a forum for research on a range of topics." Articles deal with topics such as housing prices, real estate values, land development, mortgage lending, rent control, and interest rates. The emphasis is frequently on the empirical and on the methodology that is used to find results. Most of the articles offer sophisticated mathematical and/or statistical analyses. The authors are professors of economics or business administration at American universities. The AREUEA Journal is comparable in technical level and subject scope to Journal of Urban Economics.

A typical issue includes six or seven articles, ranging from six to twenty-four pages in length. A special issue devoted to a single topic appears annually. Examples of recent topics are "Report of the President's Commission on Housing" and "An Economic Analysis of Settlement Costs." Announcement of the AREUEA program to be presented at the Allied Social Sciences Association Annual Meeting in December appear in either the summer or fall issue.

027.   Arizona Business. DATE FOUNDED: 1954. TITLE CHANGES: Arizona Business Bulletin. (1954-1972). FREQUENCY: q. PRICE: Free to Arizona residents. PUBLISHER: Arizona State University, Bureau of Business and Economic Research, College of Business Administration, Tempe, Arizona 85287. EDITOR: Mary K. Wery. INDEX. CIRCULATION: 5,300. MANUSCRIPT

SELECTION: Editor and Advisory Committee. MICROFORMS: UMI. INDEXED/
ABSTRACTED: BPIA, PAIS, PersManageAbstr. DATABASES: MC, PAIS INT. TARGET
AUDIENCE: AC, GP, SP. SAMPLE COPIES: Libraries and Individuals.

Arizona Business is a business school publication that concentrates on
business and economics topics of particular concern to its home state.
This journal has a double mission: 1) to publish articles that reflect
the research and thoughts of academics teaching in the areas of business
and economics and 2) to publish articles and data that reflect the
business conditions of the state of Arizona. Most of the articles in the
first category are written by Arizona State University faculty members
and may or may not deal with an Arizona related topic. Articles in the
second category are exclusively authored by Arizona State University
faculty or the Bureau of Business and Economic Research staff. Most
articles are non-technical in nature, but do include a considerable
amount of data. Arizona Business's parochial interest and the level of
its articles resemble the majority of business school publications.
    Each issue begins with an introductory "Report to the Reader." This
is typically followed by about three articles, each from five to eight
pages in length. Each issue includes articles on the "Arizona Business
Scene" and "A Survey of Arizona Business Conditions." Most issues
include data, short narratives, and/or charts on construction activity,
new housing starts, building permits, and economic indicators in Arizona
plus the metropolitan Phoenix consumer price index. These data are not
found in Arizona Review which publishes only full length articles.

028.   Arizona Review. DATE FOUNDED: 1952. TITLE CHANGES: Arizona
Business and Economic Review (1952-1957), Arizona Review of Business and
Public Administration (1958-1965). FREQUENCY: 2/yr. PRICE: Free.
PUBLISHER: University of Arizona, College of Business and Public
Administration, Tucson, Arizona 85721. EDITOR: Lynne Schwartz. INDEX.
CIRCULATION: 4,000 MANUSCRIPT SELECTION: Editor. INDEXED/ABSTRACTED:
PAIS. DATABASES: PAIS INT. TARGET AUDIENCE: AC, SP. SAMPLE COPIES:
Libraries and Individuals.

The Arizona Review, formerly a quarterly, is now a semi-annual business
school publication. In the two quarters that it is not published, the
College publishes the Arizona Statistical Chartbook. The Arizona Review
focuses on the "research activity of the Division of Economic and
Business Research staff as related to issues, trends, and policies
specific to the economy of Arizona." However, it does reach out beyond
the borders of Arizona with its publication of articles "describing
faculty research from throughout the College of Business and Public
Administration" of the University of Arizona. For example, 1983 and 1984
issues included articles dealing with the package software industry and
with the characteristics of Mexican nationals who shop in the U.S.
Articles are usually not theoretical in nature and do not use sophisticated quantitative analysis. However, a significant amount of data is
typically provided in each article and footnotes and/or "works cited"
are provided. This publication competes with Arizona Business, its
counterpart published by the Bureau of Business and Economic Research at
Arizona State University. Actually these two publications are quite
complementary and can both contribute to the better understanding of
business and economics topics, particularly those relating to the state
of Arizona.

The typical issue is made up of three or four articles, each averaging about ten pages in length.

029.   Arkansas Business and Economic Review. DATE FOUNDED: 1933. TITLE CHANGES: Arkansas Business Bulletin (1933-1968). FREQUENCY: q. PRICE: Free. PUBLISHER: University of Arkansas, Bureau of Business and Economic Research, College of Business Administration, Fayetteville, Arkansas 72701. EDITOR: Phillip H. Taylor. ILLUSTRATIONS. INDEX. CIRCULATION: 4,000. MANUSCRIPT SELECTION: Editorial Advisory Board. REPRINTS: Publisher. INDEXED/ABSTRACTED: BPIA, PAIS. DATABASES: MC, PAIS INT. TARGET AUDIENCE: AC, SP. SAMPLE COPIES: Libraries and Individuals.

The Arkansas Business and Economic Review is a business school publication that focuses on business and economic theory, regional and industrial problems that have implications for the Arkansas economy, and economic problems or issues of the Arkansas business community. More than half of the articles deal with economic conditions in Arkansas while the rest are concerned with economic issues of national interest. Representative examples of the latter type are "An Introduction to Social Security Benefits Computations", "The New Tax Laws and Their Impact on Investments", and "Marketing Plans: Nature, Prerequisites, and Benefits". Most articles are non-technical in nature and understandable to non-economists. The authors are academics in the fields of business, economics, and political science. Arkansas Business and Economic Review offers a mix of state and nationally oriented articles and a level of presentation that resembles many other business school publications such as the University of Nevada's Review of Business and Economics and Ball State Business Review.
    A typical issue contains four to six articles ranging in length from three to twelve pages. Each issue has an extensive statistical section featuring selected Arkansas and U.S. economic indicators. Data is given on employment, personal income, construction contracts, and consumer prices.

030.   Artha Vijnana. DATE FOUNDED: 1959. FREQUENCY: q. PRICE: $42/yr. PUBLISHER: Gokhale Institute of Politics and Economics, Pune - 411 004, India. EDITOR: B.G. Bapat. INDEX. CIRCULATION: 375. MANUSCRIPT SELECTION: Editorial Board. BOOK REVIEWS. INDEXED/ABSTRACTED: IntBibE, WAERSA. DATABASES: CAB AB. TARGET AUDIENCE: AC.

Artha Vijnana is published by an Indian research institute focusing on economics and other social sciences. This publication covers a broad range of subjects. Some articles are theoretical or methodological in nature while others are more applied and deal with specific industries, population planning, or agricultural production. A few focus on economic policy issues. Representative titles in recent issues include "Demographic Evolution of India's Family Planning Programme", "Relationship Between Farm Size, Productivity, Input Demand, and Production Cost", and "Technology and Productivity of Cement Industry in India." The articles are scholarly in treatment and most of them utilize modern quantitative methodologies. The authors are staff researchers at the Institute or academics associated with various Indian universities.
    A typical issue contains from four to six articles, each from eighteen to thirty-three pages in length. Some issues include comments

on previously published articles along with brief replies from the authors. From four to five signed book reviews appear in each issue. Occasionally, a special issue consists of an in-depth report such as the March-June 1984 double issue on "Structural Changes in Indian Economy: An Analysis with Input-Output Tables, 1951-1963."

031.   Artha-Vikas. DATE FOUNDED: 1965. FREQUENCY: 2/yr. PRICE: $4/yr. PUBLISHER: Sardar Patel University, Dept. of Economics, Vallabh Vidyanagar - 388 120, Gujarat, India. EDITORS: Mahesh Pathak, J.H. Adhvaryu. ADVERTISEMENTS. MANUSCRIPT SELECTION: Editorial Board. INDEXED/ABSTRACTED: InEcA, JEL, WAERSA. DATABASES: CAB AB, ECONLIT. TARGET AUDIENCE: AC, SP.

Artha-Vikas, subtitled Journal of Economic Development, concentrates on "articles on economic development in general and rural economic development in particular." The majority of articles deal with economic development studies in Gujarat, the state that Sardar Patel University is located. Articles present case studies of particular industries, analyses of rural energy projects, evaluations of water irrigation projects, studies of regional land utilization, and studies of regional poverty levels and unemployment. Most of the articles are expository in style. They frequently contain extensive numerical data and occasionally include regression analyses. The authors are predominantly economists associated with Sardar Patel University or its research institutes. Artha-Vikas is similar in technical level to the Indian journal, Southern Economist, but is different in geographic scope since it concentrates on regional rather than national problems.
    A typical issue contains six articles, each ten to twenty pages in length. Occasionally, a much longer article or a brief note is published. Articles vary greatly in format; some provide an abstract, extensive footnotes, a list of references, a bibliography, or an appendix. A list of contributors giving their titles and affiliations is provided near the front of each issue. Occasionally, the content of an issue is the proceedings of a special seminar.

032.   The Asian Economic Review. DATE FOUNDED: 1958. FREQUENCY: 3/yr. PRICE: $24/yr. PUBLISHER: The Indian Institute of Economics, 11-6-841, Red Hills, Hyderabad - 500 004, India. EDITOR: R.C. Lahoti. CIRCULATION: 400. MANUSCRIPT SELECTION: Editorial Board. BOOK REVIEWS. INDEXED/ABSTRACTED: WAERSA. DATABASES: CAB AB. TARGET AUDIENCE: AC, SP.

The Asian Economic Review, subtitled The Journal of the Indian Institute of Economics, is published by a research institute which concentrates on research studies dealing with the economy of India. However, the Review publishes articles covering a broader geographic scope which includes other Asian countries and Africa. Most of the articles present applied economic research but occasionally a paper offers a theoretical discussion. Representative titles of empirical studies are "Role of Income and Occupational Factors in Household Milk Consumption Pattern", "Inter-State Income Disparities Since 1960-61", and "Personal Income Taxation and Equity in India." The articles are scholarly and vary greatly in their technical level. Some employ a mathematical model and test it with empirical data while others are purely descriptive. The authors are predominantly Indian economists affiliated with universities, although occasional contributions are made by academics from other countries.

A typical issue contains three articles, ranging from fourteen to twenty-eight pages in length. Shorter articles are found in a "Notes and Memoranda" section. From one to three signed book reviews appear in each issue. In recent years, numbers one and two have been published together in a double issue.

033.   Asian Economies. DATE FOUNDED: 1972. FREQUENCY: q. PRICE: $30/yr. PUBLISHER: Research Institute of Asian Economies, Room 615, Grand Bldg., 111-12, 4-Ka, Namdaemun - Ro, Chung-ku, Seoul, South Korea. EDITOR: Taiwhan Shin. ILLUSTRATIONS. INDEX. MANUSCRIPT SELECTION: Editorial Board. INDEXED/ABSTRACTED: IntBibE, PAIS, WAERSA. DATABASES: CAB AB, PAIS INT. TARGET AUDIENCE: AC,SP.

Asian Economies receives financial assistance from The Korean Traders Scholarship Foundation. Its main area of concentration is the Korean economy but articles covering the economies of other Asian countries, economic development, and economic theory are included also. Articles in recent issues that have dealt with the Korean economy focus on topics such as the off-shore fishing industry, participation in the Middle East construction market, import-export trade, and the dairy industry. Other Asian countries represented in this publication include Japan, India, Malaysia, and Indonesia. Articles offering theoretical discussions include topics such as government spending, market growth and interest rates, optimal control theory, and the effect of international trade on economic development. The articles are scholarly and include extensive references. The level of technical treatment runs the gamut from purely descriptive to econometric modeling. About half of the authors are economists affiliated with Korean universities. Others are American, Australian, West German, Japanese, or South African economists.
A typical issue contains three full-length articles.

034.   Atlantic Economic Journal. DATE FOUNDED: 1973. FREQUENCY: q. PRICE: $55/yr. institutions, $40/yr. personal. PUBLISHER: Atlantic Economic Society, c/o John M. Virgo, Southern Illinois University, Box 101, Edwardville, Illinois 62026. EDITOR: John M. Virgo. ILLUSTRATIONS. ADVERTISEMENTS. CIRCULATION: 1,500. MANUSCRIPT SELECTION: Board of Editors. BOOK REVIEWS. SPECIAL ISSUES. INDEXED/ABSTRACTED: BPIA, PAIS. DATABASES: ABI, MC, PAIS INT. TARGET AUDIENCE: AC,SP. SAMPLE COPIES: Libraries and Individuals.

The Atlantic Economic Journal is a scholarly economics journal that pervades all fields of economics. It publishes theoretical articles in such areas as contracts, investment, location, welfare, exchange rates, and bureaucratic behavior as well as empirical papers on topics such as advertising and monopoly power, wages, concentration and import penetration, and intra-urban residential location. It also includes articles that stress methodology such as "the Simultaneity Problem in Forecasting Inflation," "Modelling a Poisson Process...", and "Tests of Exogeneity and Causality Specifications in Monetary Models of Exchange Rate Determination." Other articles deal with the history of economic thought while yet others are descriptive policy oriented discussions. It follows that articles range from being highly technical and using modern quantitative methodologies to non-technical papers written in a narrative style. The former, however, far exceed the latter. The majority of the authors are American academic economists with most of the rest being academic economists from Europe, Canada, and Israel. Occasionally an article is written by a U.S. government economist.

A typical issue contains from eight to ten articles, some of which may be addresses presented at an Atlantic Economic Society Conference. Each issue also includes from four to thirteen "Anthologies", brief papers making a "small point", reporting on research in progress, or commenting on a previously published article. Most issues have a "Book Reviews" section which contains two or three signed reviews, each dealing with a different subject area and reviewing a number of books. Two issues a year also contain abstracts of papers presented at an Atlantic Economic Society Conference. A recent issue devoted almost fifty pages to over 100 abstracts.

035.   Australian Bulletin of Labour. DATE FOUNDED: 1974. FREQUENCY: q. PRICE: $30/yr. PUBLISHER: National Institute of Labour Studies Inc., The Flinders University of South Australia, Bedford Park, South Australia 5042, Australia. EDITOR: Richard Blandy. ILLUSTRATIONS. INDEX. CIRCULA- TION: 900. MANUSCRIPT SELECTION: Editorial Board. REPRINTS: Publisher. SPECIAL ISSUES. TARGET AUDIENCE: AC,GP,SP. SAMPLE COPIES: Libraries and Individuals.

The Australian Bulletin of Labour "Analyses current trends in Australian labour markets and makes both qualitative and quantitative assessments of the likely consequences of these trends." In addition to providing periodic updates on the Australian labor market, articles deal with topics such as Australian government policies toward labour; education, training, and earnings of managers; unemployment patterns; interstate variations in strike-proneness; interstate migration; manpower forecast- ing; the determination of junior wages; limitations of the Australian consumer price index; employee attitudes toward technological change; and unionization in Australia. Articles are scholarly in nature but the majority are non-technical. Large amounts of data are presented in tables and graphs. The authors are predominantly Australian academic economists. About half of them are associated with the National Insti- tute of Labour Studies. Occasionally articles are reprinted or excerpted from a book. The Bulletin covers the same subject area as Journal of Industrial Relations.

Each issue begins with a "Main Point" section which contains brief labor news items. This is followed by three or four full length Arti- cles. Special issues are published about every two years; the two most recent ones were devoted to the results of a major study involving 1,000 young workers and to the future of Australian industrial relations.

036.   Australian Economic History Review. DATE FOUNDED: 1961. TITLE CHANGES: Business Archives and History (1961-1967). FREQUENCY: 2/yr. PRICE: $35/yr. institutions, $20/yr. personal. PUBLISHER: Sydney University Press, University of Sydney, Sydney, New South Wales, 2006, Australia. EDITORS: W.G. Rimmer, W.A. Sinclair. ILLUSTRATIONS. INDEX. ADVERTISEMENTS. CIRCULATION: 650. MANUSCRIPT SELECTION: Editorial Committee. MICROFORMS: UMI. BOOK REVIEWS. SPECIAL ISSUES: INDEXED/ ABSTRACTED: InEcA, JEL. DATABASES: ECONLIT. TARGET AUDIENCE: AC.

The <u>Australian Economic History Review</u> is published in association with the Economic History Society of Australia and New Zealand. <u>AEHR</u> focuses on the business and economic history of these two countries. Articles deal with topics such as the historical development of particular industries or regions, labor history, immigration, and the economic impact of legislative acts. Most of the articles are expository in style but some include a statistical analysis of the subject using data collected from government sources. The authors are predominantly Australian academics. Their universities, but not their specific departmental affiliations, are provided.

A typical issue includes four articles, each from ten to thirty pages in length. A book review section, which includes ten to fifteen reviews of one to two pages in length, appears in each issue. The reviews, which are signed, cover books dealing with a broad range of international economic and social issues. Each issue also has a short bibliography of books received; some of these titles have brief annotations. Occasionally a special issue is published such as the September 1983 double issue which includes the unpublished manuscripts of Professor S.J. Butlin, a prominent Australian economic historian, along with the regular features.

037.   Australian Economic Papers. DATE FOUNDED: 1962. FREQUENCY: 2/yr. PRICE: $15/yr. PUBLISHER: University of Adelaide and Flinders University of South Australia, University Relations Unit, Flinders University of South Australia, Bedford Park, South Australia 5042, Australia. ILLUS-TRATIONS. INDEX. ADVERTISEMENTS. CIRCULATION: 1,100. MANUSCRIPT SELEC-TION: Editorial Committee. REPRINTS: Authors. INDEXED/ABSTRACTED: InEcA, JEL, WAERSA. DATABASES: CAB AB, ECONLIT. TARGET AUDIENCE: AC, SP.

<u>Australian Economic Papers</u> is a publication jointly sponsored by two universities. It covers a broad range of fields such as pure economic theory and statistics, applied economics, economic history, the history of economic thought, and, occasionally, accounting. Papers dealing with applied economics focus on current conditions and problems in Australia rather than in other parts of the world. Representative titles of articles dealing with the Australian economy are "Supply and Demand for Hospital Beds in New South Wales" and "Price Trends in Wool Prices when Sydney Futures are Actively Traded". Technical treatment of articles range from purely descriptive to theoretical discussions utilizing mathematical models. Empirical data are used frequently. The authors are academics from Australia, Great Britain, Canada, and the U.S. The subject coverage of <u>Australian Economic Papers</u> overlaps with that of the <u>Australian Economic Review.</u> The latter is somewhat less scholarly and research oriented.

A typical issue contains from sixteen to twenty-two articles and notes ranging in length from four to twenty-seven pages. Articles and notes are interspersed. Articles are sometimes followed by replies, which in turn may be followed by a postscript.

038.   Australian Economic Review. DATE FOUNDED: 1968. FREQUENCY: q. PRICE: $43/yr. PUBLISHER: Institute of Applied Economic and Social Research, University of Melbourne, Parkville, Victoria 3052, Australia. EDITOR: Daina McDonald. ILLUSTRATIONS. CIRCULATION: 2,000. MANUSCRIPT

SELECTION: Editorial Board. INDEXED/ABSTRACTED: InEcA, JEL, PAIS, WAERSA. DATABASES: CAB AB, ECONLIT, PAIS INT. TARGET AUDIENCE: AC,GP,SP.

The Australian Economic Review is published by a research institute which is a "household name" in Australia (according to the Director of the Institute). Many of its reports are quoted in major daily newspapers. The Review provides "a balanced account of current economic trends together with a general view of future economic prospects in the short term." It presents "The results of original applied economic research" by members of the Institute's staff as well as by academic economists. Articles are expository in style and occasionally utilize statistical analysis. The Review complements Australian Economic Papers which is much more scholarly, is less policy oriented, offers less on the current Australian Economic scene, and employs more sophisticated quantitative analysis.

A typical issue includes two to three research articles, ranging from ten to fifteen pages in length. The research involves applied economic analysis of an actual situation. In addition, up to five articles dealing with current economic trends appear in a section called "The Economic Situation." Each issue has a "Diary" section which provides a summary of main economic events of the preceding quarter and policy statements pertaining to those events. Every other issue contains a "Statistical Appendix" which offers "annual data for the past eight financial years and forecasts for major economic variables."

039.   The Australian Journal of Agricultural Economics. DATE FOUNDED: 1957. FREQUENCY: 3/yr. PRICE: $35/yr. PUBLISHER: The Australian Agricultural Economics Society, Suite 302, Clunies Ross House, 191 Royal Parade, Parkville, Victoria 3052, Australia. EDITORS: R.R. Piggott, R.A. Powell. ILLUSTRATIONS. INDEX: ADVERTISEMENTS. CIRCULATION: 1,400. MANUSCRIPT SELECTION: Editorial Committee. BOOK REVIEWS. INDEXED/ABSTRACTED: InEcA, IntBibE, JEL, WAERSA. DATABASES: CAB AB, ECONLIT. TARGET AUDIENCE: AC.

The Australian Journal of Agricultural Economics is the official publication of a professional association of agricultural economists. The Society's aim is to encourage "the pursuit of study, research and extension work in the discipline of agricultural economics in Australia." The articles emphasize agricultural economics in Australia but occasionally contributions deal with other countries. Most of the papers present the results of applied economic research. Representative topics selected from recent issues include drought assistance policy, agricultural price supports, an econometric model of the Australian wool industry, and supply elasticity estimates for the livestock industry. The articles are scholarly in nature and employ statistics and econometric models extensively. The authors are predominantly Australian academic or government economists, but articles by foreign scholars are also published. The Journal publishes more technical articles on the Australian agricultural sector than does Quarterly Review of the Rural Economy.

A typical issue contains four or five articles, each ten to twenty pages in length. Some issues include comments on previously published articles and replies by the authors. The Journal also carries the Society's announcements about awards, annual conferences, and conference programs. From six to ten signed book reviews, ranging from one to three pages in length, appear in each issue.

040.   Bangkok Bank Monthly Review. DATE FOUNDED: 1962. FREQUENCY: m. PRICE: Free. PUBLISHER: Bangkok Bank Limited, 333 Silom Road, Bangkok, Thailand. EDITOR: Viraphong Vachratith. ILLUSTRATIONS. MANUSCRIPT SELECTION: Editor. INDEXED/ABSTRACTED: PAIS, Pred, WAERSA. DATABASES: CAB AB, PAIS INT, PF. TARGET AUDIENCE: AC, GP, SP. SAMPLE COPIES: Libraries and Individuals.

The Bangkok Bank Monthly Review reports on the current state of the Thai economy. It focuses on economic performance in general as well as the performance of certain key economic sectors. Articles are non-technical in nature but are accompanied by a variety of data that apply to the topic being discussed. While the Review is valuable for professional economists interested in the Thai economy, it is geared to members of the business community. The Review is longer and more comprehensive than other bank publications such as the Bank of Japan Monthly Economic Review, the Bank of Montreal Business Review, and the Bank of Korea Quarterly Economic Review. It offers articles on topics such as international trading companies, annual government budgets and agricultural policy. The authors are predominantly Bank economists. In those instances when an article was originally written in the Thai language, it is signed by the translator.
    The twelve issues per year are continuously paginated, totaling between 500 and 600 pages. Each issue begins with an editorial. It is followed by an economic diary, a day-by-day accounting of important economic events in Thailand. An approximately five page narrative on the "Current State of the Economy" is also presented. In addition to a "Topic of the Month", two or three articles dealing with Thai industries are included. Some issues also publish interviews with prominent Thai business leaders and a "Laws and Regulations" section. Each issue has several pages devoted to news concerning key Thai commodities such as rice, sugar, tapioca, maize, kenaf, and rubber and about ten pages of economic indicators tables.

041.   The Bangladesh Development Studies. DATE FOUNDED: 1973. TITLE CHANGES: Bangladesh Economic Review (1973-1974). FREQUENCY: q. PRICE: $25/yr. PUBLISHER: The Bangladesh Institute of Development Studies, Adamjee Court, Motijheel Commercial Area, Dhaka-2, Bangladesh. EDITOR: S.R. Osmani. ILLUSTRATIONS. INDEX. ADVERTISEMENTS. CIRCULATION: 1,200. MANUSCRIPT SELECTION: Editor and Editorial Board. BOOK REVIEWS. SPECIAL ISSUES. INDEXED/ABSTRACTED: InEcA, IntBibE, JEL, WAERSA. DATABASES: CAB AB, ECONLIT. TARGET AUDIENCE: AC,SP.

The Bangladesh Development Studies is a scholarly journal that features articles pertaining exclusively to the Bangladesh economy. Most articles deal with a topic that impacts Bangladesh's economic development. These often are concerned with an aspect of Bangladesh agriculture, demographics, or development planning. Some articles deal with the entire Bangladesh economy such as "A Macro-Econometric Model of Bangladesh" and "Some Macro-economic Implications of Higher Oil Prices for Bangladesh." Articles frequently contain mathematical models or are statistical in nature. "Estimating Distributional Weights for Bangladesh" is an example of the latter. Articles reflect that they are written by well-trained professional economists. Authors are usually either professors of economics at the University of Dhaka or research economists at the Bangladesh Institute of Development Studies.

A typical issue contain three or four fairly lengthy articles, one or two briefer notes and an extensive list of other Institute publications. Occasionally an issue will include an in-depth signed book review or a review article. Occasionally a special issue is published such as a 1980 issue on "Food Policy and Development Strategy in Bangladesh."

042.   Bank of England Quarterly Bulletin. DATE FOUNDED: 1960. FREQUENCY: q. PRICE: ₤42/yr. PUBLISHER: Bank of England, Threadneedle St., London EC2R 8AH, England. EDITOR: D.J. Reid. ILLUSTRATIONS. INDEX. CIRCULATION: 6,000. MANUSCRIPT SELECTION: Editor. MICROFORMS: UMI. INDEXED/ABSTRACTED: KeyEcS, PAIS. DATABASES: ECONAB, PAIS INT. TARGET AUDIENCE: GP.

The Bank of England Quarterly Bulletin is published by the Bank's Economics Division. It covers U.K. economic and financial developments, current banking conditions, and international finance. Many articles focus on an aspect of Britain's banking sector while others are of broader scope. These include titles such as "World Economic Stagnation and Recovery", "The Economic Scene; A Global Perspective", and "The Financial Structure and Operations of the International Monetary Fund". The articles are expository in style. Some of them are based on speeches presented at meetings or conferences while others are written specifically for this publication. The articles adopted from speeches are written by chief officers of the Bank of England. Their names appear prominently following the title. The other articles, which are unsigned, are prepared by staff writers of the Bank's Economics Division.

Each issue is divided into two sections. The first section, "Recent Economic and Financial Developments", is sub-divided into four parts: 1) "General Assessment" which presents an overview of economic conditions in the U.K. during the preceding quarter, 2) "Economic Commentary" which offers an in-depth analysis of economic conditions, 3) "Operations of Monetary Policy" which provides an account of monetary growth in the U.K. during the preceding quarter, and 4) "International Financial Developments" which supplies data on international balance of payments, banking, and capital markets, foreign exchange rates, and gold markets. The second section, "Articles and Speeches", includes four to eight articles, each from four to ten pages in length. In addition, a forty to fifty page "Statistical Annex" provides banking and financial data for both the U.K. and the world community.

043.   Bank of Israel Economic Review. DATE FOUNDED: 1955. TITLE CHANGES: Bank of Israel Bulletin (1955-1969). FREQUENCY: 2/yr. PRICE: Free. PUBLISHER: Bank of Israel, P.O.B. 780, Jerusalem 91007, Israel. EDITOR: Rama Zuta. INDEX. CIRCULATION: 1,200. MANUSCRIPT SELECTION: Editorial Board. REPRINTS: Publisher. INDEXED/ABSTRACTED: IntBibE. TARGET AUDIENCE: AC, SP. SAMPLE COPIES: Libraries and Individuals.

The Bank of Israel Economic Review is published by the Bank's research department. It includes both theoretical and applied economic research but the major emphasis is on applied research studies dealing with the

Israeli economy. The articles concentrate on macro rather than microeconomic problems. Israel's banking system and monetary policy receive a
great deal of attention. Recent issues include articles dealing with
topics such as monetary factors in Israel's inflation, the demand for
money, private sector saving in Israel, and the cost of capital. The
articles are scholarly in style and frequently include mathematical
models and empirical test results. The authors are predominantly Israeli
academics or staff economists with the Bank of Israel. This publication
is intended for professional economists as opposed to the Leumi Review
which presents an overview of the Israeli economy to a general audience.
    A typical issue includes three to five articles, ranging from ten to
forty pages in length. Each issue also contains several reports on the
increase in the money supply for previous quarters. These reports
provide tables of financial data and offer economic policy recommendations.

044.   Bank of Japan Monthly Economic Review. DATE FOUNDED: 1948. TITLE
CHANGES: Bank of Japan Monthly Review (1950-1953), Bank of Japan Quarterly Review (1948-1950). FREQUENCY: m. PRICE: Free. PUBLISHER: The Bank
of Japan, Research and Statistics Dept., Tokyo, 100-91, Japan. TARGET
AUDIENCE: AC, GP, SP. SAMPLE COPIES: Libraries and Individuals.

The Monthly Economic Review is devoted half to a narrative review of
monetary and economic trends in Japan and half to the presentation of
key current Japanese economic data. While the Review is also valuable
for professional economists interested in Japan, it is primarily aimed
at the business community. It offers an overall monthly update of the
strengths and weaknesses of the Japanese economy and follows this by
more in-depth discussions of production and shipments, commodity prices,
consumer prices, exchange rates, capital flows, money supply, and
related topics. Each discussion offers specific data which is sometimes
the result of surveys conducted by the Bank of Japan. The discussions
are non-technical in nature and can be understood by non-economists.
Authors' names are not provided, but the writing is by qualified bank
economists. The Review is shorter and less scholarly than many other
bank publications, and most closely resembles the Bank of Montreal
Business Review.
    A typical issue contains a 400 word overview of current economic
conditions plus from six to eight somewhat shorter topical discussions.
The statistical portion of the Review presents twelve different tables:
three on interest rates; the money supply; the demand and supply of
funds in particular money markets; Bank of Japan accounts; nonfinancial
business activity; machinery orders, housing starts, and retail sales;
labor statistics; Gross National Expenditures; price indices; and
international transactions.

045.   Bank of Korea Quarterly Economic Review. DATE FOUNDED: 1969.
FREQUENCY: q. PRICE: Free. PUBLISHER: Bank of Korea, Research Dept.,
Seoul, South Korea. EDITOR: Chang Kyw Lee. ILLUSTRATIONS. MANUSCRIPT
SELECTION: Editor. TARGET AUDIENCE: AC, GP, SP. SAMPLE COPIES: Libraries
and Individuals.

The Bank of Korea Quarterly Economic Review is a publication that
focuses on providing a regular update of the Korean economy. This is

aimed at professional economists interested in Korea as well as members
of the business community. The journal, in sharp contrast to most other
bank reviews, also publishes scholarly articles dealing with the Korean
Economy. Representative examples are "The Change in Quality of the Labor
Force and its Effect on the Economic Growth of Korea" and "Recent
Behavior of Money Velocity in Korea." The Review's quarterly economic
update presents a summary statement followed by more in-depth discussions of such variables as industrial production, the balance of
payments, the money supply, and prices. This portion of the Review very
much resembles the entire format of the Bank of Japan Monthly Economic
Review. The material, prepared by qualified Bank economists, is non-
technical in nature. The articles, written by Korean academic or
government economists, may be technical in nature.

A typical issue is from thirty to fifty pages in length, divided
between the Review's quarterly economic update and one article. Some
issues begin with an announcement of a major economic event, particularly a change that strongly affects the banking community. Each issue
contains a section, "Current Events and Announcements", which makes
known any changes in government regulations or rules which affect
interest rates, credit availability, and international trade. Each issue
also presents the titles of articles appearing in Chosa Wolbo, a Korean
language monthly economic review.

046.   Bank of Montreal Business Review. DATE FOUNDED: 1926. TITLE
CHANGES: Bank of Montreal Business Summary (1926-1948). FREQUENCY: m.
PRICE: Free. PUBLISHER: Bank of Montreal, P.O. Box 6002, Montreal, P. Q.
H3C3B1, Canada. EDITOR: J.D. Darish. ILLUSTRATIONS. INDEX. CIRCULATION:
100,000. MANUSCRIPT SELECTION: Editor. INDEXED/ABSTRACTED: CBPI, Pred.
DATABASES: CBI, PF. TARGET AUDIENCE: AC, GP, SP. SAMPLE COPIES: Li-
braries and Individuals.

The Bank of Montreal Business Review is published in both English and
French by the head office of the Bank of Montreal. It provides important
current information about the Canadian economy. Articles discuss
Canada's recent economic performance and economic trends. Representative
topics from recent issues include "Canada's Recent Growth Slowdown by
Industry", "Exploding Government Debt and Interest Costs", "Huge
Government Stimulus in First Quarter" and "Sectoral Free Trade with the
United States". The articles are non-technical in nature but include a
great deal of data. Articles are not signed, but clearly written by
qualified bank economists. Compared to other bank publications, the
Review is shorter and less ambitious than the Bank of England Quarterly
Bulletin, the Bank of Israel Economic Review, and the Bangkok Bank
Monthly Review. It more closely resembles the Bank of Japan Monthly
Economic Review and the Bank of Korea Quarterly Economic Review.

Most issues are eight pages in length, but some are as brief as four
pages. Each issue includes a monthly update on the Canadian economy, a
special feature or two on a particular aspect of the Canadian economy,
and a table containing the monthly and quarterly Canadian economic
indicators. The "Economic Update" section contains four or five brief
articles. A "Monetary and Financial Developments" section concentrates
on interest rates, credit availability, currency movements, and apparent
changes in fiscal or monetary policies.

047.   British Journal of Industrial Relations. DATE FOUNDED: 1963.
FREQUENCY: 3/yr. PRICE: $38/yr. institutions, $19/yr. personal. PUB-
LISHER: London School of Economics and Political Science, Houghton St.,
Aldwych, London WC2A2AE, England. EDITORS: B.C. Roberts, Ray Richardson.
ILLUSTRATIONS. INDEX. ADVERTISEMENTS. CIRCULATION: 2,500. MANUSCRIPT
SELECTION: Editors and Referees. REPRINTS. BOOK REVIEWS. SPECIAL ISSUES:
INDEXED/ABSTRACTED: BPIA, InEcA, IntBibE, JEL, WorkRelAbstr. DATABASES:
ECONLIT, MC. TARGET AUDIENCE: AC,SP. SAMPLE COPIES: Libraries.

The British Journal of Industrial Relations contains scholarly articles
that report on research done in the field of industrial relations. Some
articles focus on the British labor scene, but others deal with industrial relations in another country like Japan, France, or the U.S. Yet
other articles are comparison studies. Articles that appear in this
journal range from those that present models and empirical evidence
utilizing a fairly sophisticated quantitative approach to those that
examine and analyze particular labor laws or labor relations in a
specific industry. The authors are academics, the majority from British
institutions, but many are affiliated with universities in other
countries.
    A typical issue contains six or seven articles, each about fifteen
pages in length. Each issue includes a "Chronicle" section which covers
industrial relations events in the United Kingdom for the previous four
months. The "Chronicle" section is separated into five parts: "Statistical Background to the Industrial Relations Scene," "Government Policy
and Activities," "The Employers," "The Trade Unions", and "Major
Negotiations." The book review section includes seven to eight reviews
averaging approximately 400 words each. These are written by academics
whose affiliations are stated. There is also a list of books received,
but not reviewed. A bibliography of books and articles in industrial
relations is offered from time to time.

048.   British Review of Economic Issues. DATE FOUNDED: 1977. FRE-
QUENCY: 2/yr. PRICE: £22/yr. institutions, £8/yr. personal. PUBLISHER:
Association of Polytechnic Teachers in Economics, Thames Polytechnic,
Wellington Street, London SE186PF, England. EDITOR: A. Skouras. ILLUS-
TRATIONS. INDEX. ADVERTISEMENTS. CIRCULATION: 600. MANUSCRIPT SELECTION:
Editor and Editorial Board. BOOK REVIEWS. INDEXED/ABSTRACTED: PAIS,
WAERSA. DATABASES: CAB AB, PAIS INT. TARGET AUDIENCE: AC, SP. SAMPLE
COPIES: Libraries and Individuals.

British Review of Economic Issues is published by an Association,
established in 1972, that "aims to promote the development of economics
teaching and to encourage research into economics in Polytechnics and
other institutions of higher education." Coverage extends to a wide
variety of economics articles and topics. Some deal with aspects of
economic theory such as recent ones on "A Causality Analysis of the
Determinants of Money Growth" and "Primitive Accumulation and Optimum
Development in the Dual Economy." Others deal with issues in applied
economics including comments on current British governmental policy.
Examples from recent issues include "The Economic Significance of Common
Agricultural Policy" and "Depreciation and the Quality Adjustment of
Prices: An Investigation of the U.K. Car Market, 1980-81." Still other
papers survey or provide an exposition of the latest developments in a
particular subject or the development of a technique. Finally, this

journal also publishes articles that deal with the teaching of economics such as recent ones on "The Derivation of the LM Schedule - A Pedagogical Note" and "A Simplified Post-Keynesian Model of Inflation for Teaching Purposes." Most articles are technical in nature and employ quantitative methodologies. A few are expository in style. The authors are predominantly academic economists associated with one of the Polytechnic institutions or a British university. The Review is comparable in subject coverage and authorship to the Bulletin of Economic Research and The Manchester School of Economic and Social Studies.

A typical issue contains four articles, a note or a comment, a review section, and a list of books received. The review section contains one or two signed six-to-nine page reviews of several books that can be used to teach a specific subject.

049.   Brookings Papers on Economic Activity. DATE FOUNDED: 1970. FREQUENCY: 2/yr. PRICE: $25/yr. institutions, $20/yr. personal. PUBLISHER: The Brookings Institution, 1775 Massachusetts Ave., N.W., Washington, D.C. 20036. EDITORS: William C. Brainard, George L. Perry. ILLUSTRATIONS. INDEX. CIRCULATION: 5,000. MANUSCRIPT SELECTION: Invitation. MICROFORMS: UMI. INDEXED/ABSTRACTED: BPI, InEcA, IntBibE, JEL, PAIS, SSI. DATABASES: ECONLIT, PAIS INT, SSI. TARGET AUDIENCE: AC, GP, SP.

Brookings Papers on Economic Activity contains the articles, reports, and highlights of the discussions from the conferences of the Brookings Panel on Economic Activity. The panel members are prominent academics from the U.S. and occasionally from Great Britain. Guests of the panel are invited to make a presentation at the conference. The conferences are devoted to examining current issues of economic performance. Particular attention is devoted to economic developments that are relevant to the contemporary scene or that challenge extant economic theory. The articles are intended to be intelligible to the informed layperson, but usually require the expertise of a trained macroeconomist. The Brookings Institution is an independent organization devoted to research, education, and publication in economics, government, foreign policy, and the social sciences. Its mission is to promote public understanding of issues of national importance. The Institution claims to maintain a position of neutrality on issues of public policy. Opinions expressed in articles are those of the individual authors.

A typical issue begins with a twenty page Editor's "Summary of the Conference," presenting the topics addresssed and an overview of the papers. That is followed by three main articles of fifty to sixty pages each and accompanying discussant's comments. Each issue also includes three to four shorter reports of twenty to thirty pages in length and accompanying comments.

050.   Brookings Review. DATE FOUNDED: 1962. TITLE CHANGES: The Brookings Bulletin (1962-1982). FREQUENCY: q. PRICE: Free. PUBLISHER: The Brookings Institution, 1775 Massachusetts Avenue, N.W., Washington, DC 20036. EDITOR: Mark Goldberg. ILLUSTRATIONS. CIRCULATION: 42,000. MANUSCRIPT SELECTION: Editor. MICROFORMS: UMI. BOOK REVIEWS. SPECIAL ISSUES. INDEXED/ABSTRACTED: PAIS, Pred. DATABASES: PAIS INT, PF. TARGET AUDIENCE: AC, GP, SP. SAMPLE COPIES: Libraries and Individuals.

The Brookings Review is published by the Brookings Institution, a nonprofit organization devoted to research on issues of domestic and foreign policy. The Review is an interdisciplinary journal featuring articles on economics, foreign policy, government, and social concerns. Titles of recent representative articles dealing with economics are "Tax Incentives for Saving," "Money and Monetary Policy," and "Industrial Policy: A Dissent." These articles deal with implications of economic policy and are written in non-technical language. Most of the authors are Senior Fellows in the Economics Studies Program at Brookings. In addition to the articles, each issue contains an interview with an individual who is prominent in business, government, or education. The interview typically reveals that individual's opinions on a wide variety of topics.

A typical issue contains three or four articles, each from four to ten pages in length. The book review section presents a one to two-page unsigned analysis of new books published by Brookings. The number of reviews range from two to five. Each issue also presents a set of photographs of participants at a recent conference sponsored by the Brookings Institution.

051.   Bulletin for International Fiscal Documentation. DATE FOUNDED: 1961. FREQUENCY: m. PRICE: DFL 185/yr. PUBLISHER: International Bureau of Fiscal Documentation, P.O. Box 20237, Sarphatistraat 124, 1000 HE Amsterdam, the Netherlands. EDITOR: D.A. van Waardenburg. ILLUSTRATIONS. INDEX. ADVERTISEMENTS. CIRCULATION: 2,000. MANUSCRIPT SELECTION: Editor. MICROFORMS: Publisher. REPRINTS: SZ. SPECIAL ISSUES. INDEXED/ABSTRACTED: AcctInd, InEcA, IntBibE, JEL, PAIS. DATABASES: ACCTIND, ECONLIT, PAIS INT. TARGET AUDIENCE: AC,SP. SAMPLE COPIES: Libraries and Individuals.

Bulletin for International Fiscal Documentation is associated with the International Fiscal Association, a body concerned with "international and comparative fiscal law and the financial and economic aspects of taxation." The Bulletin aims to keep readers informed about all matters related to international taxation including actual and proposed fiscal legislation, national and international tax issues, important court decisions that affect taxation and investment, and tax policy controversies. Issues contain surveys of specific countries' tax systems, reports on tax treaties among certain countries, outlines of specific countries' fiscal year budgets, and articles discussing countries' experiences with particular tax laws or rules. Representative topics discussed in recent issues include income tax reform in developing countries, methods of income computation for world-wide combined income reporting, free trade zones, OECD activities in the field of taxation, the future financing of EEC, inflation adjusted tax base in Israel, Revenue law and practice in China, and U.S. offshore tax havens. Most articles are descriptive in style. A few contain technical analyses. The authors are academic and/or practitioner economists, accountants and tax attorneys, as well as government officials. Articles may be specifically written for the Bulletin or may be versions of speeches delivered at conferences or excerpts from court decisions, government regulations, or legislation.

A typical issue is about fifty pages long. It contains from six to nine articles, Association news, a "Bibliography" composed of about fifty brief annotations of new books, and a cumulative index. Once a year a special issue containing the proceedings of the Annual Congress of the International Fiscal Association is published.

052.   Bulletin of Economic Research. DATE FOUNDED: 1949. TITLE CHANGES: Yorkshire Bulletin of Economic Research (1949-1970). FREQUENCY: 2/yr. PRICE: $38/yr. institutions, $18.50/yr. personal. PUBLISHER: Basil Blackwell, Publisher, Ltd., 108 Cowley Rd., Oxford, OX4 1JF, England. EDITORS: John D. Hey, Peter J. Lambert. INDEX. ADVERTISEMENTS. CIRCULA-TION: 600. MANUSCRIPT SELECTION: Editor and Referees. SPECIAL ISSUES. INDEXED/ABSTRACTED: BPIA, InEcA, IntBibE, JEL. DATABASES: ECONLIT, MC. TARGET AUDIENCE: AC,SP. SAMPLE COPIES: Libraries and Individuals.

The Bulletin of Economic Research is jointly sponsored by the Depart-ments of Economics at five British universities -- Hull, Leeds, Shef-field, York, and Bradford. The articles included in this title range across a wide spectrum of economics fields. Some deal with pure economic theory, others with the history of economic thought, and most with the results of applied research. The majority of the latter study and report on some aspect of the British economy. Most of the articles are fairly technical in nature and use quite sophisticated mathematical modelling techniques. The authors are predominantly academics at British univer-sities. The Bulletin is comparable in subject coverage and authorship to The Manchester School of Economic and Social Studies and to the recently established British Review of Economic Issues.
   A typical issue contains five or six articles, ranging from six to fifteen pages in length. Brief comments on previously published articles and a reply from the original author are sometimes interspersed. Also "notes", brief comments not relating to articles in the Bulletin, are found in some issues.

053.   Bulletin of Indonesian Economic Studies. DATE FOUNDED: 1965. FREQUENCY: 3/yr. PRICE: $30/yr. PUBLISHER: Australian National Univer-sity, Research School of Pacific Studies, Department of Economics, G.P.O. Box 4, Canberra, A.C.T., 2601, Australia. EDITORS: Anne Booth, Peter McCawley, R.M. Sundrum. ILLUSTRATIONS. INDEX. CIRCULATION: 2,000. MANUSCRIPT SELECTION: Editors and Referees. REPRINTS: Publisher. BOOK REVIEWS: SPECIAL ISSUES. INDEXED/ABSTRACTED: GeoAb, InEcA, IntBibE, JEL, WAERSA. DATABASES: CAB AB, ECONLIT. TARGET AUDIENCE: AC, SP. SAMPLE COPIES: Libraries and Individuals.
   The Bulletin of Indonesian Economic Studies is the only English language journal that concentrates on economic development in Indonesia. It also covers social and political concerns of that country. Each issue contains a thirty page feature, "Survey of Recent Developments", which presents an overview of current economic conditions. This article discusses and presents data on topics such as current economic indica-tors, the national budget, tax reform, monetary policy, and government economic planning. The remaining articles deal with subject areas such as evaluation of specific agricultural industries, demographic studies, and effects of specific government economic policies. All of the articles report on applied rather than theoretical research. They are expository in style and can be understood by readers having minimal training in economics. Only tables of numerical data and graphs are utilized in the articles. The authors are either staff members of the Bulletin or academics from English-speaking countries.

A typical issue contains five or six full-length articles, including the thirty page "Survey" mentioned above. Some issues include short comments on previously published articles and replies by the authors. Up to ten signed book reviews, one to two pages each, appear in most issues. The books reviewed focus on economic concerns of Indonesia or other Southeast Asian countries.

054.   Business and Economic Review. DATE FOUNDED: 1954. FREQUENCY: q. PRICE: Free. PUBLISHER: University of South Carolina, College of Business Administration, Columbia, South Carolina. 29208. EDITOR: Jan Collins Stucker. ILLUSTRATIONS. CIRCULATION: 4,500. MANUSCRIPT SELECTION: Editor. BOOK REVIEWS. INDEXED/ABSTRACTED: PAIS, Pred. DATABASES: PAIS INT, PF. TARGET AUDIENCE: GP. SAMPLE COPIES: Libraries and Individuals.

The Business and Economic Review is a business school publication aimed at the business community of South Carolina. Its purpose is to discuss current business trends and economic issues and how they affect the business professional in general and the state of South Carolina in particular. In some issues many of the articles focus on a single topic such as "A New Economics Strategy," "Aquabusiness in South Carolina," and "Information Management." In other issues, the articles cover a wide range of topics such as "Advertising in an Age of Recessions" and "Leasing Versus Buying: A Trend for the '80s." The authors of these articles are professors at the College of Business Administration, corporate executives in South Carolina, and staff writers. Articles are non-technical in nature and most are written in a narrative style. This title is like many other periodicals published by colleges of business administration. Its level of presentation and mix of general and regional focus resembles the Illinois Business Review.
  A typical issue contains eight to nine articles ranging in length from four to seven pages. There are four "features" included in each issue: 1."Tax Strategies for the '80s" -- a short article presenting tax advice by an expert in taxation and financial planning. 2. "Information Technology Trends" -- recommendations concerning the use of computer systems. 3. "Economic Corner" -- a report of recent trends in the economy. 4. "Books" -- two to three in-depth reviews prepared by the Business Librarian plus a short annotated bibliography of new acquisitions at the Business Library of the University.

055.   Business and Society. DATE FOUNDED: 1960. FREQUENCY: 2/yr. PRICE: $3/yr. PUBLISHER: Roosevelt University, Walter E. Heller College of Business Administration, 430 South Michigan Avenue, Chicago, Illinois 60605. EDITORS: Paul Wellen, Brian Reynolds. MANUSCRIPT SELECTION: Editor MICROFORMS: UMI. INDEXED/ABSTRACTED: BPI, BPIA, PAIS, Work RelAbstr. DATABASES: MC, PAIS INT. TARGET AUDIENCE: AC, GP.

Business and Society is a journal dedicated to publishing "interdisciplinary research into the ethical and moral assumptions of business and economics." It provides a forum for individuals concerned with corporate social responsibility and the role of government in regulating the business sector. Many articles deal with the social impact of public policy. Representative examples from recent issues include "Assessing the Impact of Federal Policy on Minority Business Enterprise", "The

Displacement Effects in Public Employment Programs", and "Hard-Core
Unemployment: A Long-Term Problem." Other articles examine the social
consequences of government regulation of specific industries such as
recent ones on the savings and loan and coal industries. The articles
are written in an expository style, are non-technical, and understandable to non-economists. The authors are predominantly American academics
associated with business or economics departments. Occasionally,
business executives make contributions. Business and Society is a breed
apart from the typical business school publication that offers regional
business and economics news, continuing education concerning business
practices, or technical business and economic research papers. A
complementary publication also emphasizing corporate social responsibility is the Council on Economic Priorities Newsletter.
   Each issue contains from six to eight articles that range from five
to nine pages in length.

056.   Business Economics. DATE FOUNDED: 1965. FREQUENCY: q. PRICE:
$30/yr. PUBLISHER: National Association of Business Economists, 28349
Chagrin Blvd., Suite 201, Cleveland, Ohio 44122. EDITOR: Max Moszer.
ILLUSTRATIONS. ADVERTISEMENTS. CIRCULATION: 5,000. MANUSCRIPT SELECTION:
Editor. MICROFORMS: UMI. BOOK REVIEWS: SPECIAL ISSUES. INDEXED/ABSTRACT-
ED: BPI, BPIA, InEcA, JEL, PAIS. DATABASES: ECONLIT, MC, PAIS INT.
TARGET AUDIENCE: AC, SP.

Business Economics is published by a professional association of
economists working in private business. Its objectives include providing
" a means of communications for the exchange of experience and ideas
between the business community and educational institutions..." and
"discussion and research in matters of public policy affecting the
business community..." Some articles focus on a current economic problem
and how a particular industry may be affected by that situation.
Representative titles of this type of article are "Price Elasticities of
Demand at Retail and Wholesale Levels: An Automotive Example" and "The
Effectiveness of Orderly Marketing Agreements: The Color TV Case." Other
articles deal with government economic policies and their effect on the
U.S. economy. These are frequently based on presentations made by
nationally prominent economists at the Association's Annual Meeting. The
level of technical treatment varies from expository prose to the use of
advanced mathematical methodologies. The authors are economists affiliated with academe or the business sector. This title is the American
counterpart of The Business Economist, a British publication aimed at
economists working in the business sector.
   A typical issue contains six to eight articles, each from five to
seven pages in length. Occasionally, an issue includes short comments on
articles published in previous issues. One in depth signed book review
appears in each issue. The March issue is primarily devoted to listing
the membership of the Association and includes only one or two articles.

057.   The Business Economist. DATE FOUNDED: 1969. FREQUENCY: 3/yr.
PRICE: ₤ 17/yr. PUBLISHER: The Society of Business Economists, 11 Bay
Tree Walk, Watford, Herts WD1 3RX, England. EDITOR: R.M. Connell.
ILLUSTRATIONS. INDEX. ADVERTISEMENTS. MANUSCRIPT SELECTION: Editor. BOOK
REVIEWS. INDEXED/ABSTRACTED: WorkRelAbstr. TARGET AUDIENCE: AC, GP, SP.

The Business Economist is published by a professional association of practicing economists in the business sector in the U.K. This periodical provides a synthesis of economic issues studies by academics, government officials, and the business community. Some of the articles deal with broad economic principles such as unemployment, monetarism, exchange rates, and inflation. Others deal with specific industry concerns in Great Britain such as the cable television industry, minerals and mines, and automobile manufacturing. Occasionally, articles are adapted from presentations made at the Society's Annual Meeting. The articles are expository in style and do not utilize mathematical methodologies. The authors are predominantly British economists from academe or the business sector. This title is the British counterpart of Business Economics. However, it is less technical and its applied economic studies focus on the U.K. rather than the U.S.

A typical issue includes three articles, each from ten to twenty pages in length. Other features are an editorial offering an overview of the articles included in that issue and an extensive book review section. Each issue offers from fifteen to twenty signed reviews. Some of these are comparative reviews - two books dealing with the same topic are evaluated jointly by one reviewer.

058.   Business History. DATE FOUNDED: 1958. FREQUENCY: 3/yr. PRICE: Ⱡ35/yr. institutions, Ⱡ22/yr. personal. PUBLISHER: Frank Cass & Co. Ltd., 11 Gainsborough Road, London EII IRS, England. EDITOR: Leslie Hannah. ILLUSTRATIONS. ADVERTISEMENTS. MANUSCRIPT SELECTION: Editor. REPRINTS: Authors. BOOK REVIEWS. INDEXED/ABSTRACTED: BPI. TARGET AUDIENCE: AC,GP,SP.

Business History, although published by a commercial firm, is the intellectual offspring of the Business History Unit of the London School of Economics. Both the editor and the assistant editors are faculty members at that institution. Journal contributors are academics at various universities in the United Kingdom. This title deals with the history of business development in the United Kingdom. It also covers business development in countries formerly belonging to the British Empire and trade development with other countries. A recent issue focuses on trade between Japan and Great Britain. The articles are written in a scholarly style with copious references that can be understood by readers without training in economics. Some articles include tables of data but mathematical techniques are not used. Business History is the British counterpart of Business History Review.

A typical issue includes four to six articles of ten to twenty-five pages each and an extensive book review section of fifteen to twenty signed reviews. Most of the books reviewed are published in the U.K. Occasionally a review essay offering an in-depth evaluation of two books on the same topic is included. An annual feature is a summary of papers delivered at the Business History Seminar in London.

059.   Business History Review. DATE FOUNDED: 1926. TITLE CHANGES: Bulletin of the Business Historical Society (1926-1953). FREQUENCY: q. PRICE: $25/yr. institutions, $20/yr. personal. PUBLISHER: President and Fellows of Harvard University, Harvard University, Cambridge, Massachusetts 02138. EDITOR: Richard S. Tedlow. ILLUSTRATIONS. INDEX. ADVERTISE-

MENTS. CIRCULATION: 2,200. MANUSCRIPT SELECTION: Review Board. MICRO-
FORMS: UMI. REPRINTS: KR. BOOK REVIEWS. SPECIAL ISSUES. INDEXED/
ABSTRACTED: AcctInd, BPI, InEcA, JEL, PAIS, WorkRelAbstr. DATABASES:
ACCTIND, ECONLIT, PAIS INT. TARGET AUDIENCE: AC, SP.

The Business History Review is published for the Harvard Graduate School
of Business Administration. Articles, which are international in scope,
most often deal with the development of business enterprises or entire
industries and their influence on the economic, political, and social
environment. Some focus beyond a single industry, such as two recent
articles titled "American Business Philanthropy and Higher Education in
the 19th Century" and "Technology, Political Economy, and Professional-
ization: Central Themes of the Organizational Synthesis." Articles
typically are expository, not quantitative in nature, and often include
photographs. Both authors and members of the editorial board are
academics affiliated with universities or research institutes from all
over the world.The Review is similar in scope and format to the British
publication, Business History.

Each issue contains from four to seven articles of about twenty pages
in length. A significant portion of this journal is devoted to book
reviews. Issues contain up to forty-five reviews, usually of about 400
words each. They are written by academics and are signed. Each issue
contains a section, "The Editor's Corner," which announces future
meetings, symposia, library acquisitions, and fellowships being offered
in the field. An annual article and book review index is published in
the Winter issue and beginning with 1962, five-year cumulative indices
have been published. About once a year, a special issue is devoted to a
single topic. Recent examples are "British Business History," "Business
History and the History of Technology," and "Transportation."

060.   Business Horizons. DATE FOUNDED: 1958. FREQUENCY: 6/YR. PRICE:
$15/yr. PUBLISHER: Indiana University Graduate School of Business,
Bloomington, Indiana 47405. EDITOR: Harvey C. Bunke. ILLUSTRATIONS.
INDEX. CIRCULATION: 5,000. MANUSCRIPT SELECTION: Refereed by faculty
members. MICROFORMS: UMI. REPRINTS: Periodical Office, Indiana Univer-
sity. BOOK REVIEWS. SPECIAL ISSUES. INDEXED/ABSTRACTED: AcctInd, BPI,
BPIA, KeyEcS, PAIS, Pred, WorkRelAbstr. DATABASES: ACCTIND, ECONAB, MC,
PAIS INT, PF. TARGET AUDIENCE: AC, GP, SP. SAMPLE COPIES: Libraries and
Individuals.

Business Horizons is a business school publication that offers a broad
range of topics which are of interest to academics, business students,
and members of the business community. The editorial staff makes an
effort to strike a balance between theoretical and practical articles,
but recent issues contain more of the latter. Some explore the political, social, or cultural implications of current phenomena. Most
articles are non-technical in nature, include relatively little data,
and are written in a narrative style. The authors are predominantly
academics in economics or business and/or business consultants. They are
usually not associated with Indiana University. Business Horizons is
geared to a national readership and does not concentrate on Indiana
business and the Indiana economy as does the Business School's other
publication, Indiana Business Review.   Business Horizons resembles Mid-
South Business Journal and Akron Business And Economics Review.

Each issue contains ten to twelve articles ranging from five to fifteen pages in length. "The Editor's Chair" features a five or six-page editorial, occasionally written by a guest editor. A book review section contains three or four reviews, 300 to 600 words in length, written primarily by Indiana University academics. The book review editor tends to select books dealing with controversial topics. Each issue includes a cumulative articles and book reviews index of the volume to date so that the annual index is found in the December issue.

061.   **Business Mexico.** DATE FOUNDED: 1983. FREQUENCY: q. PRICE: $60/yr. PUBLISHER: American Chamber of Commerce of Mexico, A.C., Lucerna 78, Col. Juarez, Del Cuawhtemoc, Mexico City, 06600 Mexico, D.F. EDITOR: Merrilee A. Fuller. ILLUSTRATIONS. ADVERTISEMENTS. MANUSCRIPT SELECTION: Editor. TARGET AUDIENCE: GP.,SP.

Business Mexico is a magazine that offers a host of valuable information and analyses for American business people who conduct business in Mexico. It generally lives up to its promise of providing "a comprehensive, authoritative look at today's Mexico and its economic, investment and trade prospects." Each issue provides an overview of the Mexican economy and makes some predictions concerning its outlook. A typical issue will contain articles which cover such topics as production, employment, international trade, the current account, exchange rates, inflation, monetary policy, and banking policy. Articles also address specific economics and business issues in Mexico. Examples from recent issues include "Mexico's In-Bond Industry: Crucial Job Source and Dollar-Earner", "the National Program for Financing Development", and "the Challenge to Mexican Agriculture and Agribusiness." Articles are non-technical in nature and can be understood by non-economists. The authors are staff journalists and no by-line is provided.

A typical issue includes five to ten full-length articles, many shorter articles, and several "appendices". The latter provide detailed text of certain government regulations, rules, guidelines, and decrees. Some issues also include a "Special Section" on an important topic such as "Energy in Mexico".

062.   **Business Quarterly.** DATE FOUNDED: 1933. TITLE CHANGES: Quarterly Review of Commerce (1933-1950). FREQUENCY: q. PRICE: $22/yr. PUBLISHER: School of Business Administration, The University of Western Ontario, 1393 Western Rd., London, Ontario N6A5B9 Canada. EDITOR: Doreen Sanders. ILLUSTRATIONS. INDEX. ADVERTISEMENTS. CIRCULATION: 12,000. MANUSCRIPT SELECTION: Editor and Editorial Advisory Committee. MICROFORMS: KR, UMI. REPRINTS: Publisher. SPECIAL ISSUES. INDEXED/ABSTRACTED: BPI, BPIA, CBPI, PAIS. DATABASES: ABI, CBI, MC, PAIS INT. TARGET AUDIENCE: GP. SAMPLE COPIES: Libraries and Individuals.

Business Quarterly is a business school publication, somewhat more elaborate, but not substantively different from many American business school publications such as Indiana University's Business Horizons or Arizona State's Arizona Business. One difference is that Business Quarterly focuses on the national economy of Canada, while many of its American counterparts have a more regional interest. Most issues offer a mix of management and economics articles. Many of the former involve human resource management. The latter deal with topics such as Canada's approach to its capital markets, productivity, export stimulation, foreign owned subsidiaries in Canada, Canada's global competitiveness, industrial policy, and particular Canadian industries such as tourism and pharmaceuticals. Most articles are non-technical in nature and written in an expository style. Often they offer a point of view based on some evidence. The authors are Canadian academics in economics or business administration, Canadian business executives, or Canadian management consultants.

A typical issue contains about ten full-length articles plus a few shorter ones in regular features including "Challenging Conformity", "Viewpoint", "Art and Business", "Women in Business", and "You and the Computer". "Editor's Guest Book" introduces authors and topics in each issue. About once a year an issue includes a supplement which is comprised of a number of articles on specific topics such as "A Salute to the New Canadian Woman", "The Power of Technological Innovations", and "Managing Business/Government Relations in Canada."

063.   Business Week. DATE FOUNDED: 1929. FREQUENCY: w. PRICE: $39.95/ yr. PUBLISHER: McGraw-Hill Publications Co., 1221 Avenue of the Americas, New York, New York 10020. EDITOR: Lewis H. Young. ILLUSTRATIONS. INDEX. ADVERTISEMENTS. CIRCULATION: 850,000. MANUSCRIPT SELECTION: Editor. MICROFORMS: UMI. REPRINTS: UMI. BOOK REVIEWS. SPECIAL ISSUES. INDEXED/ABSTRACTED: AcctInd, BPI, BPIA, ComLitI, OR/MS, PAIS, Pred, RG, WorkRelAbstr. DATABASES: ACCTIND, MC, PAIS INT, PF. TARGET AUDIENCE: GP.

Business Week is one of the most well known and accepted popular business and economics magazines published in the United States. It is aimed at the same readership--business people and others interested in business and economics--and offers similar coverage as Fortune. The latter has a different format with fewer and somewhat longer articles, and is less newsy in nature since it is published half as frequently. Business Week publishes articles dealing with all facets of domestic and international economics and business. Articles often focus on specific firms, competition among firms in specific markets, or the economy as a whole. They deal with finance, marketing, and management issues of domestic and foreign firms and their international relationships. Articles are journalistic in style and non-technical. They are written by a large staff of editors and correspondents and except for commentaries are not signed.

A typical issue includes from thirty to forty articles of varying lengths. The "Cover Story" which encompasses one or more sub-stories is usually the longest. Articles are grouped into sections such as "In the News", "Economic Analysis", "Finance", "The Corporation", "Industry and Technology", "Information Processing" and "International". Each is broken down into subsections. Regular features include an updated set of indexes and data, letters to the editor, one in-depth signed book review and one or more brief unsigned reviews, sections on personal activities and investments, and three brief editorials.

064.   Cambridge Economic Policy Review. DATE FOUNDED: 1975. FREQUENCY: 2/yr. PRICE: $35/yr. PUBLISHER: Gower Publishing Co., Ltd., Gower House, Croft Rd., Aldershot, Hampshire, England. EDITOR: Cambridge Economic Policy Group. ILLUSTRATIONS. CIRCULATION: 1,000. MANUSCRIPT SELECTION: Editors. INDEXED/ABSTRACTED:IntBibE. TARGET AUDIENCE: AC, SP.

The <u>Cambridge</u> <u>Economic</u> <u>Policy</u> <u>Review</u> is published for the Department of
Applied Economics of the University of Cambridge. It is not a journal
like the <u>Cambridge</u> <u>Journal</u> <u>of</u> <u>Economics</u>, in that it does not invite
manuscripts for publication. Instead, the contents of each issue is
prepared primarily by members of the Cambridge Economic Policy Group. It
focuses only on the British economy or on how world economic developments affect the British economy. Each issue has a particular theme such
as an analysis of the U.K.'s regional growth and decay, U.K. economic
policy and its international context, and an assessment of the performance of the U.K. economy and its response to recent government policies. Much use is made of the results attained from the Cambridge
Economic Policy Group macroeconomic model for the U.K. This publication
shows evidence of careful and scholarly activity in that the authors
provide full and detailed analyses. <u>Cambridge</u> <u>Economic</u> <u>Policy</u> <u>Review</u> is
somewhat technical but is readily understandable to those with some
training in economics. The <u>Review</u> deals with the same subject area as
<u>Economic</u> <u>Review</u> and <u>National</u> <u>Institute</u> <u>Economic</u> <u>Review.</u>
A typical issue is from sixty to eighty pages in length, broken up
into several chapters, and followed by a statistical appendix. The
principle author of each chapter is sometimes named.

065.   Cambridge Journal of Economics. DATE FOUNDED: 1977. FREQUENCY:
q. PRICE: $71/yr. institutions, $35.50/yr. personal. PUBLISHER: Academic
Press Inc., High Street, Footscray, Kent DA14 5HP, England. EDITOR: Ann
Newton. ILLUSTRATIONS. INDEX. ADVERTISEMENTS. CIRCULATION: 1,800.
MANUSCRIPT SELECTION: Editorial Board and Referees. REPRINTS: Publisher.
BOOK REVIEWS. SPECIAL ISSUES. INDEXED/ABSTRACTED: InEcA, IntBibE, JEL,
PAIS, SSI, WAERSA. DATABASES: CAB AB, ECONLIT, PAIS INT, SSI. TARGET
AUDIENCE: AC, SP.

The <u>Cambridge</u> <u>Journal</u> <u>of</u> <u>Economics</u> is the journal of the Cambridge
Political Economy Society. The Society believes that "the economic
approach rooted in the traditions of Marx, Kalecki, and Keynes has much
to contribute to the understanding and treatment of current economic and
social issues." It therefore fosters the publication of "theoretical and
applied work, with strong emphasis on realism of analysis, the provision
and use of empirical evidence, and the formulation of economic policies." Articles vary greatly in subject matter. Both micro and macroeconomic topics are included. Articles deal with production and price
theory as well as unemployment and inflation. Some are quite theoretical
while others relate to a particular policy question in the U.K. Occasionally articles are in the area of economic development; recent issues
have carried some dealing with Yugoslavia, Argentina, Chile, and
Nicaragua. Also featured are serious and scholarly papers on the history
of economic thought. The authors are predominantly academic economists
from the U.K. and the U.S.
A typical issue includes from three to five articles ranging from ten
to forty pages in length. Most issues have a "Notes" section that
contains brief articles and/or a book review. Some issues have a
"Commentary" section that contains discussion and debate of current
economic problems. Occasionally an issue will include a lengthy review
article.

066.   Canadian Business Review. DATE FOUNDED: 1974. FREQUENCY: q.
PRICE: $24/yr. PUBLISHER: The Conference Board of Canada, Suite 100, 25
McArthur Avenue, Ottawa, Ontario, KIL 6R3, Canada. EDITOR: S. Scott
Hatfield. ILLUSTRATIONS. INDEX. CIRCULATION: 8,500. MANUSCRIPT SELEC-
TION: Editor. MICROFORMS: UMI. REPRINTS: WSH. INDEXED/ABSTRACTED:
AcctInd, BPI, BPIA, CanI, CBI, PAIS, Pred, WorkRelAbstr. DATABASES:
ACCTIND, CBI, MC, PAIS, INT, PF. TARGET AUDIENCE: GP, SP.

The Canadian Business Review is published by a leading Canadian inde-
pendant research institution that serves the business community. Its
stated purpose is to keep senior business decision makers informed about
current economic issues, management practices, and public affairs. The
Review features articles that discuss both the current condition of the
Canadian economy as well as its near-term prospects. Other articles deal
with a wide array of topics grouped in subject categories that include
corporate planning, public affairs, economic analysis, energy, human
resources, international finance, and international trade. The articles
are expository in style and "bridge the gap between the general reports
of the news media and the highly technical accounts of the academic
journals." Articles are devoid of mathematics. The authors are from
business, academia, and government, as well as staff members of the
Conference Board. This publication is the Canadian counterpart of Across
the Board; the Conference Board Magazine.
      A typical issue contains from nine to thirteen articles that range
from four to eight pages in length. Each issue provides an overview of
the contents detailed in an "Inside this Issue" column on the title
page. The first article in each issue is "Outlook", written by a staff
member of the Conference Board Forecasting Group. Some issues include a
special report in the form of five or six articles on a specific topic
such as "Productivity" and "Doing Business in Africa."

067.   Canadian Farm Economics. DATE FOUNDED: 1966. FREQUENCY: Ir.
PRICE: Free. PUBLISHER: Agriculture Canada, Sir John Carling Building,
Ottawa, Ontario, KIA OC7 Canada. EDITOR: M. Audrey Voitkus. ILLUSTRA-
TIONS. CIRCULATION: 6,500. MANUSCRIPT SELECTION: Editor. INDEXED/
ABSTRACTED: PAIS, WAERSA. DATABASES: CAB AB, PAIS INT. TARGET AUDIENCE:
SP. SAMPLE COPIES: Libraries and Individuals.

Canadian Farm Economics is published by the Canadian government agency
comparable to the U.S. Department of Agriculture. Its purpose is "to
provide information on agricultural economics." The publication offers
articles that evaluate the economics of specific agricultural methods
and practices, mainly as followed in Canada. Representative titles are
"An Economic Assessment of the Benefits of Captan Use in Canada",
"Energy Conservation in Canadian Greenhouses: An Economic Analysis", and
"Sustainability in the Canadian Agri-food System." The articles are
expository in style and incorporate many tables of data but do not use
advanced statistical or mathematical methodologies. Most of the authors
are staff economists at Agriculture Canada. It is quite different from
either of the two titles, Agricultural Outlook and Agricultural Economics Research, published by the U.S. Department of Agriculture. It
goes beyond merely providing data as does Agricultural Outlook, by
offering analytical studies of agricultural practices, yet it is not as
mathematically sophisticated as Agricultural Economics Research.

A typical issue includes three to five articles, ranging in length
from four to twenty-four pages. It is also available in a French
language edition.

068.   Canadian Journal of Agricultural Economics/Revue Canadienne
d'Economie Rurale. DATE FOUNDED: 1952. FREQUENCY: 3/yr. PRICE: $50/yr.
Free to Members. PUBLISHER: Canadian Agricultural Economics and Farm
Management Society, Suite 907, 151 Slater Street, Ottawa, Ontario, KIP
5H4 Canada. EDITORS: S. N. Kulshreshtha and R. C. Nicholson. ILLUSTRA-
TIONS. INDEX. ADVERTISEMENTS. CIRCULATION: 1,200. MANUSCRIPT SELECTION:
Editors and Referees. REPRINTS: Publisher. BOOK REVIEWS. SPECIAL ISSUES.
INDEXED/ABSTRACTED: InEcA, IntBibE, JEL, PAIS, WAERSA. DATABASES: CAB
AB, ECONLIT, PAIS INT. TARGET AUDIENCE: AC, SP. SAMPLE COPIES: Li-
braries.

The Canadian Journal of Agricultural Economics/Revue Canadienne d'Economie Rurale is a scholarly journal aimed at professional agricultural
economists. Almost half of the articles relate to Canadian agriculture
but many deal with an agricultural case in another country. Seldom does
an article address agricultural problems in third world countries.
Articles frequently employ a formal model and most are quite quantitative. Fairly sophisticated mathematics and statistics are used in many
of the articles and it is not unusual for articles to stress the
methodology employed more than the case for which data may be presented.
Authors are either academics (primarily at Canadian and U.S. Universities) or researchers at Agriculture Canada or another government
agricultural agency. It is comparable in subject coverage and technical
treatment to the American Journal of Agricultural Economics.
    A typical issue contains four or five articles averaging fifteen to
twenty pages in length, four or five notes averaging ten pages each, a
comment followed by a reply, about six one to two page signed book
reviews, and a list of publications received. Occasionally a review
article or an essay (the annual CAEFMS Undergraduate Prize Essay) is
also included. The proceedings of the annual meeting of the Society are
published as a supplement to the Journal.

069.   Canadian Journal of Economics/Revue Canadienne d'Economique.
DATE FOUNDED: 1968. FREQUENCY: q. PRICE: $55/yr. institutions, $35/yr.
personal, Canadian residents. PUBLISHER: University of Toronto Press,
5201 Dufferin Street, Downsview, Ontario, M3H 5T8 Canada. EDITOR:
Michael Parkin. ILLUSTRATIONS. INDEX. ADVERTISEMENTS. CIRCULATION:
3,500. MANUSCRIPT SELECTION: Board of Editors and Referees. MICROFORMS:
UMI. BOOK REVIEWS: INDEXED/ABSTRACTED: BPIA, CanI, InEcA, IntBibE, JEL,
PAIS, SSI, WAERSA, WorkRelAbstr. DATABASES: CAB AB, ECONLIT, MC, PAIS
INT, SSI. TARGET AUDIENCE: AC, SP.

The Canadian Journal of Economics/Revue Canadienne D'Economique is
published for the Canadian Economics Association. This prestigious and
scholarly journal publishes articles that are "significant contributions
to knowledge in all areas of economics." It maintains a good balance
between micro and macroeconomics topics and between theoretical and
applied work. Articles in recent issues have most often dealt with pure
economic theory, methodology, labor and demographics, international
trade, and industrial organization. Most articles present a model. Those

that engage in empirical testing emphasize Canadian economic experience. The typical article is highly technical. It employs modern mathematical and statistical methodologies. The authors are predominantly academic economists, approximately seventy-five percent at Canadian universities with most of the rest at American universities. This journal is the Canadian equivalent of the American Economic Review.

Each issue contains from nine to twelve articles ranging from ten to twenty pages in length. The majority are in English with the rest in French. Each article is prefaced by both an English and a French abstract. Some issues include a section of shorter articles and comments. Each issue has from five to seven signed book reviews, each two or three pages in length, and written by a Canadian economist. The November issue provides information about the Association and publishes the minutes of the annual meeting.

070.   Canadian Journal of Regional Science/La Revue Canadienne des Sciences Regionales. DATE FOUNDED: 1978. FREQUENCY: 2/yr. PRICE: $25/yr. institutions, $20/yr. personal. PUBLISHER: Dalhousie University, Institute of Public Affairs, Halifax, Nova Scotia, B3H 3J5 Canada and Institut National de la Recherche Scientifique-Urbanisation, 3465 rue Durocher, Montreal, Quebec, H2X 2C6, Canada. EDITORS: William J. Coffey, Mario Polese. ILLUSTRATIONS. CIRCULATION: 700. MANUSCRIPT SELECTION: Editors and Referees. REPRINTS: Publisher. BOOK REVIEWS. SPECIAL ISSUES. INDEXED/ABSTRACTED: GeoAb. TARGET AUDIENCE: AC,SP. SAMPLE COPIES: Libraries and Individuals.

The Canadian Journal of Regional Science/La Revue Canadienne des Sciences Regionales is an interdisciplinary publication covering the subjects of economics and geography. It emphasizes applied economic studies in Canada but occasionally includes articles dealing with Europe. Recent issues have included articles on topics such as economic policies of the Atlantic Provinces, potential usage of agricultural land, fisheries management on the Atlantic Coast, inter-regional migration, regional income disparities, structure of urban housing prices, interaction of federal and provincial tax rates, regional energy policy decisions, and income differences by city size. All of the articles are scholarly in style and many of them use mathematical methodology. Most of them offer empirical data in support of their hypotheses. Most of the authors are professors of economics or geography at Canadian universities. A few contributions are made by European academics, Canadian government researchers, and American academics.

The Journal includes articles in English and French. A typical issue contains six or seven full length articles and one or two shorter "research notes." Three or four signed book reviews appear in each issue. French and English abstracts of all articles are found at the back of each issue. Occasionally, special issues devoted to a specific topic are published. Recent ones dealt with "Small Regions and Economic Recession" and "Public Policy on Urban and Regional Issues."

071.   Canadian Labour/Travailleur Canadien. DATE FOUNDED: 1956. MERGER: Incorporated Canadian Labour Comment (1973-1978). FREQUENCY: 10/yr. PRICE: Free. PUBLISHER: Canadian Labour Congress, 2841 Riverside Drive, Ottawa, Ontario, KIV 8X7 Canada. EDITOR: Mary Kehoe. ILLUSTRATIONS. CIRCULATION: 25,000. MANUSCRIPT SELECTION: Editor. MICROFORMS:

MIC. INDEXED/ABSTRACTED: BPIA, CanI, CBI,PAIS, WorkRelAbstr. DATABASES:
CBI, MC, PAIS INT. TARGET AUDIENCE: GP. SAMPLE COPIES: Libraries and
Individuals.

Canadian Labour/Travailleur Canadien is published by the Canadian Labor
organization that corresponds to the AFL-CIO in the United States. The
purpose of this publication is to inform its members about current
employment conditions as well as the possible impact of federal and
provincial legislation on workers' rights. This title also deals with
broader based social concerns both in Canada and in other countries.
Some examples of topics covered in recent issues are pension plans,
corporate vs. individual taxes, affirmative action programs, corporate
profits, deregulation of industry, and the impact of technology on
employment. The articles are expository in style and aimed at a general
audience. The authors are either staff members of the Canadian Labour
Congress or officials of labor unions.
    A typical issue includes two feature articles, each up to four pages
in length. In addition there are many short news items covering recent
events such as union activities around the world, new medical care
benefits, workplace safety practices, and labor union conferences.
Occasionally, a section called "Economic Bulletin" is included which
provides data on employment rates, wages and salaries, and cost of
living adjustments. Each issue presents the entire text in both French
and English.

072.   Canadian Public Policy/Analyse de Politiques. DATE FOUNDED:
1975. FREQUENCY: q. PRICE: $35/yr. institutions, $22/yr. personal.
PUBLISHER: University of British Columbia, Department of Economics,
Vancouver, B.C., Canada and University of Guelph, Guelph, Ontario, NIG
2WI Canada. EDITOR: Anthony Scott. ILLUSTRATIONS. INDEX. ADVERTISEMENTS.
CIRCULATION: 2,400. MANUSCRIPT SELECTION: Editor. MICROFORMS: MIC.
REPRINTS: UTP. BOOK REVIEWS. SPECIAL ISSUES. INDEXED/ABSTRACTED: CanI,
CBI, InEcA, IntBibE, JEL, PAIS, SocAb, WAERSA. DATABASES: CAB AB, CBI,
ECONLIT, PAIS INT, SOCAB. TARGET AUDIENCE: AC, GP, SP. SAMPLE COPIES:
Libraries and Individuals.

Canadian Public Policy/Analyse de Politiques is a journal that has a
broad base of support in Canada. It is published jointly by two universities and receives additional financial assistance from other universities, government agencies, and corporations. Although it was established by the Canadian Economics Association, its scope has broadened
beyond economics to include all social sciences that impact on public
policy concerns. Occasionally, half of the articles in an issue will
concentrate on a single topic such as the recent issue which emphasized
"Obstacles to Recovery" and "The New Oil Price Scenario". Some of the
articles use statistical techniques, but many of them are written in a
non-technical style. Most of the authors are Canadian academics; a few
are corporate executives, and an occasional one is by an American
academic.
    A typical issue includes eight to ten articles, ranging in length
from seven to sixteen pages. Most of them are in English but each
article is prefaced with short abstracts in both French and English. A
"Views and Comments" section includes shorter (three to four page)
papers and comments from readers on previously published articles. Each
issue also includes sixteen to eighteen signed book reviews. Most of the

books deal with current economic or social concerns in Canada and are
reviewed by Canadian academics.

073.   Capital and Class. DATE FOUNDED: 1970. TITLE CHANGES: Bulletin
of the Conference of Socialist Economists (1970-1977). FREQUENCY: 3/yr.
PRICE: L25/yr. institutions, L9/yr. personal. PUBLISHER: Conference of
Socialist Economists, 25 Horsell Road, London N5, England. EDITOR:
Editorial Committee. ILLUSTRATIONS. INDEX. ADVERTISEMENTS. CIRCULATION:
1,500. MANUSCRIPT SELECTION: Editorial Committee and Referees. BOOK
REVIEWS. SPECIAL ISSUES. INDEXED/ABSTRACTED: API, LeftInd, WAERSA.
DATABASES: CAB AB. TARGET AUDIENCE: AC, GP. SAMPLE COPIES: Libraries.

Capital and Class is published by an organization "committed to the
development within the labour movement of a materialist critique of
capitalism in the Marxist tradition." All articles in this journal
reflect that commitment or mission. Many are critical of particular
British institutions including how certain industries are hurt by
capitalist actions. Some articles deal with "crises" in other countries
such as "The Current Crisis in Israel", written by an Israeli spokes-
person for the anti-zionist left. Many articles focus on the topic of
internationalization and argue that the capitalist world economy
threatens national economic strategies. Articles are non-technical in
nature, sometimes include some data, but never involve quantitative
analyses. The strong viewpoint of the Conference of Socialist Economists
is evident. Footnotes and references are typically provided. Authors are
identified by name, but no credentials and professional affiliations are
given. The editors state (in a private communication) that the authors
are academics, researchers, and sometimes government employees.
    A typical issue contains seven or eight articles, each from ten to
thirty pages in length. Most issues include one article dealing with a
contemporary situation in a "Behind the News" section. There is usually
one review article in which a recent book is examinded. Each issue lists
"Books Received".

074.   Carnegie-Rochester Conference Series on Public Policy. DATE
FOUNDED: 1976. FREQUENCY: 2/yr. PRICE: $100/yr. institutions, $46/yr.
personal. PUBLISHER: Elsevier Science Publisher B.V. (North-Holland),
P.O. Box 1919, 1000 BZ Amsterdam, The Netherlands. EDITORS: Karl
Brunner, Allan H. Meltzer. ILLUSTRATIONS. CIRCULATION: 1,500. MANUSCRIPT
SELECTION: Editors. INDEXED/ABSTRACTED: InEcA, JEL. DATABASES: ECONLIT.
TARGET AUDIENCE: AC,SP.

Carnegie-Rochester Conference Series on Public Policy are the conference
proceedings of bi-annual meetings. These conferences are supported by
the Center for the Study of Public Policy at Carnegie-Mellon University
and the Center for Research in Government Policy and Business at the
University of Rochester. Additional support is received from private and
government foundations. The conferences are aimed at directing "the
attention of economists to major problems of economic policy and
institutional arrangements." Each conference is organized around a theme
and each paper prepared for a specific conference is on that theme.
Recent conferences were devoted to topics such as "Variability in
Employment, Prices, and Money", "Monetary Institutions and the Policy
Process", and "Money, Monetary Policy, and Financial Institutions." The

articles are scholarly in style and most of them incorporate mathematical analyses in their discussions. Most of the authors are academics
at leading American universities or researchers with the National Bureau
of Economic Research. A few authors are associated with universities
outside the U.S. or leading international banks. This publication is "a
supplementary series to the Journal of Monetary Economics." Readers'
comments on papers published in the Carnegie-Rochester Conference Series
occasionally are included in the Journal.
    A typical issue begins with an introduction and summary of the papers
by the editor. This is followed by six in-depth articles (thirty to
fifty pages each) and nine or ten short comments (five to ten pages
each) on the articles. The comments include both prepared statements by
conference discussants and extemporaneous statements by conference
participants.

075.   Carroll Business Bulletin. DATE FOUNDED: 1957. FREQUENCY: 2/yr.
PRICE: $2/yr. PUBLISHER: John Carroll University, School of Business,
University Heights, Cleveland, Ohio 44118. EDITOR: Alfred Schneider.
ILLUSTRATIONS. CIRCULATION: 5,500. MANUSCRIPT SELECTION: Editor. TARGET
AUDIENCE: GP.

The Carroll Business Bulletin is a business school publication that
offers "articles of interest in accounting, administration, economics,
finance, transportation, marketing, and other areas of concern to the
business, industrial and educational communities." The editorial
view-point is on the conservative side of the political spectrum.
Representative articles in recent issues include "The Demand Curve: A
Note on Different Perspectives", "Japan's Energy Problem", "Population
Mobility for the Multinational Firm: the Captive Option." The articles
are non-technical in nature and are written in an expository style. The
authors are predominantly professors of business or economics at John
Carroll University. Occasionally an article by an academic at another
Amercian university or by an executive of a major business firm will be
included. The Carroll Business School Bulletin is far less parochial
than the majority of non-technical business school publications. In this
regard it most closely resembles Mid-South Business Journal and Indiana
University's Business Horizons.
    A typical issue contains five or six articles ranging from five to
twelve pages in length. A one to two page editorial preceeds the
articles.

076.   The Cato Journal. DATE FOUNDED: 1981. FREQUENCY: 3/yr. PRICE:
$15/yr. PUBLISHER: The Cato Institute, 224 Second Street SE, Washington,
D.C. 20003. EDITOR: James A. Dorn. ADVERTISEMENTS. CIRCULATION: 3,200.
MANUSCRIPT SELECTION: Editors. MICROFORMS: UMI. INDEXED/ABSTRACTED:
PAIS. DATABASES: ABI, PAIS INT. TARGET AUDIENCE: AC, GP.

The Cato Journal is an interdisciplinary journal of public policy
analysis. It is published by the Cato Institute, a non-profit research
foundation, that seeks to promote public policy consistent with "the
traditional American principles of limited government, individual
liberty, and peace." The Institute sponsors major policy conferences
from which papers are published in The Cato Journal. The papers cover a
wide spectrum of policy issues. Topics that might be examined include

the federal budget, Social Security, monetary policy, natural resource policy, military spending, regulation, NATO, and international trade. Recent conferences focused on "World Debt and the Monetary Order," "Social Security: continuing Crisis or Real Reform?" and "Land Use and Resource Development". The articles are written in a scholarly style with extensive footnotes but do not employ quantitative analyses. The authors are professors at American universities, researchers at government agencies, and senior executives in corporations. The Cato Journal shares the same overall subject scope as the Journal of Contemporary Studies but places greater emphasis on economic issues.

Each issue contains twelve to fourteen papers of twenty to thirty pages in length. About ninety percent of them were delivered at one of the Institute's Conferences. Many of the papers are accompanied by short comments. An editor's preface which sums up the theme of the conference appears at the beginning of each issue.

077.   **Challenge; The Magazine of Economic Affairs.** DATE FOUNDED: 1952. FREQUENCY: 6/yr. PRICE: $33/yr. institutions, $28/yr. personal. PUBLISHER: Myron E. Sharpe, 80 Business Park Drive, Armonk, New York 10504. EDITOR: Richard D. Bartel. ILLUSTRATIONS. INDEX. ADVERTISEMENTS. CIRCULATION: 5,500. MANUSCRIPT SELECTION: Editor. REPRINTS: Publisher. BOOK REVIEWS. INDEXED/ABSTRACTED: BPI, BPIA, PAIS, Pred, WorkRelAbstr. DATABASES: MC, PAIS INT, PF. TARGET AUDIENCE: GP.

Challenge; the Magazine of Economic Affairs is a publication aimed primarily at the intelligent layperson interested in current economic issues. Articles are totally expository in nature. Data is frequently provided, but no statistical, econometric, or mathematical methodology is utilized. Articles deal with a wide variety of economic issues. Some provide an analysis of a specific event such as the divestiture of AT&T, while others examine a particular economic policy or economic trend. The majority of articles deal with American economic issues, but each issue usually includes at least one article dealing with another country's economic affairs. The authors are academics or government economists and often include the "big names" in the profession. The Editorial Advisory Board consists of prominent economists, several of whom are Nobel Laureates. Challenge is aimed at the same readership as Journal of Contemporary Studies and The Cato Journal.

A typical issue contains about six articles, each from eight to ten pages in length. Each issue begins with an editorial which summarizes the articles. Some issues include an interview with a well known economist. Each issue contains a section, "The Growlery", that includes four or five two-to-three page comments, opinions and analyses. These may be excerpts of papers delivered or published elsewhere. Each issue also contains one signed in-depth book review and a list of books and articles "for further reading" on topics of that particular issue.

078.   **Chinese Economic Studies.** DATE FOUNDED: 1967. FREQUENCY: 8/yr. PRICE: $78/yr. institutions, $46/yr. personal. PUBLISHER: Myron E. Sharpe, Inc., 80 Business Park Drive, Armonk, New York 10504. EDITOR: George C. Wang. INDEX. ADVERTISEMENTS. MANUSCRIPT SELECTION: Editor. INDEXED/ABSTRACTED: InEcA, IntBibE, JEL, PAIS, WAERSA. DATABASES: CAB AB, ECONLIT, PAIS INT. TARGET AUDIENCE: AC, SP. SAMPLE COPIES: Libraries and Individuals.

Chinese Economic Studies is a journal consisting of English translations
of articles published in various Chinese journals. All of the articles
deal with current trends in China's economic situation or plans for
changes in its economic development strategies. Many of the articles
include political pronouncements interspersed with discussions of
economic policies. There is much discussion of various Five-Year Plans
that were adopted by the Chinese government. Two recent issues were
devoted to selections translated from a new Chinese journal, International Trade. The Editor noted that the establishment of this new
journal coincided with a change in China's policy that calls for
expansion of its economic relations with other countries. Examples of
articles that have appeared in current issues include "Several Problems
Involving the Current Rural Economic Policy" and "Set Up a Planned
Management System That is Appropriate for China". Although the authors'
names are given, their credentials and professional affiliations are
not. Many of them seem to be government economic planners. Very few of
the articles use any analytical techniques.
    Each issue includes five to eight articles which vary greatly in
length. A five page research article may be followed by a sixty-five
page article that translates a major economic policy address given at a
National Peoples' Congress.

079.   Colorado Business Review. DATE FOUNDED: 1928. FREQUENCY: m.
PRICE: $20/yr. - Free to Colorado Residents. PUBLISHER: Business
Reseacrh Division, Graduate Scool of Business Administration, University
of Colorado, Boulder, Colorado 80309. EDITOR: Charles R. Goeldner.
CIRCULATION: 2,100. MANUSCRIPT SELECTION: Review Board and Editor.
REPRINTS: Publisher. INDEXED/ABSTRACTED: PAIS. DATABASES: PAIS INT.
TARGET AUDIENCE: GP. SAMPLE COPIES: Libraries and Individuals.

The Colorado Business Review is a business school publication that
offers a mix of regional-interest and national-interest articles for
business people in Colorado and other Rocky Mountain states. Recent
issues carried a summary and analysis of a Colorado Business/Economics
outlook forum and a discussion of Colorado's need to expand its export
efforts. However, these issues also included articles such as "Emulating
Japan: Caveat Praefectus (Let the Manager Beware)", "Terminating
Employees", "Targeting Economic Capital Asset Formation with Certified
Development Companies" and "Joint Venture Laws and Activity in the
People's Republic of China." Articles are non-technical in nature and
expository in style. The authors are predominantly business or economics
professors at American universities, but some are researchers at
government agencies. Most are not associated with the University of
Colorado. With regard to level and coverage this publication most
resembles North Carolina Review of Business and Economics, Ball State
Business Review, and Mississippi Business Review.
    A typical issue is eight pages in length. Each of nine issues per
year contains one article of 1,500 to 2,500 words plus tables on
Colorado business indicators and local business conditions in forty-one
different Colorado metropolitan areas. The June, July and August numbers
do not include an article.

080.   Columbia Journal of World Business. DATE FOUNDED: 1965. FRE-
QUENCY: q. PRICE: $40/yr. institutions, $20/yr. personal. PUBLISHER:

Columbia University Business School, 815 Uris Hall, Columbia University, New York, New York 10027. EDITORS: Paul Dumouchelle, Richard Rollo. ILLUSTRATIONS. INDEX. ADVERTISEMENTS. CIRCULATION: 4,500. MANUSCRIPT SELECTION: Editors; Some are solicited. MICROFORMS: MIM, UMI. REPRINTS: Publisher. INDEXED/ABSTRACTED: AcctInd, BPI, BPIA, IntBibE, KeyEcS, PAIS, WAERSA, WorkRelAbstr. DATABASES: ABI, ACCTIND, CAB AB, ECONAB, MC, PAIS INT. TARGET AUDIENCE: AC, GP, SP.

The Columbia Journal of World Business publishes articles that analyze major events and issues shaping current international business. The readership is business executives, the academic community and government officials with interests in international business. Many recent issues focus on a single topic. Most, if not all of the articles of such an issue will involve some aspect of the theme topic. Examples of topics are "International Labor", "East-West Trade: Issues & Outlooks for the 1980s", "National Resources: Global Issues for the Eighties", and "Institutional Adaptation to Technological Change." These issues have guest editors who solicit and select articles as well as write an introduction to the topic. Authors are predominantly academics, but some articles are written by business executives and government officials. Authors are asked to submit articles which are global or comparative in approach and which deal with practical experience or applied theory. The result is that the articles are non-technical and non-mathematical. This publication covers the same subject area as the more technical Journal of International Business Studies.
    A typical issue contains ten or twelve articles ranging from four to ten pages in length.

081.   Comparative Labor Law. DATE FOUNDED: 1976. TITLE CHANGES: International Society for Law and Social Legislation, United States National Committee Bulletin. FREQUENCY: q. PRICE: $20/yr. PUBLISHER: School of Law, University of California, Los Angeles, 405 Hilgard Avenue, Los Angeles, CA 90024. EDITOR: Benjamin Aaron. INDEX. CIRCULA-TION: 450. MANUSCRIPT SELECTION: Editor. BOOK REVIEWS. INDEXED/ABSTRACT-ED: LRI. DATABASES: LRI. TARGET AUDIENCE: AC, SP.

Comparative Labor Law is a publication of the U.S. Branch of the International Society for Labor Law and Institute of Industrial Relations of the University of California, Los Angeles. It seeks "fuller knowledge of legal phenomena in the realm of labor relations" focusing especially on comparing the labor laws of different countries. That interest is shared by the Industrial Law Journal which, however, focuses largely on British labor law. Comparative Labor Law publishes scholarly articles which compare how different countries' labor laws treat such important concerns as unemployment assistance, child labor, safety and health of workers, fringe benefits, social security, the fixing of minimum wages, "human rights", and the position of women in the labor force. Other articles are less issue oriented and instead concentrate on the labor laws of a specific region of the world such as Asia or Latin America. Yet others probe the differences between socialist and capitalist systems. Articles are written by lawyers from all over the world, with the majority being U.S. academics. They are written primarily for other lawyers, but economists interested in labor relations or "social economics" can benefit from reading them.

Most issues contain about four articles which sometimes vary greatly in length. Most or all articles in an issue are often devoted to the same topic. Some issues include a signed book review. All issues include at least one selected bibliography on the labor law of a region of the world or a specific topic.

082.   Council on Economic Priorities Newsletter. DATE FOUNDED: 1971. FREQUENCY: m. PRICE: $25/yr. PUBLISHER: Council on Economic Priorities, 30 Irving Place, New York, New York 10003. EDITOR: Alice Tepper Marlin. ILLUSTRATIONS. MANUSCRIPT SELECTION: Editor. TARGET AUDIENCE: GP.

The Council on Economic Priorities Newsletter is published for the purpose of disseminating "unbiased and detailed information on the practices of U.S. corporations." The Council was established so that the American public could "work to ensure corporate social responsibility." Articles deal with social concerns on both a national and international scope. Titles of articles in recent issues include "Where You Bank Can Count", "Is Massive Rearmament Necessary?", "South Africa & Apartheid: What Role Should U.S. Industry Play?", and "SEC Proposes New Shareholder Rules." These and other articles provide the viewpoints that banks owned by minorities or women should be supported, a weapons increase for the NATO Alliance is unnecessary, American businesses should not invest in South Africa because of the Apartheid policy, and shareholders should receive more information on company practices involving public issues. A recent issue provided data received from state elections commissions on corporate spending for campaigns on ballot questions affecting their interests. The Newsletter is expository in nature. The articles are signed but no affiliations or credentials are provided. This publication is for social activists. Compared to the more academic orientation of Business and Society, this publication presents facts and opportunities for readers to take an active role.
    Each newsletter is only six pages in length and contains one feature article. Names and addresses of institutions or organizations providing more information on the featured topic are listed at the end of the article. Occasionally, a bibliography for further reading is included. At times, a chart listing the names of corporations having shareholder resolutions on social responsibility issues is provided.

083.   Cycles. DATE FOUNDED: 1950. FREQUENCY: 9/yr. PRICE: $30/yr. institutions, $50/yr. personal. PUBLISHER: Foundation for the Study of Cycles, Inc., 124 South Highland Ave., Pittsburgh, Pennsylvania 15206. EDITOR: Gertrude Shirk. ILLUSTRATIONS. INDEX. ADVERTISEMENTS. CIRCULA-TION: 2,000. MANUSCRIPT SELECTION: Editor. BOOK REVIEWS. INDEXED/ ABSTRACTED: PAIS, WAERSA. DATABASES: CAB AB, PAIS INT. TARGET AUDIENCE: AC, SP.

Cycles is the publication of an international, scientific, educational, non-profit foundation affiliated with the University of Pittsburgh. The Foundation continues the work of Edward R. Dewey, a pioneer in the study of cycles in the early Twentieth Century and this title still quotes from his writings. The Foundation promotes "multidisciplinary research in rhythmic fluctuations". Rhythmic fluctuations or cycles that are of interest to this organization occur in the areas of economic activity, climate, biology, and medicine. Articles emphasize the area of economics

and analyze fluctuations of commodity prices. The articles are expository in style and incorporate many charts and diagrams. Most of the
articles are written by Foundation staff members.

Each issue is from twenty-five to thirty-five pages in length and
includes four full-length articles. A regular feature, "Data Update",
lists comparative data for the previous year on production output,
construction outlays, trade, agricultural production, employment, price
indices, commodity prices, and financial statistics. Some issues include
a "Publications List" that provides information about books on cycles,
tapes of lectures presented at the Foundation's annual conference,
diskettes for microcomputers, and miscellaneous reprints. Occasioally, a
book review prepared by a staff member is included. Cycles reprints
reports from the Foundation's other publication, the Journal of Interdisciplinary Cycle Research.

084.   Czechoslovak Economic Digest. DATE FOUNDED: 1966. TITLE CHANGES:
New Trends in the Czechoslovak Economy. FREQUENCY: 8/yr. PRICE: $20/yr.
PUBLISHER: Orbis Press Agency, Features Service, 12041, Vinohradska 46,
Prague 2, Czechoslovakia. EDITOR: Vit Suchy. CIRCULATION: 600. MANU-
SCRIPT SELECTION: Editor. INDEXED/ABSTRACTED: InEcA, JEL, WAERSA.
DATABASES: CAB AB, ECONLIT. TARGET AUDIENCE: AC, GP, SP.

Czechoslovak Economic Digest is subtitled "Commentaries, Essays." It
contains articles, essays and reports regarding the Czechoslovak
economy. Some deal with its functioning while others with its social,
political and economic philosophy. Reports frequently involve the state
plan of economic and social development, economic management and trade
unions, or the implementation of government economic programs. Examples
of philosophical essays published in recent issues are: "Existential and
Social Certainties and their Realization", "Marx's Method of Political
Economy and the Present Time", and "To Observe the Principles of
Socialist Legality and Discipline." Articles do not report research and
are generally descriptive in nature. Representative examples include
"The Function of Small Enterprises in the Economy", "Coordination of
National Economic Plans of the CMEA Countries", "Investments that are
Certain to Return", "Problems of East-West Trade", "Pasture Crops: A
Resolution to the Grain Problem", and "the Monetary Policy in Banking at
the Present Stage." The authors are Czech government officials, academ-
ics, and researchers at government sponsored institutes. The Finance
Ministry, Ministry of Foreign Trade, State Planning Commission, Central
Council of Trade Unions, and the Communist Party of Czechoslovakia are
frequently represented. The Digest is less technical and more oriented
towards a non-specialist readership than Czechoslovak Economic Papers.

Czechoslovak Economic Digest has editions in English, French and
German. Most issues contain from three to six articles and essays.
Occasionally a very long report takes up all or most of an issue.

085.   Czechoslovak Economic Papers. DATE FOUNDED: 1959. FREQUENCY: a.
PUBLISHER: The Economic Institute of the Czechoslovak Academy of
Sciences, Trida Politickych veznu 7, Prague 1, Czechoslovakia. EDITOR:
Miroslav Rumler. ILLUSTRATIONS. MANUSCRIPT SELECTION: Editorial Board.
BOOK REVIEWS. INDEXED/ABSTRACTED: IntBibE, WAERSA. DATABASES: CAB AB.
TARGET AUDIENCE: AC, SP. SAMPLE COPIES: Libraries.

Czechoslovak Economic Papers is a scholarly journal that publishes both theoretical and applied economics articles. Most are either directly or indirectly concerned with the Czechoslovak economy. Articles in recent issues have dealt with the following topics: the conditions for special- ization in Czechoslovakia, a forecast of the external conditions for Czech development, application of the constant elasticity of substitu- tion production function to analyze economic growth in Czechoslovakia, external balances in a planned economy, the main theoretical foundations for the Czech management system, construction of international prices in the socialist world market, and the economic effects of the relationship between quality of products and exports. Occasionally articles are critical of capitalist approaches such as recent ones titled "the History of the Theory of the Invisible Hand" and "Towards a Consistent Theory of Inflation and Growth of Prices under Capitalism." The majority of articles are technical in nature and employ quantitative method- ologies. A few are expository and written in a narrative style. The authors are all Czech academic and/or research economists at Czech universities or research institutes. The majority are associated with the Economic Institute of the Czechoslovak Academy of Sciences in Prague. This publicaton is more technical and academically oriented than Czechoslovak Economic Digest.

A typical issue contains five or six regular articles, a section called "Scientific Life" which discusses the activities or reports of one or more commissions, and from one to four lengthy signed book reviews.

086.   Decision Sciences. DATE FOUNDED: 1970. FREQUENCY: q. PRICE: $48/yr. PUBLISHER: American Institute for Decision Sciences, University Plaza, 33 Gilmer Street; S.E. Atlanta, Georgia 30303. EDITOR: Robert E. Markland. ILLUSTRATIONS. INDEX. ADVERTISEMENTS. MANUSCRIPT SELECTION: Editors and Referees. MICROFORMS: UMI. INDEXED/ABSTRACTED: AcctInd, BPI, BPIA. DATABASES: ACCTIND, MC. TARGET AUDIENCE: AC, SP.

Decision Sciences is published by a professional association of business administration faculty and high-level corporate planning executives. The Institute is an organization dedicated to promoting "the development and application of quantitative methodology to functional behavioral problems of administration by providing a forum for the exchange of ideas, experience, and information among those who teach in collegiate schools of business." To assist in achieving that objective, this periodical publishes articles presenting "the use of behavioral, economic, and quantitative methods of analysis" in the decision-making process. All articles use quantitative methodologies from the fields of computer science, econometrics, forecasting, queing theory, and statis- tics. These are applied to managerial decision making in areas such as accounting, finance, marketing, production, and transportation. All authors are academics associated with graduate schools of business in the U.S. Decision Sciences is comparable in technical level to Managerial and Decision Economics, but empirical studies focus on the U.S. economy while MDE includes studies on an international scope.

A typical issue includes eight or nine articles, each from ten to twenty pages in length. Some issues also contain short notes which comment on previously published papers and provide authors' replies.

087.   Demography. DATE FOUNDED: 1964. FREQUENCY: q. PRICE: $53/yr.
PUBLISHER: Population Association of America, 806 15th Street, N.W.
Washington, D.C. 20005. EDITOR: Omer R. Galle. ILLUSTRATIONS. INDEX.
ADVERTISEMENTS. CIRCULATION: 4,000. MANUSCRIPT SELECTION: Editor and
Referees. MICROFORMS: UMI. REPRINTS: Publisher. INDEXED/ABSTRACTED:
InEcA, JEL, PAIS, PopIndex, SSI. DATABASES: ECONLIT, PAIS INT, SSI.
TARGET AUDIENCE: AC, SP. SAMPLE COPIES: Libraries and Individuals.

Demography is the journal of the Population Association of America, the
leading professional association of persons interested in population
studies. It is aimed at the scholar/researcher in the field. Coverage
extends to every aspect of demography. Most articles develop a model and
many include empirical test results. A significant amount of mathematics
and statistics is employed. The authors are predominantly academic
demographers in departments of economics, sociology, anthropology, and
political science or associated with population research institutes. The
majority are affiliated with American universities, but contributions
are also made by foreign scholars. Demography publishes more theoretical
articles and has a broader geographic scope for its empirical research
papers than Demography India.
      Each issue contains from ten to twelve articles ranging from fifteen
to thirty pages in length plus several shorter articles, comments, and
replies in a "Research Notes, Commentary and Debate" section. The
November issue includes the Presidential Address presented at the Annual
Meeting of the Population Association of America, an annual author
index, and a list of referees who served during the past year. A
five-year cummulative author and subject index is published.

088.   Demography India. DATE FOUNDED: 1972. FREQUENCY: 2/yr. PRICE:
$35/yr. PUBLISHER: Indian Association for the Study of Population,
Institute of Economic Growth, Delhi University, Delhi - 110007, India.
EDITOR: P. B. Desai. ILLUSTRATIONS. CIRCULATION: 500. MANUSCRIPT
SELECTION: Editorial Committee. INDEXED/ABSTRACTED: PopIndex. TARGET
AUDIENCE: AC, SP.

Demography India is the journal of the Indian Association for the Study
of Population. Its purpose is to publish articles that contribute to
"the scientific interests in population planning and research." It is a
scholarly journal aimed at academicians and other research scholars in
this field. It features demographic studies in rural and urban areas of
developing countries, especially India. The majority of articles apply
to an Indian case and use Indian data. Many articles develop a model and
report on the empirical test results. Such articles are quite mathematical and statistical in nature. Other articles emphasize methodology
such as the presentation of a procedure for estimating certain para-
meters. Occasionally, a non-quantitative "think piece" is included. The
majority of the authors are Indian, but others are American, Canadian,
English, Australian and Japanese. Most authors are academics in
departments of economics, sociology, or statistics or are researchers
associated with population research institutes. This journal rivals
Demography which contains somewhat more sophisticated articles and has a
broader geographic scope.
      A typical issue contains about a dozen articles ranging fom seven to
thirty pages on length. In recent years two numbers have frequently been
combined to constitute an entire volume.

089.   The Developing Economies. DATE FOUNDED: 1962. FREQUENCY: q.
PRICE: $50/yr. PUBLISHER: Institute of Developing Economies, 42 Ichigaya
- Hommura-cho, Chinjukuku, Tokyo 162, JAPAN. EDITOR: Editorial Board.
ILLUSTRATIONS. INDEX. ADVERTISEMENTS. CIRCULATION: 1,500. MANUSCRIPT
SELECTION: Editorial Board. MICROFORMS: MAR. BOOK REVIEWS. SPECIAL
ISSUES. INDEXED/ABSTRACTED: IntBibe, WAERSA. DATABASES: CAB AB. TARGET
AUDIENCE: AC, SP. SAMPLE COPIES: Libraries and Individuals.

The Developing Economies is the journal of the Institute of Developing
Economies, a Japanese institute founded in 1958 "for the study of basic
issues and current problems in the economies and societies of Asian and
other developing countries." This journal is international and interdisciplinary in scope and provides a forum for theoretical, empirical,
and comparative studies of the problems confronted by developing
nations. Articles are aimed at scholars in the field. Typically they
present a mathematical model and empirical results. Recent issues have
contained articles dealing with the development problems and issues in
Korea, Burma, Malaysia, Indonesia, India, Bangladesh, Tanzania, the
Philippines, Egypt, the People's Republic of China, and Japan. Articles
also discuss problems of development that transcend a number of countries and thus focus on a wide area of the world. The authors are
predominantly academic or research institute economists from Japan, and
the U.S.
    A typical issue contains from four to six articles, ranging from ten
to twenty pages in length. Comments on previously published articles,
replies, and rejoinders are sometimes included. Most issues have a book
review section that contains one or two in-depth signed book reviews.
The December issue of each volume is a "Special Issue" devoted to a
single topic. Topics of recent special issues include "Social Changes in
Rural Asia", "Chinese Economy in Search of Development", and "Trends and
Structural Changes in Pacific Asian Economies."

090.   Development and Change. DATE FOUNDED: 1970. FREQUENCY: q. PRICE:
$52/yr. institutions, $23.40/yr. personal. PUBLISHER: Sage Publications
Ltd., 28 Banner Street, London, EC1Y 8QE, England. EDITOR: Board of
Editors. ILLUSTRATIONS. INDEX. ADVERTISEMENTS. MANUSCRIPT SELECTION:
Editors. INDEXED/ABSTRACTED: IntBibE, KeyEcS, WAERSA. DATABASES: CAB AB,
ECONAB. TARGET AUDIENCE: AC, SP.

Development and Change is published for the Institute of Social Studies
at the Hague in the Netherlands. It is an interdisciplinary journal that
focuses on development problems. Recurrent themes include regional
planning, rural development, bureaucracy, educational and manpower
policies, technology transfer, and the role of multinational corporations. Most articles have empirical content, but only some employ
mathematical or statistical methodologies. The authors are a very
heterogeneous group. They include economists, sociologists and political
scientists. Some are associated with universities while others are with
research institutes. They represent nations from throughout the world.
This publication differs from the Development Policy Review which is
also published by Sage and has a similar format. DPR is not interdisciplinary and more strictly adheres to topics of economic development.
    A typical issue contains five or six articles, each from twenty to
forty pages in length. Some issues contain only articles while others

include "Discussion" and "Note and Comments" sections. Most issues have
a list of "Books Received."

091.   Development Digest. DATE FOUNDED: 1962. TITLE CHANGES: Develop-
ment Research Digest (1962-1965). FREQUENCY: 2/yr. PRICE: $6.75/yr.
PUBLISHER: Development Activities, Inc., 1606 New Hampshire Avenue,
N.W., Washington D.C. 20009. EDITOR: Gordon Donald. ILLUSTRATIONS.
INDEX. MANUSCRIPT SELECTION: Editor. INDEXED/ABSTRACTED: WAERSA.
DATABASES: CAB AB. TARGET AUDIENCE: AC, GP, SP.

Development Digest is published on behalf of the Agency for International Development. It is a journal of "excerpts, summaries and
reprints of current materials on economic and social development." Many
of the articles were originally published by United Nations or U.S.
Government agencies. AID intends this publication to be read by planners
in third world countries. It clearly reflects the view and philosophy of
the U.S. Government. Coverage extends to a wide variety of development
topics. Recent issues have devoted sections to "Private Enterprise and
the Market", "Aricultural Pricing", "Small Scale Energy", "Export
Marketing", "Newly Industrializing Countries", and "Population Trends."
Articles are non-technical in nature and written in an expository style.
Data are often included, but quantitative methodologies are not employed. The authors are predominantly economists and other social scientists
associated with the U.N. or U.S. Government agencies. They are identified, their affiliations are provided, and the source from which an
article is extracted, excerpted or adapted is cited.
    A typical issue contains three or four sections, each devoted to a
different development topic. They begin with an introductory article or
statement by the Editor or Associate Editor. This is followed by three
to six articles of varying lengths.

092.   Development Policy Review. DATE FOUNDED: 1983. FREQUENCY: 2/yr.
PRICE: $26/yr. institutions, $12.50/yr. personal. PUBLISHER: Sage
Publications Ltd., 28 Banner Street, London EC1Y 8QE, England. EDITOR:
Vincent Cable. INDEX. ADVERTISEMENTS. MANUSCRIPT SELECTION: Editor. BOOK
REVIEWS. INDEXED/ABSTRACTED: PAIS. DATABASES: PAIS INT. TARGET AUDIENCE:
AC, SP.

The Development Policy Review is published for the Overseas Development
Institute of London, England. It supersedes ODI Review. Coverage extends
to a wide variety of economic development issues that relate to countries all over the world. Recent issues have concentrated on economic
development problems in South American and African countries. Most
articles are non-technical in nature and expository in style. Only
seldom is mathematical or statistical methodology employed. The authors
are predominantly research economists specializing in economic development. They are associated with ODI, other economic development institutes, and universities. This journal, although also published by Sage
and displaying a similar format, differs significantly from Development
and Change. The latter offers a broad social service approach, while DPR
concentrates on economic development.
    A typical issue contains five or six articles, each from ten to
thirty pages in length. Approximately one-quarter of each issue is

devoted to as many as twenty or twenty-five signed book reviews of one to two pages in length.

093.   Development Research Digest. DATE FOUNDED: 1978. FREQUENCY: 2/yr. PRICE: $3.50/yr. PUBLISHER: University of Sussex, Institute of Development Studies, Brighton BN1 9RE, England. EDITOR: Zoe Mars. ADVERTISEMENTS. MANUSCRIPT SELECTION: Editor. TARGET AUDIENCE: AC, SP.

Development Research Digest offers summaries of current British research on development themes. Many of the research studies included in the Digest have not been formally published. They appear as part of a departmental reports series that many universities establish. Since access to these types of research reports is limited, this publication provides a unique service to readers interested in economic development. Each issue is devoted to one theme. Recent topics include "Agricultural and Rural Development" and "Basic Needs and Income Distribution." Articles are scholarly and offer extensive references. They are non-technical and expository in style. All of the authors are affiliated with British universities. This publication somewhat overlaps the American Development Digest.
    A typical issue begins with an introduction to the theme selected. This is an eight to ten page article with references. Although the introduction is unsigned, it appears to be written by a professional economist. The main theme is sub-divided into three or four secondary topics. Each of these subdivisions contains four or five summaries of research reports. Each summary is from four to eight pages long. The summaries are prepared by the authors of the research reports.

094.   Eastern Africa Journal of Rural Development. DATE FOUNDED: 1968. TITLE CHANGES: East African Journal of Rural Development (1968-1972). FREQUENCY: 2/yr. PRICE: $30/yr. institutions, $17/yr. personal. PUB-LISHER: Makerere University, Dept. of Agricultural Economics, P.O. Box 7062, Kampala, Uganda. EDITOR: Jossy R. Bibangambah. ILLUSTRATIONS. ADVERTISEMENTS. CIRCULATION: 1,000. MANUSCRIPT SELECTION: Editor and Referees. MICROFORMS: UMI. BOOK REVIEWS. INDEXED/ABSTRACTED: WAERSA. DATABASES: CAB AB. TARGET AUDIENCE: AC, SP. SAMPLE COPIES: Libraries.

The Eastern Africa Journal of Rural Development is sponsored jointly by the Eastern Africa Agricultural Economics Society and the Department of Agricultural Economics of Makerere University. The Journal focuses on a variety of topics pertaining to Eastern Africa including economic development, agricultural production and marketing, rural education, and social or political structures in rural areas. Some representative titles of recent articles are "The Economics of Beef Cattle Price Policy in a Developing Country: The Case of Kenya", "A Market Share Analysis of Groundnuts Exports from Nigeria, 1963-1973", and "Food Crops Production Problems and Potentials of Small Farmers in Tropical Africa." Most of the articles are expository in style and do not contain advanced quantitative analysis. They are written by academics associated with universities in Eastern Africa or researchers associated with inter-national organizations such as the World Bank or the Food and Agriculture Organization.
    A typical issue presents six or seven articles, each ranging from ten to thirty pages in length. Some of the articles are based on presenta-

tions made at conferences on the author's Ph.D. dissertation. Occasionally, issues include two or three short signed book reviews.

095.   Eastern Economic Journal. DATE FOUNDED: 1974. FREQUENCY: q. PRICE: $60/yr. institutions, $35/yr. personal. PUBLISHER: Eastern Economic Association, Temple University, School of Business Administration, Dept. of Economics, Philadelphia, Pennsylvania 19122. EDITOR: Ingrid H. Rima. ILLUSTRATIONS. INDEX. ADVERTISEMENTS. MANUSCRIPT SELECTION: Editors and Reviewers. REPRINTS: Authors. BOOK REVIEWS. SPECIAL ISSUES. TARGET AUDIENCE: AC, SP.

The Eastern Economic Journal is published by an active regional association of professional economists. It publishes articles in all fields of economics. The articles are scholarly in nature and have extensive footnotes. Some use quantitative methodology in their discussion and others are purely expository in style. The authors are predominantly professors of economics at American universities. Many of them are on the faculty of relatively little known institutions. This is in keeping with one of this journal's objectives, which is to serve as a forum for publishing papers by beginning level economists and those associated with lesser known universities. This editorial policy is not followed by the journals published by other regional economic associations such as Southern Economic Journal or Economic Inquiry.

A typical issue contains six or seven articles, each ranging from six to fourteen pages. Occasionally, the Presidential Address or the Distinguished Lecture presented at the Annual Meeting of the Eastern Economic Association is included. Some issues contain notes on previously published articles, authors' replies, and two or three signed in-depth book reviews. Occasionally, a special issue is devoted to a single topic such as a recent one on the work of the famed nineteenth century economist, Alfred Marshall.

096.   Eastern European Economics. DATE FOUNDED: 1962. FREQUENCY: q. PRICE: $170/yr. institutions, $44/yr. personal. PUBLISHER: Myron E. Sharpe, Inc., 80 Business Park Drive, Armonk, New York 10504. EDITOR: Laura D. Tyson. INDEX. ADVERTISEMENTS. MANUSCRIPT SELECTION: Editor. SPECIAL ISSUES. INDEXED/ABSTRACTED: InEcA, JEL, KeyEcS, PAIS, WAERSA. DATABASES: CAB AB, ECONAB, ECONLIT, PAIS INT. TARGET AUDIENCE: AC, SP. SAMPLE COPIES: Libraries and Individuals.

Eastern European Economics contains translations of articles from economics journals of the following countries: Albania, Bulgaria, Czechoslovakia, German Democratic Republic, Hungary, Poland, Romania, and Yugoslavia. The articles, which are selected by the editors, reflect developments in Eastern European economic theory and practice. They are of most interest to those concerned with socialist economies in general and Eastern European economies in particular. Each article lists the names of the author and the translator. Occasionally the author's affiliation is included. Bibliographical information about the original article is provided. Most of the articles are expository in style and devoid of mathematical analyses. Some articles do include tables of data.

Issues vary in format. Some contain two articles, each forty pages in length. Others include ten much briefer articles. A few issues are designated as "special issues". These have a guest editor and are entirely devoted to a particular topic. There is frequently a time lag of two to three years between the publication of an original article and the publication of its translation. Therefore, a recent change in economic conditions or policies is often not reflected in the selections appearing in this journal.

097.   Econometrica. DATE FOUNDED: 1933. FREQUENCY: 6/yr. PRICE: $83/yr. institutions, $44/yr. personal. PUBLISHER: The University of Chicago Press, Journals Division, P.O. Box 37005, Chicago, Illinois 60637. EDITOR: Angus Deaton. ILLUSTRATIONS. INDEX. ADVERTISEMENTS. CIRCULATON: 6,000. MANUSCRIPT SELECTION: Editors and Referees. MICRO-FORMS: MIM. INDEXED/ABSTRACTED: InEcA, IntBibE, JEL, KeyEcS, OR/MS, SSI, WAERSA. DATABASES: CAB AB, ECONAB, ECONLIT, SSI. TARGET AUDIENCE: AC, SP.

Econometrica is the Journal of the Econometric Society, an international organization devoted to the advancement of economic theory in its relation to statistics and mathematics. Its goal is to "promote studies that aim at the unification of the theoretical-quantitative and the empirical-quantitative approach to economic problems." In that context, coverage extends to every field of economics. Econometrica is considered to be among the most prestigious journals in economics. Articles are uniformly quantitative and usually employ sophisticated mathematics and statistics. The majority of the authors are academic economists at prestigious American universities. Quite a few articles are written by British academic economists and occasionally, economists at universities in France, Japan, Israel and Australia make contributions. Econometrica is comparable in level of scholarship to Journal of Econometrics.
    A typical issue contains about a dozen articles ranging from twelve to thirty pages in length. Most issues also include one to four shorter articles in a "Notes and Comments" section. All articles, notes, and comments are preceded by a brief abstract. Each issue has sections called "News Notes" and "Announcements." The former provides information pertaining to meetings and competitions of interest to econometricians and an occasional eulogy, while the latter informs members of the Society's plans and programs.

098.   Economia. DATE FOUNDED: 1977. FREQUENCY: 3/yr. PRICE: $35/yr. institutions, $30/yr. personal. PUBLISHER: Faculdade de Ciencias Humana, Universidade Catolica Portuguesa, Caminho de Palma de Cima, 1600 Lisbon, Portugal. EDITOR: Mario Julio Almeida Costa. ILLUSTRATIONS. INDEX. CIRCULATON: 6,000. MANUSCRIPT SELECTION: Editor. BOOK REVIEWS. INDEXED/ABSTRACTED: InEcA, JEL, WAERSA. DATABASES: CAB AB, ECONLIT. TARGET AUDIENCE: AC, SP.

Economia, a title used by a number of foreign language economic journals, can be recognized by its Portuguese sub-title, "Revista Quadrimestral". It accepts articles in Portuguese, Spanish, French, and English. About half of the articles published are in English. Articles appear in virtually all fields of economics, both micro and macro, with a concentration focusing on aspects of the Portuguese economy. Some are scholarly theoretical discussions using sophisticated mathematical models and statistical methodology. Others are policy oriented discussions, devoid of mathematics, and originally written for presentation at an economic conference. The authors are primarily academics, most at Portuguese universities, but occasionally at American or British universities. A number are Portuguese academics pursuing a Ph.D at an American university.

A typical issue contains three articles ranging from fifteen to twenty-five pages in length, two or three shorter papers in a section called communications and notes, a few Portuguese language signed book reviews, and a list of books received.

099.   Economia Internazionale. DATE FOUNDED: 1948. FREQUENCY: q. PRICE: $24/yr. PUBLISHER: Istituto di Economia Internazionale, Via Garibaldi 4, 16124 Genoa, Italy. EDITOR: Orlando D'Alauro. ILLUSTRA- TIONS. INDEX. ADVERTISEMENTS. CIRCULATON: 1,300. MANUSCRIPT SELECTION: Editorial Committee. BOOK REVIEWS. INDEXED/ABSTRACTED: InEcA, IntBibE, JEL, KeyEcS, PAIS, WAERSA. DATABASES: CAB AB, ECONAB, ECONLIT, PAIS INT. TARGET AUDIENCE: AC, SP.

Economia Internazionale is published by The Institute for International Economic Research, a Department of the Chamber of Commerce, Industry and Agriculture of Genoa. The Institute "intends to promote the study of international economics with a view to contribute to its advancement". In keeping with its stated purposes, this journal focuses on the following topics: international trade, multinational firms, currency exchange rates, trade balances, tariffs, and economics of the less developed countries. Some of the articles employ mathematical analyses and some are purely expository in nature. The authors are predominantly academic economists from English-speaking countries. The Italian language articles are written by academics at Italian universities.

A typical issue contains six to eight articles, ranging in length from ten to twenty-five pages. Up to seventy-five percent of the articles are in English, the balance are in Italian. Some issues include a substantial review article in Italian by the Editor. Each issue contains four to eight signed book reviews. The reviews are in Italian and review primarily Italian titles. Each issue contains an annotated bibliography (in Italian) of current economics books and a bibliography of recent issues of international economics periodicals with a listing of their contents.

100.   Economic Affairs. DATE FOUNDED: 1980. TITLE CHANGES: Journal of Economic Affairs (1980-1983). FREQUENCY: q. PRICE: $36/yr. institutions, $20/yr. personal. PUBLISHER: Longman Group Limited, 6th Floor, Westgate House, The High, Harlow, Essex, CM20 INE, England. EDITOR: Arthur Seldon. ILLUSTRATIONS. ADVERTISEMENTS. CIRCULATON: 400. MANUSCRIPT SELECTION: Editor. BOOK REVIEWS. INDEXED/ABSTRACTED: InEcA, JEL, WAERSA. DATABASES: CAB AB, ECONLIT. TARGET AUDIENCE: GP.

Economic Affairs is published in association with the Institute of Economic Affairs, a British research institute and educational founda- tion, that encourages support for market economies. This journal presents "informed analysis of current and impending issues in economic and related thinking and policy." It is international in perspective but emphasizes economic conditions and policies in the U.K. Recent articles dealing with economic problems in the U.K. focus on topics such as trade

union reform, national budget deficits, protectionism, defense expenditures, and government "council house" sales. Other articles deal with
situations in the U.S., France, Austria, Holland, and Yugoslavia. The
articles are expository in style and generally offer a viewpoint on how
to correct or improve conditions. Most of the authors are British
economists affiliated with universities. Occasional contributions are
made by legislators, researchers, or business executives.
    A typical issue includes four to six articles, each varying from two
to five pages in length. Regular feature sections include "Economic
Policy in the 80s" -- articles promoting policy strategies, "Commentaries" -- short essays offering analyses of specific economic situations, and "Leaders" -- short editorial messages. Up to six short signed
book reviews appear in each issue.

101.   Economic Affairs. DATE FOUNDED: 1956. FREQUENCY: q. PRICE:
$12/yr. PUBLISHER: Himansu Roy, BC/144, Sector 1, Salt Lake City,
Calcutta - 700064, India. EDITOR: Himansu Roy. INDEX. ADVERTISEMENTS.
CIRCULATION: 2,000. MANUSCRIPT SELECTION: Editor. REPRINTS: Publisher.
BOOK REVIEWS. TARGET AUDIENCE: AC,SP. SAMPLE COPIES: Libraries.

Economic Affairs is an Indian publication that concentrates on the
economy of that country. Its major emphasis is on agricultural development but it also includes the areas of finance, human resource development, public policy, and others. Articles dealing with agriculture focus
on topics such as jute cultivation, irrigation projects, farm labor,
productivity of semi-arid farming, land redistribution, energy needs of
agriculture, economics of agricultural machinery, cotton production, and
rice cultivation. Some of these articles are case studies on specific
regional situations. Articles dealing with finance may include corporation tax alternatives, monetary and fiscal policies for agricultural
expansion, rural credit, and the underground economy. The level of
technical content of the articles varies widely. Some are descriptive
and some employ quantitative analysis. The authors are economists at
Indian universities or research organizations. A few contributions are
by Indian academics teaching at universities outside of India.
    A typical issue includes six to eight articles varying in length from
six to twelve pages each. Each issue begins with a two page editorial
discussing an event of national importance. Some issues have one or two
unsigned book reviews. Short news reports of economic data are reprinted
from official sources and interspersed among the articles.

102. Economic Analysis and Policy. DATE FOUNDED: 1970. FREQUENCY: 2/yr.
PRICE: $9/yr. PUBLISHER: University of Queensland, Dept. of Economics,
St. Lucia, Brisbane, Q. 4067 Australia. EDITORS: Colin Clark, Robert
Gunton. CIRCULATION: 400. MANUSCRIPT SELECTION: Editors. BOOK REVIEWS.
INDEXED/ABSTRACTED: WAERSA. DATABASES: CAB AB. TARGET AUDIENCE: AC, SP.

Economic Analysis and Policy is published by the Queensland Branch of
the Economic Society of Australia and New Zealand. The Society's aim is
"to advance the study of economics and allied subjects" and "to invest-
igate local and general economics problems." This journal helps to
achieve that aim by concentrating on applied economic research. Many of
the articles deal with a particular economic problem that confronts all
of Australia, but some articles pertain only to the province of Queens-

land. Microeconomics is stressed although occasional macroeconomic
topics are discussed. Most of the research studies utilize statistical
or mathematical techniques. The authors are academics at Australian
universities or researchers with Australian government agencies. This
periodical offers applied economics research studies comparable to those
appearing in Australian Economic Papers.
    A typical issue includes four to five articles. Some are as brief as
four pages, while others are twenty-five pages in length. Each article
is preceded by a hundred word abstract. Some issues include two signed
book reviews of one to three pages in length. In recent years, publication problems have caused delays resulting in the production of combined
issues.

103. Economic Analysis and Workers' Management. DATE FOUNDED: 1967.
TITLE CHANGES: Economic Analysis (1967-1975). FREQUENCY: q. PRICE:
$70/yr. institutions, $30/yr. personal. PUBLISHER: Prosveta Publishing
House, Export - Import Agency, Terazije 16, 11001 Belgrade, Yugoslavia.
EDITOR: Branko Horvat. ILLUSTRATIONS. INDEX. ADVERTISEMENTS. CIRCULA-
TION: 2,000. MANUSCRIPT SELECTION: Editorial Board and Readers. RE-
PRINTS: Editorial Board. BOOK REVIEWS. INDEXED/ABSTRACTED: PAIS.
DATABASES: PAIS INT. TARGET AUDIENCE: AC, SP. SAMPLE COPIES: Libraries
and Individuals.

Economic Analysis and Workers' Management, subtitled "An International
Journal", is sponsored by nine different Yugoslav economic research
institutes and associations. It is a scholarly journal that publishes in
both the English and Serbo-Croatian languages. It concentrates on the
workers' self-management system and the Yugoslav economy. Articles in
recent issues have dealt with efficiency, investment behavior, interindustry wage structure, and alienation related to Yugoslavia's workers'
self-management experience. Other articles concern themselves with
workers' self-management proposals in Poland, German co-determination,
and cooperatives in the United States. Articles that analyze the
Yugoslav economy beyond self-management have examined economic stabilization, debt issues, the maturation period of investment, the impact of
economic reform on macro-economic policy, and a dynamic model of the
economy. The majority of articles are technical in nature and employ
modern quantitative methodologies. A few are expository in style. Most
authors are academic economists, about half at Yugoslav universities and
the rest at universities in such countries as England, Germany, Nigeria,
Canada, Sweden, and the U.S.
    A typical issue contains from three to five regular articles, one or
two shorter "communications", a "country survey" article involving an
issue in a country such as China or Sweden, a "chronicle" report on a
self-management conference, and from two to four in-depth signed book
reviews. Articles that appear in Serbo-Croatian are followed by English
summaries.

104. Economic and Industrial Democracy. DATE FOUNDED: 1980. FREQUENCY:
q. PRICE: $66/yr. institutions, $28/yr. personal. PUBLISHER: Sage
Publications, 28 Banner St., London EC1Y 8QE, England. EDITOR: Bengt
Abrahamsson. INDEX. ADVERTISEMENTS. MANUSCRIPT SELECTION: Editors. BOOK
REVIEWS. SPECIAL ISSUES. INDEXED/ABSTRACTED: BPIA, IntBibE, Work
RelAbstr. DATABASES: MC. TARGET AUDIENCE: AC, GP.

Economic and Industrial Democracy, subtitled "an international journal"
focuses on the broad field of industrial relations. Its scope encompasses the co-operative movement, workers self-management, the rights of
workers, industrial conflict, the humanization of work, organizational
behavior, women's issues in the workplace, and the issue of ownership.
Many articles are theoretical and often philosophical in nature.
Theories of political economy and ideology are explained and examined.
Other articles and sometimes entire special issues focus on practical
problems in the work place. Examples are issues devoted to public sector
human service organizations, work problems in Poland, and the working
life of women. Articles are normally expository and use little quantitative analysis. Authors are academics in the fields of economics,
political science and sociology. They are associated with universities
around the world, the majority being American, Swedish, or British.
 A typical issue begins with an editorial introduction covering all of
the articles in that issue followed by four or five regular articles
plus from one to three "current information" articles. The latter are
more factual and deal with a current industrial relations situation in a
particular country. Occasionally a review article is included and most
issues offer two or three signed book reviews.

105. The Economic and Social Review. DATE FOUNDED: 1969. FREQUENCY: q.
PRICE: $32/yr. institutions, $21/yr. personal. PUBLISHER: Economic and
Social Studies, Ltd., 4 Burlington Road, Dublin 4, Ireland. EDITORS:
John Maguire, Frances Ruane. INDEX. CIRCULATION: 600. MANUSCRIPT
SELECTION: Editors and Referees. REPRINTS: BOOK REVIEWS. INDEXED/AB-
STRACTED: BPIA, InEcA, IntBibE, JEL, PAIS. DATABASES: ECONLIT, MC, PAIS
INT. TARGET AUDIENCE: AC, GP.

The Economic and Social Review is a journal covering all aspects of the
social sciences, both theoretical and applied. It emphasizes economic
and social conditions in Ireland. Half the articles deal with economic
problems and the other half with social concerns. Representative titles
of articles dealing with economics include "Components of Growth of
Income Maintenance Expenditure in Ireland 1951-1979" and "House Prices,
Inflation and the Mortgage Market." Examples of titles of articles
dealing with social concerns include "Youth Culture in Ireland",
"Marital Choice and Quality of Relationships: A Research Note on
Hypothesis and Sampling", and "Population Trends in Late Nineteenth and
Early Twentieth Century Ireland: A Local Study." The articles are
scholarly in style. Those presenting the results of economic research
utilize mathematical or statistical methodologies. The authors are
academics at Irish universities or social scientists associated with an
Irish research institute.
 A typical issue includes three or four articles, each from ten to
twenty pages in length. Some issues contain one or two short notes. From
three to seven signed book reviews appear in each issue. The books
reviewed include textbooks, books of general interest and titles of
specific Irish interest.

106. Economic Books: Current Selections. DATE FOUNDED: 1974. FREQUENCY:
q. PRICE: $39/yr. A library may order for faculty and students at
$12.50/yr. PUBLISHER: NASA Industrial Applications Center, University of

Pittsburgh, 710 LIS Building, Pittsburgh, Pennsylvania 15260. EDITOR: Reuben E. Slesinger. INDEX. ADVERTISEMENTS. TARGET AUDIENCE: AC, SP.

Economic Books: Current Selections is a joint effort of the Department of Economics and the University Libraries of the University of Pittsburgh. It "endeavors to annotate all books that appear in the English language in the area of economics". No annotations are made for "relatively old" books or for books of less than sixty pages. The editors claim that "all annotations are reviewed and edited at meetings attended by the faculty of the Department of Economics and representatives of the University Libraries." Books are classified by subject according to a uniform theory classification scheme which has ten categories. Each listing includes the publisher of the book, its price, the International Standard Book Number, and the Library of Congress Catalog Card Number. In addition, each book is assigned a "letter category" according to the type of teaching or research library that the editor believes would be interested in purchasing it. This title, in contrast to The Wall Street Review of Books, provides no content review. Economic Books: Current Selections is closer to Economics Selections which offers about half as many entries and annotations and is less complete over a somewhat more comprehensive subject area.

This title provides annotations for about 300 titles per issue or about 1,200 per volume. Annotations average about fifty words and three to four are found on each page.

107. Economic Bulletin. DATE FOUNDED: 1964. FREQUENCY: m. PRICE: $130/yr. PUBLISHER: Gower Publishing Company, Gower House, Croft Road, Aldershot, Hampshire GU11 3HR, England. EDITOR: Dieter Teichmann. ILLUSTRATIONS. CIRCULATION: 600. MANUSCRIPT SELECTION: Editor. SPECIAL ISSUES. INDEXED/ABSTRACTED: IntBibE. TARGET AUDIENCE: AC, GP, SP.

Economic Bulletin is the English language publication of the German Institute for Economic Research/Deutsches Institute fur Wirtschaftsforschung. It is sometimes referred to as the "DIW Economic Bulletin". This title focuses on the West German economy, its current condition and the prospects for its future. It also concerns itself with the economic situation in the rest of the world, especially the effects that it has on the German economy. Articles are non-technical in nature and expository in style. Each article is signed, but no credentials or affiliations of authors are provided. Presumably, most are DIW staff economists.

The March issue provides the "major forecast" for the year and is from twenty-five to thirty pages in length. In addition to a detailed West German forecast, it also includes a world economic forecast and an appendix of key West German national account data. The June and December issues, each from ten to fifteen pages long, contain "Five Institute" forecasts which are abbreviated versions of joint analyses of the world economy and the West German economy by five major German economic institutes. Each of the remaining nine issues are about twelve pages long and contain two articles pertaining to the German economy or some international trend or event that is expected to affect the German economy.

108. Economic Bulletin For Asia and the Pacific. DATE FOUNDED: 1950.
TITLE CHANGES: Economic Bulletin for Asia and the Far East (1950-1970).
FREQUENCY: 2/yr. PRICE: $11/yr. PUBLISHER: United Nations, Development
Planning Division, ESCAP Secretariat, U.N. Building, Rajadamnern Ave.,
Bankok 10200, Thailand. ILLUSTRATIONS. INDEX. MANUSCRIPT SELECTION:
Editors. MICROFORMS: UMI. INDEXED/ABSTRACTED: IntBibE, PAIS, Pred,
WAERSA. DATABASES: CAB AB, PAIS INT, PF. TARGET AUDIENCE: AC, GP, SP.

The Economic Bulletin for Asia and the Pacific is the journal of the
United Nations Economic and Social Commission for Asia and the Pacific.
It focuses on the economic problems of the developing nations of that
part of the world and evaluates the strategies and programs that have
been suggested or implemented to alleviate those problems. It has a
significantly different format from the United Nation's Economic Bulletin for Europe. Whereas the latter is written entirely by the United
Nations Economic Commission for Europe staff and is in the form of
unsigned chapters, the Economic Bulletin For Asia and the Pacific
includes primarily signed articles or essays by academics or other
non-UNESCAP economists. Those articles written by UNESCAP staff are also
signed. Many of the authors, are associated with universities or
research institutes in the countries about which they write. Issues
frequently have a broad unifying theme. Examples from recent issues
include the environment and development, the development experience of
major South Asian economies, and aspects of public policy influences on
income distribution in Asian economies. Most articles contain quite a
bit of data and some make use of quantitative methods.
    A typical issue contains four to seven articles, each being from six
to sixteen pages in length.

109. Economic Bulletin for Europe. DATE FOUNDED: 1949. FREQUENCY: q.
PRICE: $90/yr. PUBLISHER: Pergamon Press Inc., Maxwell House, Fairview
Park, Elmsford, New York 10523. EDITOR: United Nations Economic Commis-
sion for Europe. ILLUSTRATIONS. INDEX. MANUSCRIPT SELECTION: Editors.
MICROFORMS: MIM, UMI. INDEXED/ABSTRACTED: BPIA, Pred. DATABASES: MC, PF.
TARGET AUDIENCE: AC, GP. SP.

The Economic Bulletin for Europe is the journal of the United Nations
Economic Commission for Europe. Its goal is to present studies concerning "contemporary economic problems affecting Europe and North America
in the context of the world economy." The entire contents of each issue
deals with a particular topic. Usually, but not always, it is broken
down into chapters rather than articles. Examples of topics discussed in
recent issues are: "European Agriculture Towards the End of the 20th
Century", "Trade Energy and Economic Growth - Recent Studies", and
"Aspects of Labour Market and Population Developments in Western Europe
and North America". A typical issue contains a great deal of data
presented in tables and charts, but very little mathematics or statistics is employed. The authors are predominantly UNECE staff economists.
While chapters are not signed, it is apparent that the writers are well
trained professional economists. Conference issues include signed
papers.
    Each issue is from 100 to 200 pages in length. Longer issues are
sometimes devoted to a topic of a recent conference. The final issue of
each volume is the annual "Survey of Recent Changes in Europe's Trade".

Economic Commentary. see Federal Reserve Bank of Cleveland. Economic Commentary.

110. Economic Computation and Economic Cybernetics Studies and Research. DATE FOUNDED: 1966. FREQUENCY: q. PUBLISHER: Academy of Economic Studies, 15-17, Calea Dorobantilor, Bucharest, COD 71131 R, Romania. EDITOR: Manea Manescu. ILLUSTRATIONS. INDEX. ADVERTISEMENTS. MANUSCRIPT SELECTION: Editorial Board. BOOK REVIEWS. INDEXED/ABSTRACTED: InEcA, JEL. DATABASES: ECONLIT. TARGET AUDIENCE: AC, SP.

Economic Computation and Economic Cybernetics Studies and Research is published by the leading economic research institution in Romania. This journal offers theoretical papers in the areas of cybernetics, econometrics, computer science, systems analysis, and management science. Articles dealing with applied economic problems are occasionally included. Some of the articles are reports on cybernetics conferences or economics conferences that took place in Romania. The level of treatment varies from descriptive to highly quantitative. Most of the authors are academics at Romanian universities. Occasionally, contributions are made by academics from countries such as East Germany, Israel, Iraq, and Brazil.
    Each issue begins with an editorial. This editorial frequently points out the contribution of cybernetics to the progress of the socialist economy of Romania. Occasionally the editorial quotes from speeches of Romania's President Nicolae Ceausescu or praises the leadership of President Ceausescu. The editorial is followed by six to nine articles, ranging in length from six to thirteen pages. Each article has brief abstracts in French and Russian following the text. Occasionally, an issue includes up to three signed book reviews.

111.   Economic Development and Cultural Change. DATE FOUNDED: 1952. FREQUENCY: q. PRICE: $55/yr. institutions, $30/yr. personal. PUBLISHER: University of Chicago Press, Journals Division, P.O. Box 37005, Chicago, Illinois 60637. EDITOR: Bert F. Hoselitz. ILLUSTRATIONS. INDEX. ADVERTISEMENTS. CIRCULATION: 3,700. MANUSCRIPT SELECTION: Editorial Board. MICROFORMS: KTO, UMI. BOOK REVIEWS. INDEXED/ABSTRACTED: BPI, EPIA, InEcA, IntBibE, JEL, PAIS, SSI, WAERSA, WorkRelAbstr. DATABASES: CAB AB, ECONLIT, MC, PAIS INT, SSI. TARGET AUDIENCE: AC, SP.

Economic Development and Cultural Change is a prestigious journal in the field of economic development. The editorial board is composed of academics from the top ten universities in the U.S. Most of the authors teach at those same schools. Many of the articles present case studies of specific economic factors in particular countries. These case studies frequently employ quantitative analysis in their discussion. Examples of this kind of article include "Irrigation Water Distribution Along Branch Canals in Egypt: Economic Effects" and "Growth and Fluctuations of Fiji's Exports, 1875-1978". Some articles deal with development theory such as "The Trickle-Down Myth" and others examine social structure such as "Yemenite Jewish Women in Israeli Rural Development: Female Power Versus Male Authority". This publication is comparable in level of scholarship to Journal of Development Economics.
    A typical issue includes eight to ten articles, each from twelve to twenty-five pages in length. Each issue has a book review section. This

section features a six to ten page "Review Article" which is an in-depth evaluation of a book expected to become a "classic". Five to seven other signed book reviews, some of them as extensive as the "Review Article", are included. Each issue provides a list of books received.

112. **Economic Education Bulletin.** DATE FOUNDED: 1960. FREQUENCY: m. PRICE: $17/yr. PUBLISHER: American Institute for Economic Research, Great Barrington, Massachusetts 01230. EDITOR: Ernest P. Welker. CIRCULATION: 9,500. MANUSCRIPT SELECTION: Editor. REPRINTS: Publisher. INDEXED/ABSTRACTED: PAIS. DATABASES: PAIS INT. TARGET AUDIENCE: GP. SAMPLE COPIES: Libraries and Individuals.

The Economic Education Bulletin is published by a non-profit educational foundation whose main objective is to provide economic and finance education to the general public. The Bulletin focuses on subjects in consumer finance and general economic theory but occasionally includes articles on public policies, political problems, and philosophy. Recent articles covering consumer finance dealt with subjects such as life insurance, annuities, health insurance, wills, and benefits of home ownership. Articles dealing with general economic theory emphasize the monetary system, the banking system and inflation. Non-economic articles deal with subjects such as the U.S. defense capability, U.S. policies towards South Africa, and theory of knowledge. The articles are expository in style and contain graphs, charts, and tables of data. Some of the articles express a definite viewpoint on policy issues. For example, they display strong support for re-introducing a gold standard and for high levels of military expenditures. Most of the articles are written by the same few authors. They have backgrounds in economics but no professional affiliations are given.

Each issue contains one article. Most range from twenty to forty pages. Occasionally an issue is only four to eight pages in length.

113. **Economic Eye.** DATE FOUNDED: 1980. FREQUENCY: q. PRICE: $12/yr. PUBLISHER: Keizai Koho Center, Otemachi Bldg., 6-1, Otemachi 1- Chome, Chiyoda - ku, Tokyo 100, Japan. EDITOR: Editorial Board. ILLUSTRATIONS. ADVERTISEMENTS. MANUSCRIPT SELECTION: Editorial Board. INDEXED/ABSTRACTED: PAIS. DATABASES: PAIS INT. TARGET AUDIENCE: AC, GP, SP.

Economic Eye is a publication of the Japan Institute for Social and Economic Affairs, a private non-profit organization that works in cooperation with Keidanren/Japan Federation of Economic Organizations to provide information about the Japanese economy. Economic Eye contains full or partial English translations of recent Japanese magazine articles dealing with current economic topics plus data and analysis concerning the current condition of the Japanese economy. Coverage extends to a wide variety of economic topics including the Japanese budget, Japanese labor markets, Japanese industrial policy, and Japanese trade with other countries. Articles are non-technical in nature and written in a narrative style. The authors typically hold Ph.D's in economics and are either professors at Japanese universities or researchers with Japanese government ministries. Economic Eye is comparable in subject coverage and technical level to Japanese Economic Studies.

Each issue is thirty-three pages in length and contains six or seven translated articles, an "Overview" article, one or two "Spotlight" articles, and a statistical section. The latter provides current data on Japanese national accounts, prices, industrial production, balance of payments, the yen-dollar exchange rate, monetary indexes, and the labor market. The "Overview" article is a three page summary of the current condition of the Japanese economy written by a senior professor of economics at a Japanese university. "Spotlight" articles present points of view of prominent Japanese government or business leaders.

114.   Economic Forum. DATE FOUNDED: 1970. TITLE CHANGES: Intermountain Economic Review (1970-1978). FREQUENCY: 2/yr. PRICE: $15/yr. institutions, $8/yr. personal. PUBLISHER: University of Utah, Department of Economics, College of Business, Salt Lake City, Utah 84112. EDITOR: Ann Jennings. ILLUSTRATIONS. ADVERTISEMENTS. CIRCULATION: 500. MANUSCRIPT SELECTION: Editors and Referees. BOOK REVIEWS. SPECIAL ISSUES. INDEXED/ ABSTRACTED: InEcA, JEL, PAIS. DATABASES: ECONLIT, PAIS INT. TARGET AUDIENCE: AC, SP. SAMPLE COPIES: Libraries.

Economic Forum is sponsored by departments of economics at twenty-two different universities. Most prominent in the effort and the location at which the journal is edited is the Department of Economics at the University of Utah. This journal is edited by students and encourages student publication. It emphasizes heterodoxy and expounds a viewpoint outside the mainstream of extant economic thought. Articles typically reflect institutionalist economic thought and are very critical of neoclassical economic theory. Articles also frequently possess a strong political viewpoint critical of U.S. political, social, and economic policies. Representative titles from recent issues include "Finanz-kapital in El Salvador" and "Causes of the Great Depression, or What Reagan Doesn't Know About the 1920s". The authors are predominantly academics at departments of economics, history, or sociology. About twenty percent of the articles are written by students.
A typical issue contains five or six articles. Most, but not all issues, include several signed book reviews. From time to time a "Special Issue" replaces a regular issue. Special issues are devoted to a single topic such as "Militarism and the U.S. Economy" and "Value Theory". In 1983 an Economic Forum "Special Supplement" was published, which consisted of a single article, "On Monetary Circulation and the Rate of Exploitation".

115.   Economic Geography. DATE FOUNDED: 1925. FREQUENCY: q. PRICE $18.50/yr. institutions, $15/yr. personal. PUBLISHER: Clark University, 950 Main Street, Worcester, Massachusetts 01610. EDITOR: Gerald J. Karaska. ILLUSTRATIONS. INDEX. CIRCULATION: 4,000. MANUSCRIPT SELECTION: Editor and Referees. REPRINTS: Authors. BOOK REVIEWS. SPECIAL ISSUES. INDEXED/ABSTRACTED: BPIA, InEcA, IntBibE, JEL, PAIS, SSI, WAERSA. DATABASES: CAB AB, ECONLIT, MC, PAIS INT, SSI. TARGET AUDIENCE: AC, GP.

Economic Geography is a journal concentrating on the fields of economic geography and urban geography. These interdisciplinary fields combine economics, geography, urban studies, and regional studies. Many of the articles present studies dealing with location of industrial sites or retail establishments. Some articles present population studies concerned with migration of people from urban to suburban regions. Studies deal with situations in the U.S. and other countries. The use of econometric models is incorporated in a good many of the articles. The authors of the articles are academics associated with U.S. universities. Most of the articles are intended for professional economists or geographers with quantitative skills.

A typical issue contains five articles, ranging from ten to twenty pages in length. Each issue also includes from ten to seventeen book reviews. These signed reviews, one to five pages in length, evaluate books on a broad range of topics. Examples of topics covered, in addition to economics and urban geography, are energy, the environment, political science, and agriculture. Occasionally, an entire issue is devoted to a specific topic and is directed by a guest editor.

116. The Economic History Review. DATE FOUNDED: 1927. FREQUENCY: q. PRICE: Ŀ12/yr. institutions, Ŀ14/yr. personal. PUBLISHER: Titus Wilson & Son Ltd., 28 Highgate, Kendal, Cumbria LA9 4TB, England. EDITORS: R.A. Church, A.T. Hopkins. ILLUSTRATIONS. INDEX. ADVERTISEMENTS. CIRCULATION: 4,500. MANUSCRIPT SELECTION: Editors. REPRINTS: KR. BOOK REVIEWS. INDEXED/ABSTRACTED: InEcA, JEL, KeyEcS, SSI, WorkRelAbstr. DATABASES: ECONAB, ECONLIT, SSI. TARGET AUDIENCE: AC, SP.

The Economic History Review is the journal of the Economic History Society, the foremost such society in England. It, together with the Journal of Economic History, published in the U.S., are the leading journals in this field. Its scope includes all aspects of economic and social history, but it focuses more on British economic history than that of any other country. Articles are scholarly in nature and approach. Some provide tables of data to support their theories, and a few make use of mathematical and statistical methodology. The authors are predominantly academics at British universities. Occasionally, articles by U.S., Canadian, Australian or European scholars are published.

A typical issue begins with a fifteen to twenty page article in a section called "Surveys and Speculations". This is followed by four or five additional full length papers in an "Articles" section that usually includes several responses to previously published articles and rejoinders. Most issues include a review article of a book, a scholar's writings, or a theme in a section called "Essays in Bibliography and Criticism". The final section, "Reviews", is quite extensive. The first issue of each year begins this section with an overview article of the periodical literature of two years past. Each issue offers from forty to fifty 700 to 900 word signed book reviews. These are separated into books dealing with British economic history and those pertaining to other countries.

117. Economic Indicators. DATE FOUNDED: 1948. FREQUENCY: m. PRICE: $27/yr. PUBLISHER: U.S. Council of Economic Advisers, Executive Office of the President, Executive Office Building, Washington,, D.C. 20506. EDITOR: William A. Niskanan. ILLUSTRATIONS. MICROFORMS: UMI. INDEXED/ ABSTRACTED: PAIS. DATABASES: PAIS INT. TARGET AUDIENCE: AC, GP, SP.

Economic Indicators is prepared by the U.S. President's Council of Economic Advisers for the Joint Economic Committee of the U.S. Congress. This publication contains no articles or narrative of any sort. Its contents are made up entirely of economic data prepared in the form of tables and charts. The monthly issuance of this title allows it to present the state of the economic health of the United States on as current a basis as possible. Economic Indicators presents data for thirteen different "Total Output, Income, and Spending" variables, seven different "Employment, Unemployment, and Wage" variables, six "Production and Business Activity" variables, five different "Prices", eight "Money, Credit, and Security Markets" variables, three "Federal Finance" accounts, and three "International Statistics" variables. This is the best single current source on this variety of leading and lagging economic indicators for the United States. This title is therefore useful to economists, business people, and the public at large.

Each issue is thirty-eight pages in length. A Table of Contents for the forty-five variables included is found on the back cover.

118.   Economic Inquiry. DATE FOUNDED: 1962. TITLE CHANGES: Western Economic Journal (1962-1973). FREQUENCY: q. PRICE: $100/yr. institutions, $50/yr. personal. PUBLISHER: Western Economic Association International, 7400 Center Avenue, Suite 109, Huntington Beach, California 92647. EDITORS: Thomas E. Borcherding, John F. Chant. INDEX. ADVERTISEMENTS: CIRCULATION: 4,000. MANUSCRIPT SELECTION: Editors. MICROFORMS: UMI. REPRINTS: HJM. INDEXED/ABSTRACTED: BPIA, InEcA, IntBibE, JEL, PAIS, SSI, WAERSA. DATABASES: CAB AB, ECONLIT, MC, PAIS INT, SSI. TARGET AUDIENCE: AC, SP. SAMPLE COPIES: Libraries and Individuals.

Economic Inquiry is the professional journal of the Western Economics Association. While this is a regional association in the U.S., the journal is a prestigious title and well earns that reputation. The Association is dedicated "to encouraging economic research and discussion and to disseminating economic knowledge." This journal publishes "scholarly research and analysis, covering all economic areas." Articles run the gamut from fairly theoretical papers to applied economic research, to interesting observations on and approaches to economic phenomena. Many articles deal with microeconomic topics, but more with macroeconomics. Most articles are treated in a scholarly fashion, offer sophisticated discussion, and include extensive footnotes and references. Almost all are technical in nature and employ mathematical and/or statistical methodologies. Most of the authors are academic economists at American or Canadian universities and a few are associated with universities or research institutes in other countries. This journal is comparable in level of scholarship to the Southern Economic Journal published by the Southern Economic Association.

A typical issue includes from ten to fifteen articles, ranging from ten to twenty pages in length.

119.   The Economic Journal. DATE FOUNDED: 1891. FREQUENCY: q. PRICE: $98/yr. PUBLISHER: Cambridge University Press, 32 East 57th St., New York, New York 10022. EDITORS: C.H. Feinstein, J.P. Hutton. ILLUSTRATIONS. INDEX. ADVERTISEMENTS: CIRCULATION: 7,200. MANUSCRIPT SELECTION: Editors. MICROFORMS: UMI. REPRINTS: ISI, Publisher (25 minimum). BOOK REVIEWS. SPECIAL ISSUES. INDEXED/ABSTRACTED: BPIA, InEcA, IntBibE, JEL, KeyEcS, PAIS, SSI, WAERSA. DATABASES: CAB AB, ECONAB, ECONLIT, MC, PAIS

INT, SSI. TARGET AUDIENCE: AC, SP. SAMPLE COPIES: Libraries and Individuals.

The Economic Journal is the journal of the Royal Economic Society in England. This scholarly and very prestigious publication covers all fields of economics, theoretical and applied, and represents a variety of schools of thought. Most articles present a model and many provide empirical test results. Articles are typically quantitative in character and make use of sophisticated mathematical and statistical methodologies. Frequently a mathematical appendix is attached to an article. Those that have empirical content most often use data from the U.K. The authors are predominantly academics from prestigious American, British and other (Canadian, Israeli, Italian, and Australian) universities. The Economic Journal is comparable in level of scholarship to other prestigious periodicals such as the American Economic Review, the Journal of Political Economy, and the Quarterly Journal of Economics.

A typical issue contains from six to twelve articles, ranging from eight to twenty pages in length. Most, but not all issues, also include one to three comments or brief papers in a "Notes and Memoranda" section. A substantial portion of this journal is devoted to information about new books. Each issue contains from twenty to thirty signed book reviews averaging between one and two pages in length. In addition the "Book Notes" section contains from fifty to ninety approximately 300 word signed annotations of new books. Also included in each issue is a list of "Books Received" which includes hundreds of books separated into English Language, Foreign Language, Textbooks, and Official Publications. Some issues list Thesis Titles for Degrees in the U.K., and others provide short descriptions of the completed projects of Social Science Research Council and Economic and Social Research Council grants.

120.   Economic News From Italy. DATE FOUNDED: 1946. FREQUENCY: bw. PRICE: $26/yr. PUBLISHER: Elite Publishing Corporation, 11-03 46th Ave., Long Island City, New York 11101. EDITOR: Peter G. Treves. CIRCULATION: 1,000. MANUSCRIPT SELECTION: Editor. INDEXED/ABSTRACTED: Pred. DATABASES: PF. TARGET AUDIENCE: AC, GP. SP.

Economic News from Italy is a newsletter that reviews current developments concerning the Italian economy and provides a summary of important political events in Italy. It focuses on news concerning specific Italian industries and developments in foreign trade. News items are non-technical in nature, contain a substantial amount of data, but do not include analyses of data or events. Economic News From Italy provides the reader with translated summaries of articles that appear on the front page and business pages of leading Italian newspapers. All news items are prepared by the Editor.

Each issue is divided into eight sections. The first, Political and Economic Developments, is a one page current overview. The remaining seven sections, Food and Agricultural News; News from Italian Industries; Health, Labor, Emigration; Foreign Trade Developments; Government Finances; Money, Banking, Insurance; and Corporation Finance - Stock Markets are further divided into topical sub-headings that contain brief news items. Two of the sections, News from Italian Industries and Foreign Trade Developments, typically contain from ten to fifteen news items each. The other sections have only from two to six items each.

121.   Economic Notes. DATE FOUNDED: 1933. FREQUENCY: m. PRICE: $10/yr.
institutions, $6/yr. personal. PUBLISHER: Labor Research Association, 80
East 11th Street, Room 634, New York, New York, 10003. EDITOR: Gregory
Tarpinian. ILLUSTRATIONS. CIRCULATION: 3,000. MANUSCRIPT SELECTION:
Editor and Board of Editors. SPECIAL ISSUES. TARGET AUDIENCE: GP. SAMPLE
COPIES: Libraries and Individuals.

Economic Notes is a pro-labor publication aimed at trade unionists,
labor educators, and the general public. It is journalistic in style and
does not report on economic research. It's goal is to "provide clear,
concise, and current reports on the economy and labor issues." This
non-scholarly publication's articles carry strong political overtones.
Many articles are normative in nature, yet provide information on the
economy or some particular labor issue. Titles of representative
articles include "U.S. Has Brink of War Economy", "Who Bears the Tax
Burden?", "Unemployment Numbers Game", "It Pays to Belong to a Union",
"How Corporations Hide Profits", and "Monopoly Price Gouging Causes
Inflation." Articles are signed, but full affiliations are usually not
provided. The editor characterizes authors as "economists from universities, trade unions, and labor education programs, and active trade
unionists." Economic Notes is similar in scope of coverage, viewpoint,
and format to Labor Notes.
    The typical issue is about twelve pages in length. It includes an
average of about ten articles. Most issues have a "special focus topic"
of interest to trade unionists. Regular columns on certain industries
such as steel and labor issues such as contract negotiations are
included. There are cartoons interspersed with the text.

122.   Economic Notes by Monte dei Paschi di Siena. DATE FOUNDED: 1972.
FREQUENCY: 3/yr. PUBLISHER: Monte dei Paschi di Siena, Piazza Salimbeni,
3, 53100 Siena, Italy. EDITOR: Lorenzo Maccari. ILLUSTRATIONS. INDEX.
MANUSCRIPT SELECTION: Editor. BOOK REVIEWS. SPECIAL ISSUES. TARGET
AUDIENCE: AC, SP.

Economic Notes by Monte dei Paschi di Siena is the English edition of
Note Economiche; Revista Economica del Monte dei Paschi di Siena. Monte
dei Paschi di Siena is a large Italian bank with international operations. Economic Notes presents papers "On economic, financial, and
monetary subjects with particular reference to applied economics and to
the economics of banking." The articles concentrate on macroeconomics.
Topics cover interest rates, multinational investment, exchange rates,
and inflation. Occasionally papers deal with an economic problem in
Italy, but the major emphasis of this journal is international. Some of
the papers use quantitative methodologies and some use straight exposition. Most of the authors are economists associated with universities or
research institutes in Italy. Some are from other European countries and
a few from the U.S.
    A typical issue contains three to five articles from ten to thirty
pages in length. In addition, six to seven articles are included in a
"Notes and Comments" section, but these are frequently as long as the
regular articles. The book review section is divided into "Reviews of
Books" and "Bibliographical Notes" with no discernible difference in
review length between the two divisions. A total of five to six books,
most of them Italian, are evaluated in signed reviews. A special issue
was published in 1982 to mark the tenth anniversary of the founding of

the journal. This issue, which was devoted to the theme "Experiences and Problems of the International Monetary System" includes thirteen articles written by some of the world's leading economists.

123.   Economic Outlook. DATE FOUNDED: 1977. FREQUENCY: m. PRICE: $170/yr. PUBLISHER: Gower Publishing, Gower House, Croft Rd., Aldershot, Hampshire GU11 3HR, England. EDITORS: P.W. Robinson and G.R. Dicks. ILLUSTRATIONS. CIRCULATION: 1,200. MANUSCRIPT SELECTION: Editors. INDEXED/ABSTRACTED: PAIS. DATABASES: PAIS INT. TARGET AUDIENCE: AC, GP, SP.

Economic Outlook is the publication of the Centre for Economic Forecasting of the London Business School. The Centre was established in 1976 to extend the work on forecasting and model-building which had begun in the London Business School's Econometric Forecasting Unit. The Centre aims to provide "economic forecasts for use in policy discussion and corporate planning" in England. The Centre is supported by the Social Science Research Center and a consortium of major British banks and industrial firms. Economic Outlook publishes general forecast articles as well as articles that focus on particular variables such as inflation, wages, employment, and business costs. Fairly detailed analysis of about fifty different U.K. sectors and a host of forecast tables are provided. No sophisticated quantitative techniques are employed. The authors are professional economists associated with the Centre for Economic Forecasting.
     While Economic Outlook is a monthly, each volume is made up of three "major forecast" issues (October, February, and June) plus nine intermediate "Forecast Releases". Major Forecast issues are about eighty to eighty-five pages in length while the Releases are only from four to eight pages long. A typical major Forecast issue begins with a two page "Forecast Summary" and a fifteen page "Forecast in Detail." This is followed by two signed articles, "Economic Viewpoint" and "Briefing Paper", each from seven to ten pages in length.

124.   Economic Outlook USA. DATE FOUNDED: 1974. FREQUENCY: q. PRICE: $27/yr. institutions, $13/yr. personal for faculty and students. PUBLISHER: Survey Research Center, The University of Michigan, 426 Thompson St., P.O. Box 1248, Ann Arbor, Michigan 48106. EDITOR: F. Thomas Justen. ILLUSTRATIONS. INDEX. MANUSCRIPT SELECTION: Editor and Editorial Board. INDEXED/ABSTRACTED: BPI, PAIS, Pred, SSI. DATABASES: PAIS INT, PF, SSI. TARGET AUDIENCE: AC, GP, SP.

Economic Outlook USA is the publication of a leading university survey research institute. It is "designed to aid private and public decision makers in achieving a better understanding of the economic and social environment in which they will be operating." The analyses in the articles found in this title "incorporate direct measurements of the expectations, attitudes and plans of both consumers and business firms with the economic and financial variables traditionally used in forecast models." Articles generally focus on data of the recent past and project future economic developments. Roughly half of the articles are written by Survey Research Center economists, while the other half are divided among other University of Michigan economists, political scientists at the University of Michigan's Center for Political Studies, and econo-

mists associated with other universities or research institutes.
Articles typically include data presented in tables and charts, but do
not employ sophisticated mathematical or statistical methodologies.
A typical issue contains from four to six articles, each three or
four pages in length. Each issue also includes current and constant
dollar Gross National Product projections in the form of two charts, a
table of actual and projected economic indicators, charts showing four
different SRC measures of consumer attitudes, and eight charts picturing
some key measures of national economic activity.

125.   Economic Papers. DATE FOUNDED: 1982. FREQUENCY: q. PRICE:
$16.60/yr. PUBLISHER: Economic Society of Australia, c/o R.L. Wood, Hill
Samuel Australia Ltd., P.O. Box H68, Australia Square, NSW 2000,
Australia. EDITORS: D.J. Collins, H.H. Goldberg. CIRCULATION: 3,000.
MANUSCRIPT SELECTION: Editorial Committee. SPECIAL ISSUES. INDEXED/
ABSTRACTED: PAIS. DATABASES: PAIS INT. TARGET AUDIENCE: AC, SP.

Economic Papers is intended to be a "forum for the presentation and
discussion of the views of a wide range of professional economists from
the business, government, and academic communities." It deals "with
issues in business economics, applied economics, or economic policy" and
has "a contemporary relevance to policy-makers and business economists
in Australia." This publication is a complement to the Economic Record,
another publication of the Economic Society of Australia. The Record
emphasizes economic theory and employs mathematical models whereas most
of the articles in Economic papers offer non-quantitative discussions of
practical economic problems in Australia. Examples of the latter include
"Australian Personal Income Tax Liabilities, 1960-1980" and "Outbound
and Inbound Diversification in Australian Manufacturing Industries".
Most of the authors are economists associated wtih Australian universities. A few of the authors are Americans who participated in economics
conferences in Australia.
A typical issue of Economic papers includes six to eight articles.
They vary in length from short papers of five pages to more in-depth
discussions of twenty pages. Occasionally a "Special Edition" is
published, such as the recent issue dedicated to Sir Keith Campbell, an
outstanding Australian businessman and civic leader. That issue contained the papers presented at a Conference dedicated to his work.

Economic Perspectives. see Federal Reserve Bank of Chicago. Economic
Perspectives.

126.   Economic Planning. DATE FOUNDED: 1965. FREQUENCY: 6/yr. PRICE:
$14/yr. PUBLISHER: Academic Publishing Co., 3400 Jean Talon West, Suite
35, Montreal, H3R2E9 Canada. EDITOR: Peter Harsany. ADVERTISEMENTS.
CIRCULATION: 5,000. MANUSCRIPT SELECTION: Editor. BOOK REVIEWS. INDEXED/
ABSTRACTED: PAIS, WAERSA. DATABASES: CAB AB, PAIS INT. TARGET AUDIENCE:
AC, SP. SAMPLE COPIES: Libraries.

Economic Planning is a publication that is designated by its publisher
as a "journal for agriculture and related industries." Most of the
articles are in the areas of economic planning in agriculture, the world
food supply, and agricultural policy. Occasionally articles only
remotely related to agriculture are included. Examples in recent issues

are articles on the transfer of management know-how, when to refinance
residential property, and capital budgeting. Many articles focus on the
agricultural policy of a specific country, including socialist countries. Articles are sketchy and often of a fairly low level. Almost no
use is made of mathematicl or statistical analysis. Occasionally an
article is reprinted from documents supplied by Agriculture Canada, a
Canadian government agency. Most of the authors are academics in
departments of economics, business, or geography at little known
colleges and universities in the U.S. and Canada.

Most issues are twelve pages in length, with some extending to twenty
pages. An issue contains from one to three brief articles. Some issues
have a listing of "Books Received" with most titles accompanied by a
brief annotation. Other issues have a one to two page signed book
review.

127.   Economic Policy Issues. DATE FOUNDED: 1981. FREQUENCY: 4/yr.
PRICE: Free to Associates of the Conference Board. PUBLISHER: The
Conference Board, Economic Policy Research, 845 Third Avenue, New York,
New York 10022. EDITOR: Michael E. Levy. ILLUSTRATIONS. MANUSCRIPT
SELECTION: Editor. TARGET AUDIENCE: GP, SP.

Economic Policy Issues is the publication of a leading nonprofit
business and economics research organization. It is aimed at policy
makers in the private sector of the United States. The entire contents
of an issue is devoted to a single topic or theme involving current
American economic policy. Articles are typically thoughtful analyses of
such policy initiatives. The contents of each issue is determined by the
Director and three associate directors of the Economic Policy Research
division of the Conference Board. Some issues are written entirely by
this group. More often, issues include one or two articles written by
other economists, either Conference Board economists in other sections
or economists associated with financial institutions or government
committees. Articles are non-technical in nature, do not employ sophisticated quantitative methodologies, and can be understood by informed
business executives.

Each issue is fifteen pages in length. The first number of each
volume deals with U.S. monetary policy and financial markets. The second
issue provides facts and analysis concerning the federal government
budget of that year. The third number presents an international perspective. The final issue of each volume is the only one without a set
agenda. Its focus may be on any U.S. economic policy pursued by the
current administration.

128.   The Economic Record. DATE FOUNDED: 1925. FREQUENCY: q. PRICE:
$36/yr. institutions, $27/yr. personal. PUBLISHER: Economic Society of
Australia, c/o M.R.H. Scott, 5 Sidaway St., Chapman, ACT, 2611 Aus-
tralia. EDITORS: J.W. Freebairn, R.G. Gregory. ILLUSTRATIONS. INDEX.
ADVERTISEMENTS. CIRCULATION: 1,200. MANUSCRIPT SELECTION: Editors and
Referees. MICROFORMS: UMI. BOOK REVIEWS. INDEXED/ABSTRACTED: InEcA,
IntBibE, JEL, KeyEcS, WAERSA, WorkRelAbstr. DATABASES: CAB AB, ECONAB,
ECONLIT. TARGET AUDIENCE: AC, SP.

The Economic Record is the publication of the major professional
association of economists in Australia. The Record covers "all areas of

major interest to economists" and endeavors to offer "a mixture of
theoretical and empirical articles." The empirical articles focus on
economic conditions in Australia. Recent issues contain a survey article
which reviews the state of the economy or discusses significant public
policies, or presents syntheses of recent developments in economic
theory. The articles are of a scholarly nature and many of them employ
statistical or mathematical methodologies. Most of the authors are
academics at Australian universities. A few are associated with British
or American universities. The Record complements Economic Papers, a
journal published by the same professional society, which emphasizes
applied economics of Australia.

A typical issue contains seven to nine articles ranging from seven to
seventeen pages in length. Some issues, include one or two short
comments on previously published articles and the author's reply. Each
issue includes from three to eight signed book reviews of one to two
pages in length. An annotated bibliography of "Books Received" includes
thirty to forty titles of economic interest. A "News and Notes" section
announces future economics conferences to be held in Australia, visiting
economists expected from abroad, and other news of interest to economists.

129.   Economic Report. DATE FOUNDED: 1964. FREQUENCY: 3/yr. PRICE:
Free. PUBLISHER: Security Pacific National Bank, Economics Department,
H8-13, P.O. Box 2097 Terminal Annex, Los Angeles, California 90051.
ILLUSTRATIONS. TARGET AUDIENCE: GP, SP. SAMPLE COPIES: Libraries and
Individuals.

The Economic Report is a bank publication that focuses on presenting an
economic outlook for the California economy, the U.S. national economy,
and the international economy. It is aimed at the business community and
the general public. Each issue emphasizes one of these three, but all
include at least one article on the U.S. national economy. The California outlook issue will typically contain articles on California's
near-term outlook, California's industry trends, and the economic
outlook for important regions of the state. The U.S. outlook issue
emphasizes the long-term outlook for the national economy and includes
articles on the determinants of long-term growth, growth in particular
industries and sectors of the U.S., as well as a five-year policy
overview. The international outlook issue presents separate articles on
the economic outlook for the industrial countries and for developing
countries. It also includes one or more articles on the outlook for
world trade. Articles are written by staff members of the Bank's
Economics Department. They typically include a significant amount of
data but are devoid of mathematical or statistical analysis. Very little
formal economic theory is employed.

A typical issue contains four or five articles, each from four to
eight pages in length.

130.   Economic Review. DATE FOUNDED: 1970. FREQUENCY: m. PRICE:
$45/yr. PUBLISHER: Economic and Industrial Publications, P.O. Box 7843,
Al-Masiha, 47 - Abdullah Haroon Road, Karachi - 3, Pakistan. EDITOR:
Iqbal Haidari. ILLUSTRATIONS. ADVERTISEMENTS. CIRCULATION: 50,000.
MANUSCRIPT SELECTION: Editor. BOOK REVIEWS. SPECIAL ISSUES. INDEXED/
ABSTRACTED: BPIA, PAIS. DATABASES: MC, PAIS INT. TARGET AUDIENCE: GP.

Economic Review, subtitled Pakistan's journal of economic development, provides information on economic and business conditions in that country. It covers all aspects of the economy such as agriculture, banking and finance, economic policy and planning, energy needs, industry, mineral resources, and labor. Recent issues have included articles on the federal budget, taxation proposals, fisheries development, industrial policy, productivity gains, computerization, economic forecasts, agricultural mechanization, the brain drain, public sector employment, and the sugar industry. The articles are descriptive and incorporate tables of data. The names of authors, but not their professional affiliations, are given. According to the editor, they are "leading economists, bankers, and finance experts."

A typical issue includes ten to twenty short articles. Regular sections include "Economic Diary", a calendar of business news released during the month; "People", biographical sketches of newly appointed executives, government officials, and military officers; "Comments", opinion pieces on current developments; and "Book Review", two or three signed reviews.

131.   Economic Review. DATE FOUNDED: 1983. FREQUENCY: 2/yr. PRICE: ₤20/yr. PUBLISHER: The City University Business School, Frobisher Crescent, Barbican Centre, London EC2Y 8HB, England. EDITOR: Editorial Board. ILLUSTRATIONS. MANUSCRIPT SELECTION: Editorial Board. TARGET AUDIENCE: AC, GP, SP.

Economic Review is intended to be "of practical use and interest to the financial and economic community, to policy makers in government and corporations and to the interested lay public." The articles contained in this publication are "exclusively based upon research that has taken place at the City University Business School." Many make use of a model of the U.K. economy that has been developed at the Business School. It is claimed to be "novel" in that it incorporates important supply-side variables in addition to the traditional demand-side factors. Some articles appraise the whole British economy while others focus on a particular sector such as distribution or manufacturing. Invariably, one article provides an economic outlook for the U.K. and another discusses monetary developments. Other articles deal with topics ranging from the determinants of oil prices, to work incentives in the U.K., to the economics of Cable TV. Many articles are expository in style, make use of data in tables and charts, and keep quantitative methodologies to a minimum. Articles are written by Business School teaching or research faculty. This publication deals with the same subject area as Cambridge Economic Policy Review and National Institute Economic Review.

Each issue begins with a one to two page editorial. This is followed by from three to five articles of varying lengths in a section called "Economic Assessment." The final section of this publication, "Economic Briefing", contains from two to four articles on topical issues.

132.   Economic Studies. DATE FOUNDED: 1959. FREQUENCY: q. PRICE: $10/yr. PUBLISHER: Economic Studies & Journals Publishing Co., 2, Private Road, Dum Dum, Calcutta - 700074, India. EDITOR: D.N. Mukherjea. ADVERTISEMENTS. CIRCULATION: 7,000. MANUSCRIPT SELECTION: Editor and Editorial Board. BOOK REVIEWS. TARGET AUDIENCE: GP.

Economic Studies is an interdisciplinary journal covering economics, political science, and sociology relating to India. Its major emphasis is the Indian economy. Many articles discuss various government planning schemes for economic development. Other articles deal with commercial banks, wage differentials, the dollar crisis, foreign trade, life insurance programs, the annual budget, transportation services, population problems, industrial outlook, export-import policies, and development of tourism. Articles also deal with socialization of different classes, management problems, executive-legislative relations, and motivation of workers. Most of the articles are descriptive in style. Some incorporate numerical data while others discuss conceptual ideas. The authors, all Indian, come from the ranks of academics, journalists, government officials, and business executives. Economic Studies differs from other Indian publications like Economic Affairs, Margin, and Indian Journal of Agricultural Economics, in that it does not deal with agricultural concerns and rarely uses quantitative treatment of its subjects.
    A typical issue begins with an editorial and includes ten to twelve articles, four to eight pages each. A section "Company Promotion" reports on two or three industrial firms in India. Two signed book reviews appear in each issue.

133.   The Economic Studies Quarterly. DATE FOUNDED: 1950. FREQUENCY: 3/yr. PRICE: $29/yr. PUBLISHER: Japan Association of Economics and Econometrics, Toyo Keizai Shinpo Sha, 1-4 hongokucho, Nihonbashi, Chuo-ku, Tokyo 103 Japan. EDITORS: Kotaro Suzumura, Toshihisa Toyoda, Shunsoku Nishikawa. ILLUSTRATIONS. INDEX. MANUSCRIPT SELECTION: Editors. BOOK REVIEWS. INDEXED/ABSTRACTED: InEcA, JEL. DATABASES:ECONLIT. TARGET AUDIENCE: AC, SP.

The Economic Studies Quarterly is subtitled "the Journal of the Japan Association of Economics and Econometrics." It is a scholarly journal that concentrates on microeconomic and macroeconomic theory, applied economic research and econometric techniques. Articles are typically highly technical and employ sophisticated modern quantitative methodologies. Representative theoretical and applied topics discussed in recent issues include foreign exchange rates, demand-supply adjustments in the labor market for economists, Japanese macro policy alternatives for higher oil prices, quality uncertainty and the theory of money, the labor market and stagflation, Japanese banking firms, relative price changes of Japanese goods related to technical change biases, and equilibria in an industry made up of a cartel and a competitive fringe. Other articles focus on techniques used in regression models, feedback control methods, and various econometric tests. The majority of authors are academic economists at Japanese universities. A few are American academics, some of whom co-author with Japanese economists. Occasionally Japanese government or U.N. researchers make contributions.
    A typical issue contains from four to seven full-length articles, one or two shorter articles in a "Notes and Communications" section, and from one to four signed book reviews. All of the book reviews and about twenty percent of the articles are in Japanese. A brief English summary is provided for articles written in Japanese.

134.   Economica. DATE FOUNDED: 1921. TITLE CHANGES: Economica, A Journal of the Social Sciences (1921-1933). FREQUENCY: q. PRICE: $42/yr. institutions, $25/yr. personal. PUBLISHER: The London School of Economics and Political Science, Economica Publishing Office, Houghton Street, London, WC2A 2AE, England. EDITORS: Frank Cowell, James Davidson, David de Meza. ILLUSTRATIONS. INDEX. ADVERTISEMENTS. CIRCULATION: 3,000. MANUSCRIPT SELECTION: Editors and Referees. REPRINTS: DAW. BOOK REVIEWS. SPECIAL ISSUES. INDEXED/ABSTRACTED: InEcA, IntBibE, JEL, KeyEcS, SSI, WAERSA. DATABASES: CAB AB, ECONAB, ECONLIT, SSI. TARGET AUDIENCE: AC, SP. SAMPLE COPIES: Libraries and Individuals.

Economica is "devoted to economics, economic history, statistics, and closely related problems." It publishes articles in all areas of economics, both theoretical and empirical. Economica is a scholarly journal that enjoys a very prestigious reputation among professional economists. Articles often contain theoretical or methodological innovations on new empirical findings. Most are quite sophisticated in nature and employ mathematical and/or statistical methodologies. Many present a model and the results of empirical testing. The authors are predominantly academics although many are associated with major economic research organizations. The majority are British or American, but recent articles have been written by authors from Canada, Israel, Australia, Korea, France, Germany, Belgium, and the Scandinavian countries. Economica is comparable in level of scholarship to the Oxford Economic Papers.
  A typical issue contains from seven to ten articles (occasionally as many as fifteen appear in a single issue), ranging from ten to twenty pages in length. In addition, an average of ten one-to-two page signed book reviews are included. the number is not uniform; as few as three appear in one issue and as many as eighteen in another. Each issue also lists "Books Received", usually an extensive list of at least 100 books.

135.   Economics Letters. DATE FOUNDED: 1978. FREQUENCY: 8/yr. PRICE: $140/yr. institutions, $62/yr. personal. PUBLISHER: North Holland Publishing Company, P.O. Box 103, 1000 AC AMSTERDAM, The Netherlands. EDITOR: Jerry Green. ILLUSTRATIONS. INDEX. ADVERTISEMENTS. MANUSCRIPT SELECTION: Editor. MICROFORMS: Elsev. INDEXED/ABSTRACTED: MathR. DATABASES: MATHFILE. TARGET AUDIENCE: AC, SP. SAMPLE COPIES: Libraries and Individuals.

Economics Letters was conceived out of a concern about the proliferation of economics journals and the "concomitant labyrinth of research to be conquered in order to reach the specific information" required by many research economists. "As a letters Journal, it consists of concise communications (letters) that provide a means of rapid and efficient dissemination of new results, models and methods in all fields of economics research." The editor is an academic economist at Harvard University and the twenty-eight advisory editors are also associated with prestigious American and foreign universities. A typical article begins with a brief abstract, offers a short introduction, a model, some empirical findings, and a brief conclusion. Articles are invariably quite mathematical. Sophisticated statistics or econometrics may also be employed. Authors are either academics or associated with economic research organizations such as Brookings, Rand, or the National Bureau of Economic Research. Approximately half of the authors are at American

institutions while the other half are associated with prestigious universities located in many different countries.
The editor requests that contributions be limited to four printed pages. Many are only four pages in length, a few are only three pages, but the majority are from four to six pages long, with an occasional eight to ten page "letter" also published. Approximately 130 articles are published each year.

136.   Economics of Planning. DATE FOUNDED: 1960. TITLE CHANGES: Oest -Oekonomi (1960-1962). FREQUENCY: 3/yr. PRICE: ₤16/yr. PUBLISHER: University of Birmingham, Centre for Russian and East European Studies, P.O. Box 363, Birmingham B15 2TT, England. EDITOR: Mario Nuti. ILLUSTRATIONS. ADVERTISEMENTS. CIRCULATION: 1,200. MANUSCRIPT SELECTION: Editors and Referees. MICROFORMS: SZ. BOOK REVIEWS. INDEXED/ABSTRACTED: InEcA, JEL. DATABASES: ECONLIT. TARGET AUDIENCE: AC, SP. SAMPLE COPIES: Libraries and Individuals.

The Economics of Planning is published by the University of Birmingham's Centre for Russian and East European Studies. The Centre, established for the purpose of conducting research in Russian affairs, is interested in "Soviet economic organization and policy and economic planning (including mathematical methods)" as well as Soviet sociological problems. The journal covers theoretical discussions of economic planning models incorporating sophisticated econometric methodology as well as case studies of particular economic conditions in specific countries. Some of the articles offer a quantitative treatment of economic planning such as "Firm Response to Planner Initiative in a Centrally Planned Economy." Others offer a discussion of a particular situation such as "Restrictive Contract Clauses in East-West Trade Licenses: Case Study of Poland." Many of the case studies are of Eastern European countries, but some are of Asian countries such as India and Pakistan. Most of the authors are academics from England, Poland, the U.S. and India. Some author's affiliations are not given. This publication is comparable in level of scholarship and subject scope to Journal of Comparative Economics.
A typical issue includes three or four articles, each from ten to twenty pages in length. Some issues include one page signed book reviews. Each issue prints a Russian translation of the table of contents.

137.   Economics Selections. DATE FOUNDED: 1954. FREQUENCY: q. PRICE: $91/yr. PUBLISHER: Gordon and Breach, Science Publishers, Inc., One Park Avenue, New York, New York 10016. EDITOR: Maurice B. Ballabon. INDEX. MANUSCRIPT SELECTION: Editor. TARGET AUDIENCE: AC, SP.

Economics Selections is an international annotated bibliography covering new English language books in economics and related disciplines. Titles are arranged according to the area or subject specialization. Ten fairly broad categories, further divided into forty subcategories are used. All but two of the broad categories - -"Economic Statistics, Computer Methodology and Information Systems" and "Administration, Business Finance, Marketing and Accounting" - -are the traditional subject divisions in the field of economics. Each entry includes publication data, a 100 to 300 word annotation, an indication as to whether or not

it includes a glossary, and an appraisal of the level of presentation.
No content review is provided in this title which contrasts with The
Wall Street Review of Books. Economics Selections is closer to Economic
Books: Current Selections which offers about twice as many entries and
annotations and is more complete over a somewhat less comprehensive
subject area.
    Each issue contains approximately 150 new titles. All but those which
are under fifty pages in length are annotated. An author index is
provided in each issue. The same annotations are also available in
cummulative volumes. The years 1954 to 1981 are covered in four volumes
prepared by Maurice B. Ballabon, the editor of Economics Selections.

138.   De Economist. DATE FOUNDED: 1852. FREQUENCY: q. PRICE: $56/yr.
PUBLISHER: H. E. Stenfert Kroese B.V., P.O. Box 33, 2300 AA LEIDEN, The
Netherlands. EDITOR: S.K. Kuipers. ILLUSTRATIONS. ADVERTISEMENTS.
CIRCULATION: 1,000. MANUSCRIPT SELECTION: Editorial Board. REPRINTS:
Author. BOOK REVIEWS. SPECIAL ISSUES: INDEXED/ABSTRACTED: InEcA, JEL,
KeyEcS, PAIS, WAERSA. DATABASES: ABI, CAB AB, ECONAB, ECONLIT, PAIS INT.
TARGET AUDIENCE: AC, SP.

De Economist is a well established journal published in the Netherlands.
It has been continuously published since 1852. Its scope encompasses the
entire field of economics, both theoretical and applied and both
microeconomics and macroeconomics. Articles dealing with applied
economics usually focus on economic conditions in the Netherlands but
occasionally study other European countries. Many of the articles use
quantitative methodology and offer either a statistical analysis or
construct an econometric model. Most of the authors are economists
associated with universities in The Netherlands. Many of these authors
are also on the Board of Editors. Other authors are from a wide variety
of countries including England, Greece, Israel, and the U.S. Several
issues contain articles written in honor or in memory of prominent Dutch
economists.
    A typical issue includes five to six articles ranging from seven to
twenty-two pages in length. Most issues include an extensive book review
section. From ten to fifteen carefully prepared one to three page signed
reviews appear in most issues. A few of the reviews are in Dutch. An
annotated bibliography of "Publications Received" is included. These
annotations are in Dutch.

139.   Economy and Society. DATE FOUNDED: 1972. FREQUENCY: q. PRICE:
$48/yr. institutions, $29/yr. personal. PUBLISHER: Routledge & Kegan
Paul, Broadway House, Newton Road, Henley-on-Thames, Oxon, RG9 IEN,
England. EDITOR: Editorial Board. INDEX. ADVERTISEMENTS. CIRCULATION:
2,000. MANUSCRIPT SELECTION: Editorial Board. MICROFORMS: UMI. REPRINTS:
Publisher. BOOK REVIEWS. INDEXED/ABSTRACTED: IntBibE, WAERSA. DATABASES:
CAB AB. TARGET AUDIENCE: AC, SP. SAMPLE COPIES: Libraries.

Economy and Society is a publication that focuses on social science
analysis "for Marxist scholarship." It is a specialized journal that
presents viewpoints outside the mainstream of economics. This journal's
general social science and philosophical approach can be recognized by
the following examples of articles that have appeared in recent issues:
"Durkheim: the Sacred Language", "The Limits of Expropriation", "Prus-

sian agriculture - German Politics", and "Notes on Body Pain and Truth in Medieval Christian Ritual." However, articles more clearly critical of extant mainstream economic thought also appear. Examples from recent issues are "The Case of Full Employment", "Can Economics be Scientific?", "Monetarism and Economic Ideology" and "Was Economic Policy Ever Keynesian?" Articles are non-technical in nature and expository in style. The members of this journal's editorial board are all British academics. Authors are predominantly at British universities, but a few are associated with other European institutions. some are economists, but more are sociologists or general social scientists.

A typical issue contains three or four, thirty-to-fifty page articles plus a ten-to-twelve page review article. Some issues also include a "Debate" section which contains comments on previously published articles and rejoinders to those comments.

140.   Empirical Economics. DATE FOUNDED: 1976. FREQUENCY: q. PRICE: DM 165/yr. PUBLISHER: Physica-Verlag, Institute for Advanced Studies, Stumpergasse 56, A-1060 Vienna, Austria. EDITOR: Bernhard Bohn. ILLUSTRATIONS. ADVERTISEMENTS. MANUSCRIPT SELECTION: Editor and Editorial Board. INDEXED/ABSTRACTED: InEcA, JEL. DATABASES: ECONLIT. TARGET AUDIENCE: AC, SP.

Empirical Economics is a scholarly journal published by a leading Austrian research institute. It publishes articles "in the field of empirical economic research using advanced statistical methods and tackling the economic problems of our time." The editors give preference to articles "in the field of economic policy and control." The journal publishes "studies about all industrialized countries with special emphasis to the European economies." Most articles in this highly technical journal make use of sophisticated mathematical and statistical methodologies. The authors are predominantly academics at American or European universities. Occasionally, a contribution is made by a Canadian, Australian or third world economist.

A typical issue contains from four to six articles. Some are as brief as five pages while others are thirty pages or more in length. It is not uncommon to find a lengthy mathematical or statistical appendix attached to an article. Each article is preceeded by a brief abstract.

141.   Energy Economics. DATE FOUNDED: 1979. FREQUENCY: q. PRICE: L88./yr. PUBLISHER: Butterworth Scientific, P.O. Box 63, Westbury House, Bury Street, Guildford, Surrey GU2 5BH, England. EDITOR: Homa Motamen. ILLUSTRATIONS. INDEX. ADVERTISEMENTS. CIRCULATION: 4,000. MANUSCRIPT SELECTION: Editor and Referees. REPRINTS: Publisher. BOOK REVIEWS. INDEXED/ABSTRACTED: GasAbstr, GeoAb, InEcA, JEL, PAIS. DATABASES: ECONLIT, PAIS INT. TARGET AUDIENCE: AC, SP. SAMPLE COPIES: Libraries and Individuals.

Energy Economics is the British counterpart of the American journal, The Energy Journal. It focuses on the economic analysis of energy issues. Energy Economics "provides a forum for papers concerned with economic theory and its application, methodology, statistics and mathematical modelling." It is a scholarly journal written by professional energy economists for an audience of their peers. The Editorial Board of thirty prominent economists is about forty percent British, with the remainder

being American, Canadian, European, or Japanese. The list of authors is
even more international in scope.
A typical issue contains from seven to ten articles, ranging from
five to fifteen pages in length. Many issues include a brief comment
concerning a previously published article and the author's reply. Each
issue contains a book review section with signed reviews of one or two
energy related books. There is also a "Recent Papers" section that lists
a wide selection of journal articles and working papers on energy
economics.

142.   The Energy Journal. DATE FOUNDED: 1980. FREQUENCY: q. PRICE:
$75/yr. institutions, $48/yr. personal. PUBLISHER: Oelgeschlager, Gunn &
Hain, Publishers, Inc., 1278 Massachusetts Avenue, Cambridge, Mass-
achusetts 02138. EDITOR: Helmut J. Frank. ILLUSTRATIONS. INDEX. ADVER-
TISEMENTS. CIRCULATION: 1,800. MANUSCRIPT SELECTION: Editor and Refer-
ees. REPRINTS: Publisher. BOOK REVIEWS. SPECIAL ISSUES: INDEXED/
ABSTRACTED: BPI. TARGET AUDIENCE: AC, SP. SAMPLE COPIES: Libraries and
Individuals.

The Energy Journal is a publication of the Energy Economics Educational
Foundation in association with the International Association of Energy
Economists. This scholarly and prestigious journal extends coverage to
all aspects of energy economics and policy. Articles deal with theoretical energy economics, applied problems in energy economics, and current
energy policy. Most articles are technical in nature and employ sophisticated mathematical and statistical methodologies. The authors are
prominent energy economists associated with prestigious universities,
research institutes, and corporations. The majority are American. This
journal is at about the same level and covers about the same subject
area as the British title, Energy Economics.
Most issues contain six sections. The first, "Announcements",
presents information concerning conferences and symposia in the field of
energy economics. The second section, "Research Reports", contains from
four to eight major articles that vary greatly in length. The third
section, "Energy Policy Forum" contains several more articles that are
shorter and more topical. A fourth section, "Notes and Comments",
contains papers that either concisely address specific points of
interest to energy economists or comment on (often with a reply)
previously published articles. The fifth section, "Book Review (s)"
contains from one to three fairly brief signed book reviews. Some issues
include a sixth section, "Letters to the Editor."

143.   The Engineering Economist. DATE FOUNDED: 1955. FREQUENCY: q.
PRICE: $22/yr. institutions, $12/yr. personal. PUBLISHER: American
Society for Engineering Education and Institute of Industrial Engineers,
25 Technology Park/Atlanta, Norcross, Georgia 30092. EDITOR: Gerald J.
Thuesen. ILLUSTRATIONS. INDEX. CIRCULATION: 2,700. MANUSCRIPT SELECTION:
Referees. MICROFORMS: UMI. BOOK REVIEWS. INDEXED/ABSTRACTED: AcctInd,
BPI, BPIA, InEcA, JEL, KeyEcS. DATABASES: ACCTIND, ECONAB, ECONLIT, MC.
TARGET AUDIENCE: AC, SP.

The Engineering Economist, subtitled "a journal devoted to the problems
of capital investment", is a joint publication of two professional
engineering societies. It presents articles, reviews, and case studies

in the area of managerial economics with an emphasis on the problems of capital budgeting. A secondary area of interest is regulated industries such as public utilities. This journal also includes articles on topics in accounting, benefit cost analysis, decision analysis, production economics, and resource allocation theory. Most of the authors are academics at American universities with a few being executives with public utility firms. All of the articles use mathematical techniques to present their arguments and conclusions.

A typical issue includes four or five articles, each twelve to twenty-two pages in length. A "technical note" section includes one or two short papers. Some issues have a "reader's forum" which offers one or two short papers dealing with engineering economy education or comments on published papers. The annual index appears in the summer issue. Society news such as award recipients and conference programs are included. Each issue also features four or five signed reviews of books relevant to the journal's scope of interest.

144.   Euromoney. DATE FOUNDED: 1969. FREQUENCY: m. PRICE: $89/yr. PUBLISHER: Euromoney Publications Ltd., Nestor House, Playhouse Yard, London EC4V 5EX England. EDITOR: Padraic Fallon. ILLUSTRATIONS. INDEX. ADVERTISEMENTS. CIRCULATION: 18,000. MANUSCRIPT SELECTION: Editor. MICROFORMS: UMI. REPRINTS: Publisher. SPECIAL ISSUES: INDEXED/ABSTRACT-ED: BPI, BPIA, PAIS, Pred. DATABASES: MC, PAIS INT, PF. TARGET AUDIENCE: GP, SP. SAMPLE COPIES: Libraries and Individuals.

Euromoney is a British publication that focuses on the world of international banking and finance. The articles are written primarily for bankers, financiers, and investment advisors but can be understood by general readers with an interest in these areas. This publication provides information about international investments, financial conditions in specific countries, international bond issues, exchange rates, and short-term interest rates. The articles are descriptive in nature and incorporate charts, graphs, and tables of data. Some of the authors are staff journalists: others are professionals employed by banks and investment firms. Euromoney overlaps the subject scope of Intereconomics which is also non-technical in nature.

Each issue contains regular feature sections plus a number of articles dealing with economic conditions in a specific country. The regular feature sections are: "Editorial" -- a one page commentary on a significant event in the banking world, "Front End" -- short news items about international finance, "Cover Story" -- a ten to twenty page article about an important financial event that is depicted on the cover of that issue, "American Section" -- reports about financial conditions in the U.S., "Market Commentary" -- data on recent bank loans, U.S. bond markets, London dollar CDs, and financial futures, and "Facts and Figures" -- data on currency exchange rates and interest rates. Articles dealing with specific countries are grouped together under headings such as "Japanese International Finance" or "The German Economy." This periodical has a magazine-like format in that it appears on glossy paper and is illustrated with ample photographs. Supplements which provide a public relations function are frequently issued. They generally deal with a specific country, and present an overview of economic conditions in that country.

145.   European Economic Review. DATE FOUNDED: 1969. FREQUENCY: 9/yr.
PRICE: $219.25/yr. PUBLISHER: Elsevier Science Publishers B.V. (North
Holland), P.o. Box 211, 1,000 AE Amsterdam, The Netherlands. EDITOR:
Jean Waelbroeck, Herbert Glejser. ILLUSTRATIONS. INDEX. ADVERTISEMENTS.
MANUSCRIPT SELECTION: Editorial Board. MICROFORMS: MIM. REPRINTS:
Publisher, Special Services Department. SPECIAL ISSUES: INDEXED/AB-
STRACTED: BPIA, InEcA, IntBibE, JEL, KeyEcS, PAIS, SSI. DATABASES:
ECONAB, ECONLIT, MC, PAIS INT, SSI. TARGET AUDIENCE: AC, SP. SAMPLE
COPIES: Libraries and Individuals.

The European Economic Review is the journal of the Association Scientif-
ique Europeenne d'Economie Appliquee. ASEPELT is an association which
groups together the major European economic research centers for the
purpose of promoting research in applied economics and disseminating
research results. This scholarly journal emphasizes applied economic
work but also publishes theoretical articles which are relevant to
applied economic research. It covers virtually all fields of economics.
From time to time it also publishes an article which presents a point of
view on an issue deemed to be of international significance. This
prestigious journal contains primarily articles that present a model and
the results of empirical testing. Most articles employ a significant
amount of mathematics and/or statistics. The journal's editorial board
is composed of economists from seventeen different countries, the only
non-European being Canada and Israel. However, the authors, mostly
academics from prestigious universities, are as often American as they
are European.
    A typical issue contains seven to twelve papers, ranging from three
page comments or notes to twenty-five page articles with appendices. An
occasional special issue employing guest editors is published. Two
recent examples are an issue composed of ten papers on "Market Competition, Conflict and Collusion" and one that published the seven papers
and seven discussions that comprised the "International Seminar on
Macroeconomics."

146.   European Economy. DATE FOUNDED: 1978. FREQUENCY: q. PRICE:
$23/yr. PUBLISHER: Commission of the European Communities, Directorate-
General for Economic and Financial Affairs, rue de la Loi 200, 1049
Brussels, Belgium. MANUSCRIPT SELECTION: Editor. INDEXED/ABSTRACTED:
PAIS. DATABASES: PAIS INT. TARGET AUDIENCE: SP.

European Economy is published by an international organization composed
of the countries in the European Economic Community (EEC) plus Greece.
It focuses on financial and economic conditions in the ten member
countries. The articles are descriptive in style and include large
amounts of data in tabular or graphic form. They are prepared by staff
members and are unsigned. The subject coverage of European Economy
overlaps with the contents of European Trends. It has a more professional orientation and provides more comprehensive statistical data than
the latter.
    There is little uniformity among the four issues published in each
volume. One issue is divided into two sections -- "Economic Trends and
Prospects" and "Special Studies." The "Economic Trends and Prospects"
section presents an overview of the current situation in the world
economy and the European Communities and then presents a detailed
analysis of the economic situation in each of its ten member countries.

The "Special Studies" section has a report on unit labor costs in manufacturing industries and two opinion reports by the Economic Policy Committee of the Commission. Another issue is devoted to an "Annual Economic Review" which presents a comprehensive summary of the economic conditions during the previous year. This summary covers the economic outlook, the balance of payments, prices and costs, monetary policy, labor markets, capital markets, and external trade. The remaining two issues function as "special issues" as they are devoted to specific topics. Two recent issues focused on "The European Monetary System" and "Borrowing and Lending Activities of the Community in 1981."

147.   European Industrial Relations Review. DATE FOUNDED: 1974. FREQUENCY: m. PRICE: Ŀ140./yr. PUBLISHER: Eclipse Publications Ltd., 67 Maygrove Road, London NW6 2EJ, England. EDITOR: Michael Gold. INDEX. CIRCULATION: 2,000. MANUSCRIPT SELECTION: Editor. REPRINTS: Publisher. INDEXED/ABSTRACTED: WorkRelAbstr. TARGET AUDIENCE: AC, GP, SP. SAMPLE COPIES: Libraries and Individuals.

The European Industrial Relations Review is a publication that provides information on current industrial relations developments in eighteen countries in Europe. Its scope is collective bargaining agreements, labor registration, social security benefits, and occupational safety and health. Recent issues have presented articles on topics such as reform of the Austrian state pension system, Swedish labor market policy, role of the Irish Labour Court, analysis of nationalized steel industry workforces in three European countries, an analysis of a comprehensive labor agreement in Spain, youth employment opportunities in France, and problems of managerial and supervisory staff in Belgium. The articles are descriptive in style. All authors are staff writers or special correspondents outside of England. Articles are not signed.

A typical issue contains from five to seven articles, each from two to four pages in length. There are three regular feature sections: "News" which provides brief reports of current developments in industrial relations in individual countries and in the EEC as a whole, "Documents" which reproduces the text (in English) of all important labor laws and agreements, and "Statistics" which tabulates the consumer price indices for eighteen European countries plus the U.S. and Japan. A comprehensive annual index appears in the January issue.

148.   European Review of Agricultural Economics. DATE FOUNDED: 1973. FREQUENCY: q. PRICE: $65/yr. institutions, $32.50/yr. personal. PUBLISHER: Mouton Publishers, c/o Walter de Gruyter, 200 Saw Mill River Road, Hawthorne, New York, 10532. EDITOR: Kees Burger. ILLUSTRATIONS. CIRCULATION: 1,200. MANUSCRIPT SELECTION: Editors. BOOK REVIEWS. INDEXED/ABSTRACTED: IntBibE, WAERSA. DATABASES: CAB AB. TARGET AUDIENCE: AC, SP.

The European Review of Agricultural Economics serves as a forum "for discussions about the development of theoretical and applied agricultural economics research in Europe and for stimulating ideas regarding the economics problems of agriculture in Europe and other parts of the world." These articles cover a range of topics within agricultural economics. They deal with production economics, farm management problems, agricultural policy, regional planning and rural development, international trade and development, and others. Most of the articles incorporate statistical and/or economic methods in their discussions and are intended for a readership of professional agricultural economists. The authors, with backgrounds similar to the intended readership, are associated with universities or government planning or research agencies. They are from countries all over the world. The Review most closely resembles the Journal of Agricultural Economics in technical level, subject coverage, and geographic scope.

A typical issue presents five articles, each from ten to twenty-five pages in length. Some issues include a short note of four to eight pages in length. Most issues include from three to five signed book reviews. The reviews, two to four pages in length, cover books on agricultural economics.

149.   European Trends. DATE FOUNDED: 1964. FREQUENCY: q. PRICE: $105/yr. institutions, $140/yr. personal. PUBLISHER: Economist Intelligence Unit Ltd., 27 St. Jame's Place, London SWIA INT England. EDITOR: INDEX. MANUSCRIPT SELECTION: Editor. MICROFORMS: WMI. SPECIAL ISSUES: Annual Supplement. INDEXED/ABSTRACTED: KeyEcS, WAERSA. DATABASES: CAB AB, ECONAB. TARGET AUDIENCE: GP, SP. SAMPLE COPIES: Libraries and Individuals.

European Trends is a publication that presents news of current economic developments in Western Europe. It is aimed primarily at business people who have interests in Western Europe. Most countries in Western Europe belong to one of two economic cooperative organizations, the European Economic Community (EEC) made up of Belgium, France, Italy, Luxemburg, Netherlands, Denmark, Ireland, United Kingdom, and West Germany or the European Free Trade Association (EFTA) made up of Austria, Finland, Iceland, Norway, Portugal, Sweden, and Switzerland. European Trends focuses on developments within the EEC countries but also includes statistical data on the EFTA countries. Articles deal with many different business and economics topics such as the robotics challenge to Western Europe, the physical distribution of goods in Western Europe, and the problems and progress of specific industries. Articles are descriptive and do not incorporate quantitative methodologies. The authors are named, but no professional affiliations or credentials are provided. European Trends somewhat overlaps the subject coverage of European Economy. The latter provides more comprehensive statistical data.

A typical issue contains five regular features: 1) "Issues in the News" -- brief news reports of economic events and decisions, 2) "Agricultural Report" -- a four page report on agricultural production and marketing, 3) "Special Report" -- an in-depth report on a current topic, 4) "Special Series" -- an in-depth report on a topic of the year, and 5) "Statistical Appendix" -- tables of data presenting various economic indicators and trade figures for both EEC and EFTA countries. An annual supplement presents a summary of all the trade agreements established by European countries since the end of World War II.

150.   Explorations in Economic History. DATE FOUNDED: 1963. TITLE CHANGES: Explorations in Entreprenuerial History. FREQUENCY: q. PRICE: $72/yr. PUBLISHER: Academic Press, 111 Fifth Avenue, New York, New York 10003. EDITOR: Larry Neal. INDEX. MANUSCRIPT SELECTION: Editor. INDEXED/

ABSTRACTED: InEcA, JEL, SSI. DATABASES: ECONLIT, SSI. TARGET AUDIENCE:
AC, SP.

Explorations in Economic History "publishes research papers of scholarly
merit on a wide range of topics in economic history." Topics may include
"economic development, income distribution, urbanization, poverty, human
resource development, as well as the more traditional topics of business
enterprises, finance, agriculture, manufacturing, and transportation
improvements." The articles deal with as broad a range of topics as
stated in the editorial policy. They emphasize historical studies in the
U.S. and Great Britain but occasionally present studies from other parts
of the world. There is a balance between articles using quantitative
methods of analysis and articles using expository narrative. Occasionally, an article dealing with the use of theoretical analysis in
economic history is included. The articles are scholarly in nature and
are extensively footnoted. Most of the authors are academics from
American universities. This journal deals with more comprehensive
historical trends than does Business History Review which emphasizes
historical analyses of specific industries.
    A typical issue includes five to seven articles ranging from ten to
twenty-five pages in length.

151.   Far Eastern Economic Review. DATE FOUNDED: 1946. FREQUENCY: w.
PRICE: $72/yr. PUBLISHER: Far Eastern Economic Review Ltd., GPO Box 160,
Hong Kong. EDITOR: Derek Davies. ILLUSTRATIONS. INDEX. ADVERTISEMENTS.
CIRCULATION: 58,000. MANUSCRIPT SELECTION: Editors. MICROFORMS: UMI.
REPRINTS: Editor. BOOK REVIEWS. SPECIAL ISSUES. INDEXED/ABSTRACTED:
KeyEcS, SSI, WAERSA. DATABASES: CAB AB, ECONAB, SSI. TARGET AUDIENCE:
GP.

Far Eastern Economic Review is a news magazine covering all the countries of Asia. While economics, business, trade, and financial affairs
of the area are emphasized, many articles deal with politics, international relations, and social and cultural affairs. The magazine is
aimed at "Asia's elite," senior executives both in the private and
public sectors as well as professionals. Communist and socialist nations
are covered as well as those with open economies and democracies, but
articles tend to reflect the relative success of the latter. Most
articles are signed, but no other information is provided. Writers are
mostly professional journalists who have excellent academic qualifica-
tions and experience in the region. Occasionally articles are written by
academics, managers, or government officials, but in those cases their
affiliations are identified. All articles are written exclusively for
the Review which reprints no agency or feature service.
    Each issue runs between seventy and one hundred and fifty pages in
length. Typically an issue contains thirty to thirty-five articles. The
contents page groups them into "Regional" and "Business" affairs. There
are also a number of "Regular Features" which include letters to the
editor, brief news items, several regular columns, company financial
results, stockmarket results, price trends, an economic monitor of a
particular Asian country, and some signed book reviews.

152.   Federal Home Loan Bank Board Journal. DATE FOUNDED: 1968.
FREQUENCY: m. PRICE: $35/yr. PUBLISHER: Federal Home Loan Bank Board,

Washington, D.C. 20552. EDITOR: Jeff Sconyers. ILLUSTRATIONS. INDEX.
MANUSCRIPT SELECTION: Editor. INDEXED/ABSTRACTED: AcctInd, PAIS, Pred.
DATABASES: ACCTIND, PAIS INT, PF. TARGET AUDIENCE: AC, GP, SP.

The Federal Home Loan Bank Board Journal supersedes the same agency's
Digest published since 1958. The Federal Home Loan Bank Board is a U.S.
government agency which supervises the nation's savings and home
financing industry. The Journal is published for the benefit of "savings
and loan officials and other lenders, builders, developers, educators,
planners, public officials, economists, librarians ..." Its scope covers
all aspects affecting the thrift industry. Examples of article topics in
recent issues are the "all-savers" experience, home equity conversion,
fidelity insurance, fund availability to the real estate industry,
antitrust merger criteria for savings and loans, mutual to stock
conversions of savings and loans, and how housing is financed in other
countries such as England, Germany, Korea, and Switzerland. Authors are
economists or financial experts either associated with the Board,
another government agency, a financial institution, or a university.

   Most issues include about four articles plus four other sections:
"News," "News in the Districts," "Regulations, Rulings, and Opinions,"
and "Statistical Series." These cover Board policies, regulations, and
programs; industry and government achievements; and statistics on
mortgage and housing markets, savings and loan associations, Federal
Home Loan Banks, FSLIC finances, and general financial data. The April
issue is the Federal Home Loan Bank Board's Annual Report. The December
issue contains an annual subject index.

153.   Federal Reserve Bank of Atlanta. Economic Review. DATE FOUNDED:
1915. TITLE CHANGES: Federal Reserve Bank of Atlanta. Monthly Business
Review (1915-1927). Federal Reserve Bank of Atlanta. Monthly Review
(1927-1977). FREQUENCY: m. PRICE: Free. PUBLISHER: Federal Reserve Bank
of Atlanta, Information Center, PO Box 1731, Atlanta, Georgia 30301.
EDITOR: Gary W. Tapp. ILLUSTRATIONS. INDEX. ADVERTISEMENTS. CIRCULATION:
30,000. MANUSCRIPT SELECTION: Editor. MICROFORMS: BLH, MIM, UMI. SPECIAL
ISSUES. INDEXED/ABSTRACTED: FedP, PAIS. DATABASES: ABI, PAIS INT. TARGET
AUDIENCE: AC, GP, SP. SAMPLE COPIES: Libraries and Individuals.

Federal Reserve Bank of Atlanta. Economic Review's stated purpose is to
"inform the public about Federal Reserve policies and the economic
environment and in particular to narrow the gap between specialists and
concerned laymen." Articles are generally non-technical and employ
almost no sophisticated mathematical or statistical analysis. Of the
twelve district Federal Reserve Banks which publish an economic review
serial, this one is the most readable for laymen. The Federal Reserve
Bank of Philadelphia Business Review is a close second, while those
published by the Federal Reserve Banks of St. Louis, Minneapolis, San
Francisco, and Richmond offer the greatest contrast. The Federal Reserve
Bank of Atlanta Economic Review has a very wide scope. Subjects covered
in recent issues include the role of robots, the economic condition of
farmers, competition in banking, the consumer do-it-yourself movement,
international debt, and the prospects for specific industries. Many
articles emphasize the implications of an event or trend on the Southeast region of the U.S. The authors are well qualified staff researchers
or academics who are serving as visiting scholars with the Atlanta
Federal Reserve Bank.

Regular issues usually contain five or six articles averaging about ten pages in length. Some issues have a "Special Section" with two or three articles on the same topic while other issues are designated "Special Issue" and deal entirely with a single topic. Each issue contains a four-page statistical summary covering Southeast economic data.

154.   Federal Reserve Bank of Boston. New England Economic Indicators. DATE FOUNDED: 1969. FREQUENCY: m. PRICE: Free. PUBLISHER: Federal Reserve Bank of Boston, 600 Atlantic Ave., Boston, Massachusetts 02106. EDITOR: Marguerite Coughlin. ILLUSTRATIONS. INDEX. MANUSCRIPT SELECTION: Editor. INDEXED/ABSTRACTED: FedP. TARGET AUDIENCE: GP, SP. SAMPLE COPIES: Libraries and Individuals.

The Federal Reserve Bank of Boston. New England Economic Indicators differs from that Bank's New England Economic Review in that it deals almost exclusively with the economy of New England (Connecticut, Maine, Massachusetts, New Hampshire, Rhode Island and Vermont) and is devoid of technical articles while the former contains research articles on varied national economic issues and problems. New England Economic Indicators provides tables of data and/or charts on variables such as production, employment, construction, consumption, commercial and savings bank deposits, and energy in each New England state and all of New England combined. All articles are written and all tables and charts are prepared by Boston Federal Reserve economists.

About half of the issues include only a single article, "New England Economic Survey." The other half include an additional article dealing either directly with the New England economy or with important implications for it. Examples of the former are "Men in Massachusetts: A Scarce Resource," "Gross State Product in New England and Selected States," and "New England State Governments - Looking Ahead to a Better Fiscal Year." The latter are exemplified by "Municipal Fiscal Distress," and High Technology and Regional Economic Development."

155.   Federal Reserve Bank of Boston. New England Economic Review. DATE FOUNDED: 1969. FREQUENCY: 6/yr. PRICE: Free. PUBLISHER: Federal Reserve Bank of Boston, Research Department, 600 Atlantic Ave., Boston, Massachusetts 02106. EDITOR: Ruth Norr. ILLUSTRATIONS. INDEX. CIRCULATION: 10,000. MANUSCRIPT SELECTION: Editor. MICROFORMS: MIM, UMI. REPRINTS: UMI. INDEXED/ABSTRACTED: FedP, InEcA, JEL, PAIS. DATABASES: ECONLIT, PAIS INT. TARGET AUDIENCE: AC, GP, SP. SAMPLE COPIES: Libraries and Individuals.

Federal Reserve Bank of Boston. New England Economic Review superseded its New England Business Review published since 1920. It is one of twelve Federal Reserve District Bank reviews. It is closest in coverage to those published by the Federal Reserve banks of Cleveland, Kansas City, Philadelphia, Dallas, and Chicago. Articles vary greatly in scope, covering both topics in micro as well as macroeconomics. Many focus on national economic problems while others deal with topics pertaining specifically to the New England economy. Some articles are fairly technical in nature but sophisticated mathematical and statistical methodologies are generally avoided. Tables of data, charts and diagrams accompany many articles. Articles deal almost exclusively with contemporary U.S. economic issues and are policy oriented. The authors are well credentialed and qualified economists with the Federal Reserve Bank of Boston. Occasionally an article is coauthored by an academic economist. Most issues contain four articles ranging from ten to twenty pages in length. Many are accompanied by a brief appendix. Occasionally an address delivered at a conference by the President of the Federal Reserve Bank of Boston is included.

156.   Federal Reserve Bank of Chicago. Economic Perspectives. DATE FOUNDED: 1977. FREQUENCY: 6/yr. PRICE: Free. PUBLISHER: Federal Reserve Bank of Chicago, Public Information Center, Box 834, Chicago, Illinois 60690. EDITOR: Edward G. Nash. ILLUSTRATIONS. INDEX. CIRCULATION: 36,000. MANUSCRIPT SELECTION: Editorial Committee. MICROFORMS: BLH, UMI. REPRINTS: UMI. SPECIAL ISSUES. INDEXED/ABSTRACTED: FedP, Pred. DATABASES: PF. TARGET AUDIENCE: AC, GP, SP. SAMPLE COPIES: Libraries and Individuals.

Federal Reserve Bank of Chicago. Economic Perspectives superseded the Chicago Federal Reserve Bank's Business Conditions which it published since 1921. It is more limited in scope than some of the other Federal Reserve district bank reviews as it covers primarily banking topics. In terms of format and coverage it is closest to the reviews published by the Federal Reserve Banks of Cleveland and Philadelphia. It presents more reviews of past economic events and more outlook discussions than do other Federal Reserve Bank reviews. Most articles deal with national banking topics, but some concentrate on the Chicago market or the Midwest. Articles generally offer data in the form of tables and charts but avoid sophisticated technical material. Occasionally a more technical article does appear. Authors are primarily senior economists at the Chicago Federal Reserve Bank, but some articles are written by academic economists, economists with the Board of Governors of the Federal Reserve System, and other qualified experts.
     A typical issue is about twenty-five pages and contains two or three articles. Occasionally an entire issue is devoted to a single topic such as the perspectives on a precious metal, or the analysis of a particular piece of banking legislation. An annual chronology of economic events of the previous year appears in the first issue of each volume.

157.   Federal Reserve Bank of Cleveland. Economic Commentary. DATE FOUNDED: 1975. FREQUENCY: bw. PRICE: Free. PUBLISHER: Federal Reserve Bank of Cleveland, Research Department, P.O. Box 6387, Cleveland, Ohio 44101. EDITOR: Patricia Wren. CIRCULATION: 13,000. MANUSCRIPT SELECTION: Editor. INDEXED/ABSTRACTED: FedP. TARGET AUDIENCE: GP, SP. SAMPLE COPIES: Libraries and Individuals.

Federal Reserve Bank of Cleveland. Economic Commentary is a bulletin focusing primarily on banking issues. It differs from the Cleveland Federal Reserve Bank's Economic Review in that articles are much briefer and less technical in nature. Occasionally a research article published in the latter title appears in summary form in Economic Commentary. Tables and charts accompany most articles, but no mathematical or statistical methodologies are employed. Recent issues have concentrated on current problems in the banking sector such as the international debt situation, the treasury debt that is held by commercial banks, banking without interstate barriers, and other issues involving the degree of regulation of U.S. banks. Occasionally articles appear on non-banking issues such as the loss of tax revenues due to the issuance of industrial development bonds, and the cost advantage that Japanese auto firms have over their U.S. competitors. Articles are signed. Almost all are written by economists with the Cleveland Federal Reserve Bank. Occasionally the author is an intern with the Bank.

Each issue is comprised of a single four-page article. Articles are footnoted and end with a separate "summary" or "Conclusion" paragraph.

158.   Federal Reserve Bank of Cleveland. Economic Review. DATE FOUNDED: 1921. TITLE CHANGES: Federal Reserve Bank of Cleveland. Monthly Business Review (1921-1963). FREQUENCY: q. PRICE: Free. PUBLISHER: Federal Reserve Bank of Cleveland, Box 6387, Cleveland, Ohio 44101. EDITOR: Pat Wren. ILLUSTRATIONS. INDEX. CIRCULATION: 4,200. MANUSCRIPT SELECTION: Editor. INDEXED/ABSTRACTED: FedP, PAIS. DATABASES: PAIS INT. TARGET AUDIENCE: AC, GP, SP. SAMPLE COPIES: Libraries and Individuals.

Federal Reserve Bank of Cleveland. Economic Review contains a mix of technical and non-technical articles. Of the twelve Federal Reserve District Bank reviews, it is closest to those published by the Federal Reserve Bank of Boston, Chicago, and Kansas City. It contains less technical and scholarly articles than typically found in the St. Louis, San Francisco, Minneapolis, and Richmond reviews, but is less aimed at the general public than are the Atlanta and Philadelphia Federal Reserve Bank reviews. It focuses on banking and monetary policy topics, but the contents of recent issues have been influenced by the relative decline of smoke stack industries in the state of Ohio. Articles on location of plants, plant closings, wage laws, capital stock needs and cash management have appeared. Most articles are written by economists at the Federal Reserve Bank of Cleveland, with an occasional one written by an academic economist or one employed by a government agency.

Issues average about twenty-five pages in length and contain two articles. Occasionally a one-page "Review" (really a summary) of a technical working paper by a Federal Reserve Bank of Cleveland research economist is included. A list of available working papers is also included in some issues.

159.   Federal Reserve Bank of Dallas. Economic Review. DATE FOUNDED: 1982. FREQUENCY: 6/yr. PRICE: Free. PUBLISHER: Federal Reserve Bank of Dallas, Station K, Dallas, Texas 75222. ILLUSTRATIONS. CIRCULATION: 17,000. MANUSCRIPT SELECTION: Editor. MICROFORMS: BLH, MIM. INDEXED/ABSTRACTED: FedP, PAIS, WAERSA. DATABASES: CAB AB, PAIS INT. TARGET AUDIENCE: AC, SP. SAMPLE COPIES: Libraries and Individuals.

Federal Reserve Bank of Dallas. Economic Review supersedes the Bank's Voice published from 1978 to 1981 which superseded its Review (1977-1978), Business Review (1957-1977) and Monthly Business Review, the latter dating back to 1916. It is one of twelve District Bank reviews. Its level and scope is closest to those published by the Federal Reserve Banks of Cleveland, Kansas City, New England, and Chicago. The majority of articles deal with national macroeconomic problems and banking issues. The remainder deal with regional topics. For example, recent issues have included articles which have focused on Mexican immigration

to the U.S., the effects of natural gas deregulation, U.S. vulnerability
toward oil supply disruptions, Texas agricultural productivity, and the
availability of capital in the Southwestern United States. Articles are
scholarly in nature, often quite empirical in content, and more technical than is suitable for a lay readership. Many articles employ
mathematical equations and make use of statistical and econometric
methodologies. The majority of the authors are research economists with
the Dallas Bank. A considerable number of academics, either consultants
or visiting scholars at the Dallas Bank, have their works published as
well.
    A typical issue contains two articles, each from ten to fifteen pages
in length.

160.   Federal Reserve Bank of Kansas City. Economic Review. DATE
FOUNDED: 1921. TITLE CHANGES: Federal Reserve Bank of Kansas City.
Monthly Review. FREQUENCY: 6/yr. PRICE: Free. PUBLISHER: Federal Reserve
Bank of Kansas City, Research Division, 925 Grand Ave., Kansas City,
Missouri 64198. EDITOR: T. E. Davis. ILLUSTRATIONS. INDEX. CIRCULATION:
29,000. MANUSCRIPT SELECTION: Staff of Research Division. MICROFORMS:
BLH, MIM, UMI. INDEXED/ABSTRACTED: BPIA, FedP, PAIS, WAERSA. DATABASES:
ABI, CAB AB, MC, PAIS INT. TARGET AUDIENCE: AC, GP, SP. SAMPLE COPIES:
Libraries and Individuals.

Federal Reserve Bank of Kansas City. Economic Review is fairly "middle
ground" among the twelve different reviews that are published by
district Federal Reserve Banks. It is more research oriented than its
Atlanta, Philadelphia, or Chicago counterparts, but somewhat less
technical than the reviews published by the St. Louis, Minneapolis, San
Francisco or Richmond Federal Reserve Banks. Only about half the
articles in this review are related directly to banking, monetary
policy, and interest rates while the other half deal with a myriad of
topics including productivity, oil, international trade, agricultural
policy, and taxation. Only occasionally do articles take a district
perspective. Articles range from theoretical papers employing mathematical models to policy discussions that informed non-economists can
understand. Technical articles make use of economic jargon and diagrams.
Authors are professional economists who are either with the Federal
Reserve Bank of Kansas City's Research Division on a permanent basis or
as visiting scholars.
    Most issues of the Review are between thirty-five and forty pages in
length and contain either two or three articles. Occasionally an
impressive list of available "Research Working Papers" produced by
Kansas City Federal Reserve Bank economists is published.

161.   Federal Reserve Bank of Kansas City. Financial Letter. DATE
FOUNDED: 1974. TITLE CHANGES: Federal Reserve Bank of Kansas City.
Financial Developments (1972-1975). FREQUENCY: m. PRICE: Free. PUB-
LISHER: Federal Reserve Bank of Kansas City, Federal Reserve Station,
Kansas City, Missouri 64198. EDITOR: Scott Hoober. ILLUSTRATIONS.
CIRCULATION: 6,500. MANUSCRIPT SELECTION: Editor. INDEXED/ABSTRACTED:
FedP. TARGET AUDIENCE: GP. SAMPLE COPIES: Libraries and Individuals.

The Federal Reserve Bank of Kansas City. Financial Letter is aimed
primarily at the business community of the Tenth District (Colorado,

Kansas, Missouri, Nebraska, New Mexico, Oklahoma, and Wyoming). It is far less technical and has less of a national perspective than does the Federal Reserve Bank of Kansas. City Economic Review. Financial Letter focuses on current economic conditions in the Tenth District or those importantly affecting the Tenth District. The lead articles deal with such topics as consumer interest rates, housing sales, monetary aggregates, inflation, the strength of the dollar, productivity, business inventory, employment, and agricultural credit conditions. Four issues per year present a survey of agricultural credit conditions based on the results of the Bank's quarterly survey of about 180 banks in the Tenth District. Articles are usually accompanied by statistical tables and charts, but are devoid of economic jargon and mathematical or statistical analysis. Articles are only occasionally signed and always written by staff economists in the Bank's Research Division.

Financial Letter is a four-page bulletin featuring a single article. Each issue regularly presents a table on the latest banking and monetary aggregates and one providing Tenth District depository institution statistics. The latter is accompanied by a half-page narrative statement.

162.   Federal Reserve Bank of Minneapolis. Quarterly Review. DATE FOUNDED: 1977. FREQUENCY: q. PRICE: Free. PUBLISHER: Federal Reserve Bank of Minneapolis, Research Dept., 250 Marquette Ave., Minneapolis, Minnesota 55480. EDITORS: Richard M. Todd, Patricia Lewis. ILLUSTRATIONS. CIRCULATION: 20,000. MANUSCRIPT SELECTION: Editors. MICROFORMS: BLH, MIM, UMI. REPRINTS: UMI. SPECIAL ISSUES. INDEXED/ABSTRACTED: FedP, InEcA, JEL, PAIS, Pred. DATABASES: ECONLIT, PAIS INT, PF. TARGET AUDIENCE: AC, GP, SP. SAMPLE COPIES: Libraries and Individuals.

Federal Reserve Bank of Minneapolis. Quarterly Review supersedes Federal Reserve Bank of Minneapolis Ninth District Quarterly. It primarily presents economic research aimed at improving policymaking by the Federal Reserve System and other government authorities. The level is mixed. Many articles are written at an advanced level for scholars in the field. These employ sophisticated mathematical and statistical methodologies. Others are written at a level understandable by college undergraduate economics students and informed laymen. The selection of articles reflects the view of Minneapolis Federal Reserve economists that "whenever possible, policy questions should be analyzed according to the criteria of welfare economics ... developed with reference to general equilibrium models." By contrast to most other Federal Reserve District Bank reviews, almost half of the articles published in this review are written by academic economists. The remainder are written by professional economists employed by the Minneapolis Bank.

Most issues are about twenty to twenty-five pages in length and contain two articles and one "District Conditions" review. Only about fifteen percent of the space is devoted to the latter which provides a report on current economic conditions in the district covering Minnesota, Montana, North Dakota, South Dakota and the northern portions of Wisconsin and Michigan.

163.   Federal Reserve Bank of New York. Quarterly Review. DATE FOUNDED: 1976. FREQUENCY: q. PRICE: Free. PUBLISHER: Federal Reserve Bank of New York, 33 Liberty St., New York, New York 10045. EDITOR:

Peter Fousele. ILLUSTRATIONS. CIRCULATION: 40,000. MANUSCRIPT SELECTION:
Research Department Officers. MICROFORMS: BLH, MIM, UMI. REPRINTS: UMI.
INDEXED/ABSTRACTED: BPI, BPIA, FedP, InEcA, IntBibE, JEL, PAIS. DATA-
BASES: ECONLIT, MC, PAIS INT. TARGET AUDIENCE: AC, GP, SP. SAMPLE
COPIES: Libraries and Individuals.

Federal Reserve Bank of New York. Quarterly Review supersedes the
Federal Reserve Bank of New York Monthly Review which had been published
since 1925. It is a much more substantial publication featuring more
articles than its eleven counterpart Reviews published by other Federal
Reserve District Banks. It covers both domestic and international
economic topics whereas most of the other Federal Reserve Bank Reviews
concentrate on domestic issues. The great majority of articles deal with
domestic monetary and fiscal policy matters and with foreign trade and
international finance. Each issue contains a report on the U.S. Treasury
and Federal Reserve foreign exchange operations. Most issues have one
article on New York's economic performance. Articles also appear on a
whole host of other economic topics including state and local government
issues and social security systems. Articles are technical but an effort
is made to minimize the use of sophisticated quantitative methodologies. Authors are professional research economists employed by the
Federal Reserve Bank of New York.
    A typical issue contains from six to nine articles rather than the
two to three articles that comprise most of the other Federal Reserve
Bank Reviews. Recent issues of this title have an "In Brief, Economic
Capsules" section that offers several one to two-page discussions of
varied current economic topics.

164.   Federal Reserve Bank of Philadelphia. Business Review. DATE
FOUNDED: 1921. TITLE CHANGES: Federal Reserve Bank of Philadelphia.
Business and Financial Conditions (1921-1923). FREQUENCY: 6/yr. PRICE:
Free. PUBLISHER: Federal Reserve Bank of Philadelphia, 10 Independence
Mall, Philadelphia, Pennsylvania 19106. EDITOR: Judith Farnbach.
ILLUSTRATIONS. INDEX. CIRCULATION: 23,000. MANUSCRIPT SELECTION: Editor.
MICROFORMS: BLH, MIM, UMI. REPRINTS: UMI. INDEXED/ABSTRACTED: FedP,
PAIS, Pred. DATABASES: PAIS INT, PF. TARGET AUDIENCE: AC, GP. SAMPLE
COPIES: Libraries and Individuals.

Federal Reserve Bank of Philadelphia. Business Review is among the
shortest and least technical of the twelve District Federal Reserve Bank
Reviews. Only the Federal Reserve Bank of Atlanta. Economic Review is
designed for an even more general audience. The scope of this title is
very wide. Its greatest concentration is on banking topics, interest
rates, and monetary policy in the U.S. But recent issues have included
articles on clean air, forecasting with the Index of Leading Indicators,
health care, housing, and the stock market. Occasionally articles of
regional interest are included such as "The Casino Industry in Atlantic
City" and "Targeting High Tech in the Delaware Valley." Articles are
non-technical in nature and except for an occasional brief mathematical
appendix are devoid of sophisticated quantitative analysis. The authors
are economists employed by the Philadelphia Federal Reserve Bank or
academics affiliated with the Bank.
    Most issues are from twenty to twenty-five pages in length and
contain two articles. Liberal use is made of boxed inserts offering a
separate explanation of a concept or providing an alternative viewpoint.

The last issue of each volume carries a combined table of contents for the past year.

165.   Federal Reserve Bank of Richmond. Economic Review. DATE FOUNDED: 1921. TITLE CHANGES: Federal Reserve Bank of Richmond . Monthly Review (1921-1974). FREQUENCY: 6/yr. PRICE: Free. PUBLISHER: Federal Reserve Bank of Richmond, Box 27622, Richmond, Virginia 23261. EDITOR: Thomas M. Humphrey. ILLUSTRATIONS. INDEX. CIRCULATION: 27,000. MANUSCRIPT SELEC-TION: Editor. MICROFORMS: BLH, MIM, UMI. INDEXED/ABSTRACTED: FedP, PAIS. DATABASES: ABI, PAIS INT. TARGET AUDIENCE: AC, SP. SAMPLE COPIES: Libraries and Individuals.

Federal Reserve Bank of Richmond. Economic Review is a scholarly and technical journal. It is aimed at financial and economic analysts, academic economists, bankers, and participants in financial markets. It contrasts greatly with some other Federal Reserve Bank Reviews, notably those published by the Atlanta and Philadelphia district banks. It is most like the St. Louis, San Francisco, and Minneapolis bank reviews. It is considerably more specialized than the other Federal Reserve Bank Reviews, concentrating heavily on monetary theory and policy and the analysis of financial markets. It has strong empirical content and makes use of fairly sophisticated mathematical models and quantitative techniques. Forecasts of economic activity, with particular emphasis on the Fifth District, appear in some issues. Occasionally articles which provide a historical assessment of monetary policies are included. The editor is careful not to advocate a particular viewpoint, but many of the articles do exhibit a monetarist approach. Authors are professional research economists at the Richmond Federal Reserve Bank or at a university.
    Issues range from fifteen to thirty-five pages in length and usually contain two articles. The January/February issue also contains a three to five-page economic forecast for that year.

166.   Federal Reserve Bank of San Francisco. Economic Review. DATE FOUNDED: 1975. FREQUENCY: q. PRICE: Free. PUBLISHER: Federal Reserve Bank of San Francisco, Box 7702, San Francisco, California 94120. EDITOR: Gregory J. Tong. ILLUSTRATIONS. INDEX. CIRCULATION: 16,000. MANUSCRIPT SELECTION: Editorial Committee. MICROFORMS: BLH, MIM, UMI. REPRINTS: UMI. INDEXED/ABSTRACTED: FedP, InEcA, JEL, PAIS. DATABASES: ECONLIT, PAIS INT. TARGET AUDIENCE: AC, SP. SAMPLE COPIES: Libraries and Individuals.

Federal Reserve Bank of San Francisco. Economic Review supersedes its Monthly Review and then Business Review which date back to 1921. The San Francisco Bank's Economic Review is among the most scholarly and technical of the twelve Federal Reserve District Bank Reviews. In this respect it is on a par with the reviews published by the St. Louis, Richmond, and Minneapolis Federal Reserve Banks. Articles have a strong empirical content and make use of mathematical and statistical mechod-ologies. Occasionally a "viewpoint" article is included. This journal focuses on banking, monetary and fiscal theory and policy, and financial markets. Articles appear on such topics as the demand for money, velocity, mortgage rates, real interest rates, risk, and deposit insurance. Occasionally an article will concentrate on a topic of interest in California or on a topic that concerns the Pacific Basin, especially Japan. Most authors are professional research economists with the Federal Reserve Bank of San Francisco, but occasionally an article is written by an academic economist who is serving as a visiting scholar at the Bank.

Issues vary from thirty to seventy-five pages in length and contain from two to four articles. Some issues begin with a one to three-page introduction which summarizes the articles in that issue.

167.   Federal Reserve Bank of San Francisco. Weekly Letter. DATE FOUNDED: 1973. TITLE CHANGES: Federal Reserve Bank of San Francisco. Business and Financial Letter (1973-1978). FREQUENCY: w. PRICE: Free. PUBLISHER: Federal Reserve Bank of San Francisco, P.O. Box 7702, San Francisco, California 94120. EDITOR: Gregory Tong. ILLUSTRATIONS. CIRCULATION: 19,000. MANUSCRIPT SELECTION: Editor. INDEXED/ABSTRACTED: FedP, Pred. DATABASES: PF. TARGET AUDIENCE: GP. SAMPLE COPIES: Libraries and Individuals.

Federal Reserve Bank of San Francisco. Weekly Letter is this Bank's publication for the general public. While the scope is essentially the same as its quarterly Economic Review, the latter contains much more technical articles aimed at professional economists. Weekly Letter is much like the Federal Reserve Bank of Cleveland's Economic Commentary, which also publishes less technical articles than Cleveland's Economic Review. Some issues of the Weekly Letter are part of a series of digests of articles that first appeared in the San Francisco Bank's Economic Review. The editor states that "these digests are intended to make the major findings of research conducted at the San Francisco Bank available to a wider audience." Articles focus on national rather than regional economic issues and problems. Many deal with banking such as deposit insurance, bank regulation, and the insurance and management of bank risk taking. Others are broader and deal with topics such as U.S. income taxes, savings in the U.S., unemployment versus employment statistics, budget deficits, and the U.S. international balance of payments problem. Articles are written by professional economists with the Federal Reserve Bank of San Francisco.

Each issue is four pages in length, three of which are devoted to that week's article. The fourth page provides up-to-date banking data for the Twelfth Federal Reserve District.

168.   Federal Reserve Bank of St. Louis. Monetary Trends. DATE FOUNDED: 1967. FREQUENCY: m. PRICE: Free. PUBLISHER: Federal Reserve Bank of St. Louis, P.O. Box 442, St. Louis, Missouri 63166. EDITORS: Albert E. Burger, R. Alton Gilbert, R. W. Hafer, Daniel L. Thornton. ILLUSTRATIONS. MANUSCRIPT SELECTION: Editors. INDEXED/ABSTRACTED: FedP. TARGET AUDIENCE: AC, GP, SP. SAMPLE COPIES: Libraries and Individuals.

Federal Reserve Bank of St. Louis. Monetary Trends is a unique publication containing comments and data on U.S. monetary aggregates. It is a very important source of data for economists and business people who are influenced by monetarist theories and predict or act according to changes in monetary aggregates. Monetary Trends complements the St. Louis Federal Reserve Bank's Review which contains full-length research articles and its National Economic Trends which provides data on the economic condition of the U.S. economy. Monetary Trends contains tables and charts showing annual rates of change on a monthly basis for the M1 and M2 money stock, a number of different demand and time deposit variables, the monetary base, reserves, bank loans and investments, and federal government expenditures. Data on Federal Reserve credit, federal government debt, and federal government budgets is also provided for the current period. Introductory comments are made by professional economists with the St. Louis Federal Reserve Bank.

Each issue is sixteen pages in length, fifteen of which are tables and charts.

169.   Federal Reserve Bank of St. Louis. National Economic Trends. DATE FOUNDED: 1965. TITLE CHANGES: Federal Reserve Bank of St. Louis. National Economic Indicators (1965-1967). FREQUENCY: m. PRICE: Free. PUBLISHER: Federal Reserve Bank of St. Louis, P.O. Box 442, St. Louis, Missouri 63166. EDITORS: Keith M. Carlson, John A. Tatom. ILLUSTRATIONS. MANUSCRIPT SELECTION: Editors. INDEXED/ABSTRACTED: FedP. TARGET AUDIENCE: AC, GP, SP. SAMPLE COPIES: Libraries and Individuals.

Federal Reserve Bank of St. Louis. National Economic Trends provides up-to-date information, primarily in the form of statistical tables and charts, on the economic condition of the U.S. economy. It complements but does not overlap with the same Bank's Review which contains full-length research articles and Monetary Trends which largely provides U.S. money supply data. National Economic Trends is aimed at professional economists as well as business people who have an interest in seeing the changes taking place in important U.S. economic variables. Annual rates of change on a monthly basis are provided for U.S. employment, consumer and producer prices, industrial production, personal income, retail sales, unit labor costs, productivity, gross national product, the GNP price deflator, personal consumption expenditure, gross private domestic investment, government purchases, disposable personal income, and corporate profits. Introductory comments are made by research economists with the St. Louis Federal Reserve Bank.

Each issue is twenty pages in length, nineteen of which are tables and charts. The back cover is devoted to a chart comparing business inventories to sales.

170.   Federal Reserve Bank of St. Louis. Review. DATE FOUNDED: 1917. TITLE CHANGES: Federal Reserve Bank of St. Louis. Monthly Review (1921-1962). FREQUENCY: 10/yr. PRICE: Free. PUBLISHER: Federal Reserve Bank of St. Louis, Box 442, St. Louis, Missouri 63166. EDITOR: Daniel P. Brennan. ILLUSTRATIONS. INDEX. CIRCULATION: 40,000. MANUSCRIPT SELECTION: Editor. MICROFORMS: BLH, UMI. REPRINTS: UMI. INDEXED/ABSTRACTED: BPI, InEcA, IntBibE, JEL, PAIS, WAERSA. DATABASES: CAB AB, ECONLIT, PAIS INT. TARGET AUDIENCE: AC, SP. SAMPLE COPIES: Libraries and Individuals.

Federal Reserve Bank of St. Louis. Review has a unique reputation among economists. It is known as a technical journal which espouses a monetarist viewpoint. The so-called St. Louis equation is used to show the effectiveness of monetary as opposed to fiscal policy. Of the other eleven Federal Reserve District Bank Reviews the one that comes closest in coverage, viewpoint, and use of technical economic methodologies is the Federal Reserve Bank of Richmond Economic Review. Next to the

Federal Reserve Bank of New York Quarterly Review, the St. Louis Review
has the greatest amount of international economics content. Articles are
included which contrast monetary policies in other nations to those of
the U.S. Many articles in this title examine monetary theory and policy,
often attempting to measure velocity, the money multiplier, and the
monetary base. The tools of the professional economist--mathematical
models, diagrams, econometrics, and statistics--are liberally employed.
Little space is devoted to Eighth District interests per se, but an
occasional article with that perspective does appear. Authors are
professional research economists, primarily employed by the St. Louis
Federal Reserve Bank, but sometimes associated with a university.
     A typical issue is from thirty-five to forty pages in length and
contains three or four articles. Each issue begins with an "In this
Issue" section which provides a one to two-page introduction to the
articles in that issue.

171.   Federal Reserve Bulletin. DATE FOUNDED: 1915. FREQUENCY: m.
PRICE: $20/yr. PUBLISHER: Federal Reserve System, Board of Governors,
Publications Services, Rm. MS-138, Washington D.C. 20551. EDITOR: Joseph
R. Coyne. ILLUSTRATIONS. INDEX. CIRCULATION: 26,000. MANUSCRIPT SELEC-
TION: Publications Committee. MICROFORMS: MIM, UMI. REPRINTS: UMI.
INDEXED/ABSTRACTED: BPI, BPIA, FedP, InEcA, IntBibE, JEL, KeyEcS, PAIS.
DATABASES: ECONAB, ECONLIT, MC, PAIS INT. TARGET AUDIENCE: AC, GP, SP.

The Federal Reserve Bulletin is the premier publication of the Federal
Reserve System, the central bank of the United States. It includes
articles, reports, statements, and position papers which make known the
views and policies of the Federal Reserve System as well as a host of
financial and business statistics. The scope is wide and covers not only
the Federal Reserve's monetary policy and foreign exchange operations,
but also its perspectives on topics such as consumer finances, the
underground economy, American agriculture, the U.S. labor market, the
U.S. housing market, and business investment. Articles usually include
tables of data and charts but are non-technical and non-mathematical in
nature. The authors are predominantly economists in the Federal Reserve's Division of Research and Statistics or its Division of International Finance. Occasionally an article is taken from a presentation
made by a member of the Board of Governors.
     About half of each issue--approximately seventy pages--is devoted to
the presentation of financial and business statistics in the form of
tables. The other half usually includes an article, one or more reports
to Congress, a summary of a signed staff study, a news release on
industrial production testimony before the Congress by the Chairman or
another Federal Reserve official, announcements of new appointments,
announcements of meetings to be held, a list of new admissions to
membership, the record of the policy actions of the Federal Open Market
Committee, and a report on legal developments.

172.   Finance and Development. DATE FOUNDED: 1964. TITLE CHANGES: Fund
and Bank Review (1964-1967). FREQUENCY: q. PRICE: Free. PUBLISHERS:
International Monetary Fund, 700 19th Street, Washington, D.C. 20431 and
World Bank, 1818 H Street, Washington, D.C. 20433. EDITOR: Bahram
Nowzad. ILLUSTRATIONS. INDEX. ADVERTISEMENTS. CIRCULATION: 110,000.
MANUSCRIPT SELECTION: Editor. MICROFORMS: UMI. BOOK REVIEWS. INDEXED/

ABSTRACTED: AcctInd, BPI, BPIA, InEcA, JEL, KeyEcS, PAIS, SSI, WAERSA.
DATABASES: ACCTIND, CAB AB, ECONAB, ECONLIT, MC, PAIS INT, SSI. TARGET
AUDIENCE: GP. SAMPLE COPIES: Libraries and Individuals.

Finance and Development is jointly published by two international
organizations whose purposes are to assist countries in financial
matters and to promote the economic growth of developing countries. The
journal explains the operations of the two institutions and discusses
development and financial topics of general interest. The journal,
available in six languages, aims at presenting economic material in
non-technical form to a wide audience. Articles deal with all aspects of
international finance and development. Most of the articles are written
by staff members, who are international in background and primarily
economists by training. Many of the articles are based on longer,
in-depth technical research reports published by the IMF or World Bank.
Some representative article titles are: "Interest Rates and Exchange
Rates," "Private Investment in Developing Countries," "Industrial Policy
in Small Developing Countries," and "Toward a More Orderly Exchange Rate
System." Finance and Development complements the scholarly International
Monetary Fund Staff Papers published by this same organization.
    Each issue includes about twelve short articles. Occasionally several
of the articles focus on the same topic. Some issues have a review
article which presents an overview of a particular aspect of the world
economy. Each issue has three or four signed book reviews and from six
to ten annotations in a "books received" section. An annual index
appears in the December issue.

173.   Finance and Trade Review. DATE FOUNDED: 1952. FREQUENCY: a.
PRICE: Free. PUBLISHER: Volkskas Limited, P.O. Box 578, Pretoria 0001.,
South Africa. EDITOR: Economic Division, Volkskas Limited. ILLUSTRA-
TIONS. CIRCULATION: 3,000. MANUSCRIPT SELECTION: Editor. INDEXED/
ABSTRACTED: InEcA, IntBibE, JEL, KeyEcS. DATABASES: ECONAB ECONLIT.
TARGET AUDIENCE: AC, SP. SAMPLE COPIES: Libraries and Individuals.

Finance and Trade Review is published by a South African bank "to
promote a wider knowledge overseas of economic conditions in South
Africa." The journal presents articles dealing with economics, finance
and trade in South Africa. Most of the articles use sophisticated
technical methodologies and are intended for professional economists.
Some offer a substantial amount of data. Some articles deal with actual
economic situations while others offer theoretical discussions of public
policy issues. Examples of the former are "On the Velocity of Circulation of the Money Supply in the South African Economy," and "Industrializing the National States: The Bophuthatswana Example." Representative examples of the latter are "Some Issues in South African Personal
Income Tax Reform," and "Technology: An Investment for Tomorrow."
Authors are academics, bankers, and government economists in South
Africa. Compared to Journal for Studies in Economics and Econometrics,
the Review is narrower in subject scope and deals exclusively with South
Africa.
    Each issue contains two articles. This periodical recently changed
its publication frequency from twice a year to an annual edition. The
only annual to date is eighty pages long and is divided equally between
the two articles.

Finances Publiques. see Public Finance/Finances Publiques.

Financial Letter. see Federal Reserve Bank of Kansas City. Financial
Letter.

174.   Financial Review. DATE FOUNDED: 1965. TITLE CHANGES: The Appala-
chian Financial Review (1965-1971). FREQUENCY: q. PRICE: $30/yr.
institutions, $20/yr. personal. PUBLISHER: Eastern Finance Association,
School of Management, State University of New York at Buffalo, Buffalo,
New York 14214. EDITOR: James Boness. ILLUSTRATIONS. ADVERTISEMENTS.
CIRCULATION: 1,000. MANUSCRIPT SELECTION: Editor. REPRINTS: DATCO. BOOK
REVIEWS. INDEXED/ABSTRACTED: BPIA, PAIS. DATABASES: ABI, MC, PAIS INT.
TARGET AUDIENCE: AC, SP.

The Financial Review is the journal of a regional professional association of economists, business managers, and academics. The region
encompasses the eastern part of the U.S. and Canada. The Review publishes "empirical, theoretical, and methodological articles on topics of
micro and macro-finance." It also deals with financial education and the
relationship between economics and finance. Most of the authors are
academics from American and Canadian universities with a few contributors from the business and government sectors. The articles are scholarly in style, using mathematical methodologies, tables of data, and
extensive references. The Review overlaps in subject coverage and
technical level with two other journals sponsored by regional finance
associations, The Journal of Financial Research and Journal of Financial
and Quantitative Analysis. However, these do not include the extra
feature of finance education.
    Each issue is divided into four sections. The "Articles" section
includes four to six papers of ten to twenty pages each. The "Notes and
Conjectures" section presents two to four shorter papers of up to ten
pages in length. The "Education" section presents a variety of papers
relevant to financial education. A recent issue includes a summary of
lecture notes for a course on financial management and a literature
review of the market disequilibrium concept. The fourth section, "Book
Reviews," includes two or three signed reviews.

The Finnish Journal of Business Economics. see Liiketaloudellinen
Aikakauskirja/The Finnish Journal of Business Economics.

175.   Food Policy. DATE FOUNDED: 1975. FREQUENCY: q. PRICE: $116/yr.
PUBLISHER: Butterworth Scientific Ltd., Journals Div., P.O. Box 63,
Westbury House, Bury St., Guildford GU2 5BH, England. EDITOR: Colin
Blackman. ADVERTISEMENTS. MANUSCRIPT SELECTION: Editor and Referees.
REPRINTS: Publisher. BOOK REVIEWS. INDEXED/ABSTRACTED: WAERSA. DATA-
BASES: CAB AB. TARGET AUDIENCE: AC, GP, SP. SAMPLE COPIES: Libraries.

Food Policy is a journal that covers many aspects of "the economics,
planning and politics of food, nutrition, and agriculture." Articles
deal with national government agricultural policies, international
organizations' agricultural policies, food supplies in specific countries, specific commodity markets, food aid, nutrition problems in

specific countries, and agricultural production. There is a broad range
in the level of complexity of articles. Some use mathematical methodologies, some use diagrams and charts based on statistical data, and
some consist entirely of expository text. All of them include documentation. Many articles are written to promote changes in national or
international agricultural policies. About half the authors are American
academics or researchers while the rest are academics, researchers, and
journalists from other countries.

Each issue includes five or six research papers of eight to ten pages
in length. In addition, a "Viewpoint" section presents three shorter
papers offering controversial opinions. Two regular sections are "Food
Business," brief news and comments on food matters, and "Grapevine,"
brief personal views of current developments in the field. A "Review"
section offers three signed book reviews, reports of the highlights of
food conferences, and a listing of new publications. A calendar of
forthcoming international meetings of interest to readers is included in
the book.

176.   Food Research Institute Studies. DATE FOUNDED: 1960. TITLE
CHANGES: Studies in Agricultural Economics, Trade, and Development
(1968-1976). FREQUENCY: 2/yr. PRICE: $20/yr. PUBLISHER: Stanford
University, Food Research Institute, Stanford, California 94305. EDITOR:
Walter P. Falcon. ILLUSTRATIONS. INDEX. ADVERTISEMENTS. MANUSCRIPT
SELECTION: Editors. REPRINTS: Publisher. INDEXED/ABSTRACTED: Agrindex,
BibAg, BioAg, FldCropAbstr, InEcA, JEL, NutrAbstrRev, PAIS, WAERSA.
DATABASES: AGRIS, CAB AB, ECONLIT, PAIS INT. TARGET AUDIENCE: AC, SP.

Food Research Institute Studies is the scholarly journal of a distinguished university agricultural economics department. It covers a wide
range of agricultural economics subjects that are applied to an equally
wide range of countries. Topics in recent issues include price policies,
competition, growth of agriculture, supply and demand with respect to a
food product, population prospects, marketing systems, irrigation and
drainage schemes, and hedging and speculation in futures markets. Most
articles have substantial empirical content. They use data from countries such as Kenya, the Philippines, Korea, India, Mexico, Peru,
Argentina, Egypt, Pakistan, Ghana, El Salvador, Bangladesh, Denmark, and
the U.S. Most articles are technical in nature but few employ sophisticated mathematical models. They typically contain a substantial amount
of data and employ some statistical methodologies. The authors are
predominantly agricultural economists associated with universities or
research institutes. A disproportionate number are with the Stanford
University Food Research Institute.

Most issues contain four or five articles which average from twenty
to twenty-five pages in length. Each volume contains three issues, but
no more than two are published in any one year.

177.   Foreign Agricultural Trade of the United States. DATE FOUNDED:
1936. TITLE CHANGES: Foreign Crops and Markets (1936-1946). FREQUENCY:
6/yr. PRICE: $19/yr. PUBLISHER: U.S. Department of Agriculture, Economic
Research Service, 500 12th Street SW, Washington, DC 20250. EDITOR: T.
A. Warden. ILLUSTRATIONS. ADVERTISEMENTS. CIRCULATION: 2,000. MANUSCRIPT
SELECTION: Editor. REPRINTS: NTIS. SPECIAL ISSUES. TARGET AUDIENCE: SP.
SAMPLE COPIES: Libraries and Individuals.

Foreign Agricultural Trade of the United States is a government publication focusing on foreign trade in agricultural products. The articles
deal with all aspects of trade and cover areas such as volume of
agricultural exports and imports, dollar amount of agricultural exports
and imports, exports and imports by type of commodity, strength of the
dollar, volume of exports by state, regional markets for U.S. agricultural products, commodity prices, and government-financed agricultural
exports. The articles are short summaries supported by statistical data.
Some of the articles include short forecasts of market conditions. The
articles are written by staff members of the U.S.D.A.'s Economic
Research Service. FATUS differs from Foreign Agriculture in that it
includes imports as well as exports and concentrates on presenting
detailed statistics instead of news stories of the foreign trade
situation.
     Each issue begins with a "Digest" section which presents short
summaries of each article. FATUS presents four to six articles of two to
three pages each supported by extensive tables of data. Some articles
may have up to fifty pages of data. FATUS publishes two annual supplements, a fiscal year statistical report and a calendar year statistical
report. Both of these statistical references present current and
historic data on U.S. foreign trade in agricultural products. Each
supplement is between 200 and 300 pages in length.

178.   Foreign Agriculture. DATE FOUNDED: 1962. FREQUENCY: m. PRICE:
$16/yr. PUBLISHER: U.S. Department of Agriculture, Foreign Agricultural
Service, Washington, D.C. 20250. EDITOR: Lynn K. Goldsbrough. ILLUSTRA-
TIONS. ADVERTISEMENTS. CIRCULATION: 13,000. MANUSCRIPT SELECTION:
Editor. MICROFORMS: UMI. INDEXED/ABSTRACTED: Pred, WAERSA. DATABASES:
CAB AB, PF. TARGET AUDIENCE: AC, GP, SP.

Foreign Agriculture is published by the U.S.D.A. as a service to
business firms selling U.S. farm products overseas. This periodical
presents current information useful to agricultural exporters. It
includes articles dealing with topics such as international franchising,
foreign business restrictions, foreign markets, markets for particular
commodities, international trade exhibits, and the world food situation.
Most of the authors are staff members of the Foreign Agricultural
Service but contributions from business executives, foreign service
personnel, and employees of other government agencies are also included.
The articles are non-technical and lavishly illustrated with photographs. This journal differs from Foreign Agricultural Trade of the
United States in that it deals only with exports and it provides very
little data.
     Each issue includes seven to eight short articles. In addition there
are regular features such as "Marketing News" which presents brief
reports on specific markets in foreign countries, "Country Briefs" which
presents reports on specific commodity demand in foreign countries, and
"Trade Updates" which presents data on foreign countries' purchases of
specific commodities.

179.   Foreign Trade Review. DATE FOUNDED: 1966. FREQUENCY: q. PRICE:
$15/yr. PUBLISHER: Indian Institute of Foreign Trade, Ashok Bhawan, 93
Nehru Pl., New Delhi 1100 19 India. EDITOR: Hartirath Singh. ILLUSTRA-
TIONS. INDEX. ADVERTISEMENTS. MANUSCRIPT SELECTION: Editor. BOOK

REVIEWS. SPECIAL ISSUES. INDEXED/ABSTRACTED: KeyEcS, WAERSA. DATABASES: CAB AB, ECONAB. TARGET AUDIENCE: AC, SP.

The Foreign Trade Review is a publication whose major emphasis is international finance and trade from the Indian perspective. Many of the articles deal with an aspect of India's foreign trade problems such as the shipping industry and the balance of payments. Others deal with India's trade relations with specific countries or regions. Some articles discuss trade relations of other Asian countries such as Japan, Bangladesh, Nepal and Sri Lanka. Additional articles deal with economic theory such as complementarity or direct foreign investment. The level of difficulty of the articles varies widely. The theoretical articles employ mathematical methodologies while the applied articles are expository in style with supporting data. The authors are predominantly staff researchers at the Institute or academics from Indian universities. A few authors are from American universities.

A typical issue contains eight or nine articles of eight to sixteen pages each. Some issues have a signed review article or a short signed book review. Occasionally an issue is devoted to a trade seminar that took place in India and includes selected papers from that seminar. Recent seminars were "Trading with Eastern Europe" and "UNCTAD-VI."

180.   Fortune. DATE FOUNDED: 1930. FREQUENCY: sm. PRICE: $39/yr. PUBLISHER: Time Inc., Time and Life Bldg., New York, New York 10020. EDITOR: William S. Rukeyser. ILLUSTRATIONS. INDEX. ADVERTISEMENTS. CIRCULATION: 675,000. MANUSCRIPT SELECTION: Editor. MICROFORMS: BLH, MIM, UMI. REPRINTS: UMI. BOOK REVIEWS. INDEXED/ABSTRACTED: AcctInd, BPIA, OR/MS, PAIS, RG, WorkRelAbstr. DATABASES: ACCTIND, MC, PAIS INT. TARGET AUDIENCE: GP.

Fortune is one of the most well-known and accepted popular business and economics magazines published in the United States. It is aimed at the same readership--business people and others interested in business and economics--and offers similar coverage as Business Week. The latter has a different format with more and briefer articles and is somewhat more newsy in nature. Fortune publishes articles dealing with competition in American and foreign markets, management, selling, technology, money and financial markets, corporate performance, politics and economic policy, and the past, present and anticipated condition of the American economy. All articles are written in a journalistic and non-technical style. Authors are primarily associate editors and reporters for Fortune and while articles are signed, no information about the authors is provided. Occasionally a well-known economist or business leader writes a guest article.

Most issues include about ten multi-page articles and a number of shorter pieces. Regular features of each issue include "The Editor's Desk," a brief editorial statement, "News Trends," brief news items, "Follow-Up," further information on previously published articles, "Letters to Fortune," "Keeping Up," tidbits of interest, "Personal Investing," "On Your Own Time," a note on leisure activities, and "Books & Ideas," a signed book review. An important regular annual feature is the publication of individual company data in a number of categories, the most important of which are the "Fortune 500," on the largest U.S. industrial firms, the "Service 500," on the largest U.S. non-industrial firms, and the "International 500," on the largest non-U.S. industrial firms.

181.   GATT FOCUS. DATE FOUNDED: 1981. FREQUENCY: 10/yr. PRICE: Free. PUBLISHER: General Agreement on Tariffs and Trade, Centre William Rappard, 154 rue de Lausanne, CH-1211 Geneva 21, Switzerland. EDITOR: John Croome. INDEX. CIRCULATION: 5,500. MANUSCRIPT SELECTION: Editor. REPRINTS: Publisher. TARGET AUDIENCE: AC, SP. SAMPLE COPIES: Libraries and Individuals.

GATT FOCUS is published by the General Agreement on Tariffs and Trade, an international organization composed of about ninety member countries. FOCUS presents information on all activities of this organization. It includes articles on GATT ministerial decisions implementation and operation of specific trade agreements, trading systems and policies, international trade, trade disputes, new working parties, GATT and developing countries, and trends in international trade. Some representative article titles are "International Trade Recovery in 1983", "Satisfactory Implementation of Most Tokyo Round Agreements" "The International Dairy Council" and "The Multifibre Arrangement". All articles are unsigned and written by staff members. They are non-technical and occasionally incoporate graphs and tables of data. FOCUS is published in English, French, and Spanish editions.

Each issue, a four page newsletter, contains ten to fifteen short articles. Regular features include "Coming GATT Activities" a schedule of meetings, "GATT Publications" a listing of new publications, and In Brief" a report of GATT committee recommendations. An anual index is published.

182.   The George Washington Journal of International Law and Economics. DATE FOUNDED: 1966. TITLE CHANGES: Journal of International Law and Economics (1971-1981). Journal of Law and Economic Development (1968-1970). Studies in Law and Economic Development (1966-1967). FREQUENCY: 3/yr. PRICE: $15/yr. PUBLISHER: George Washington University, National Law Center, Washington, D.C. 20052. EDITOR: LaDawn Naegle. INDEX. ADVERTISEMENTS: CIRCULATION: 750. MANUSCRIPT SELECTION: Editorial Board. MICROFORMS: UMI. REPRINTS: WSH. BOOK REVIEWS. INDEXED/ABSTRACTED: BPIA, ILP, PAIS. DATABASES: LEXIS, MC, PAIS INT. TARGET AUDIENCE: AC, SP.

The George Washington Journal of International Law and Economics is run and edited by the students of the George Washington University Law School. It is the membership publication of the Washington Foreign Law Society. It deals with a "variety of topics covering a broad area of international law and economics, including those dealing with some aspect of the substantive or procedural law of any nation, as well as problems international in scope having any impact on a nation's legal, social, economic or financial policy." Recent articles covered aspects of international trade agreements, the U.S. antitrust laws, legal decisions in other countries and their economic implications, and U.S. patent laws infringement problems. The articles are written in a scholarly style and are amply documented by references. Some of the articles deal with broad public policy implications and can be understood by a general audience while others deal with legal technicalities

of specific laws and treaties and require readers to have legal training.
    A typical issue contains six articles divided between an "Articles"
section and a "Notes" section. The former section includes contributions
by practicing attorneys while the latter section includes contributions
by student members of the journal's editorial board. Each issue has
either one signed book review or an annotated list of "Books Received."
The last issue of each volume includes the annual index.

183.   Georgia Business and Economic Conditions. DATE FOUNDED: 1936.
TITLE CHANGES: Georgia Business (1936-1981). FREQUENCY: 6/yr. PRICE:
$12/yr. PUBLISHER: University of Georgia, College of Business Adminis-
tration, Athens, Georgia 30602. EDITOR: Lorena M. Akioka. ILLUSTRATIONS.
CIRCULATION: 1,000. MANUSCRIPT SELECTION: Editor. INDEXED/ABSTRACTED:
PAIS. DATABASES: PAIS INT. TARGET AUDIENCE: GP.

Georgia Business and Economic Conditions is a publication whose primary
purpose is to disseminate information on economic conditions in Georgia.
Most of the articles discuss an aspect of the state economy such as
"Comparative Economic Growth in Georgia, 1950-1981", "Manufacturing
Exports from Georgia", and "Unemployment patterns in Georgia: 1975,
1979, and 1982". A few of the articles discuss a national economic issue
and may include its implication for Georgia. Examples of the latter are
"Economic Outlook for Support for the Arts in the U.S. and Georgia",
"Prospects for Energy Prices", and "America's Stake in International
Business." The articles do not use technical terms or quantitative
analyses and are understandable to the general reader. Most of the
authors are staff writers or academics from the University of Georgia.
This title resembles Arizona Business, Kentucky Economy: Review &
Perspective, Indiana Business Review, and Montana Business Quarterly,
other business school publications which concentrate on economic
conditions in their home state.
    In addition to two articles, each issue includes composite indexes of
leading and coincident Georgia economic indicators and Georgia business
statistics. The latter includes data for employment, weekly earnings,
retail sales, building permits, and total personal income.

184.   Government College Economic Journal. DATE FOUNDED: 1966.
FREQUENCY: 2/yr. PRICE: Rs.30/yr. institutions, Rs.50/yr. personal.
PUBLISHER: Government College, Department of Economics, Lahore, Pakis-
tan. EDITOR: A.S. Khalid. ILLUSTRATIONS. CIRCULATION: 250. MANUSCRIPT
SELECTION: Editorial Board. TARGET AUDIENCE: AC, SP. SAMPLE COPIES:
Libraries and Individuals.

Government College Economic Journal is the journal of the Department of
Economics at Government College, Lahore. It focuses on the economic
problems of Pakistan with an occasional article on a development problem
of another country or on a more general economic development topic.
Recurring topics concerning the Pakistan economy include its strategies
and policies to attain economic growth, how it can earn more foreign
exchange, the merits of protectionism, manpower planning, and income
distribution. Articles vary greatly in type and level. Some offer models
and empirical results, others are "think pieces", but most have a simple
hypothesis supported by some data. The authors are predominantly

academic economists at Pakistan universities. Occasionally an article is published by an American economist. The Journal covers the same subject area but is less technical than The Pakistan Development Review and Pakistan Economic and Social Review.

For the past several years both numbers of each volume have been published in a single issue. Such a double issue contains from three to five articles which range from ten to four pages in length. Most issues include two or three signed book reviews.

185.   Government Union Review. DATE FOUNDED: 1980. FREQUENCY: q. PRICE: $10/yr. PUBLISHER: Public Service Research Foundation, 8330 Old Courthouse Road, Suite 600, Vienna, Virginia 22180. EDITOR: George C. Bevel. CIRCULATION: 1,800. MANUSCRIPT SELECTION: Editor. SPECIAL ISSUES: INDEXED/ABSTRACTED: PAIS, WorkRelAbstr. DATABASES: PAIS INT. TARGET AUDIENCE: AC, GP, SP. SAMPLE COPIES: Libraries and Individuals.

Government Union Review, subtitled "a quarterly Journal on Public Sector Labor Relations", is published by the Public Service Research Foundation. The purpose of this non-profit public foundation is "to increase research, scholarship, and public awareness in the area of public policy regarding public sector employer-employee relations, with emphasis on the influence by public sector unions on the nation's federal, state and local governments." This periodical assists the Foundation in fulfilling its purpose by publishing articles that cover many aspects of public sector collective bargaining both in the U.S. and in foreign countries such as the U.K. and Canada. Some of the areas covered are public employee work stoppages, binding arbitration in public employment, the federal compensation system, and contracting out in federal employment. Some of the articles discuss the philosophical implications of these topics while other articles deal with case studies of actual situations. Although the editor states that this periodical does not advocate a particular view, most of the articles present arguments in support of limiting the power of public sector unions. The contributors are professors of economics and management, attorneys, and labor mediators. Many of the contributors are also members of the journal's "Board of Fellows". The Review covers the same subject areas as Journal of Collective Negotiations in the Public Sector. However, it offers more policy-oriented articles, while the Journal emphasizes empirical research results.

Each issue has from four to six articles, averaging fifteen pages in length. Occasionally, an issue is devoted to a single topic such as "Public Services and the Private Alternative", the subject of a recent seminar in England.

186.   Greek Economic Review. DATE FOUNDED: 1979. FREQUENCY: 3/yr. PRICE: $25/yr. institutions, $20/yr. personal. PUBLISHER: Society for Economic Research, Central Post Office, Box 4085, Athens, 102 10, Greece. EDITORS: George C. Bitros, Nicholas C. Garganas. MANUSCRIPT SELECTION: Editor and Editorial Board. REPRINTS: Authors. BOOK REVIEWS. INDEXED/ABSTRACTED: InEcA, JEL. DATABASES: ECONLIT. TARGET AUDIENCE: AC, SP.

The Greek Economic Review receives financial assistance from the Ionian and Popular Bank of Greece. It is a scholarly journal that publishes both economic theory and empirical studies. Empirical studies use predominantly data obtained from Greek sources, but occasionally utilize data from other European countries. Articles dealing with economic theory cover topics such as tax structure and balance of payments, unemployment benefits and labor supply, adjustment cost models of capital and labor, general equilibrium theory, and pure theory of international trade. Empirical studies include topics such as financial structure in Greece, male-female pay differentials in Greece, and investments in the Athens Stock Exchange during the years 1955 to 1975. Most of the articles are technical in nature and utilize advanced mathematical methodology. About half of the authors are Greek economists affiliated with institutions in Greece, the U.K., or the U.S. Other contributions are made by an international roster of economists or financial experts.

A typical issue has five or six articles, each between fifteen and forty pages in length. One or two signed book reviews, which may be as long as ten pages, appear in most issues.

187.   Growth and Change; A Journal of Public, Urban, and Regional Policy. DATE FOUNDED: 1970. TITLE CHANGES: Growth and Change; A Journal of Regional Development. (1970-1982). FREQUENCY: q. PRICE: $20/yr. institutions, $15/yr. personal. PUBLISHER: University of Kentucky, College of Business and Economics, 451 Commerce Building, Lexington, Kentucky 40506. EDITOR: Charles W. Hultman. ILLUSTRATIONS. INDEX. CIRCULATION: 1,200. MANUSCRIPT SELECTION: Editor and Referees. MICRO-FORMS: UMI. REPRINTS: Publisher. BOOK REVIEWS. SPECIAL ISSUES. INDEXED/ABSTRACTED: BPIA, InEcA, IntBibE, JEL, KeyEcS, PAIS, UAA, WAERSA. DATABASES: ABI, CAB AB, ECONAB, ECONLIT, MC, PAIS INT. TARGET AUDIENCE: AC, SP. SAMPLE COPIES: Libraries and Individuals.

Growth and Change; a Journal of Public, Urban, and Regional Policy is a publication that covers a broad range of topics in the social sciences. This interdisciplinary journal includes articles in economics, sociology, geography, history, political science, and related areas. Recent issues have focused mainly on economic development issues. The style and level of complexity of the articles vary with the discipline. Articles dealing with economics tend to be of a more quantitative nature than those dealing with social concerns which tend to be expository in nature although they are supported by charts, graphs, and statistical data. The authors are American academics in a wide variety of disciplines. Growth and Change is somewhat less quantitative than the International Regional Science Review. The Review includes articles dealing with many different countries while this journal concentrates on the U.S.

A typical issue includes six to eight articles. The articles are five to ten pages in length. Each issue includes eight to fifteen signed book reviews. A regular feature is a section named "The Grapevine". This section lists upcoming meetings, new publications from nonprofit organizations, and articles in other journals that might be of interest to readers. An annual index appears in the October issue.

188.   Harvard Business Review. DATE FOUNDED: 1922. FREQUENCY: 6/yr. PRICE: $30/yr. PUBLISHER: Harvard Business School, Soldiers Field, Boston, Massachusetts, 02163. EDITOR: Kenneth R. Andrews. ILLUSTRATIONS. INDEX. ADVERTISEMENTS: CIRCULATION: 232,000. MANUSCRIPT SELECTION:

Editorial Board. MICROFORMS: UMI. REPRINTS: Publisher. BOOK REVIEWS. INDEXED/ABSTRACTED: AcctInd, BPI, BPIA, IntBibE, KeyEcS, PAIS, Pred, WorkRelAbstr. DATABASES: ACCTIND, ECONAB, MC, PAIS INT, PF. TARGET AUDIENCE: AC, GP, SP.

Harvard Business Review is published by one of the leading Graduate Schools of Business Administration in the U.S. The Review aims at increasing business executives' understanding of the concepts and methods of professional management and keeping them informed of new ideas and approaches in management. Although the primary focus of this journal is business management, a secondary area of interest relates to economic theories and policies. Articles in the latter category focus on topics such as the international monetary system, industrial policy for the U.S., vertical integration, and international trade policy. The articles are expository in style, with occasional graphs, charts, or tables. The majority of contributors are academics from American Schools of Business with the rest being business executives and consultants.
   A typical issue contains ten to twelve articles of ten to twelve pages each. Regular features include "Letter from the Editor", an overview of the issue, "For the Manager's Bookshelf", two to four signed book reviews, "Growing Concerns," articles of interest to owners and managers of small businesses, and "Ideas for Action", practical suggestions for managers. An annual index is found in the November/December issue.

189.   Harvard Business School Bulletin. DATE FOUNDED: 1921. FREQUENCY: 6/yr. PRICE: $24. PUBLISHER: Harvard Business School, Soldiers Field, Boston, Massachusetts 02163. EDITOR: Deborah E. Blagg. ILLUSTRATIONS. ADVERTISEMENTS: CIRCULATION: 44,000. MANUSCRIPT SELECTION: Editor. BOOK REVIEWS. SPECIAL ISSUES. TARGET AUDIENCE: GP.

The Harvard Business School Bulletin is published primarily for the purpose of keeping HBS alumni informed about developments at the school and in the personal and professional lives of their fellow graduates. It does include some articles which concentrate on business management, current economic conditions, international trade and economic development, but these occupy a small fraction of the space in the publication. Some of these articles may be based on interviews with alumni. Others may be based on conference or seminar sessions. The authors are staff writers or free-lance writers. No educational credentials are given. The articles are written in a popular, journalistic style and understandable to a general audience. This publication differs sharply in emphasis from its sister publication Harvard Business Review which offers informational articles on current trends in management and is written primarily by academics.
   Each issue has several regular features. These include "News", brief news items about HBS; "Faculty", news items about HBS faculty; "Authors", two or three unsigned book reviews; and "Who's News", a listing of career changes of HBS alumni taken from the Wall Street Journal. Over one hundred pages are devoted to "Class Notes", a chronological listing of alumni activities. The October issue focuses on that year's 25th Class Reunion and reports on class members' achievements.

190.   Harvard College Economist. DATE FOUNDED: 1976. TITLE CHANGES:
Harvard Undergraduate Journal of Economics. FREQUENCY: 2/yr. PRICE:
$15/yr. institutions, $10/yr. personal. PUBLISHER: Harvard Economics
Association, c/o Economics Tutorial Office, Littauer Hall, Cambridge,
Massachusetts 02138. EDITOR: Renata Villers. ILLUSTRATIONS. ADVERTISE-
MENTS: MANUSCRIPT SELECTION: Editor. BOOK REVIEWS. TARGET AUDIENCE: AC,
GP.

The Harvard College Economist is published for the purpose of providing
a forum for papers written by undergraduate students of economics. Some
of these papers are based on the student's honors thesis. Although this
journal does accept articles in any field of economics, each recent
issue concentrated on a single topic and most articles addressed that
topic. Examples are international banking and development, the firm,
economic history, and industrial organization. Some articles are
actually interviews of well known economists by student reporters. The
articles are of a level to be understood by a senior economics major. A
few articles employ quantitative analysis but most are written in an
expository style. Some articles provide substantial references.
    Each issue includes four or five articles from three to six pages in
length. A book review section provides two signed reviews of current
books.

191.   History of Political Economy. DATE FOUNDED: 1969. FREQUENCY: q.
PRICE: $32/yr. institutions, $24/yr. personal. PUBLISHER: Duke Univer-
sity Press, Crowell Hall, East Campus, Duke University, Durham, North
Carolina 27708. EDITOR: Craufurd D.W. Goodwin. ILLUSTRATIONS. INDEX.
ADVERTISEMENTS: CIRCULATION: 1,500. MANUSCRIPT SELECTION: Editors and
Advisory Board. MICROFORMS: MIM, UMI. REPRINTS: ISI, UMI. BOOK REVIEWS.
INDEXED/ABSTRACTED: HistAb, InEcA, IntBibE, JEL, KeyEcS, SSI. DATABASES:
ECONAB, ECONLIT, HISTAB, SSI. TARGET AUDIENCE: AC, SP.

History of Political Economy focuses on the history of economic thought.
It is a scholarly journal that contains articles on a wide variety of
topics which have as a common thread the goal of clarifying the economic
contributions of the past in order to better understand modern economics. Many articles analyze the works of the great masters of political
economy such as J.B. Clark, J.M. Keynes, Marshall, Marx, Mill, Pareto,
Ricardo, Schumpeter, Adam Smith, Veblen, and Wicksell. Other articles
attempt to show how less well known economists such as Babbage, Barton,
Malynes, and Snyder made important contributions. Still other articles
focus on the contributions made during a particular period of time or on
the development of an idea over time rather than on an individual
economist. The authors are predominantly academic economists associated
wtih U.S., Canadian, and European universities. Most articles require
the reader to have an in-depth knowledge of economic theory.
    A typical issue contains about ten articles averaging about ten pages
in length and from three to ten carefully prepared signed book reviews.

192.   Hitotsubashi Journal of Economics. DATE FOUNDED: 1960. FRE-
QUENCY: 2/yr. PUBLISHER: Hitotsubashi University, Kunitachi, Tokyo, 186,
Japan. EDITORS: Kazuhiko Tokoyama, Ryoshin Minami. MANUSCRIPT SELECTION:
Editors. INDEXED/ABSTRACTED: InEcA, IntBibE, JEL, KeyEcS, PAIS. DATA-
BASES: ECONAB, ECONLIT, PAIS INT. TARGET AUDIENCE: AC, SP.

The Hitotsubashi Journal of Economics is published by the university of the same name for the purpose of supporting and encouraging research by its own faculty members. Most of the authors are from Hitotsubashi University with an occasional contribution by Australian and American economists. The journal's primary emphasis is empirical, theoretical, and historical aspects of the Japanese economy. The journal also includes articles on general economic theory, Soviet economic theory, international trade policy issues, and specific industry studies. Many of the articles use sophisticated mathematical or econometric techniques. Others are expository in style and incorporate graphs and tables of data. All articles have extensive references. Some representative article titles are "Australia's Trade with Asia: Some Policy Issues", "Mechanical power in the Industrialization of Japan: A Case Study of the Spinning Industry," and "The Process of Writing the General Theory as 'A Monetary Theory of Production'".

A typical issue includes four to six articles, each from ten to twenty pages in length. Once a year a listing of publications received is included in an issue.

193.   Hokudai Economic Papers. DATE FOUNDED: 1969. FREQUENCY: a. PRICE: Free. PUBLISHER: Hokkaido University, Faculty of Economics and Business Administration, Hokkaido Daigaku Keizaigakubu, North 9, West 7, Kita-ku, Sapporo, 060, Japan. EDITOR: Akio Ishizaka. ILLUSTRATIONS. CIRCULATION: 500. MANUSCRIPT SELECTION: Editor. REPRINTS: Publisher. BOOK REVIEWS. TARGET AUDIENCE: AC, SP. SAMPLE COPIES: Libraries and Individuals.

Hokudai Economic Papers publishes articles in both economics and business. While it is a general economics and business journal, it includes more articles in the fields of economic history and the history of economic thought than do other Japanese journals such as The Kyoto University Economic Review, KSU Economic and Business Review, and Kansai University Review of Economics and Business. Articles range from being highly technical and employing modern quantitative methodologies to being descriptive in nature. Articles dealing with business subjects discuss topics such as personnel management, labor and business in a new international economic order, education for executives, the mechanism of Japanese management, and the venture business booms in Japan. Economics topics discussed in recent issues include flexible exchange rates, the welfare effect of price stabilization policy, research efficiency in a Cournot duopoly model, and the usefulness of input-output analysis for studying price movements in Japan. The authors are members of, or affiliated with, the Faculty of Economics and Business Administration at Hokkaido University.

Each issue contains from four to seven articles of various lengths. Occasionally one signed book review is included. Except for one German language article in the 1978-79 issue, all articles are in English.

194.   The Hungarian Economy. DATE FOUNDED: 1972. FREQUENCY: q. PRICE: $9.50/yr. PUBLISHER: Hirlapkiado Vallalat, Blaha Lujzater 3, Budapest 8, Hungary. EDITOR: Janos Follinus. ILLUSTRATIONS. ADVERTISEMENTS: CIRCULATION: 11,000. MANUSCRIPT SELECTION: Editors. INDEXED/ABSTRACTED: Pred. DATABASES: PF. TARGET AUDIENCE: GP.

The Hungarian Economy is subtitled "a quarterly economic and business review." It is a special publication of the Economic Weekly/Figyelo. It is in a newspaper format and articles are journalistic in style. Its aim is to provide information to the business community of English speaking countries. It reports on economic progress in Hungary, especially in its trade relations to other countries. This non-scholarly and non-technical publication does provide some interesting economic data from time to time. The authors of lead articles are predominantly government officials such as the Deputy Minister of Industry, the Minister of Foreign Trade, the Minister of Home Trade, and the Chairman of the National Planning Board. Occasionally such an article is written by an academic. Secondary articles are unsigned and presumably written by staff journalists. Articles deal primarily with foreign trade and economic cooperation with other countries. Examples include "Anglo-Hungarian Commerce", "Joint Ventures in Hungary", "Hungary-India Trade", "Hungarian-American Trade," and "CMEA-The Perspective of Cooperation." Other articles aim to enhance Hungary's economic image such as those discussing its successful farming projects in developing countries, the country's first nuclear power station, and how economic growth has become more balanced.

Most issues contain from ten to twelve articles of various lengths. A large percentage of each issue is devoted to advertisements by Hungarian export firms.

195.   IDS Bulletin. DATE FOUNDED: 1969. TITLE CHANGES: Institute of Development Studies Bulletin (1969-1975). FREQUENCY: q. PRICE: ₺10/yr. PUBLISHER: University of Sussex, Institute of Development Studies, Brighton BN1 9RE England. EDITOR: Ann Segrave. ILLUSTRATIONS. ADVERTISE- MENTS. CIRCULATION: 3,500. MANUSCRIPT SELECTION: Editor. REPRINTS: Publisher. INDEXED/ABSTRACTED: WAERSA. DATABASES: CAB AB. TARGET AUDIENCE: AC, SP.

The IDS Bulletin is published by a research institute in England whose aim is to present current information on development problems to a wide audience of students, teachers, and government administrators. Each issue focuses on one topic and all the articles deal with that topic. Recent topics covered are the history of UNCTAD (United Nations Conference on Trade and Development), health care in developing countries, food aid, rural women, and agricultural development. The articles are written in a non-technical style with the occasional use of supporting data and photographs. Authors are from many countries and are IDS researchers, academics, or officials from various international organizations. Many of them have training in economics.

A typical issue has ten articles of four to ten pages in length. Each issue begins with an editorial which provides an overview to the subject of that issue. A "Notes on Contributors" section offers a brief biographical sketch of the authors. Summaries of all articles are provided in English, Spanish, and French.

196.   Illinois Business Review. DATE FOUNDED: 1944. FREQUENCY: 6/yr. PRICE: Free. PUBLISHER: University of Illinois, Bureau of Economic and Business Research, 428 Commerce Bldg; West, 1206 S. Sixth St., Champaign, Illinois 61820. EDITOR: William Bryan. ILLUSTRATIONS. INDEX. CIRCULATION: 6,000. MANUSCRIPT SELECTION: Editor. MICROFORMS: UMI.

REPRINTS: UMI. INDEXED/ABSTRACTED: BPIA, PAIS. DATABASES: MC, PAIS INT. TARGET AUDIENCE: GP. SAMPLE COPIES: Libraries and Individuals.

Illinois Business Review is a graduate business school publication not unlike Ball State Business Review, Nevada Review of Business and Economics, and the University of South Carolina's Business Economic Review, all of which offer a mix of articles, some pertaining only to state interests, but others dealing with more general economic and business issues and problems. Its stated purpose is to "provide businessmen of the State and other interested persons with current information on business conditions." Titles of recently published articles which exemplify strict state concerns include "Service Industries in Illinois", "The Illinois Timber Industry" and "Trends in Illinois Personal Income 1967-1981". Titles of articles of more general economic interest include "A Summary of Supply-Side Economics", "Indexed Bonds", and "A Balanced Budget - The Modern Holy Grail". Articles are non-technical in nature and do not employ mathematical, statistical, or econometric methodologies. They do include tables of data and charts. Authors are either reseachers at the University of Illinois Bureau of Economic and Business Research or academics at the University of Illinois or other universities located in Illinois.

A typical issue is twelve pages long and includes four articles. A feature of each issue is an article dealing with a development in real estate. Also each issue contains a lengthy table of current Illinois business indexes.

197.   ILO Information. DATE FOUNDED: 1972. FREQUENCY: 5/yr. PRICE: Free. PUBLISHER: International Labor Office, Washington Branch, 1950 New York Avenue, N.W., Washington, D.C. 20006. EDITOR: Jan Vitek. ILLUSTRATIONS. CIRCULATION: 40,000. MANUSCRIPT SELECTION: Editor. INDEXED/ABSTRACTED: WorkRelAbstr. TARGET AUDIENCE: GP. SAMPLE COPIES: Libraries and Individuals.

ILO Information is published on behalf of the 150 member International Labor Organization, an agency associated with the United Nations. This publication covers many aspects of international labor concerns such as employment, occupational safety and health, workers' rights, conditions of employment, multinational firms, growth in developing countries, labor migration, and employment of handicapped workers, women, and youth. The articles are written in a non-technical journalistic style. The articles themselves are unsigned but some are based on ILO research studies whose bibliographic citations are provided. This publication appears in fifteen languages. It covers the same general topics as another ILO publication, Social and Labour Bulletin but it is only an eight page newsletter compared to the Bulletin's 200 page issue.

In addition to ten to fifteen short articles, there are some even briefer reports which offer information on new trade agreements, forthcoming meetings, committee recommendations, appointments of personnel, summaries of conference, and employment data in specific countries. Occasionally a two page African Supplement is included.

198.   ILR Report. DATE FOUNDED: 1964. TITLE CHANGES: Industrial and Labor Relations Report (1964-1981). FREQUENCY: 2/yr. PRICE: Free. PUBLISHER: New York State School of Industrial and Labor Relations,

REPRINTS: UMI. INDEXED/ABSTRACTED: BPIA, PAIS. DATABASES: MC, PAIS INT.
TARGET AUDIENCE: GP. SAMPLE COPIES: Libraries and Individuals.

Illinois Business Review is a graduate business school publication not
unlike Ball State Business Review, Nevada Review of Business and Economics, and the University of South Carolina's Business Economic Review,
all of which offer a mix of articles, some pertaining only to state
interests, but others dealing with more general economic and business
issues and problems. Its stated purpose is to "provide businessmen of
the State and other interested persons with current information on
business conditions." Titles of recently published articles which
exemplify strict state concerns include "Service Industries in Illinois", "The Illinois Timber Industry" and "Trends in Illinois Personal
Income 1967-1981". Titles of articles of more general economic interest
include "A Summary of Supply-Side Economics", "Indexed Bonds", and "A
Balanced Budget - The Modern Holy Grail". Articles are non-technical in
nature and do not employ mathematical, statistical, or econometric
methodologies. They do include tables of data and charts. Authors are
either researchers at the University of Illinois Bureau of Economic and
Business Research or academics at the University of Illinois or other
universities located in Illinois.
A typical issue is twelve pages long and includes four articles. A
feature of each issue is an article dealing with a development in real
estate. Also each issue contains a lengthy table of current Illinois
business indexes.

197.   ILO Information. DATE FOUNDED: 1972. FREQUENCY: 5/yr. PRICE:
Free. PUBLISHER: International Labor Office, Washington Branch, 1950 New
York Avenue, N.W., Washington, D.C. 20006. EDITOR: Jan Vitek. ILLUSTRA-
TIONS. CIRCULATION: 40,000. MANUSCRIPT SELECTION: Editor. INDEXED/
ABSTRACTED: WorkRelAbstr. TARGET AUDIENCE: GP. SAMPLE COPIES: Libraries
and Individuals.

ILO Information is published on behalf of the 150 member International
Labor Organization, an agency associated with the United Nations. This
publication covers many aspects of international labor concerns such as
employment, occupational safety and health, workers' rights, conditions
of employment, multinational firms, growth in developing countries,
labor migration, and employment of handicapped workers, women, and
youth. The articles are written in a non-technical journalistic style.
The articles themselves are unsigned but some are based on ILO research
studies whose bibliographic citations are provided. This publication
appears in fifteen languages. It covers the same general topics as
another ILO publication, Social and Labour Bulletin but it is only an
eight page newsletter compared to the Bulletin's 200 page issue.
In addition to ten to fifteen short articles, there are some even
briefer reports which offer information on new trade agreements,
forthcoming meetings, committee recommendations, appointments of
personnel, summaries of conference, and employment data in specific
countries. Occasionally a two page African Supplement is included.

198.   ILR Report. DATE FOUNDED: 1964. TITLE CHANGES: Industrial and
Labor Relations Report (1964-1981). FREQUENCY: 2/yr. PRICE: Free.
PUBLISHER: New York State School of Industrial and Labor Relations,

Cornell University, P.O. Box 1000, Ithaca, New York 14853. EDITOR: Mary
T. Cullen. ILLUSTRATIONS. ADVERTISEMENTS: CIRCULATION: 7,000. MANUSCRIPT
SELECTION: Editor. INDEXED/ABSTRACTED: BPIA, PAIS. DATABASES: MC, PAIS
INT. TARGET AUDIENCE: AC, GP. SAMPLE COPIES: Libraries and Individuals.

The ILR Report is published by the oldest school of industrial and labor
relations in the U.S. It serves a dual purpose: 1) a public relations
function by disseminating information about the school and 2) an
educational function by publishing articles dealing with various aspects
of labor. The ILR Report deals with a broad range of topics having
implications for workers and labor unions. Each issue is devoted to a
single topic and all of the articles focus on it. Recent issues examined
"Illegal Immigration from Mexico", "Collective Bargaining in the
Entertainment Industry", "Productivity", and "Labor and Politics". Most
of the articles promote the establishment and maintenance of labor
unions to contribute to the welfare of workers. The articles are written
in an easy-to-read, non-technical style. About half of the authors are
professors of industrial relations at the New York State School or
another university. Many of the remainder are executives or researchers
with various unions. The latter frequently are graduates of the School.
     Each issue includes five or six articles, each from three to six
pages in length. Regular features include "Report from the School" a
description of programs offered by the School, "Profile" an interview of
a prominent graduate, and "Short Reports" news items about faculty,
staff, students, and new publications.

199.   The Indian Economic and Social History Review. DATE FOUNDED:
1963. FREQUENCY: q. PRICE: $35/yr. institutions, $10/yr. personal.
PUBLISHER: Vikas Publishing House PVT LTD, Vikas House, 20/4 Industrial
Area, Sahibabad Distt, Ghaziabad, U.P. India. EDITOR: Dharma Kumar.
ILLUSTRATIONS. INDEX. ADVERTISEMENTS. CIRCULATION: 1,000. MANUSCRIPT
SELECTION: Editors. MICROFORMS: UMI. REPRINTS: UMI. BOOK REVIEWS.
INDEXED/ABSTRACTED: HistAb. DATABASES: HISTAB. TARGET AUDIENCE: AC, SP.

The Indian Economic and Social History Review is a scholarly journal of
high repute. It focuses on the economic-social history of India.
Articles are very specialized in nature concentrating on a particular
time period in a particular region of India. Areas of interest include
industrialization, communal conflict, the effect of certain types of
education, racial discrimination, and folk traditions. Some articles
focus on how to conduct research in economic history and the sources
that can be most helpul. Many articles include tables of data and charts
but rarely do authors employ the statistical and econometric methods of
the "new economic history". Authors are for the most part Indian
academics, but articles by Australian, British, Canadian, and American
Academics are published as well.
     An issue contains from four to eight articles depending on their
length. Articles are frequently as long as thirty or forty pages. The
journal also features book reviews. From eight to fifteen signed reviews
appear in each issue. These are often three or four pages in length and
reviewed by American academics.

200.   The Indian Economic Journal. DATE FOUNDED: 1953. FREQUENCY: q.
PRICE: $20/yr. PUBLISHER: Indian Economic Association, University of

Bombay, Dept. of Economics, Bombay 400032, India. EDITOR: Editorial
Board. INDEX. ADVERTISEMENTS: CIRCULATION: 2,000. MANUSCRIPT SELECTION:
Editorial Board. MICROFORMS: UMI. REPRINTS: UMI. INDEXED/ABSTRACTED:
InEcA, JEL, KeyEcS, WAERSA. DATABASES: CAB AB, ECONAB, ECONLIT. TARGET
AUDIENCE: AC, SP.

The Indian Economic Journal is a high level journal in the mainstream of
economics. Its scope in terms of fields covers the whole range of
economics. More than half of the articles are theoretical in nature
while the remainder are either empirical or reflective. The latter
appear only occasionally and are usually the written version of an
address given by a prominent economist at the Indian Economic Association Meetings. Theoretical articles often reappraise the work of past
"masters" such as Keynes, Smith, Sraffa, or Schumpeter. Articles that
provide empirical results more often than not use Indian data. Most
articles are technical in nature and make heavy use of mathematics and
statistics. Authors are mainly academic economists associated with
Indian and American universities. Occasionally articles appear by
British, Canadian and Greek professors. The scope and level approximates
that of the Indian Journal of Economics, and is broader and more
sophisticated than some other Indian Journals such as The Indian Economic and Social History Review.
      Most issues contain from seven to ten articles and notes. The latter
are typically much shorter in length and are interspersed among the
articles. Occasionally a "special number" is published on a specific
topic such as a recent one containing eight articles on monetary
economics.

201.   The Indian Economic Review. DATE FOUNDED: 1952. FREQUENCY: 2/yr.
PRICE: $18/yr. institutions, $12/yr. personal. PUBLISHER: University of
Delhi, School of Economics, Delhi 110007, India. EDITOR: S.D. Tendulkar.
ILLUSTRATIONS. INDEX. CIRCULATION: 600. MANUSCRIPT SELECTION: Editor and
Editorial Board. BOOK REVIEWS. INDEXED/ABSTRACTED: InEcA, JEL, WAERSA.
DATABASES: CAB AB, ECONLIT. TARGET AUDIENCE: AC, SP.

The Indian Economic Review "publishes papers on theoretical and applied
economics including econometrics, though it concentrates on subjects
relating to the Indian Economy." In the latter regard it differs from
such other technical Indian economics journals as The Indian Economic
Journal and The Indian Journal of Economics which concentrate far less
on the Indian economy. While The Indian Economic Review covers many
different issues and problems pertaining to the Indian economy, the
proponderence of articles deal with economic planning and development,
income distribution, productivity, labor markets, and agriculture.
"Surveys of research in the area of economic development, special
detailed reviews of official reports on the Indian economy and review
articles are frequently published." Most articles, however, are research
articles which present models and empirical results. These make use of
sophisticated mathematical and statistical methods. Most articles are
written by Indian academics. Their affiliation is not always given.
      A typical issue contains about seven articles, most from twenty to
thirty pages long and three or four in-depth book reviews. The signed
reviews are usually three or four pages in length and occasionally as
long as ten pages.

202.   Indian Journal of Agricultural Economics. DATE FOUNDED: 1946. FREQUENCY: q. PRICE: $30/yr. institutions, $20/yr. personal. PUBLISHER: Indian Society of Agricultural Economics, 46-48 Esplanade Mansions, Mahatma Gandhi Road, Fort, Bombay - 400023, India. EDITOR: Shri V. M. Jakhade. INDEX. ADVERTISEMENTS: CIRCULATION: 1,800. MANUSCRIPT SELECTION: Editor and Referees. REPRINTS: Res Rep. BOOK REVIEWS. SPECIAL ISSUES. INDEXED/ABSTRACTED: WAERSA. DATABASES: CAB AB. TARGET AUDIENCE: AC, SP. SAMPLE COPIES: Libraries.

The Indian Journal of Agricultural Economics is the publication of a professional association. The Journal covers a broad range of social and economic problems of agriculture and rural areas. Specific topics covered include land economics, agrarian structure, agricultural cooperation, marketing, finance, production economics, agricultural policies, rural development, poverty and income distribution, and farm management. Most of these topics are applied to India and the research makes use of Indian data and case studies. Occasionally articles deal with agricultural situations in countries such as the Philippines and Sri Lanka. Many of the articles use quantitative analysis. Others are expository in style but include supporting statistics. Most of the authors are economists at universities or government agencies in India. Some are from American universities.

A typical issue includes three articles of thirteen to sixteen pages each and four "research notes" of four to ten pages. The book review section is extensive. An average of fifteen books are evaluated each in a two to three page signed review. Four or five others have a brief unsigned annotation. A list of publications received provides a bibliography of new titles in agricultural economics. An annual "Conference Number" publishes selected papers presented at the Society's annual meeting.

203.   Indian Journal of Economics. DATE FOUNDED: 1916. FREQUENCY: q. PRICE: $25/yr. PUBLISHER: University of Allahabad, Dept. of Economics and Commerce, Allahabad 211002, Uttar Pradesh, India. EDITOR: D.K. Ghose. ILLUSTRATIONS. INDEX. ADVERTISEMENTS: CIRCULATION: 500. MANUSCRIPT SELECTION: Editor and Editorial Board. BOOK REVIEWS. SPECIAL ISSUES. INDEXED/ABSTRACTED: IntBibE, WAERSA. DATABASES: CAB AB. TARGET AUDIENCE: AC, SP.

The Indian Journal of Economics was founded by the prominent economist, H. Stanley Jevons, in 1916. It covers "every branch of economic science." Articles in recent issues have dealt with such diverse topics as price instability and expected profits, growth models, game theory, x-inefficiency, the supply of public goods, economic planning, the demand for and the supply of money, portfolio theory, and the consumption function. Some articles are theoretical, others empirical, and a few expository. Many are case studies and employ data pertaining to a particular country. India leads a long list that also includes Japan, England, Greece, Nigeria, and the U.S. Most articles are technical in nature and make liberal use of the economist's tools. Articles use sophisticated diagrams, mathematics, and statistics. The authors are predominantly academic economists, most from India, England, Nigeria, and the U.S., but some from the Netherlands, Japan, Australia, Malaysia, and Taiwan. This journal covers more diverse topics, is more interested in economic theory per se, and deals with a broader geographic area than

many other Indian economics journals including The Indian Economic
Review, and The Indian Economic and Social History Review.
  A typical issue contains five to eight full-length articles, one
brief article in a "Notes and Memoranda" section, and one or two signed
book reviews. Occasionally a "Special Number" in memory of someone and
dealing with a single broad topic such as "Contemporary Economic Theory
and Present Day Economics" is published.

204.   Indian Journal of Industrial Relations. DATE FOUNDED: 1964.
FREQUENCY: q. PRICE: $15/yr. PUBLISHER: Shri Ram Centre for Industrial
Relations and Human Resources, 5, S. Vaswani Marg, New Delhi 110005,
India. EDITOR: C.K. Johri. INDEX. ADVERTISEMENTS: CIRCULATION: 750.
MANUSCRIPT SELECTION: Editor. BOOK REVIEWS. INDEXED/ABSTRACTED: PsyAb,
WAERSA, WorkRelAbstr. DATABASES: CAB AB, PSYAB. TARGET AUDIENCE: AC, GP,
SP.

The Indian Journal of Industrial Relations is a publication that covers
the areas of industrial psychology, personnel management, labor-management relations, labor unions, and rural employment. Most of the articles
discuss aspects of these areas in India but occasionally situations in
countries such as Bangladesh, Nigeria, and the Philippines are included.
Examples of specific topics covered in recent issues are leadership
effectiveness, industrial relations law, participative management,
impact of mechanization on agricultural employment, counseling problem
employees, worker motivation, steel industry unions, development of
rural areas, and labor-management relations. The articles are expository
in style with extensive references. An occasional quantitative paper is
included. Most of the authors are economists, psychologists, or sociologists affiliated with universities, research institutes, or government agencies in India. A few contributions from Nigerian academics or
Indian academics in Canada are included. The Journal covers somewhat the
same subject area as The Indian Journal of Labour Economics but it
places a greater emphasis on industrial psychology. It is broader in
scope than Manpower Journal which emphasizes education and employment.
  A typical issue has three to six full-length articles and two to four
shorter communications and discussions. Two or three signed book reviews
appear in each issue. Most issues include a bibliography of periodical
articles in the field of industrial relations in India.

205.   The Indian Journal of Labour Economics. DATE FOUNDED: 1958.
FREQUENCY: q. PRICE: $10.50/yr. PUBLISHER: Indian Society of Labour
Economics, University of Lucknow, Department of Economics, Lucknow,
India. EDITOR: R.S. Mathur. CIRCULATION: 500. MANUSCRIPT SELECTION:
Editor. BOOK REVIEWS. SPECIAL ISSUES. INDEXED/ABSTRACTED: WAERSA.
DATABASES: CAB AB. TARGET AUDIENCE: AC, GP, SP.

The Indian Journal of Labour Economics is the publication of the
professional association of labor economists in India. It covers various
aspects of Indian labor concerns such as collective bargaining, productivity, special employment generation schemes, labor relations in
agriculture, motivation and job satisfaction, and wage-employment
relationships in developing countries. The Journal includes three types
of articles -- theoretical discussions, empirical case studies, and

descriptive reports. Examples of these include "Methods of Employment Growth Accounting", "Study of Employee Motivation in a Steel Firm," and "Employment in Karnatka Agriculture." The theoretical discussions employ quantitative methodology, the empirical case studies incorporate tables of data, and the descriptive reports are entirely narrative in style. The authors are predominantly academics at Indian universities. The Journal covers somewhat the same subject area as the Indian Journal of Industrial Relations but has fewer articles dealing with industrial psychology. It is broader in scope than Manpower Journal which concentrates on employment and training.

A typical issue includes six to eight full-length articles. The last issue of each volume is the "Conference Number" and contains the papers delivered at the Society's annual conference. Some issues include three or four signed book reviews.

206.   **Indiana Business Review.** DATE FOUNDED: 1926. FREQUENCY: 11/yr. PRICE: Free. PUBLISHER: Indiana University, Graduate School of Business, Division of Research , Bloomington, Indiana 47405. EDITOR: Morton J. Marcus. ILLUSTRATIONS. INDEX. CIRCULATION: 4,000. MANUSCRIPT SELECTION: Editor. TARGET AUDIENCE: GP. SAMPLE COPIES: Libraries and Individuals.

Indiana Business Review is a graduate business school publication much like Arizona Business, Arkansas Business and Economic Review, and Montana Business Quarterly, all of which concentrate on business topics and the economic condition of their respective states. IBR does publish an occasional article that is more general and therefore of national interest. Examples of recently published articles with a state theme are "Indiana Banking Profile", "Housing in Indiana", "Indiana Population Projections to the Year 2020", "Hoosiers in Interstate Migration" and "Educational Attainment and Retention in Indiana." Some articles are even more narrow in geographic scope such as "Community Attitudes Toward Industry in Terre Haute" and "Progress on the South Shore". Articles are written mainly by research economists with the Business School's Division of Research and by business and economics professors at Indiana University. Occasionally articles are solicited from business executives and academics from other universities such as several 1982 articles which focused on the steel industry. Articles are usually accompanied by tables of data and charts, but are non-technical and devoid of quantitative methodologies.

Issues range from eight to thirty-five pages in length and contain from one to five articles. Two issues per year are devoted to an economic outlook for the nation, Indiana, and ten Indiana regions.

207.   **Industrial and Labor Relations Review.** DATE FOUNDED: 1947. FREQUENCY: q. PRICE: $18/yr. institutions, $14/yr. personal. PUBLISHER: New York State School of Industrial and Labor Relations, Cornell University, Ithaca, New York 14853. EDITOR: Donald E. Cullen. ILLUSTRA-TIONS. INDEX. ADVERTISEMENTS: CIRCULATION: 4,500. MANUSCRIPT SELECTION: Editor and Referees. MICROFORMS: UMI. REPRINTS: UMI. BOOK REVIEWS. SPECIAL ISSUES. INDEXED/ABSTRACTED: BPI, BPIA, InEcA, IntBibE, JEL, PAIS, SSI, WorkRelAbstr. DATABASES: ABI, ECONLIT, MC, PAIS INT, SSI. TARGET AUDIENCE: AC, SP. SAMPLE COPIES: Libraries.

Industrial and Labor Relations Review is the foremost journal in the broad field of industrial and labor relations. It includes more research articles and fewer articles based on symposia presentations than Industrial Relations. Articles are more technical and cover a wider geographic scope than the British Industrial Relations Journal. The ILR Review considers itself an interdisciplinary journal that covers all aspects of industrial and labor relations. Recent issues have included articles dealing with such diverse domestic labor issues as the effect of illegal immigrants on domestic employment, the losses from strikes, compensation for death from asbestos, wage differentials among blacks, hispanics, and whites, cost of living escalators, grievances in the coal industry, union effects on teacher productivity, and labor-force participation of older workers. Occasionally articles dealing with other countries' labor issues, such as recent ones on Swiss and on British experiences, are included. Articles are scholarly and make ample use of econometrics. Most authors are academic economists at U.S. universities. A few are research economists at government agencies or research institutes.

A typical issue of the ILR Review includes eight articles of from ten to twenty pages in length and fifteen to twenty signed book reviews separated into ten different categories. Also there is a section, "Research In Progress" which includes from ten to fifteen statements about research being conducted at major universities and institutes throughout the world. Each volume includes a bibliography of some 2,000 new books, articles, monographs, and legislative hearings.

208.   The Industrial Law Journal. DATE FOUNDED: 1972. FREQUENCY: q. PRICE: ₤16/yr. PUBLISHER: Sweet & Maxwell, Ltd., 11 New Fetter Lane, London, EC4P 4EE, England. EDITOR: Paul L. Davies. INDEX. ADVERTISEMENTS. CIRCULATION: 1,800. MANUSCRIPT SELECTION: Editor and Referees. BOOK REVIEWS. SPECIAL ISSUES. INDEXED/ABSTRACTED: ILP. TARGET AUDIENCE: AC, SP. SAMPLE COPIES: Libraries and Individuals.

The Industrial Law Journal is the publication of the Industrial Law Society of England. Its scope is labor law in the U.K. Most articles analyze a philosophy, an issue, a labor law, or a case pertaining to British labor relations. Occasionally articles examine labor relations in another country such as France or the U.S. in order to provide information about alternative ways of dealing with problems. It focuses far less on comparing labor laws of different countries than does Comparative Labor Law. Articles are written mainly for legal practitioners but economists who specialize in labor relations can benefit from reading them. Topics dealt with in recent issues include the effect of anti-wage-inflation strategies on labor law, trade union immunities, the closed shop, sex discrimination in pension schemes, union recognition, worker cooperatives, and equal pay for work of equal value. Articles are scholarly in nature but usually do not dwell on a minute legal point. Authors are predominantly academics at British law schools or departments, but some are economists specializing in industrial relations.

Most issues contain two lengthy articles plus sections on recent legislation, recent cases, reports and awards, and book reviews. The book review section usually includes one or two brief signed reviews. Some issues provide a bibliography of the periodical literature on British and Irish labor law for a recent time period.

Bibliography   119

209.   Industrial Relations. DATE FOUNDED: 1961. FREQUENCY: 3/yr.
PRICE: $20/yr. institutions, $15/yr. personal. PUBLISHER: University of
California, Berkeley, Institute of Industrial Relations, Berkeley,
California 94720. EDITOR: David Bowen. ILLUSTRATIONS. INDEX. ADVERTISE-
MENTS. CIRCULATION: 2,500. MANUSCRIPT SELECTION: Board of Editors and
Referees. MICROFORMS: Johnson, UMI. REPRINTS: UMI. SPECIAL ISSUES.
INDEXED/ABSTRACTED: BPI, BPIA, FedTaxArt, InEcA, IntBibE, JEL, PAIS,
WAERSA, WorkRelAbstr. DATABASES: CAB AB, ECONLIT, MC, PAIS INT. TARGET
AUDIENCE: AC, SP. SAMPLE COPIES: Libraries and Individuals.

Industrial Relations is a journal dealing with all aspects of the
employment relationship. Its scope is the same as Industrial and Labor
Relations Review but it carries fewer full-length articles and more
symposia papers and brief research notes. Articles are more technical
and more concerned with U.S. labor relations than the British Industrial
Relations Journal. Recent research articles and notes in Industrial
Relations have focused on such topics as interindustry comparisons of
strike activity, minimum wage non-compliance, unionism and employee
discrimination, pay discrimination in specific industries, and absen-
teeism. Articles and notes are usually technical in nature, making use
of statistical and econometric methodologies. Authors are mainly
academics at U.S. universities.
    Many issues include from four to six discussion papers presented at a
symposium in addition to several research articles. Recent topics of
symposia were "The Future of Industrial Relations" and "Labor Relations
and High Unemployment Abroad." Other issues contain up to six research
articles. Generally research articles are more technical than symposium
papers. Most issues include from three to five "Research Notes",
technical research reports that are shorter than articles. Some issues
have a "Current Topics" section with from one to three additional
articles, usually less technical in nature than either articles or
research notes.

Industrial Relations (Canada). see Relations Industrielles/Industrial
Relations.

210.   Industrial Relations Journal. DATE FOUNDED: 1970. FREQUENCY: q.
PRICE: 627/yr. PUBLISHER: Associated Business Press, Ludgate House, 110
Fleet St., London EC4, England. EDITOR: Brian Towers. ILLUSTRATIONS.
INDEX. ADVERTISEMENTS. MANUSCRIPT SELECTION: Editor and Editorial Board.
MICROFORMS: UMI. BOOK REVIEWS. INDEXED/ABSTRACTED: ANB, BPIA, Work-
RelAbstr. DATABASES: MC. TARGET AUDIENCE: AC, SP.

Industrial Relations Journal is a leading labor journal published in
England. It focuses more on the British labor scene and labor relations
in Australia and OECD countries than does either Industrial Relations or
Industrial and Labor Relations Review. Compared to these latter two
journals, IRJ also has a more practical bent. Its' editor writes of
wanting to "bridge thought and practice in industrial relations" and
that IRJ is aimed at "practitioners and practice oriented academics."
Articles often reflect the current economic and political climate in
England such as the papers in recent issues which dealt with the
responses of government, management, and trade unions to recession and
unemployment. Other articles cover more usual industrial relations

themes such as training, strikes, discrimination, and pensions. Articles are scholarly, often make use of data, but are generally non-technical in nature. Most authors are academics in British departments of economics, sociology or law. Some are research fellows, government officials, economists at research institutes and even personnel managers.

A typical issue contain ten articles of about ten pages each. Each issue has an abstract of each article in both English and French, a "Law Commentary" section of four or five pages on legal changes, and a "Book Review" section of three to six signed reviews. Some issues include a "Register of Current Research" and the first issue of each volume contains an editorial article.

211.   Industry of Free China. DATE FOUNDED: 1954. FREQUENCY: m. PRICE: $32/yr. PUBLISHER: Council for Economic Planning and Development, 1198 Hwai Ning Street, Taipei, Taiwan, Republic of China. ILLUSTRATIONS. INDEX. CIRCULATION: 2,300. MANUSCRIPT SELECTION: Editor. INDEXED/ ABSTRACTED: PAIS, WAERSA. DATABASES: CAB AB PAIS INT. TARGET AUDIENCE: AC, SP.

Industry of Free China is published by a government planning agency of Taiwan. It covers all aspects of the state of the economy of Taiwan. Some articles cover specific industries such as the food processing industry and the machinery industry. Other articles deal with agriculture, rural industrialization, and regional development. Additional articles deal with trade and economic development. Most of the articles are written in an expository style with extensive documentation. The authors are researchers at government agencies or academics at universities in Taiwan and the U.S. The greater part of each issue is devoted to "Taiwan Economic Statistics". These statistics are prepared partly by the government planning agency and partly by a U.N. agency. They include data on national income, agricultural production, industrial production, transportation, foreign trade, finance, and prices.

Each issue is in both English and Chinese. It includes two articles of about ten to fifteen pages each and a section named "Domestic Economic News in Brief". This section presents short announcements of current developments in trade, production, investment, contracts, and banking. The last issue of each volume contains a cumulative index.

212.   Information Economics and Policy. DATE FOUNDED: 1983. FREQUENCY: q. PRICE: $80/yr. PUBLISHER: North-Holland Publishing Company, P.O. Box 211, 1000 AE Amsterdam, The Netherlands. EDITOR: Editorial Board. ILLUSTRATIONS. ADVERTISEMENTS. MANUSCRIPT SELECTION: Editorial Board. TARGET AUDIENCE: AC, SP. SAMPLE COPIES: Libraries.

Information Economics and Policy is a new international and interdisciplinary journal in the broadly defined field of information economics. It is aimed at researchers, expert consultants, and policy-makers in the field. Telecommunications economics and policy is its intended core, but it also covers related issues on information economics and media policy. This scholarly journal is technical in nature and many articles make use of advanced economic theory and quantitative methodologies. Articles cover the economics of information in specific domestic and international markets and how trade and competition is affected. Another special interest is the economics and policy surrounding the transfer of

data and knowhow as well as the economics of information networks and
the analysis of new information technology including direct satellite
broadcasting, teleconferencing, and viewdata. The journal has a very
distinguished international Editorial Board, a few of whom have written
articles in early issues. Authors are academics in departments of
economics, engineering, law, and production management or research
economists, practicing engineers, or administrators with public or
private institutes.

Early issues have had five to seven articles averaging fifteen pages
each. Each issue begins with a brief biographical sketch of the contributors.

213.   Inquiry. DATE FOUNDED: 1963. FREQUENCY: q. PRICE: $35/yr.
PUBLISHER: Blue Cross and Blue Shield Association, 676 North St. Clair
Street, Chicago, Illinois 60611. EDITOR: Lewis E. Weeks. INDEX. CIRCU-
LATION: 3,500. MANUSCRIPT SELECTION: Editor and Referees. MICROFORMS:
UMI. REPRINTS: Authors. BOOK REVIEWS. INDEXED/ABSTRACTED: BPI, BPIA,
Imed, PAIS. DATABASES: MC, Medline, PAIS INT. TARGET AUDIENCE: AC, SP.
SAMPLE COPIES: Libraries and Individuals.

Inquiry is subtitled the Journal of Health Care Organization, Provision,
and Financing. This publication's primary focus is on health care
economics. Articles deal with hospital financial planning, medical
insurance plans, government regulations, medicare and medicaid, HMOs,
and health care costs. Most of the articles pertain to the situation in
the U.S. but some articles discuss conditions in Canada, the U.K., and
Western Europe. A secondary area of concentration is the provision of
health care. Those articles deal with geographic distribution of
physicians, medical training, and utilization of hospitals. Many of the
articles use some form of quantitative analysis in their discussion.
Some construct a model and test its validity with empirical data. Much
use is made of statistical methods of analysis. All of the articles
employ extensive references. The authors come from a variety of disciplines. Contributions are made by staff members of the U.S. Public
Health Service, researchers at private foundations and associations, and
professors in medical schools, management, political science, and
economics departments. Inquiry is less technical and emphasizes microeconomic analysis more than Journal of Health Economics.

Each issue contains seven to nine articles of eight to fifteen pages
in length. From three to five signed book reviews are included together
with an annotated list of new publications.

214.   Institute of Economic Affairs Occasional Papers. DATE FOUNDED:
1963. FREQUENCY: ir. PRICE: $55/yr. PUBLISHER: The Institute of Economic
Affairs, 2 Lord North Street, Westminster, London SW1P 3LB, England.
EDITOR: Martin Wassell. MANUSCRIPT SELECTION: Editor. TARGET AUDIENCE:
AC, GP, SP.

The Institute of Economic Affairs Occasional Papers is published by a
research and educational organization in London that "specializes in the
study of markets and pricing systems as technical devices for register-
ing preferences and apportioning resources." The Papers cover a wide
range of topics in modern economic thought and practice such as the
merits of capitalism, the monetary system, productivity, inflation, and

unemployment. Most Papers focus on the British economy although a few relate to the entire European community. Most of the Papers reflect the philosophy that the role of government has grown too powerful in modern times and must be curtailed in favor of free enterprise. The Papers are written in an expository style and do not use mathematical analysis. Some do present data and diagrams. The authors are predominantly English or American economists although occasionally a business executive is represented. Some of the English economists are on the staff of the Institute. The American economists include two Nobel Laureates.

Each paper focuses on a single topic, is generally written by one person, and averages thirty to forty pages. Some of the Papers were originally delivered as lectures and are published for the purpose of wider dissemination. A few "Special Papers" are comprised of essays by more than a single author. Each Paper begins with a two or three page preface providing background material on the topic and a short biographical sketch of the author.

215.   Institute of Public Affairs Review. DATE FOUNDED: 1947. TITLE CHANGES: IPA Review (1947-1982). FREQUENCY: q. PRICE: $22/yr. PUBLISHER: Institute of Public Affairs, 83 William Street, Melbourne, 3000, Victoria, Australia. EDITOR: Rod Kemp. ADVERTISEMENTS. CIRCULATION: 21,000. MANUSCRIPT SELECTION: Editor. TARGET AUDIENCE: GP.

The Institute of Public Affairs Review is published by a non-profit educational organization for the purpose of advancing "the cause of free business enterprise in Australia". The Review's aim is "to inform the Australian public of the facts of our economic system and to raise the level of economic literacy in Australia". The Review concentrates on public policy issues such as tax reform, government spending, economic regulation, and constitutional reform. Most of the articles deal with public policies of Australia. Occasionally articles deal with the same topics in the U.K., the U.S. and France. Examples of articles in the former group are "Problems with Government Planning", "Railways: Haemorrhage of the Body Politic," and "Cheap Resources into Expensive Energy". Examples of articles in the latter group are "Air Line Deregulation", "Privatization in the U.K." and "France: the Collapse of the Mitterand Experiment". The articles are written in a non-technical style for general readers. Most of the authors are academics, business executives, or journalists in Australia. A few are from the U.K. or the U.S.

A typical issue includes five to seven articles, each five or six pages in length. Each issue also features an editorial and many one to two page articles expressing a viewpoint on current economic or political events. Occasionally an issue is devoted to speeches presented at the annual meeting of the Institute.

216.   Inter-American Economic Affairs. DATE FOUNDED: 1947. FREQUENCY: q. PRICE: $25/yr. PUBLISHER: Inter-American Affairs Press, P.O. Box 181, Washington, D.C. 20044. EDITOR: Simon G. Hanson. INDEX. MANUSCRIPT SELECTION: Editor. MICROFORMS: UMI. INDEXED/ABSTRACTED: IntBibE, KeyEcS, PAIS, SSI, WAERSA. DATABASES: CAB AB, ECONAB, PAIS INT, SSI. TARGET AUDIENCE: AC, GP, SP.

Inter-American Economic Affairs is a publication that deals with the politics, economics, history, and social concerns of Latin America, Central America, and the Caribbean. This interdisciplinary journal concentrates on political issues but includes economic concerns as a secondary field. Articles deal with U.S. - Mexico relations, Latin-American military establishments, protectionist policies and industry growth, agricultural policies, and political conditions in specific countries. Many articles offer a historical analysis of economic development of a particular industry in Latin America. The articles are written for the general reader as well as the specialist and do not use technical terms or mathematical methodologies. Some do use diagrams and data. Many have extensive references. The authors are professors of political science, economics, finance, and history at American universities.

Each issue includes five or six articles varying from ten to thirty pages in length. Some issues include a "Government Documents" section which contains material taken from congressional hearings, U.S. Department of Agriculture publications, or other official sources. An annual index of the preceding volume appears in the first number of each volume.

217.   Intereconomics. DATE FOUNDED: 1965. FREQUENCY: 6/yr. PRICE: $24/yr. PUBLISHER: HWWA-Institut fuer Wirtschaftsforschung-Hamburg, Neuer Jungfernstieg 21, 2000 Hamburg 36, West Germany. EDITOR: Klaus Kwasniewski. INDEX. ADVERTISEMENTS: CIRCULATION: 2,500. MANUSCRIPT SELECTION: Editor. INDEXED/ABSTRACTED: IntBibE, PAIS, Pred, WAERSA. DATABASES: CAB AB, PAIS INT, PF. TARGET AUDIENCE: GP. SAMPLE COPIES: Libraries and Individuals.

Intereconomics, subtitled Review of International Trade and Development, is published by a West German institute of economic research. It covers current developments in international trade and economic policies. More specifically, it includes the following topics: the world economy, Bretton Woods institutions, the European Community (EC), the General Agreement for Trade and Tariffs (GATT), monetary policy, regional development, protectionism, multinational firms, and trade policies. The articles are aimed at a general readership and do not make use of technical jargon and quantitative methodologies. They do use statistical data to support their arguments. Most of the authors are from West Germany, either staff researchers or academics. A few are academics from the U.S. and Canada or staff researchers in UN agencies. Intereconomics overlaps the subject scope of Euromoney which can also be understood by a general audience.

Each issue contains six or seven articles of five to ten pages each. Regular feature sections include an editorial which focuses on a specific topic, "Economic Trends" which offers current information on economic conditions in a specific country and the HWWA Index of World Market Prices of Raw Materials, and "Report" which offers an analysis of past economic performance in a specific country or region.

218.   International Economic Conditions. DATE FOUNDED: 1978. FRE-QUENCY: q. PRICE: Free. PUBLISHER: Federal Reserve Bank of St. Louis, P.O. Box 42, St. Louis, Missouri 63166. ILLUSTRATIONS. INDEXED/AB-

STRACTED: FedP. TARGET AUDIENCE: AC, GP, SP. SAMPLE COPIES: Libraries and Individuals.

International Economic Conditions is one of several important data source titles published by the Federal Reserve Bank of St. Louis. Just as it publishes National Economic Trends and Monetary Trends to provide domestic data, International Economic Conditions provides economic data for ten foreign countries (Belgium, Canada, France, Germany, Italy, Japan, Netherlands, Sweden, Switzerland and United Kingdom). International Economic Conditions superseded Rates of Change in Economic Data for Ten Industrial Countries and U.S. International Transactions and Currency Review. It includes detailed U.S. international transactions tables and charts of exchange rates as well as charts illustrating inflation in each of the foreign countries relative to the U.S. and effective exchange rate changes for all ten currencies. It also provides the annual rates of change on a quarterly basis of each of the ten countries' money supply, price level, gross national product, employment, industrial production and imports and exports.

Each issue of International Economic Conditions is about sixty pages long, all but the first page composed of tables and charts.

219.   International Economic Review. DATE FOUNDED: 1960. FREQUENCY: 3/yr. PRICE: $66/yr. institutions, $36/yr. personal. PUBLISHER: University of Pennsylvania, Economics Department, McNeil Building CR, Philadelphia, Pennsylvania 19104. EDITORS: Robert A. Pollak, Masanao Aoki. ILLUSTRATIONS. INDEX. ADVERTISEMENTS. CIRCULATION: 2,000. MANUSCRIPT SELECTION: Editors. INDEXED/ABSTRACTED: BPIA, InEcA, IntBibE, JEL, KeyEcS, SSI, WAERSA. DATABASES: CAB AB, ECONAB, ECONLIT, MC, SSI. TARGET AUDIENCE: AC.

The International Economic Review is a joint venture of the University of Pennsylvania Economics Department and the Osaka University Institute of Social and Economic Research. This journal publishes "articles on quantitative economics" and "welcomes contributions of empirical works, as well as those in mathematical economics and statistical theory related to quantitative aspects of economics." All of the articles in this publication offer an econometric analysis of an economic concept. They construct a theoretical model and then either show how empirical data fits the model or how mathematical theorems can offer proof of the validity of the model. The authors are economists from universities in many countries. Most of them are from English speaking countries and Japan. The editorial board reflects the international character of this journal. The Review provides econometric studies on an international scope that are comparable to those published in Journal of Econometrics.

Each issue contain fifteen to seventeen articles varying in length from eight to thirty pages. A bibliography of "Publications Received" is included in each issue. An author index is published annually.

220.   International Journal of Game Theory. DATE FOUNDED: 1971. FREQUENCY: q. PRICE: $44/yr. PUBLISHER: Physica-Verlag, Schottengasse 7/5, A-1011 Vienna, Austria. EDITOR: Reinhard Selten. ILLUSTRATIONS. ADVERTISEMENTS. MANUSCRIPT SELECTION: Editor and Referees. TARGET AUDIENCE: AC.

The International Journal of Game Theory is a publication that focuses on a narrow speciality of mathematical economics. It was founded by Oskar Morgenstern, "Father" of game theory. Game theory is used as a tool of quantitative economic analysis for microeconomic problems. It is frequently used in managerial economics, industrial organization, and decision sciences. This publication is advised by a large editorial board whose members are academics from prestigious universities around the world. The authors are economists and mathematicians, mostly faculty members from institutions of like ranking and prestige. Some of the articles are completely theoretical while others demonstrate how the results can have practical applications. An example of the former type is "Persistent Equilibria in Strategic Games" and an example of the latter is "Game Theory and the Tennessee Valley Authority". The articles are written for a readership with advanced training in mathematical economics. This publication is comparable in technical level to Journal of Economic Theory, Journal of Mathematical Economics, and Journal of Economic Dynamics and Control.

A typical issue contains four to five articles ranging from five to twenty pages in length. Some issues also have a section named "Listing Service" which announces research memoranda and discussion papers in game theory published elsewhere.

221.   International Journal of Industrial Organization. DATE FOUNDED: 1983. FREQUENCY: q. PRICE: $176/yr. institutions, $68/yr. personal. PUBLISHER: North-Holland Publishing Co., P.O. Box 1991, Molenwerf 1, 1991 BZ Amsterdam, The Netherlands. EDITOR: Keith Cowling. ILLUSTRA- TIONS. INDEX. ADVERTISEMENTS. MANUSCRIPT SELECTION: Board of Editors. TARGET AUDIENCE: AC, SP. SAMPLE COPIES: Libraries.

The International Journal of Industrial Organization is a relatively new venture with strong roots in Europe, Japan and the United States. It aims at "a full coverage of both theoretical and empirical questions within the field of industrial organization broadly defined." It covers the traditional issues of market structure and performance as well as issues of internal organization of firms, all facets of technological change, productivity analysis, and the macroeconomic implications of alternative industrial structures. Special attention is directed at "international issues, including industrial structure aspects of trade, investment, technology and development, involving both market and planned economies, and industrialized and industrializing economies." Articles are scholarly and very technical in nature. Most articles present a mathematical model and some contain the empirical results of testing the model. Authors are predominantly academic economists or researchers with private or public research institutions. Most are European and American, but some are associated with Japanese and Israeli institutions. This publication is similar in subject coverage and technical level to The Journal of Industrial Economics.

Early issues contain from four to seven articles varying from about ten to over thirty pages in length. Each issue contains a "News Items" or "Announcment" page telling of forthcoming events such as meetings of interest to industrial organization economists.

222.   International Journal of Manpower. DATE FOUNDED: 1980. FRE- QUENCY: q. PRICE: $180/yr. PUBLISHER: MCB University Press Ltd., 62

Toller Lane, Bradford, West Yorkshire, BD8 9BY, England. EDITOR: David
Ashton. ADVERTISEMENTS. CIRCULATION: 400. MANUSCRIPT SELECTION: Editor.
REPRINTS: Publisher. SPECIAL ISSUES. INDEXED/ABSTRACTED: BPIA, Work-
RelAbstr. DATABASES: MC. TARGET AUDIENCE: AC, GP, SP. SAMPLE COPIES:
Libraries and Individuals.

The International Journal of Manpower is a publication that covers a
broad range of areas related to employment. Some articles deal with
unemployment problems both in specific countries such as Canada and
Australia and in philosophical discussions of possible solutions. Other
articles deal with topics in industrial psychology such as job satisfaction and worker behavior. Another focus of the journal is on the
importance of vocational-technical training to maintain a skilled labor
force and the quality of education available in various countries. The
Journal also covers the topic of union activities by including articles
that analyze differences in strike frequencies among several countries
and that demonstrate the relationship between trade unions and productivity. The articles are predominantly expository in style and frequently have extensive references. The majority of authors are academics
or government officials in the U.K., Canada, Australia, and New Zealand.
    A typical issue includes three or four articles. Some issues have a
"Bookshelf" section which contains about ten unsigned annotations of
recent books. Frequent "Special Issues" are devoted to specific topics.
Recent examples include "Economic Development and the Labour Market in
Iraq" and "Changes in the Structure of the Australian Labor Market".

223.   International Journal of Social Economics. DATE FOUNDED: 1974.
FREQUENCY: 7/yr. PRICE: $269.95/yr. PUBLISHER: MCB University Press
Ltd., 198/200 Keighley Rd., Bradford, West Yorkshire, BD9 4JQ, England.
EDITOR: John Conway O'Brien. ILLUSTRATIONS. ADVERTISEMENTS. CIRCULATION:
600. MANUSCRIPT SELECTION: Editor. REPRINTS: Publisher. BOOK REVIEWS.
SPECIAL ISSUES. INDEXED/ABSTRACTED: BPIA, IntBibE, PAIS. DATABASES: MC,
PAIS INT. TARGET AUDIENCE: AC, SP. SAMPLE COPIES: Libraries and Indi-
viduals.

The International Journal of Social Economics is loosely tied to the
International Institute of Social Economics based in England. It
publishes articles considered to be an alternative to mainstream
economics. Areas of primary interest are socio-economic systems,
manpower policy, social indicators, environmental economics, income
distribution and policy, social services, and demographic trends.
Articles vary greatly in terms of their technical nature. Some are
expository in style while others make use of diagrams and quantitative
methodologies. The editorial advisory board as well as the authors of
articles are mostly academics and represent prominent universities and
institutes in the United States, Canada, Japan, Israel, and Europe.
    The format of this journal is quite variable. Some entire issues are
devoted to a single topic by a single author, while others contain
articles on different topics written by different individuals. The
former is exemplified by recent issues on "Leon Walras: The Pure
Scientist Versus the Social Reformer" and "The Economics of Social
Measurement Processes". The latter type of issues usually contain from
three to six articles. Some issues include from one to three signed book
reviews and a list of "Publications Received".

224.   International Labor and Working Class History. DATE FOUNDED:
1972. TITLE CHANGES: Newsletter of European Labor and Working Class
History (1972-1975). FREQUENCY: 2/yr. PRICE: $20/yr. institutions,
$12/yr. personal. PUBLISHER: Study Group on International Labor and
Working Class History, Dept. of History, Hall of Graduate Studies, Yale
University, New Haven, Connecticut 06520. EDITOR: David Montgomery.
ADVERTISEMENTS. CIRCULATION: 750. MANUSCRIPT SELECTION: Editors. BOOK
REVIEWS. TARGET AUDIENCE: AC, SP. SAMPLE COPIES: Libraries and Indi-
viduals.

International Labor and Working Class History is the publication of the
Study Group that bears its name. ILWCH serves as a forum for the
exchange of scholarly ideas. Most articles are discussions, exchanges,
review essays, or reports on meetings rather than research articles in
the usual sense. The subject matter is interdisciplinary, primarily
bridging the fields of economics and history but also covering other
social sciences such as sociology and political science. The center of
interest is the history of the working class. Discussions focus on
topics such as the interpretation of Marx's theory of the working class,
technological diffusion and industrialization, women in labor movements,
and industrial relations policies. The journal thrives on controversy
emphasizing different scholarly interpretations of the same historical
occurences. Writers are predominantly academics; a few are trade
unionists. ILWCH maintains a formal cooperative network with scholars
who study the working class in France, Canada, Germany, Italy, Japan and
other countries enabling it to receive news, reports of conferences, and
works in progress from around the world.
    Most issues feature a scholarly "Controversy" in the form of an essay
followed by several responses. "Letters" responding to previously
published essays are included. Issues usually contain three or four
"Review Essays", each covering a number of works surrounding a particular topic. A typical issue contains as many as eight to twelve "Reports" on conferences and the same number of two to three page signed
book reviews.

225.   International Labour Review. DATE FOUNDED: 1921. FREQUENCY:
6/yr. PRICE: $28.50/yr. PUBLISHER: International Labour Office, CH-1211
Geneva 22, Switzerland. INDEX. ADVERTISEMENTS: CIRCULATION: 9,500.
MANUSCRIPT SELECTION: Editor. MICROFORMS: UMI. REPRINTS: UMI. BOOK
REVIEWS. INDEXED/ABSTRACTED: BPIA, InEcA, JEL, KeyEcS, PAIS, WAERSA,
WorkRelAbstr. DATABASES: CAB AB, ECONAB, ECONLIT, MC, PAIS INT. TARGET
AUDIENCE: AC, GP, SP.

The International Labour Review is published by the International Labour
Office which is the operational agency for the International Labour
Organization. This organization was established for the purpose of
promoting the welfare of workers. The Review publishes articles on
economic and social topics of international interest affecting labor.
Some articles present general policy discussions such as the improvement
of the quality of working life in the industrial nations or the effect
of technological developments on employment. Other articles deal with
employment conditions in specific countries such as migration and the
urban labor market in India or the role of government programs in
Thailand. Additional articles cover the employment of women, trends in
collective bargaining, and judicial decisions in labor law. Each of the

articles is carefully researched and documented and may include supporting data. Most of the authors are ILO staffers but a few are associated
with universities. The Review differs from both the Social and Labour
Bulletin and ILO Information. Neither of those publications offer
research articles. The former provides notes on current events in the
international labor field excerpted from printed sources, while the
latter is a newsletter that aims at informing the public about new
developments in the international employment picture.

A typical issue contains seven or eight articles of ten to twenty
pages each. A "Bibliography" section includes "ILO publications" an
annotated list of new publications, "Book Notes" a list of new books and
one page reviews, and "Books received" an annotated list of new titles
received. Neither the annotations nor reviews are signed. An annual
index provides general, author, and country listings.

226.   International Monetary Fund Staff Papers. DATE FOUNDED: 1950.
FREQUENCY: q. PRICE: $6/yr. institutions, $12/yr. personal. PUBLISHER:
International Monetary Fund, Washington, D.C. 20431. EDITOR: Norman K.
Humphreys. INDEX. CIRCULATION: 7,000. MANUSCRIPT SELECTION: Editor.
MICROFORMS: UMI. REPRINTS: UMI. INDEXED/ABSTRACTED: BPI, InEcA, IntBibE,
JEL, KeyEcS, PAIS, SSI, WAERSA. DATABASES: CAB AB, ECONAB, ECONLIT, PAIS
INT, SSI. TARGET AUDIENCE: AC, SP.

The International Monetary Fund Staff Papers serves as a vehicle for
making available some of the work of members of the IMF staff. The IMF
staff, most of whom are professional economists, conduct research on
international monetary and financial problems. The Staff Papers deals
with international trade, the balance of payments, exchange rates,
monetary systems, monetary analysis, fiscal analysis, and public
finance. Some articles offer a discussion of an economic concept or
theory. Other articles present a discussion of a current economic
situation in specific countries. Occasionally an article provides an
historical analysis of an aspect of a national economy. Examples of
these three kinds of articles are respectively: "On the Monetary
Analysis of an Open Economy", "A test of the Efficacy of Exchange Rate
Adjustments in Indonesia", and "The Underground Economy in the United
States: Annual Estimates, 1930-80". All of the articles are technical in
nature and use econometric models, graphs, or tables of data. The Staff
Papers are the scholarly complement to the International Monetary Fund's
popular Finance and Development.

Each issue includes six to seven articles varying in length from
twenty to sixty pages. Summaries of up to 300 words each are found in
English, French, and Spanish. The December issue contains an annual
index.

227.   International Regional Science Review. DATE FOUNDED: 1975.
FREQUENCY: 3/yr. PRICE: $30/yr. institutions, $16/yr. personal. PUB-
LISHER: Regional Science Association, 107-109 Observatory, 901 S.
Mathews, University of Illinois, Urbana, Illinois 61801. EDITOR: Andrew
M. Isserman. INDEX. CIRCULATION: 3,300. MANUSCRIPT SELECTION: Editor and
Referees. REPRINTS: Publisher. INDEXED/ABSTRACTED: InEcA, JEL, PopIndex,
WAERSA. DATABASES: CAB AB, ECONLIT. TARGET AUDIENCE: AC, SP. SAMPLE
COPIES: Libraries.

International Regional Science Review is published by the Regional
Science Association and co-sponsored by the Graduate Program in Urban
and Regional Planning and the Departments of Economics and Geography of
the University of Iowa. The Review covers an interdisciplinary field
combining economics and geography. More specifically, it deals with
regional economic development, industrial location, population distribution, land use, environment, natural resources, and transportation.
This is a scholarly and professional journal. A majority of the articles
use quantitative techniques such as input-output analysis and econometric models. Occasionally an in-depth review of the literature is
included. All of the articles have extensive references. The authors are
academics from departments of business administration, economics,
geography, and regional science. The Review differs from Growth and
Change in that it puts greater emphasis on quantitative economic
analysis and includes more theoretical in-depth research papers.
     A typical issue includes five articles of sixteen to twenty-four
pages each. Each issue offers abstracts of the articles in French,
Italian, Japanese, and Spanish. A special feature is an annual subject
and author index of the contents of twenty-six journals in regional
science and related fields.

International Review of Economics and Business. see Rivista Internazionale Di Scienze Economiche E. Commerciali/International Review of
Economics and Business.

228.   International Social Security Review. DATE FOUNDED: 1950. TITLE
CHANGES: International Social Security Association Bulletin (1950-1966).
FREQUENCY: q. PRICE: $10/yr. PUBLISHER: International Social Security
Association, Case postale 1, CH-1211 Geneva 22, Switzerland. INDEX.
ADVERTISEMENTS. CIRCULATION: 5,000. MANUSCRIPT SELECTION: Editor. BOOK
REVIEWS. INDEXED/ABSTRACTED: PAIS. DATABASES: PAIS INT. TARGET AUDIENCE:
AC, GP, SP.

The International Social Security Review is published by the Association
of the same name. It covers all aspects of social security systems on a
worldwide basis. Many articles offer descriptive studies of social
security systems in different countries such as "Social Security in
Switzerland: Main Features of the Schemes and Current Problems". Other
articles deal with financing problems of social security systems such as
"Problems and Perspectives in the Financing of Social Security in Latin
America". Additional articles deal with only one aspect of social
security systems such as medical care, disability allowances, and
prevention of occupational accidents. The articles are expository in
nature but use extensive documentation. The authors are experts in the
field. Some of them are government employees with the U.S. Department of
Health and Human Services or other countries' equivalent agencies.
Others are academics or executives of health insurance organizations.
The Review presents an international picture of social security systems
while the Social Security Bulletin focuses on the U.S. system.
     A typical issue includes seven articles from seven to sixteen pages
in length. Regular feature sections are "Social Security News" -brief
reports of legislative changes in social security systems in different
countries, "International News" - reports of international meetings that
have implications for social security systems, "ISSA News" - reports of

Association developments such as meetings and seminars, and "Bibliography" - short unsigned annotations of new books. Occasionally an issue is devoted to an important conference such as the Twenty-First General Assembly of ISSA.

229.   Israel Economist. DATE FOUNDED: 1944. FREQUENCY: m. PRICE: $48/yr. PUBLISHER: Kollek & Son Ltd., 6 Hazanovitch St., P.O. B. 7052, Jerusalem 91070 Israel. EDITORS: J. Kollek, M. Jur. ILLUSTRATIONS. ADVERTISEMENTS. CIRCULATION: 11,000. MANUSCRIPT SELECTION: Editors. MICROFORMS: UMI. REPRINTS: Publisher. SPECIAL ISSUES. INDEXED/ABSTRACTED: Pred. DATABASES: PF. TARGET AUDIENCE: GP. SAMPLE COPIES: Libraries and Individuals.

The Israel Economist is a publication that offers a broad view of the current state of affairs in Israel. It provides news of economic, social, political, and scientific developments. Although the major emphasis is on business and economics, a secondary area of concentration is Israeli innovations in science and technology. Many issues offer an in-depth report on a specific industry such as the citrus fruit products industry or the aerospace industry. The articles are written in a popular "news magazine" style generally by staff writers who have background in economics, business, and political science. Occasionally there are guest writers who are specialists or academics. The articles are aimed at readers outside of Israel who might be potential investors or business partners.
    Each issue includes twenty to twenty-five articles, each one to three pages in length. The articles are grouped into four sections: "The Economy," "Business", "Special Report", and "Departments". The latter section includes an editorial and discussions about taxes, investments, and law. Many issues include "Economic Indicators", a summary of financial statistics of the Israeli economy. Some issues include articles dealing with art, medicine, sports, and the environment. Occasionally a special issue is published such as the recent double size issue highlighting the Jerusalem Economic Conference.

230.   Jahrbuch der Wirtschaft Osteuropas/Yearbook of East-European Economics. DATE FOUNDED: 1970. FREQUENCY: 2/yr. PRICE: $31/yr. PUBLISHER: Hans Raupach, Osteuropa-Institut, Munchen, Scheinerstr. 11, D-8000 Munchen 80, West Germany. EDITOR: Franz-Lothar Altmann. ILLUSTRATIONS. ADVERTISEMENTS. CIRCULATION: 450. MANUSCRIPT SELECTION: Editor and Referees. INDEXED/ABSTRACTED: IntBibE. TARGET AUDIENCE: AC, SP. SAMPLE COPIES: Libraries and Individuals.

Jahrbuch der Wirtschaft Osteuropas/Yearbook of East-European Economics is a publication that covers both theoretical and empirical studies on the centrally planned economies of the Council for Mutual Economic Assistance (CMEA) countries, which include Bulgaria, Czechoslovakia, East Germany, Hungary, Poland, Romania, and the USSR. Some articles provide a philosophical discussion of topics such as employment policies in socialist countries, Yugoslav workers' management system, decentralization of planning decisions, distribution of goods in a socialist economy and Soviet demand theory. Other articles offer empirical studies on topics such as the effect of CMEA on the Hungarian economy, employment structure of CMEA countries from 1950-1975, the effect of technology transfer to socialist countries, Eastern Europe's foreign trade,

and analysis of the Soviet grain market from 1928-1938. The articles
vary in technical level. Some use econometric models but many are
expository essays devoid of quantitative analysis. The authors are
academic economists from the U.S., Canada, West Germany, Austria, and
the U.K. or research economists affiliated with the United Nations. This
publication provides the same subject coverage as Soviet Studies.
    Each issue is divided into two sections. One includes four or five
articles on the "Theory of Planning." The other includes the same number
of articles on "Empirical Studies." About eighty percent of the articles
are in English, the rest in German. Each article has summaries in both
English and German.

231.   Japan Labor Bulletin. DATE FOUNDED: 1962. FREQUENCY: m. PRICE:
3,600 Yen/yr. PUBLISHER: The Japan Institute of Labour, Chutaikin Bldg.,
7-6 Shibakoen 1-chome, Minato-ku, Tokyo 105, Japan. EDITOR: Kayao
Kobayashi. ILLUSTRATIONS. INDEX. ADVERTISEMENTS. CIRCULATION: 2,300.
MANUSCRIPT SELECTION: Editors. TARGET AUDIENCE: AC, GP, SP. SAMPLE
COPIES: Libraries and Individuals.

The Japan Labor Bulletin is the only monthly English language serial
which specializes in Japanese industrial relations. It is a news
bulletin which offers expert analysis of labor news rather than a
scholarly labor journal. It covers a broad range of labor topics,
including the current unemployment situation in Japan, pending and new
labor legislation, news about specific labor disputes, the policies of
the Japanese Ministry of Labor, issues of older workers and retirement,
the demographics of labor dealing both with age and sex, discrimination
among labor groups, the relationship between education and employment
and international labor relations. Articles are non-technical in nature,
but do frequently include data in the form of tables and charts.
Articles are not signed. They are written by staff economists who are
members of the Editorial Committee of the Institute and simultaneously
teach at Japanese universities.
    Each issue is eight pages long. Occasionally an additional insert,
such as a Directory of Unions is included. Most issues contain about
fifteen short articles and one much longer one. These are placed in six
separate sections: "General Survey," "Working Conditions and the Labor
Market," "Labor Disputes and Trade Unions," "International Relations,"
"Public Policy," and "Special Topic." The December issue includes a
subject index for the year.

232.   Japanese Economic Studies. DATE FOUNDED: 1972. FREQUENCY: q.
PRICE: $170/yr. institutions, $44/yr. personal. PUBLISHER: M. E. Sharpe,
Inc; 80 Business Park Drive, Armonk, New York 10504. EDITOR: Kazuo Sato.
ILLUSTRATIONS. INDEX. ADVERTISEMENTS. MANUSCRIPT SELECTION: Editor.
INDEXED/ABSTRACTED: PAIS. DATABASES: PAIS INT. TARGET AUDIENCE: AC, SP.

Japanese Economic Studies is a publication that "contains translations
of economic material from Japanese sources, primarily scholarly journals
and books." This journal includes articles on a broad range of topics
but emphasizes current developments in the Japanese economy. Recent
issues presented articles dealing with labor markets, structure of
financial markets and institutions, history of postwar inflation,
industrial organization, land use policies, economic growth, and fiscal

reform. Many articles deal with Japanese management policies and how they compare with American management policies and whether they can be successfully utilized in American corporations. Another area of interest is trade relations with neighboring countries, such as the USSR and the People's Republic of China. The articles are expository in style and non-technical. They occasionally use charts, diagrams, graphs, and tables of data. The authors are Japanese economists affiliated with universities, government agencies, or corporations. This publication is comparable in subject coverage and technical level to Economic Eye.
   A typical issue includes two to four in-depth articles. Frequently an issue is devoted to a single topic. The original source and date of publication are provided for each article. The time lag between orginal publication and appearance of the translation may be up to two years.

233.   Japanese Finance and Industry. DATE FOUNDED: 1949. TITLE CHANGES: Survey of Japanese Finance and Industry (1949-1975). FREQUENCY: q. PRICE: Free. PUBLISHER: The Industrial Bank of Japan, Reference and Statistics Center, 3-3, Marunuchi 1-chome, Chiyoda-ku, Tokyo, Japan. ILLUSTRATIONS. INDEX. MANUSCRIPT SELECTION: Editor. INDEXED/ABSTRACTED: PAIS. DATABASES: PAIS INT. TARGET AUDIENCE: AC, GP, SP. SAMPLE COPIES: Libraries and Individuals.

Japanese Finance and Industry is an economic survey publication prepared by the research department of a major Japanese bank. It offers a combination of reports on the general industrial conditions of the Japanese economy and in-depth analyses of specific Japanese industries or major economic trends that impact Japanese industries. Compared to Bank of Japan Monthly Economic Review, which provides a general review of Japanese monetary and economic trends, this publication focuses on Japanese industry. It covers some of the same topics offered in Economic Eye, but the latter is much more diverse in its coverage. The level is higher than either of these other Japanese publications. The articles in Japanese Finance and Industry are non-technical in nature, but are carefully prepared analyses based on an abundance of data. Articles are written by staff researchers. Most are not signed, but it is evident that they are prepared by competent economists.
   Issues range from twenty-five to sixty pages in length. They contain from one to three articles plus a number of industry-trend tables. Articles range from three to fifty pages in length. Some issues devote much more space to recent trends and future prospects of industries than do others.

234.   Journal for Studies in Economics and Econometrics/Tydskrif vir Studies in Ekonomie en Ekonometrie. DATE FOUNDED: 1977. FREQUENCY: q. PRICE: R30/yr. PUBLISHER: University of Stellenbosch, Bureau for Economic Research, Private Bag 5050, Stellenbosch, 7600 South Africa. EDITOR: A.J.M. de Vries. ILLUSTRATIONS. CIRCULATION: 500. MANUSCRIPT SELECTION: Editor. SPECIAL ISSUES. TARGET AUDIENCE: AC, SP.

Journal for Studies in Economics and Econometrics/Tydskrif vir Studies in Ekonomie en Ekonometrie is a scholarly journal that publishes both in the English and Afrikaans language. It focuses on analyzing different aspects of the South African economy, such as trade-offs between real wages and employment in the manufacturing sector, the pricing of coal, the business cycle, macroeconomic consequences of the drought, inflation problems, energy substitution responses by manufacturers, the demand for construction, the size mobility of firms, and the impact of political tensions on the price of gold. Occasionally articles deal with topics not specifically associated with South Africa. Some recent examples include ones on the Nigerian foreign trade sector, the social discount rate, prediction performance of certain forecasting models, and labor employment in developing countries. The majority of articles are technical and make use of some quantitative methodologies. Others are expository in nature. Virtually all authors are South African economists, most academics at South African universities and a few research economists with government agencies or institutes. The Journal offers a somewhat broader geographic scope than Finance and Trade Review.

Most issues contain from three to five articles. Usually only one of them is in Afrikaans, but no English summary is provided for that article. Recently a special issue containing thirteen articles was published on the occasion of the retirement of the director of the Bureau for Economic Research.

235.   Journal of Accounting and Economics. DATE FOUNDED: 1979. FREQUENCY: 3/yr. PRICE: $71.50/yr. institutions, $27/yr. personal. PUBLISHER: Elsevier Science Publishers B.V. (North-Holland), P. O. Box 1991, 1000 BZ Amsterdam, The Netherlands. EDITORS: Ross L. Watts, Jerold L. Zimmerman. INDEX. ADVERTISEMENTS. MANUSCRIPT SELECTION: Editors. MICROFORMS: Elsev. REPRINTS: Publisher. INDEXED/ABSTRACTED. AcctInd, BPIA, InEcA, JEL. DATABASES: ABI, ACCTIND, ECONLIT, MC. TARGET AUDIENCE: AC, SP. SAMPLE COPIES: Libraries and Individuals.

The Journal of Accounting and Economics is published by North-Holland Publishers in collaboration with The Graduate School of Management of The University of Rochester. The JAE publishes articles that deal with "the application of economic theory to the explanation of accounting phenomena." Some of the topics included in this area are theory of the firm, public choice, government regulation, agency theory, and financial economics. Some examples of representative articles are "Toward Understanding the Role of Auditing in the Public Sector," "Taxes and Firm Size," and "The Economic Consequences of Accounting Choice: Implications of Costly Contracting and Monitoring." JAE offers high quality research papers. Over eighty percent of submitted papers are rejected. The articles employ sophisticated methodologies, including both formal mathematical models and empirical studies. Most of the articles deal with accounting practices in the U.S. The authors are primarily American academics from well-known universities.

Each issue contains three articles of twenty to thirty pages in length. Each article begins with an abstract and ends with an extensive list of references. A page of "Editorial Data" that summarizes the distribution of manuscripts received during the preceding twelve months is included in each issue.

236.   Journal of Agricultural Economics. DATE FOUNDED: 1928. TITLE CHANGES: Journal of Proceedings of the Agricultural Economics Society (1928-1954). FREQUENCY: 3/yr. PRICE: ₤15/yr. institutions, ₤12/yr. personal. PUBLISHER: Agricultural Economics Society, Department of Agricultural Economics, the University College of Wales, Aberystwyth

SY23 3DD, U.K. EDITOR: D. I. Batemen. ILLUSTRATIONS. INDEX. ADVERTISE-
MENTS. CIRCULATION: 1,800. MANUSCRIPT SELECTION: Editors and Referees.
BOOK REVIEWS. INDEXED/ABSTRACTED: IntBibE, PAIS, WAERSA. DATABASES: CAB
AB, PAIS INT. TARGET AUDIENCE: AC, SP.

The Journal of Agricultural Economics is the publication of the leading
agricultural economics association in England. Its scope is all of
agricultural economics. It offers theoretical, methodological, empirical, and policy oriented articles. Most are quite technical research
papers. Many introduce a formal model using mathematical equations and
then show the results of empirical testing. Articles that contain
empirical content often use British cases, but recent issues have also
examined cases in Scotland, the Philippines, Egypt, Canada, Nepal,
Tanzania, Haiti, Ecuador, Mexico, and Venezuela. The authors are
research economists, both academics and researchers at agricultural
economics institutes. The great majority are British but some are
associated with other European, Australian, U.S., African, and Philippine universities and institutes. The Journal most closely resembles
European Review of Agricultural Economics in subject coverage, geographic scope, and technical level.
    Most issues contain from six to ten research articles plus from four
to six "Notes." The latter include brief articles, comments on previously published articles, and replies. Each issue includes a book
review section, under a separate editor, with from eight to twelve
one-to-two page signed reviews. Issues also include sections on books
received, higher degrees in agricultural economics awarded by British
universities, and notices concerning essay competitions and meetings.
The September issue includes the presidential address and other "main
papers" presented at the annual meeting of the Agricultural Economic
Society.

237.   Journal of Agricultural Economics and Development. DATE FOUNDED:
1971. FREQUENCY: 2/yr. PRICE: $12/yr. PUBLISHER: Philippine Agricultural
Economics and Development Association, Inc., College of Development
Economics and Management, U.P. at Los Banos, College, Laguna, Phil-
ippines. EDITOR: Amono M. Dalisay. ILLUSTRATIONS. ADVERTISEMENTS.
MANUSCRIPT SELECTION: Editor. BOOK REVIEWS. SPECIAL ISSUES. INDEXED/
ABSTRACTED: WAERSA. DATABASES: CAB AB. TARGET AUDIENCE: AC, SP.

The Journal of Agricultural Economics and Development is a general
economic development journal that focuses on development issues and
problems in the Philippines. Occasionally an article deals with an
overview of development problems in all of Asia or in some other
developing nation such as Bangladesh or Malaysia. Most articles concern
themselves with policy issues in Philippine agriculture, the findings of
major national research programs, and the results of empirical research
on a topic of Philippine agricultural economics. Policy issues dealt
with in recent issues include marketing policies for agriculture,
manpower training strategies for countryside development, and policies
for loan repayment and technical assistance. Entire issues are devoted
to technical papers and documents on such major government sponsored
programs as the Agricultural Diversification and Markets Project and the
Agricultural Market Development Project. Empirical research reported
upon includes such studies as consumer preferences for agricultural
products, fertilizer use by rice farmers, and the factors affecting

technology transfer in rice production at the regional level. Articles range from quite technical to merely descriptive. The authors are mostly Philippine economists who are associated with the University of the Philippines at Los Banos and/or one of a number of Philippine Agricultural research institutes. The Journal of Agricultural Economics and Development is more scholarly and broader in scope than the Philippine Economy and Industrial Journal.

Each issue contains about six articles, ranging from ten to thirty-five pages in length. A "Notes and Comments" section usually contains a brief article, a report or two on a recently held symposium, lecture series, or meeting, and abstracts of graduate theses in agricultural economics at the University of the Philippines at Los Banos. Most issues include two in-depth signed book reviews.

238.   Journal of Australian Political Economy. DATE FOUNDED: 1976. FREQUENCY: 3/yr. PRICE: $A25/yr. institutions, $A15/yr. personal. PUBLISHER: Australian Political Economy Movement, Box 76, Wentworth Building, University of Sydney, Sydney N.S.W. 2006, Australia. EDITOR: Editorial Collective. ILLUSTRATIONS. ADVERTISEMENTS. CIRCULATION: 300. MANUSCRIPT SELECTION: Editorial Collective. BOOK REVIEWS. SPECIAL ISSUES. TARGET AUDIENCE: GP.

The Journal of Australian Political Economy is a publication with a strong socialist and Marxist point of view. All articles have either implicit or explicit underlying themes designed to convince readers of the benefits of socialism and the evils of capitalism. The articles are non-technical in nature and may be understood by people with virtually no formal training in economics. Examples of topics discussed in recent issues are the contemporary applicability of Marx's concept of the "reserve army of labour," how a 1973 Australian report on education has perpetuated inequitable income distribution, the restructuring of the Australian retailing industry so as to raise economic concentration, the merits of a socialist incomes policy, why the Laffer Curve is invalid, how workers are being replaced by labor-saving technology in Australia's steel industry, and monopoly trends in the Australian brewing and mining industries. Most articles contain footnotes and references and a few include bibliographies. Some articles present data in the form of tables and/or charts. The majority of authors are academics in departments of economics, government, or sociology at Australian universities. The rest are graduate students, government workers, and labor unionists. The Journal provides the same general viewpoint as Review of Radical Political Economics and Studies in Political Economy: a Socialist Review.

A typical issue begins with an editorial which includes an introduction to each article, four to six articles, one to four in-depth signed book reviews, and several brief unsigned annotations called "Booknotes." Interspersed throughout the journal are cartoons which may or may not be related to the article in the issue.

239.   Journal of Bank Research. DATE FOUNDED: 1970. FREQUENCY: q. PRICE: $30/yr. PUBLISHER: Bank Administration Institute, 60 Gould Center, Rolling Meadows, Illinois 60008. EDITOR: R. Gerald Fox. ILLUSTRATIONS. INDEX. ADVERTISEMENTS. CIRCULATION: 12,000. MANUSCRIPT SELECTION: Editors and Board of Referees. REPRINTS: Publisher, UMI. SPECIAL ISSUES. INDEXED/ABSTRACTED. ABA BankLit, AcctInd, BPIA, DPD,

InEcA, IntBibE, JEL, PAIS. DATABASES: ABI, ACCTIND, ECONLIT, MC, NEXIS, PAIS INT. TARGET AUDIENCE: AC, SP. SAMPLE COPIES: Libraries.

The Journal of Bank Research is a scholarly journal dealing with a wide variety of topics bearing on banking and investment problems. "Papers may describe original research or may be survey-review articles of research efforts or unique and significant applications." Topics dealt with in recent issues include: banking deregulation, international banking competition, bank acquisitions, electronic payments technology, foreign ownership of U.S. banks, net interest margin sensitivity, consumer credit, NOW accounts, fixed rate lending, and portfolio theory. Most of the articles report on research results. Many introduce a model and present empirical results. The majority of the articles are technical and make use of mathematical and statistical methodologies. The authors are a diverse group of economic and finance researchers. About half are academics with the rest associated with the Federal Reserve System, Federal Home Loan Bank, investment banking houses, research institutions and corporations.

A typical issue contains about six full-length articles plus a couple of shorter papers in a "Research Commentary" section. Each issue begins with the Editor's "Management Summary," a concise statement designed for bank managers that gives the purpose and results of each article in the issue. In addition, an abstract by the author proceeds each article. Special issues covering a number of papers and discussions presented at a conference are published about once a year. The Spring issue includes an index for the previous volume.

240.   Journal of Banking and Finance. DATE FOUNDED: 1977. FREQUENCY: q. PRICE: $116/yr. institutions, $48/yr. personal. PUBLISHER: North-Holland Publishing Co., Box 211, 1000 AE Amsterdam, The Netherlands. EDITOR: Editorial Board. ILLUSTRATIONS. INDEX. ADVERTISEMENTS. MANU-SCRIPT SELECTION: Editorial Board. MICROFORMS: Elsev. BOOK REVIEWS. SPECIAL ISSUES. INDEXED/ABSTRACTED. BPI, BPIA, CREJ, IntBibE, PAIS. DATABASES: ABI, MC, PAIS INT. TARGET AUDIENCE: AC, SP. SAMPLE COPIES: Libraries and Individuals.

The Journal of Banking and Finance is published in cooperation with several European finance associations. It publishes "scholarly research concerning financial institutions and the money and capital markets within which they function." It emphasizes applied and policy-oriented research as it is "intended to improve communications between and within the academic and other research communities and those members of financial institutions . . . who are responsible for operational and policy decisions." Most articles deal with some aspect of commercial banking. Topics include: portfolio management, credit rationing, investment trusts, equity risk, the capital asset pricing model, bank holding companies, the Eurodollar market, Federal Reserve actions, the concentration of world banking, and the acquisition of non-banks by banks. Articles deal with banking issues and problems in many different countries as well as the international banking community. Most articles are very technical in nature, introduce mathematical models, and present empirical research results using sophisticated quantitative techniques. The authors are research economists at universities or institutions such as the Federal Reserve System. At least half are U.S. academics, but Israel, Canada, and the U.K. are also well represented. The level is a bit higher, the subject about the same, and the geographic scope considerably broader than the Journal of Bank Research.

A typical issue contains ten articles, a note, two signed book reviews, a list of forthcoming papers, and an announcement or two. About once a year a special issue is devoted to publishing the proceedings of a conference. Recent topics have been: "Company and Country Risk Models" and "International Banking, Its Market and Institutional Structure."

241.   The Journal of Behavioral Economics. DATE FOUNDED: 1972. FREQUENCY: 2/yr. PRICE: $16/yr. institutions, $13/yr. personal. PUB-LISHER: Western Illinois University, Center for Business and Economic Research, Macomb, Illinois 61455. EDITOR: Richard E. Hattwick. ILLUSTRA-TIONS. CIRCULATION: 350. MANUSCRIPT SELECTION: Editor and Referees. BOOK REVIEWS. SPECIAL ISSUES. INDEXED/ABSTRACTED. BPIA, InEcA, JEL. DATA-BASES:ECONLIT, MC. TARGET AUDIENCE: AC, SP. SAMPLE COPIES: Libraries.

The Journal of Behavioral Economics is an interdisciplinary journal whose goals are "to further knowledge of real economic phenomena by integrating psychological and sociological variables into economic analysis" and "to promote interdisciplinary research by academicians and practitioners dealing in economics, the behavioral sciences, and public policy." In keeping with its editorial policy, JBE publishes articles dealing with a wide range of topics from mainly economic, such as "Plant Scale and Multiplant Production as Determinants of Industrial Concen-tration" to mainly psychological, such as "The Psychoeconomics of Human Needs: Maslow's Hierarchy and Marshall's Organic Growth." Articles vary in their degree of complexity--some use mathematical methodologies and others are expository in style. Contributors are primarily professors of economics at American universities. There is a large external editorial board composed of academics at various state universities and an internal editorial board made up of representatives from the departments of sociology, anthropology, economics, and management at Western Illinois University.

Each issue contains five to seven articles, ranging from ten to twenty pages in length. A recently added feature of each issue is "Business Role Models." This section provides a biographical account of a successful business leader's career. Occasionally a signed book review is included.

242.   Journal of Business. DATE FOUNDED: 1928. FREQUENCY: q. PRICE: $35/yr. institutions, $22/yr. personal. PUBLISHER: University of Chicago Press, 5801 Ellis Avenue, Chicago, Illinois 60637. EDITOR: Merton Miller. ILLUSTRATIONS. INDEX. ADVERTISEMENTS. CIRCULATION: 5,000. MANUSCRIPT SELECTION: Board of Editors and Referees. MICROFORMS: MIM, UMI. REPRINTS: ISI, UMI. BOOK REVIEWS. SPECIAL ISSUES. INDEXED/AB-STRACTED: AcctInd, BPI, BPIA, InEcA, IntBibE, JEL, KeyEcS, ManI, PAIS, Pred, WorkRelAbstr. DATABASES: ACCTIND, ECONAB, ECONLIT, MC, PAIS INT, PF. TARGET AUDIENCE: AC, SP.

The Journal of Business is published in cooperation with the Graduate School of Business and the Department of Economics of the University of Chicago. Many consider it the most scholarly and prestigious of all business school publications. It is not directed toward a general business audience as it publishes "only papers that make an original and substantive contribution to knowledge." Its scope is accounting, economics, finance, and marketing, but most papers deal with topics in finance and economics. Recent issues have carried finance articles concerned with stock trading, value of corporate debt, the capital asset pricing model, mutual fund performance, measurement of risks, future contracts, and the returns from hedging options against stock. Economics articles have concentrated in the fields of industrial organization and public finance. Articles are very technical in nature. They frequently introduce mathematical models and use sophisticated statistical and econometric methods in showing the results of empirical testing. The authors are mainly academics at U.S. universities. A few are associated with universities in the U.K., Canada, and Australia and occasionally an article is written by a research economist at a bank or institute. This publication is comparable in level of scholarship and subject coverage to Journal of Financial Economics.

Most issues contain about six articles, a lengthy "Books Received" section, and a section of "Notes" covering appointments, grants, leaves, promotions, etc. at graduate schools of business. Some issues include a signed book review. Occasionally a special issue (part two of a regular issue) is devoted to the proceedings of a conference.

243.   Journal of Business & Economic Statistics. DATE FOUNDED: 1983. FREQUENCY: q. PRICE: $28/yr. PUBLISHER: American Statistical Association, 806 15th St., NW, Washington, DC 20005. EDITOR: Arnold Zellner. ILLUSTRATIONS. INDEX. ADVERTISEMENTS. MANUSCRIPT SELECTION: Editor and Referees. TARGET AUDIENCE: AC, SP.

The Journal of Business & Economic Statistics is published by an association of professional statisticians. It publishes articles "dealing with applied problems in business and economic statistics." Articles deal wtih topics such as seasonal adjustment, money supply measurement, time series modeling, forecasting, energy models, statistical analysis of discrimination in employment, pricing models, models of demand for medical care, predicting insurance losses, and housing-demand statistical analysis. All of the articles employ advanced statistical methodology and are aimed at readers having a thorough background in statistics. The authors are associated with academic institutions, corporations, or government agencies in countries around the world. The editorial board is made up of individuals from similar organizations. The universities represented are generally well-known and prestigious institutions. Articles in the Journal are comparable in technical complexity to those in Oxford Bulletin of Economics and Statistics and The Review of Economics and Statistics.

A typical issue includes nine to ten articles, varying in length from ten to twenty pages. Each article includes an abstract and extensive references. Some issues have a lengthy research paper and as many as eight comments on that paper plus a reply from the author. Other issues have comments on a paper published in a previous issue plus the author's reply. An annual index is included in the final issue of each volume.

244.   The Journal of Business and Social Studies. DATE FOUNDED: 1977. FREQUENCY: 2/yr. PRICE: $18/yr. PUBLISHER: University of Lagos, Faculty of Social Sciences, Akoka, Lagos, Nigeria. EDITOR: Oladejo O. Okediji.

ADVERTISEMENTS. CIRCULATION: 1,500. MANUSCRIPT SELECTION: Editorial
Board. BOOK REVIEWS. TARGET AUDIENCE: AC.

The Journal of Business and Social Studies is a Nigerian publication
that covers a broad range of topics. It offers articles in the fields of
economics, business administration, sociology, political science,
psychology, and history. Most of these articles are concerned with
aspects of these subjects in Nigeria. However, a few offer a philosophical discussion or an empirical study using data from other African
countries. Many articles focus on economic development problems in
Nigeria. Others deal with education, psychological studies, political
structures, and cultural comparisons among different population groups
in Nigeria. Some of the articles employ quantitative methodology, but
most of them are purely expository in style. The majority of the authors
are academics from universities in Nigeria. They represent a variety of
social science and business disciplines. The Journal is less technical
than The Nigerian Journal of Economic and Social Studies.
     A typical issue contains four to six articles, each from eight to
twenty pages in length. Many of the articles have extensive references.
Some issues include a signed book review.

245.   Journal of Business Finance & Accounting. DATE FOUNDED: 1974.
FREQUENCY: q. PRICE: $77.50/yr., $41.70/yr. personal. PUBLISHER: Basil
Blackwell Publisher, 108 Cowley Road, Oxford, OX4 1JF, England. EDITORS:
Richard J. Briston, John R. Perrin. INDEX. ADVERTISEMENTS. CIRCULATION:
1,200. MANUSCRIPT SELECTION: Editors and Referees. REPRINTS: Publisher.
INDEXED/ABSTRACTED: AcctInd, BPIA. DATABASES: ACCTIND, MC. TARGET
AUDIENCE: AC, SP. SAMPLE COPIES: Libraries and Individuals.

The Journal of Business Finance & Accounting publishes articles of
research results on a variety of topics in accounting practices and
financial management. It supercedes the Journal of Business Finance
which was published from 1969 to 1973. Some of the articles bridge the
gap between financial analysis and a broader economic assessment.
Articles offer both theoretical and empirical studies of financial
practices in many industrialized countries. Some topics covered in
recent issues include economic depreciation of a capital budgeting
project, economic analysis of value to the owner, applications of the
theory of the firm, enterprise theory, utility functions, and the
relationship between systematic risk and price elasticity of demand.
Virtually all the articles employ mathematical methodology in their text
and are aimed at readers with good quantitative backgrounds. Half of the
authors are American academics while the other half are from Canada,
Australia, the U.K., and Europe. JBFA is similar in subject concentration and technical level to Journal of Accounting & Economics. The
former is more international in scope.
     Each issue contains nine to eleven full-length papers and two to four
shorter notes, comments, and replies. An annual index is included in the
final issue of each volume.

246.   The Journal of Business Forecasting Methods & Systems. DATE
FOUNDED: 1981. FREQUENCY: q. PRICE: $45/yr. PUBLISHER: Graceway Pub-
lishing Co., P.O. Box 159, Station C, Flushing, New York 11367. EDITOR:
C.L. Jain. ILLUSTRATIONS. ADVERTISEMENTS. CIRCULATION: 3,500. MANUSCRIPT

SELECTION: Editorial Board. REPRINTS: Publisher. BOOK REVIEWS. SPECIAL
ISSUES. INDEXED/ABSTRACTED: AcctInd, BPIA, OR/MS. DATABASES: ACCTIND,
MC. TARGET AUDIENCE: AC, SP. SAMPLE COPIES: Libraries and Individuals.

The Journal of Business Forecasting Methods & Systems has as its primary
focus the dissemination of information on various forecasting methods or
systems. These forecasting methods are used primarily by business
planners. The publication's secondary aim is to provide both data and
trends of the business and economic outlook for the next year. Articles
that concentrate on forecasting methods include case studies of forecasting methods used in specific firms, descriptions of specific
indexes, comparative evaluations of accuracy of forecasting services,
and variations in the mathematical models used in forecasting techniques. In addition, some articles deal with computer software packages
available for use in forecasting. Articles that have more direct bearing
on economic issues deal with projected economic growth, corporate
earnings, and public policy changes. Articles are written in a popular
style but do include mathematical equations and statistical terms. The
authors are either professors of business administration at American
universities or forecasting practitioners with business or consulting
firms. The Journal is less scholarly and technical than the Journal of
Forecasting.
    Recent issues have been divided into three sections. The first
section includes four to six articles. The second, "Business and
Economic Outlook" includes three short articles plus tables of forecasts
of various economic indicators. A third section, "Regular Features"
contains a forecasting program, an evaluation of a commercially available software package, and a signed book review. Occasionally a special
issue is devoted to a single topic.

247.   Journal of Business Research. DATE FOUNDED: 1973. TITLE CHANGES:
Southern Journal of Business (1966-1972). FREQUENCY: q. PRICE: $95/yr.
institutions, $52/yr. personal. PUBLISHER: Elsevier Science Publishing
Co., Inc., 52 Vanderbilt Ave., New York, New York, 10017. EDITOR: Arch
G. Woodside. ILLUSTRATIONS. INDEX. ADVERTISEMENTS. MANUSCRIPT SELECTION:
Editors and Referees. MICROFORMS: MIM, UMI. BOOK REVIEWS. SPECIAL
ISSUES. INDEXED/ABSTRACTED: BPI, BPIA. DATABASES: MC. TARGET AUDIENCE:
AC, SP. SAMPLE COPIES: Libraries.

The Journal of Business Research "applies theory developed from business
research to actual business situations." It publishes articles focusing
on "theoretical and empirical advances in buyer behavior, finance,
organizational theory and behavior, marketing, risk and insurance and
international business." It offers a mixture of business and economics
articles. JBR is more directly business oriented and considerably more
interested in marketing than is the Journal of Business. It does,
however, publish articles on such topics as capital expenditure decision
making, the effects of inflation on consumer choice, the antitrust
implications of the state of ownership and control in the modern
corporation, and currency exchange rates. Most articles are quite
technical and make use of modern quantitative methodologies. Almost all
the authors are academics at American universities.
    A typical issue contains from eight to ten articles. Almost half the
issues are "special" in that either all the articles or some substantial
portion of the articles focus on a single topic. Less than half the

issues include a book review section. When they do, it contains one or two signed reviews.

248.   Journal of Collective Negotiations in the Public Sector. DATE FOUNDED: 1972. FREQUENCY: q. PRICE: $51/yr. institutions, $27/yr. personal. PUBLISHER: Baywood Publishing Company, Inc., 120 Marine St., P.O. Box D, Farmingdale, New York, 11735. EDITOR: Harry Kershen. INDEX. ADVERTISEMENTS. MANUSCRIPT SELECTION: Editor and Referees. REPRINTS: Authors. BOOK REVIEWS. INDEXED/ABSTRACTED: BPIA, EdAAb, HLitI, PAIS, WorkRelAbstr. DATABASES: ABI, MC, PAIS INT. TARGET AUDIENCE: AC, GP, SP. SAMPLE COPIES: Libraries and Individuals.

The Journal of Collective Negotiations in the Public Sector focuses on "approaches for dealing with the complexities and ramifications of public sector labor relations." Articles focus on U.S. public sector labor relations but occasionaly an article deals with a situation in another country such as Canada, England, or Israel. Many articles discuss the experience resulting from a piece of labor legislation or tax legislation in a particular state. A favorite topic is teacher unions, both K-12 and college faculty. Other topics that articles frequently deal with include public sector union security, permissible strike authorization, public sector strike behavior, and public versus private union attitudes. Most articles report on empirical research. Data is compiled from public records or from survey research conducted by the author(s). Some use is made of statistical methodologies, but most articles avoid sophisticated quantitative techniques. The authors are mostly academics in departments of economics, labor relations, management, education, finance, marketing, and political science. Some are attorneys or school administrators. The Journal emphasizes empirical research results whereas Government Union Review, which covers the same subject area, emphasizes public policy discussions.
   Most issues contain from six to eight articles which average about ten pages in length. Some issues include a book review which may or may not be signed. Each article begins with an abstract and ends with a biographical sketch and full address of the author(s).

249.   Journal of Common Market Studies. DATE FOUNDED: 1962. FREQUENCY: q. PRICE: $70/yr. institutions, $45.70/yr. personal. PUBLISHER: Basil Blackwell Publisher, Ltd., 108 Cowley Rd., Oxford OX4 1JF, England. EDITOR: Peter Robson. INDEX. ADVERTISEMENTS. CIRCULATION: 1,500. MANUSCRIPT SELECTION: Editor and Editorial Advisory Board. MICROFORMS: ROTH. BOOK REVIEWS. SPECIAL ISSUES: INDEXED/ABSTRACTED: BPI, BPIA, InEcA, IntBibE, JEL, KeyEcS, PAIS. DATABASES: ECONAB, ECONLIT, MC, PAIS INT. TARGET AUDIENCE: AC, SP. SAMPLE COPIES: Libraries and Individuals.

The Journal of Common Market Studies is the publication of the University Association for Contemporary European Studies. It focuses on "experiments in integration throughout the international system, from a political, economic, legal, or historical perspective, with a particular emphasis on the integration process in Western Europe." Many articles can be characterized as applied economics or political economy. Recent issues have included articles on economic integration in the European Community with regard to banking, aerospace, energy, textiles, information technology, and agriculture. Other articles focus on integration elsewhere such as East Africa, Northern and Southern Ireland, and the Andean Group made up of Boliva, Columbia, Ecuador, Peru, and Venezuela. Still other articles deal more in the abstract, speculating on traditional versus Marxist approaches to economic integration and the feasibility of a functioning monetary union. Articles are scholarly, but not very technical in nature. Data is frequently provided in a simple form. Most of the authors are academics associated with European universities.

Most issues contain four or five articles averaging about twenty pages in length. A book review section including from eight to fifteen brief signed reviews appears in every issue. Occasionally a double special issue arises out of a special conference such as the 1982 issue on "The European Community: Past, Present, and Future."

250.   Journal of Comparative Economics. DATE FOUNDED: 1977. FREQUENCY: q. PRICE: $66/yr. PUBLISHER: Academic Press, 111 Fifth Avenue, New York, New York 10003. EDITOR: John Michael Montias. ILLUSTRATIONS. INDEX. ADVERTISEMENTS. MANUSCRIPT SELECTION: Editor and Referees. REPRINTS: Authors. BOOK REVIEWS. SPECIAL ISSUES. INDEXED/ABSTRACTED: InEcA, IntBibE, JEL, PAIS, SSI, WAERSA. DATABASES: CAB AB, ECONLIT, PAIS INT, SSI. TARGET AUDIENCE: AC, SP.

The Journal of Comparative Economics is a publication co-sponsored by the Association for Comparative Economic Studies. It publishes both "theoretical and empirical articles on the comparison of economic systems and subsystems." Most of the comparative studies deal with market-based vs. centrally planned economies but occasional articles compare two countries having similar systems such as Japan and the U.S. or Hungary and Yugoslavia. A few articles offer an analysis of an economic system rather than a comparison. Many studies focus on the U.S.S.R. Some articles offer a purely theoretical study. Many articles deal with labor-managed firms. The Journal contains scholarly studies most of which are highly technical in nature. The majority of authors are economists from American universities. A few are from Israel, Western Europe, and Japan. The Journal of Comparative Economics overlaps with the Jahrbuch der Wirtschaft Osteuropas in that both deal with CMEA countries. The former is more scholarly and quantitative in orientation while the latter concentrates on Eastern Europe and offers descriptive rather than comparative studies.

A typical issue includes four or five full length articles and one or two short comments. An average of six signed book reviews appear in each issue. Occasionally a special issue is devoted to a single topic under the direction of a guest editor. Recent special issues focused on Soviet fertility and the labor-force and on Hungarian economic reforms.

251.   The Journal of Consumer Affairs. DATE FOUNDED: 1967. FREQUENCY: 2/yr. PRICE: $55/yr. institutions, $30/yr. personal. PUBLISHER: American Council on Consumer Interests, 162 Stanley Hall, University of Missouri, Columbia, Missouri 65211. EDITOR: David Eastwood. ADVERTISEMENTS. CIRCULATION: 2,600. MANUSCRIPT SELECTION: Editor and Referees. MICRO-FORMS: MIM. BOOK REVIEWS. INDEXED/ABSTRACTED: BPIA, IntBibE, ManI, PAIS, WAERSA. DATABASES: CAB AB, MC, PAIS INT. TARGET AUDIENCE: AC, SP.

The Journal of Consumer Affairs is published "to foster and disseminate professional thought and scholarly research advancing the consumer interest." The scope of The Journal includes "consumer economics, consumer education, consumer policy and consumer behavior." The major emphasis of this publication is consumer economics. Recent issues have presented articles dealing with windfall income, consumer cooperatives, home ownership, consumer expenditure patterns, retirement savings goals, and competition in health care. The articles are scholarly and either report the results of empirical studies or discuss theoretical hypotheses. Most use quantitative analyses of data gathered in their studies. Authors are professors of economics, home economics, and marketing at American and Canadian universities. The Journal of Consumer Affairs deals predominantly with actual consumer behavior while the Journal of Consumer Research concentrates on consumer psychology. Both are more technical journals than the Journal of Consumer Policy which concentrates on government policies and their social and economic consequences.

Each issue includes four or five research articles plus six or seven shorter research notes. A book review section includes six in-depth signed reviews.

252.   Journal of Consumer Policy. DATE FOUNDED: 1977. FREQUENCY: q. PRICE: $66/yr. institutions, $26/yr. personal. PUBLISHER: D. Reidel Publishing Company, P.O. Box 17, 3300 AA Dordrecht, The Netherlands. EDITORS: Folke Olander, Norbert Reich, Gerhard Scherhorn. ILLUSTRATIONS. INDEX. ADVERTISEMENTS. MANUSCRIPT SELECTION: Editors. BOOK REVIEWS. SPECIAL ISSUES. INDEXED/ABSTRACTED: PAIS. DATABASES: PAIS INT. TARGET AUDIENCE: AC, SP.

The Journal of Consumer Policy "is an international scholarly journal which encompasses a diverse range of issues to do with consumer affairs." Articles analyze "the consumer's dependence upon existing social and economic structures", seek "to define the consumer's interest" and "discuss the ways in which this interest can be fostered - or restrained - through actions and policies of consumers, industry, organizations, government, educational institutions, and mass media." Most articles take the perspective of the consumer, but a few present the producer's viewpoint. Topics dicussed in recent issues are the expansion of consumer cooperatives, the impact of trade restrictions on U.S. consumers of apparel, and the consumer information deficit. Most articles are non-technical and do not employ quantitative analysis. Both the Journal of Consumer Affairs and the Journal of Consumer Research are more technical. The former emphasizes consumer economics and the latter concentrates on the psychological analysis of consumer behavior. The majority of the articles in the Journal of Consumer Policy are written by academics in departments of economics and business administration at U.S. and European universities. The rest are by government economists and lawyers.

A typical issue contains three regular articles, one or two more in sections called "Notes and Reports" and "Current Developments in Consumer Law", one or two communications, four or five signed book reviews, and from fifteen to twenty brief unsigned "Book Notes". German language summaries appear at the end of each article. Occasionally a special issue on a single topic with guest editors is published.

253.   Journal of Consumer Research. DATE FOUNDED: 1974. FREQUENCY: q.
PRICE: $56/yr. PUBLISHER: University of California, Los Angeles,
Graduate School of Management, Los Angeles, California 90024. EDITORS:
Harold H. Kassarjian, James R. Bettman. ILLUSTRATIONS. INDEX. ADVERTISE-
MENTS. CIRCULATION: 3,200. MANUSCRIPT SELECTION: Editors and Referees.
MICROFORMS: UMI. REPRINTS: Authors. INDEXED/ABSTRACTED: BPI, BPIA,
InEcA, JEL, PsyAb, SocAb. DATABASES: ECONLIT, MC, PSYAB, SOCAB. TARGET
AUDIENCE: AC, SP. SAMPLE COPIES: Libraries and Individuals.

The Journal of Consumer Research is an interdisciplinary publication
presenting articles on research in consumer behavior. Disciplines
represented in this periodical include psychology, sociology, marketing,
management, and economics. The primary focus of this publication is the
psychological analysis of consumer behavior. Secondary areas of coverage
include marketing studies, social surveys, advertising effectiveness,
and consumer economics. The articles report the results of research
studies. They are scholarly, extensively footnoted, and frequently
employ quantitative analysis. The authors are American academics
associated with business, psychology, and social science departments.
Occasional papers are co-authored with graduate students. JCR concentrates on the psychological aspects of consumer behavior whereas The
Journal of Consumer Affairs focuses on consumer economics. The Journal
of Consumer Policy is less technical and deals more with government
policies in the consumer sphere and with their social and economic
consequences.
   A typical issue includes ten to eleven articles varying in length
from eight to fifteen pages. Some issues also present shorter notes and
comments. An annual index is included with the last issue of the volume.

254.   Journal of Contemporary Studies. DATE FOUNDED: 1978. TITLE
CHANGES: Taxing & Spending (1978-1980). FREQUENCY: q. PRICE: $15/yr.
PUBLISHER: Institute for Contemporary Studies, 785 Market Street, Suite
750, San Francisco, California 94103. EDITORS: Patrick Glynn, Walter J.
Lammi. INDEX. ADVERTISEMENTS. CIRCULATION: 2,000. MANUSCRIPT SELECTION:
Editors. MICROFORMS: UMI. REPRINTS: Publisher, UMI. BOOK REVIEWS.
INDEXED/ABSTRACTED: PAIS. DATABASES: PAIS INT. TARGET AUDIENCE: AC, GP,
SP. SAMPLE COPIES: Libraries.

The Journal of Contemporary Studies is published by the institute of the
same name and serves as a forum for debate on current public policy
issues in a broad range of subject area. Some articles deal with
political situations, both on the domestic and international scene.
Others are concerned with the U.S. education system. About half the
articles discuss public policy issues having direct economic consequences. Topics covered in recent issues include structural unemployment, job-training programs, wages, transportation, FTC regulations,
industrial policy, immigration policy, protectionism, flat rate taxes,
and monetarism at the Federal Reserve. The articles are written in
expository style without any quantitative analysis but are scholarly
with extensive references. The authors are American academics from a
variety of disciplines - political science, sociology, and economics.
This Journal is more interdisciplinary than The Cato Journal as it

offers articles dealing with a wider range of topics. The latter
concentrates more on economic issues.
    A typical issue contains six to eight articles. They vary in length
from ten to twenty-five pages. Occasionally a special issue is published
that is devoted to responses to a previously published provocative
article. An issue including five in-depth signed book reviews is
designated as "Special Book Review Issue."

255.   Journal of Cultural Economics. DATE FOUNDED: 1977. FREQUENCY:
2/yr. PRICE: $30/yr. institutions, $15/yr. personal. PUBLISHER: Univer-
sity of Akron, Department of Urban Studies, Akron, Ohio 44325. EDITOR:
William S. Hendon. ILLUSTRATIONS. CIRCULATION: 300. MANUSCRIPT SELEC-
TION: Editor and Referees. REPRINTS: Publisher. BOOK REVIEWS. INDEXED/
ABSTRACTED: InEcA, JEL. DATABASES: ECONLIT. TARGET AUDIENCE: AC, SP.
SAMPLE COPIES: Libraries.

The Journal of Cultural Economics is published in cooperation with the
Association of Cultural Economics. Its scope is economics applied to
cultural topics in the arts, historic preservation and pop culture.
Topics addressed include markets for the arts, economic support for the
arts, the earnings gap in the performing arts, government and the arts,
the economics of cultural industries, managerial economics for the arts,
and economics of historic preservation. Articles vary greatly in type
and technical content. Articles appearing in recent issues included
technical ones such as "An Economic Model of Artistic Behavior", "The
Economics of Collectible Goods", "Competition, Pricing and Concentration
in the U.S. Recorded Music Industry" and "Demand Elasticities for
Symphony Orchestras". Others are descriptive such as "The Classical
Record Industry in the United States", "Keynes and the Economics of the
Arts", and "Film and Video: An Institutional Paradigm and Some Issues of
National Policy." The authors are predominantly academic economists, but
some are researchers with the National Endowment for the Arts. The
majority are American, but British, Australian, Swiss, and Canadian
scholars also make contributions.
    A typical issue contains six articles of varying lengths. Some issues
include a short note and others an in-depth signed book review.

256.   The Journal of Developing Areas. DATE FOUNDED: 1966. FREQUENCY:
q. PRICE: $20/yr. institutions, $15/yr. personal. PUBLISHER: Western
Illinois University, 900 West Adams Street, Macomb, Illinois 61455.
EDITOR: Nicholas C. Pano. ILLUSTRATIONS. INDEX. ADVERTISEMENTS. CIRCULA-
TION: 1,500. MANUSCRIPT SELECTION: Editors. BOOK REVIEWS. INDEXED/
ABSTRACTED: BPI, BPIA, HistAb, InEcA, IntBibE, JEL, KeyEcS, PAIS,
WAERSA. DATABASES: ABI, CAB AB, ECONAB, ECONLIT, HISTAB, NEXIS, PAIS
INT. TARGET AUDIENCE: AC, SP.

The Journal of Developing Areas is an interdisciplinary journal that has
as its purpose to "stimulate the descriptive, theoretical, and comparative study of regional development, past and present." Articles vary
greatly in type and sophistication. Some are basically descriptive such
as an account of development policy in Tanzania or public choice and
policy in Latin America. Others are more evaluative such as the examination of certain technology importation policies, food policies or even
specific programs such as Swaziland's and Kenya's rural development

programs, or the Andean auto program. Still others are empirical in nature such as estimating the size of the subsidy of the Cuban-Soviet sugar trade. Some articles are much more technical such as those that deal with the application of a certain methodology or present a formal model and test its validity. Most articles are written by American academics from a great variety of disciplines including geography, political science, economics, sociology, demographics, history, education, finance, and marketing. World Development examines the same subject area as the Journal, but from a traditional economic approach.

A typical issue contains five or six articles, a "News and Notes" section, and extensive sections devoted to book reviews and books received. Issues contain twenty to twenty-five one-to-three page signed reviews and a three to four page list of books received.

257.   Journal of Development Economics. DATE FOUNDED: 1974. FREQUENCY: 9/yr. PRICE: $220.25/yr. institutions, $77/yr. personal. PUBLISHER: North-Holland Publishing Co., P.O. Box 211, 1000 AE Amsterdam, The Netherlands. EDITOR: Lance Taylor. ILLUSTRATIONS. INDEX. ADVERTISEMENTS. MANUSCRIPT SELECTION: Editors. MICROFORMS: Elsev. REPRINTS: Publisher. BOOK REVIEWS. INDEXED/ABSTRACTED: BPIA, CREJ, InEcA, IntBibE, JEL, PAIS, SSI, WAERSA. DATABASES: ABI, CAB AB, ECONLIT, MC, PAIS INT, SSI. TARGET AUDIENCE: AC, SP. SAMPLE COPIES: Libraries and Individuals.

The Journal of Development Economics publishes articles relating to "all aspects of economic development -- from immediate policy concerns to structural problems of underdevelopment." It is a scholarly technical economics journal which focuses on economic theory and empirical work that makes use of modern quantitative methodologies. It does not take a more general social science perspective such as The Journal of Development Studies. A typical article in the Journal of Development Economics begins with an introduction, followed by a model expressed in mathematical terms, a section attempting to provide empirical verification, and ending with some conclusions. Articles deal with topics such as human capital divestment, capital mobility and growth, income distribution, terms of trade, manpower flows, export taxes, nutrition demand, rural-urban migration, and the instability of exports. Many are case studies involving a particular developing country. The editors, co-editors and associate editors are academic economists at prestigious universities in the U.S. and a few other countries. The authors reflect that authority to a considerable degree. The Journal is comparable in level of scholarship to Economic Development and Cultural Change.

Three volumes, each containing three issues are published annually. Frequently two and sometimes three issues are combined. Each issue contains six or seven articles. Most issues include a book review section with from one to three in-depth signed reviews. An author index appears in the third issue of each volume.

258.   The Journal of Development Studies. DATE FOUNDED: 1964. FREQUENCY: q. PRICE: L55 /yr. institutions, L28/yr. personal. PUBLISHER: Frank Cass & Co. Ltd., Gainsborough House, Gainsborough Rd., London E11 IRS, England. EDITOR: Editorial Board. ILLUSTRATIONS. INDEX. ADVERTISEMENTS. CIRCULATION: 1,900. MANUSCRIPT SELECTION: Managing Editors and Referees. BOOK REVIEWS. SPECIAL ISSUES. INDEXED/ABSTRACTED: BPIA, BritHumI, InEcA, IntBibE, JEL, KeyEcS, PAIS, SocAb, SSI, WAERSA,

WorkRelAbstr. DATABASES: CAB AB, ECONAB, ECONLIT, MC, PAIS INT, SOCAB, SSI. TARGET AUDIENCE: AC, SP. SAMPLE COPIES: Libraries.

The Journal of Development Studies is devoted to all aspects of development studies. It features economic development, but is a broad based social science journal that also covers social and political development. This is reflected in the diversity of authors. While the majority are economists -- at universities, government agencies, or institutions such as the World Bank and International Monetary Fund -- many are sociologists and political scientists. Most are British and American, but other countries are also represented. Articles vary greatly in their technical nature. Some present a model and make use of quantitative methods, while others rely on some data but are basically expository. The average article is far less rigorous than those typically found in the Journal of Development Economics.

Each issue contains from five to seven articles averaging about twenty pages in length. Some issues include a review article covering four or five books on the same topic such as housing in Asia or women in development. All issues have "Books Received", "Short Notes on Some Books Received", and "Book Reviews" sections. A typical issue contains from ten to fifteen signed reviews. Occasionally a special issue on a specific topic, with guest editors, is published. An author index appears in the July issue.

259.   Journal of Econometrics. DATE FOUNDED: 1973. FREQUENCY: 9/yr. PRICE: $260/yr. institutions, $97.50/yr. personal. PUBLISHER: Elsevier Sequoia SA, Box 851, 1001 Lausanne 1, Switzerland. EDITORS: Dennis Aigner, Takeshi Amemiya, Arnold Zellner. ILLUSTRATIONS. INDEX. ADVERTISEMENTS. MANUSCRIPT SELECTION: Editors and Referees. MICROFORMS: Elsev. REPRINTS: Elsev. SPECIAL ISSUES. INDEXED/ABSTRACTED: BPIA, CREJ, InEcA, JEL, MathR, SSI, STMA, WAERSA. DATABASES: CAB AB, ECONLIT, MATHFILE, MC, SSI. TARGET AUDIENCE: AC, SP. SAMPLE COPIES: Libraries and Individuals.

The Journal of Econometrics publishes articles in both theoretical and applied econometrics. They deal with "estimation and other methodological aspects of the application of statistical inference to economic data" as well as with "the application of econometric techniques to substantive areas of economics." The Journal of Econometrics together with Econometrica, the Journal of the Econometric Society, publish the most new knowledge in this important field. By nature the material is very technical as econometrics combines mathematics and statistics with economic theory. The journal is international in scope. While its present three editors are American, its short list of associate editors includes economists from eight different countries. Authors, who are mainly academic economists, reflect the same international distribution.

The nine issues per year are published in three volumes of three issues each. One issue in each volume is a special issue edited by a guest editor and devoted to a specific topic in applied economics. Recent examples are: "Insurance Modelling", "Pre-Test and Stein-Rule Estimators, Some New Results", "Censored or Truncated Regression Models", and "Interfaces Between Econometrics and Psychometrics." Regular issues include from seven to twelve articles plus some announcements. The last issue of each volume includes an author index.

260.   Journal of Economic Behavior and Organization. DATE FOUNDED:
1980. FREQUENCY: q. PRICE: $84.90/yr. institutions, $34.60/yr. personal.
PUBLISHER: North-Holland Publishing Co., Box 211, 1000 AE Amsterdam, The
Netherlands. EDITORS: Richard H. Day, Sidney T. Winter. ILLUSTRATIONS.
INDEX. ADVERTISEMENTS. MANUSCRIPT SELECTION: Editors and Editorial
Board. REPRINTS: Publisher. SPECIAL ISSUES. INDEXED/ABSTRACTED: BPIA,
CREJ. DATABASES: MC. TARGET AUDIENCE: AC, SP. SAMPLE COPIES: Libraries
and Individuals.

The Journal of Economic Behavior & Organization is devoted to "theoretical and empirical research concerning economic decision, organization,
and behavior." Its aim is to foster improved understanding of "how human
cognitive, computational, and informational characteristics influence
the working of economic organizations and market economies." JEBO's
scope does not correspond to a traditional field of specialization in
economics but rather falls within the range of what may be referred to
as behavioral theory, adaptive economics, disequilibrium theory, bounded
rationality, and biological economics. It is a scholarly journal that
reconsiders extant economic theory and searches in the field of funda-
mental theoretical models and concepts. A few articles are expository in
style, but most use sophisticated simulation modeling or statistical and
mathematical analysis. The authors are predominantly academic economists
associated with prestigious universities in the U.S., U.K., Canada,
Israel, Germany, and others.
    Most issues contain from five to eight articles. Occasionally replies
to previously published articles and rejoinders are included. Recently a
special issue, JEBO's first, was published on "The Dynamics of Market
Economics" in commemoration of the birth of Joseph Schumpeter. The
December issue includes an author index.

261.   Journal of Economic Dynamics and Control. DATE FOUNDED: 1979.
FREQUENCY: 6/yr. PRICE: $220.25/yr. institutions, $57.75/yr. personal.
PUBLISHER: North-Holland Publishing Co.,, Box 211, 1000 AE Amsterdam,
The Netherlands. EDITORS: Mansanao Aoki, Stephen J. Turnovsky. ILLUSTRA-
TIONS. INDEX. ADVERTISEMENTS. MANUSCRIPT SELECTION: Editors and Editor-
ial Board. MICROFORMS: Elsev. REPRINTS: Publisher. BOOK REVIEWS. SPECIAL
ISSUES. INDEXED/ABSTRACTED: BPIA, CREJ, InEcA, JEL, MathR. DATABASES:
ECONLIT, INSPEC, MATHFILE, MC. TARGET AUDIENCE: AC, SP. SAMPLE COPIES:
Libraries and Individuals.

The Journal of Economic Dynamics and Control is among the most technical
and mathematical journals in economics. The theoretical areas covered
are: economic dynamics, stability, controllability, deterministic
stochastic and adaptive control, decentralized control, differential
gains, estimation, and measurement. Articles that apply theory cover the
full range of areas of economic analysis. Recent issues have included
application articles on investment, taxation, military expenditures,
output-inflation tradeoffs, currency diversification, oil extraction
decision making, monetary policy choices, advertising decisions, and
income distribution. Both theoretical and applied articles make use of
sophisticated quantitative methodologies including simulation modeling
and statistical and mathematical analysis. The authors are predominantly
research economists at universities, but some are associated with
government agencies and institutes. The majority are American, British,
and Canadian, but authors from as many as a dozen different countries

have published their work in recent issues. This journal is comparable in technical level to Journal of Mathematical Economics and Journal of Economic Theory.
A typical issue contains four or five articles. Briefer notes are sometimes included. Double issues are not uncommon. The last issue of each of the two annual volumes contains an author index. Occasionally a special issue is published such as a 1983 issue on modeling languages.

262.   Journal of Economic Education. DATE FOUNDED: 1969. FREQUENCY: q. PRICE: $25/yr. institutions, $13/yr. personal. PUBLISHER: Heldref Publications, 4000 Albermarle St., NW, Washington, DC 20016. EDITOR: Donald W. Paden. ILLUSTRATIONS. INDEX. ADVERTISEMENTS. CIRCULATION: 1,200. MANUSCRIPT SELECTION: Editors. MICROFORMS: UMI. REPRINTS: UMI. BOOK REVIEWS. INDEXED/ABSTRACTED: CIJE, InEcA, IntBibE, JEL. DATABASES: ECONLIT. TARGET AUDIENCE: AC, SP. SAMPLE COPIES: Libraries and Individuals.

The Journal of Economic Education is published by a nonprofit educational foundation in cooperation with the Joint Council on Economic Education, the Advisory Committee of the American Economic Association, and the Department of Economics of the University of Illinois. It is intended to promote the teaching and learning of economics in college, junior colleges, and high schools. The journal includes articles that deal with the effectiveness of teaching methods, with the evaluation of teaching effectiveness, and with some of the topics and issues that are to be taught. Examples of the first type are articles dealing with the classroom lecture, televised instruction, programmed learning, games and simulation, computerized teaching, length of the principles course, examination formats, and the teaching of particular concepts. Articles focusing on the evaluation of teaching effectiveness report on studies involving academic performance, economic understanding, faculty evaluation and reward systems. Most articles that report on research in economic education make use of modern statistical methodologies. The authors are predominantly academic economists at American universities. Expository type articles by very well known economists like Friedman, Stigler, and Tobin are included in some issues.
A typical issue contains about five "Research in Economic Education" articles, one "Content" article, one or two "Innovation in Economic Instruction" articles, one or two "The Teaching of Economics" articles, and a "Professional Information" section which usually includes one article, one signed book review, and some announcements.

263.   Journal of Economic History. DATE FOUNDED: 1941. FREQUENCY: q. PRICE: $30/yr. institutions, $20/yr. personal. PUBLISHER: Economic History Association, P.O. Box 3630, Wilmington, Delaware 19807. EDITOR: Richard Sylla. ILLUSTRATIONS. INDEX. ADVERTISEMENTS. CIRCULATION: 3,600. MANUSCRIPT SELECTION: Editor and Referees. MICROFORMS: KR., UMI. BOOK REVIEWS. INDEXED/ABSTRACTED: InEcA, JEL, KeyEcS, PAIS, SSI, WorkRelAbstr. DATABASES: ECONAB, ECONLIT, PAIS INT, SSI. TARGET AUDIENCE: AC, SP. SAMPLE COPIES: Libraries and Individuals.

The Journal of Economic History publishes articles dealing with a wide range of topics in economic history and related areas. The subject is covered on an international scope and without limitations of time periods. The primary area of concentration focuses on Modern Europe and North America in the 19th and 20th Centuries but a secondary area covers Medieval times and Asia, Africa, and South America. The articles are scholarly in style, employ extensive footnotes, and occasionally use quantitative analysis, graphs, and charts. Most of the authors are economists at Universities in English speaking countries. A few are historians. The Journal compares favorably to The Economic History Review in level of scholarship but has a broader geographic and chronologic scope.

A typical issue includes six to eight in-depth research papers and three to five shorter notes. Each issue includes one or two review articles. A section "Editors' Notes" reports on news items of interest to members such as fellowships, prizes, awards, and forthcoming conferences. The book review section provides an average of forty signed book reviews grouped into "Medieval", "Modern Europe", "Asia, Africa and Latin America," "United States", and "Economic Thought". One issue per year contains papers presented at the annual meeting of the Economic History Association.

264.   Journal of Economic Issues. DATE FOUNDED: 1967. FREQUENCY: q. PRICE: $25/yr. institutions, $22/yr. personal. PUBLISHER: Department of Economics, California State University, Sacramento, California 95819. EDITOR: Marc R. Tool. ILLUSTRATIONS. INDEX. ADVERTISEMENTS. CIRCULATION: 2,200. MANUSCRIPT SELECTION: Editor and Editorial Board. MICROFORMS: UMI. REPRINTS: KRC, UMI. BOOK REVIEWS. SPECIAL ISSUES. INDEXED/ABSTRACTED: BPI, BPIA, InEcA, IntBibE, JEL, PAIS, SocAb, SSI. DATABASES: ECONLIT, MC, PAIS INT, SOCAB, SSI. TARGET AUDIENCE: AC, SP. SAMPLE COPIES: Libraries and Individuals.

The Journal of Economic Issues is the publication of the Association for Evolutionary Economics, a group of economists interested in institutional economics. The latter is associated with the works and views of such economists as John R. Commons, Clarence Ayres, Thorstein Veblen, and John Kenneth Galbraith. The articles published deal with "Basic economic problems, economic policy, methodology, the organization and control of economies, and all of the specialized fields of economics", but in the main are critical of extant mainstream economic views. Some articles report on research involving a model and some empirical testing, but most are essays putting forth heterodox viewpoints in the realm of political economy. These may or may not involve the use of some quantitative methodologies. Most of the authors are American academic economists.

Regular issues contain from eight to fifteen articles and a "Notes and Communications" section which includes brief essays, comments on previously published articles, replies, and rejoinders. There is an extensive book review section usually offering ten to twelve signed reviews plus two or three separate reviews by different people on a single book of particular interest. One issue of each volume is a special issue devoted to the proceedings of the annual meeting of the Association for Evolutionary Economics. Other special issues may be published as a 1984 number which contained thirteen solicited essays on "Economic Policy for the Eighties and Beyond".

265.   Journal of Economic Literature. DATE FOUNDED: 1969. FREQUENCY: q. PRICE: $100/yr. institutions, includes subscription to American

Economic Review, $49/yr. personal, includes membership to AEA and subscription to American Economic Review. PUBLISHER: American Economic Association, 1313 21st Avenue South, Suite 809, Nashville, Tennessee 37212. EDITOR: Moses Abramovitz. ILLUSTRATIONS. INDEX. ADVERTISEMENTS. CIRCULATION: 26,000. MANUSCRIPT SELECTION: Editor and Board of Editors. MICROFORMS: MIM, UMI. BOOK REVIEWS. INDEXED/ABSTRACTED: BPIA, InEcA, IntBibe, JEL, KeyEcS, PAIS, SSI, WAERSA. DATABASES: CAB AB, ECONAB, ECONLIT, MC, PAIS INT, SSI. TARGET AUDIENCE: AC, SP. SAMPLE COPIES: Libraries.

The Journal of Economic Literature is both a journal of articles and book reviews and a journal of abstracts. The latter function had previously been provided by the Journal of Economic Abstracts (1963-1969). JEL complements the American Economic Review, the other publication of the American Economic Association. While the AER contains only research articles, JEL contains the "tools for research and study." Its scope covers all areas of applied and theoretical economics. Articles do not report on the research of the author, but are review articles covering the literature concerning some problem or issue in economics. In most instances a reader can learn about the most important research and ideas that the profession has to date on a particular topic.

A typical issue contains from two to four review articles, each thirty or forty pages in length. Some issues have a "Communications" section with one or two brief comments and/or replies regarding previously published articles. Each issue contains an extensive book review section which includes from thirty to fifty one-to-two page signed reviews separated according to subject category. Each issue also includes an annotated listing of hundreds of new books classified according to subject, the table of contents of a large number of current economics periodicals, a subject index of the articles in current periodicals, and hundreds of selected abstracts of articles arranged in a classified schedule.

266.   Journal of Economic Psychology. DATE FOUNDED: 1981. FREQUENCY: q. PRICE: $60/yr. institutions, $38.50/yr. personal. PUBLISHER: Elsevier Science Publishers B.V. (North-Holland) P.O. Box 1991, 1000 BZ Amsterdam, The Netherlands. EDITOR: W. Fred van Raaij. ILLUSTRATIONS. INDEX. ADVERTISEMENTS. MANUSCRIPT SELECTION: Editorial Board. REPRINTS: Publisher. BOOK REVIEWS. INDEXED/ABSTRACTED: BPIA. DATABASES: MC. TARGET AUDIENCE: AC, SP. SAMPLE COPIES: Libraries and Individuals.

The Journal of Economic Psychology is published under the auspices of the International Association for Research in Economic Psychology. This publication is an interdisciplinary journal that presents studies describing the psychological mechanisms that underlie consumption and other economic behavior. Articles deal with preferences, choices, decisions, and factors influencing economic behavior and how the consequences of the latter provide satisfaction of consumer needs. Articles relate to "different levels of aggregation, from the household and the individual consumer to the macro level of whole nations." The editorial board is international in scope with heavy representation from Western Europe. The articles are written in a scholarly style with extensive references. Some of the articles employ quantitative techniques and many of them use data gathered from consumer surveys. The authors are academics from universities around the world. About half are

from departments of business and economics and half from departments of
psychology. This Journal somewhat overlaps the subject field of Journal
of Consumer Research but it is more theoretical than the latter and
includes studies of macro levels whereas the Journal of Consumer Research concentrates on individual consumers' behavior.

A typical issue contains four or five articles of fifteen to twenty-
five pages in length. One or two signed book reviews are included. The
first issue published in a calendar year has an "Agenda" section which
announces forthcoming conferences of interest for readers.

267.   Journal of Economic Studies. DATE FOUNDED: 1974. FREQUENCY: q.
PRICE: $179.95/yr. PUBLISHER: MCB University Press Ltd., 198/200
Keighley Road, Bradford, West Yorkshire, BD9 4 JQ, England. EDITOR:
Frank H. Stephen. ADVERTISEMENTS. CIRCULATION: 500. MANUSCRIPT SELEC-
TION: Editor. REPRINTS: Publisher. BOOK REVIEWS. INDEXED/ABSTRACTED:
InEcA, JEL, PAIS, WAERSA. DATABASES: CAB AB, ECONLIT, PAIS INT. TARGET
AUDIENCE: AC, SP. SAMPLE COPIES: Libraries and Individuals.

The Journal of Economic Studies, which supercedes Economic Studies
published by the same press, provides readers with "Current developments
in all fields of economics, but particularly international and development economics." Recent issues have presented articles on developing
countries such as Chile, Egypt, and Pakistan. Other articles run the
gamut of economic problems and issues such as monetary policy, size of
the firm, capital utilization, the housing market, income inequality,
trade theory, health care, and peak-load pricing. Some issues include
articles on the history of economic thought and occasionally an entire
volume is devoted to such essays. Most of the articles utilize quantitative analysis by offering a model and testing its validity with empirical data. The Journal is assisted by an editorial advisory board made
up of academics primarily from the U.K., the U.S., Australia and Canada.
The authors have similar affiliations.

Each issue includes four to six articles varying in size from five to
fifteen pages. A brief abstract precedes each article. A review article
offering an in-depth evaluation of a current book is included in most
issues. Each issue contains a book review section with from one to four
signed reviews.

268.   Journal of Economic Theory. DATE FOUNDED: 1969. FREQUENCY: 6/yr.
PRICE: $237/yr. PUBLISHER: Academic Press, Inc., 111 Fifth Ave., New
York, New York 10003. EDITOR: Karl Shell. ILLUSTRATIONS. INDEX. ADVER-
TISEMENTS. MANUSCRIPT SELECTION: Editor. INDEXED/ABSTRACTED: BPIA,
InEcA, IntBibe, JEL, SSI. DATABASES: ECONLIT, MC, SSI. TARGET AUDIENCE:
AC, SP.

The Journal of Economic Theory is a highly technical journal covering
economic theory at the frontier of knowledge. It comes as close to
publishing pure economic theory as any extant journal. Articles offer
virtually no empirical content. Most present an introduction, a model,
and a conclusion. Some devote a large part of the article to proving
theorems. This journal is very mathematical, the mathematics often
taking precedence over the economics. Articles deal with many different
areas of economics, but more with micro than macroeconomics. Many
concern themselves with topics in price theory including duopoly theory

and utility theory. Variables are often observed under conditions of risk and/or uncertainty. Some articles deal with statistical theory. The authors are primarily academic research economists who specialize in pure theory. The majority are associated with American universities, but quite a few are European and Israeli. This publication offers the same level of technical complexity as Journal of Economic Dynamics and Control, International Journal of Game Theory, and The Review of Economic Studies.

Most issues contain from seven to ten regular articles plus several brief notes in a "Notes, Comments, and Letters to the Editor" section. "Comments" refer to papers previously published in the journal and replies are also included in this section. Three volumes of two issues each are published annually. An author index appears in the last issue of each volume.

269.   Journal of Economics and Business. DATE FOUNDED: 1949. TITLE CHANGES: Economic and Business Bulletin (1949-1971). FREQUENCY: q. PRICE: $64/yr. institutions, $32/yr. personal. PUBLISHER: Elsevier Science Publishing Co., 52 Vanderbilt Ave., New York, New York 10017. EDITOR: Robert H. Deans. ILLUSTRATIONS. INDEX. ADVERTISEMENTS. CIRCULA-TION: 1,000. MANUSCRIPT SELECTION: Editor and Referees. MICROFORMS: UMI. REPRINTS: Publisher. SPECIAL ISSUES. INDEXED/ABSTRACTED: BPI, BPIA, InEcA, JEL, PAIS, WAERSA. DATABASES: CAB AB, ECONLIT, MC, PAIS INT. TARGET AUDIENCE: AC, SP. SAMPLE COPIES: Libraries and Individuals.

The Journal of Economics and Business is published in cooperation with the School of Business Administration of Temple University. It presents the results of "professional and academic research in economics, finance, management, marketing, and related fields." The articles emphasize finance and applied economics. Studies in the above areas include municipal bond markets, black-owned banks, optimal portfolio composition, implications of the Bankruptcy Reform Law, capital needs of electric utilities, and oil prices and world inflation. A few articles offer the results of research on theoretical economic concepts such as oligopoly models, market entry decisions, theory of the firm, and international monetary systems. Most of the research studies employ advanced quantitative analytic methodologies. The authors are either academics or researchers with financial institutions.

A typical issue contains twelve articles of ten to twenty pages each. Each article is preceded by an abstract and concludes with a list of references. Occasionally, a special issue is published. Such an issue is devoted to a single topic and is under the direction of a guest editor. A recent one dealt with "Financial Analysis, Planning and Forecasting."

270.   Journal of Energy and Development. DATE FOUNDED: 1975. FRE-QUENCY: 2/yr. PRICE: $24/yr. institutions, $14/yr. personal. PUBLISHER: International Research Center for Energy and Economic Development, 216 Economics Building, Box 263, University of Colorado, Boulder, Colorado 80309. EDITOR: Ragaei El Mallakh. ILLUSTRATIONS. INDEX. ADVERTISEMENTS. CIRCULATION: 2,100. MANUSCRIPT SELECTION: Editor and Referees. REPRINTS: Authors. BOOK REVIEWS: INDEXED/ABSTRACTED: InEcA, JEL, PAIS, Pred. DATABASES: ECONLIT, PAIS INT, PF. TARGET AUDIENCE: AC, GP, SP. SAMPLE COPIES: Libraries and Individuals.

The Journal of Energy and Development is an interdisciplinary publication presenting studies relevant to both energy and economic development. It is international in scope and deals with a broad range of topics related to energy concerns. Recent articles focusing on international concerns include topics such as West European energy supplies, the Japan-Indonesia oil trade, Norwegian gas reserves, Nigerian oil policies, and the Mexican oil industry. Some articles deal with domestic energy concerns and cover topics such as energy development for the Western U.S., energy resources of Colorado, electricity consumption in the U.S., and energy economics and taxation. The articles avoid excessive technical jargon and quantitative methods and rarely use a mathematical model in constructing a hypothesis. The authors are predominantly economists affiliated with universities, government agencies, and energy companies.

Each issue includes ten articles, varying in length from six to twenty pages each. There is an extensive book review section. An average of ten books are evaluated in an in-depth review by individuals with similar credentials as the authors of full length papers.

271.   Journal of Environmental Economics and Management. DATE FOUNDED: 1974. FREQUENCY: q. PRICE: $72/yr. PUBLISHER: Academic Press, Inc., 111 Fifth Avenue, New York, New York 10003. EDITORS: Allen V. Kneese, Ralph C. D'Arge. ILLUSTRATIONS. INDEX. ADVERTISEMENTS. CIRCULATION: 1,100. MANUSCRIPT SELECTION: Editors. REPRINTS: Authors. INDEXED/ABSTRACTED: BPIA, InEcA, JEL, PAIS, WAERSA. DATABASES: CAB AB, ECONLIT, MC, PAIS INT. TARGET AUDIENCE: AC, SP.

The Journal of Environmental Economics and Management publishes both "theoretical and empirical papers devoted to specific environmental issues." The Journal presents papers covering economic analyses of environmental concerns or resource management topics. A major emphasis in recent issues has been environmental pollution controls. Other topics covered in recent issues include studies on secondary material markets (i.e. scrap steel, wastepaper), exhaustible natural resources, fisheries management, soil conservation, and pesticide efficacy. The articles are scholarly in style and employ advanced quantitative methodologies. The authors are economists from the U.S., Canada, Western Europe, and Israel. Most are affiliated with universities but some are with private research institutes or government agencies. The editorial board includes individuals from distinguished universities in the U.S., Canada, Western Europe, and Japan.

A typical issue includes six or seven articles of ten to fifteen pages each and one or two notes of four pages each. Each issue lists the officers of the Association of Environmental and Resource Economists, a professional organization having a close relationship with the Journal.

272.   The Journal of European Economic History. DATE FOUNDED: 1972. FREQUENCY: 3/yr. PRICE: Free. PUBLISHER: Banco di Roma, Via del Corso, 307, 00186 Rome, Italy. EDITOR: Luigi de Rosa. ILLUSTRATIONS. INDEX. CIRCULATION: 3,500. MANUSCRIPT SELECTION: Editor and Editorial Board. REPRINTS: Publisher. BOOK REVIEWS. INDEXED/ABSTRACTED: InEcA, IntBibE, JEL, PAIS. DATABASES: ECONLIT, PAIS INT. TARGET AUDIENCE: AC, SP. SAMPLE COPIES: Individuals.

The Journal of European Economic History is devoted to "the study of the
economic history of various European countries." The Journal covers the
history of specific industries, the influence of public policies on
economic development, and European trade. Recent issues have dealt with
the Russian beet sugar industry, the British cotton textile industry,
and the mining industry of Germany. Topics dealing with public policies
include fiscal policy in 19th century Germany, economic policies in the
Netherlands in the 19th and 20th centuries, and economic reform in
Hungary in the 1950's. Articles focusing on European trade include
topics such as the Baltic trade in the 18th Century, the wheat trade in
17th century Sicily, and the rise of trade in the port of Rowen. The
articles span the time from the medieval period to the present. Some
articles deal with historical analysis according to Marxist writers. The
articles are expository in style and may incorporate tables of data. The
authors are academics at universities in the U.S., Canada, Australia,
and Europe. Most of the members of the Editorial Board are faculty from
European universities. This publication most closely resembles Journal
of Economic History in subject coverage.
   A typical issue includes three to four full length articles and three
to five shorter notes. There is an extensive book review section. From
eight to eleven books are reviewed by professors from various universities.

273.   The Journal of Finance. DATE FOUNDED: 1946. FREQUENCY: 5/yr.
PRICE: $40/yr. institutions, $25/yr. personal. PUBLISHER: New York
University, Graduate School of Business, 100 Trinity Place, New York,
New York 10006. EDITORS: Edwin J. Elton, Martin J. Gruber. ILLUSTRA-
TIONS. INDEX. ADVERTISEMENTS. CIRCULATION: 7,000. MANUSCRIPT SELECTION:
Editors and Editorial Board. MICROFORMS: KR, MIM. REPRINTS: UMI. BOOK
REVIEWS. SPECIAL ISSUES. INDEXED/ABSTRACTED: AcctInd, BPI, BPIA,
FedTaxArt, InEcA, IntBibE, JEL, KeyEcs. DATABASES: ACCTIND, ECONAB,
ECONLIT, MC. TARGET AUDIENCE: AC, SP.

The Journal of Finance is the publication of the American Finance
Association and is the foremost journal in this field. It publishes
research articles in all areas of finance. Articles deal mainly with
problems and issues having to do with financial markets, corporate
financial policy, optimal portfolio selection, capital structure theory,
and the banking industry. Articles typically are concerned with topics
such as futures markets, auctions, arbitrage pricing theory, stocks,
bonds, interest rate determination, tax effects, takeover bids, inflation effects, option pricing, fixed versus variable rate loans, and the
deregulation of the banking industry. Most articles are technical in
nature. Many introduce a formal model expressed in mathematical equations and present empirical verification using statistical and econometric methodologies. Most authors are academics at graduate schools of
business and economics departments, but some are researchers with
institutes or private firms. The majority are American, but quite a few
are Canadian or British. Articles cover about the same subject area, but
are a bit less theoretical, quantitative and economics oriented than The
Journal of Financial Economics.
   Each of four issues per year contains from twelve to fifteen full-
length articles, two to five shorter notes, some comments and replies,
and from four to seven one-to-two page signed book reviews. A fifth
issue (July) is devoted to publishing the papers and proceedings of the

annual meeting of the American Finance Association. A subject and author
index is included in the December issue.

274.   Journal of Financial and Quantitative Analysis. DATE FOUNDED:
1966. FREQUENCY: q. PRICE: $30/yr. institutions, $20/yr. personal.
PUBLISHER: University of Washington, Graduate School of Business
Administration, Seattle, Washington 98195. EDITOR: Robert C. Higgins.
ILLUSTRATIONS. INDEX. ADVERTISEMENTS. CIRCULATION: 2,400. MANUSCRIPT
SELECTION: Editor and Referees. MICROFORMS: KR, MIM, UMI. REPRINTS: UMI.
INDEXED/ABSTRACTED: AcctInd, BPI, BPIA, InEcA, JEL, PAIS. DATABASES:
ACCTIND, ECONLIT, MC, PAIS INT. TARGET AUDIENCE: AC, SP.

The Journal of Financial and Quantitative Analysis published by the
University of Washington is also the Journal of the Western Finance
Association. Its purpose is to publish articles that "develop new
theories, empirical tests of theories in issues in public policy and
financial affairs of individuals, firms, and institutions." Topics
covered in recent issues include arbitrage pricing theory, stock
returns, refunding noncallable debt, the effectiveness of hedging,
portfolio choice, the asset substitution problem, the capital asset
pricing model, put prices, returns to owners of merged firms, negotiated
brokerage commissions, and floating rate notes. Most articles contain
some empirical work. A few are contributions as statistical studies, but
even these relate to some financial problem or issue. The typical
article is quite technical using both mathematics and statistics. Almost
all the authors are academics associated with American business schools.
The scope and coverage is very close to the Journal of Finance, which
publishes slightly more sophisticated works by authors at more prestigious universities.
   A typical issue contains nine articles, each about fifteen pages in
length. The December issue contains fewer regular articles but includes
selected papers from the Western Finance Association Annual Meeting.

275.   Journal of Financial Economics. DATE FOUNDED: 1974. FREQUENCY:
q. PRICE: $122/yr. institutions, $46/yr. personal. PUBLISHER: Elsevier
Science Publishers B.V., P.O. Box 1991, 1000 BZ, Amsterdam, The Nether-
lands. EDITOR: Editorial Board. ILLUSTRATIONS. INDEX. ADVERTISEMENTS.
MANUSCRIPT SELECTION: Editorial Board. MICROFORMS: Elsev., MIM. SPECIAL
ISSUES. INDEXED/ABSTRACTED: BPIA, CREJ, InEcA, JEL. DATABASES: ECONLIT,
MC. TARGET AUDIENCE: AC, SP. SAMPLE COPIES: Libraries and Individuals.

The Journal of Financial Economics is published in collaboration with
the Graduate School of Management of the University of Rochester. It is
a high-level technical journal in the general area of financial economics. It publishes analytical, mathematical and empirical contributions in the major areas of "consumption and investment decisions under
uncertainty, portofolio analysis, theories of market equilibrium, the
dynamic behavior of asset prices in the financial and real sectors and
the concept of efficient markets, relationships between the financial
and real sectors, and normative theory of financial management." It
covers the same over-all subject areas, but is somewhat more theoretical, quantitative and oriented toward economics than the Journal of
Finance. Both are prestigious journals. The majority of authors are
American academics in graduate departments of business and economics.

Occasionally a paper appears by a Canadian, British, Australian, or Israeli researcher.
Most issues contain from five to seven articles. Occasionally a special issue is published such as the one that included three papers of a symposium on futures pricing (1981) or a special volume such as the nearly 500 page (fifteen papers) on "The Market for Corporate Control: The Scientific Evidence" published in 1983.

276.   The Journal of Financial Research. DATE FOUNDED: 1978. FRE-QUENCY: q. PRICE: $40/yr. institutions, $18/yr. personal. PUBLISHER: School of Business Administration, Georgetown University, Washington, DC 20057. EDITOR: David A. Walker. ILLUSTRATIONS. INDEX. ADVERTISEMENTS. MANUSCRIPT SELECTION: Editors. TARGET AUDIENCE: AC, SP.

The Journal of Financial Research is the official and joint publication of the Southern Finance Association and the Southwestern Finance Association. The editorial policy of the Journal interprets "financial research" to include financial management, investments, financial institutions, capital market theory and portfolio theory. Its focus is on financial decision-making and policy-making at the level of the individual unit of operation as opposed to the macroeconomic level. While its scope and interest very much overlaps with the Journal of Finance, the Journal of Financial Economics and the Journal of Financial and Quantitative Analysis, it is closest to the latter in its micro focus. Of these four journals, The Journal of Financial Research presents fewest formal models. Most articles have a substantial amount of empirical content. They are technical in nature and employ mathematical and statistical methodologies. The authors are primarily academics associated with American schools of business and departments of economics.
Most issues contain either eight or nine articles ranging from ten to fifteen pages in length. An author index appears in the December issue.

277.   Journal of Forecasting. DATE FOUNDED: 1982. FREQUENCY: q. PRICE: $69.50/yr. PUBLISHER: John Wiley & Sons Ltd., Baffins Lane, Chichester, Sussex, PO19 1UD, England. EDITOR: Spyros Makridakis. INDEX. ADVERTISE-MENTS. CIRCULATION: 1,250. MANUSCRIPT SELECTION: Editor and Referees. MICROFORMS: UMI. REPRINTS: UMI. BOOK REVIEWS. SPECIAL ISSUES. INDEXED/ABSTRACTED: BPIA, PAIS. DATABASES: MC, PAIS INT. TARGET AUDIENCE: AC, SP. SAMPLE COPIES: Libraries and Individuals.

The Journal of Forecasting is an interdisciplinary publication in that it covers the use of forecasting systems in both the management area (marketing, accounting, production, finance, and organizational behavior) and the social sciences (psychology, sociology, demography, and economics). JOF also includes articles that deal with the evaluation of various forecasting methodologies, econometric forecasting, time series forecasting, impact of uncertainty on decision making, and financial forecasting. JOF presents articles that deal with theoretical aspects of forecasting methodologies as well as articles that deal with practical applications. The articles are scholarly in style with extensive references. Most of them incorporate mathematical and/or statistical methodologies. The authors are academics from departments of business, economics, or social science. About half are from American universities.

The others are from Canada and Western Europe. JOF is more scholarly
than the Journal of Business Forecasting Methods & Systems.
    A typical issue contains six to nine full length articles. Occasion-
ally a special issue is dedicated to a specific topic under the direction of guest editors. Some issues include several shorter comments and
replies to the comments on an important paper published in an earlier
issue. Each issue includes two to four signed book reviews. Some issues
have a "Clearinghouse" section listing papers that have not been
published but that can be obtained from the author.

278.   The Journal of Futures Markets. DATE FOUNDED: 1981. FREQUENCY:
q. PRICE: $120/yr. PUBLISHER: John Wiley & Sons, Inc., 605 Third Ave.,
New York, New York, 10158. EDITOR: Mark J. Powers. ILLUSTRATIONS. INDEX.
ADVERTISEMENTS. MANUSCRIPT SELECTION: Editors and Referees. MICROFORMS:
UMI. INDEXED/ABSTRACTED: AcctInd, BPIA, PAIS. DATABASES: ACCTIND, MC.
PAIS INT. TARGET AUDIENCE: AC, SP.

The Journal of Futures Markets is published in affiliation with the
Center for the Study of Futures Markets, Columbia Business School. It is
devoted to the "exploration of ideas and professional discussion of a
wide range of issues affecting all aspects of futures." This journal is
aimed at academics, practitioners and regulators. It, together with
Review of Research in Futures Markets, are the only professional
journals that are exclusively devoted to the study of futures. Articles
deal with the performance and contribution of organized futures markets
to society. They address questions such as "What is the role of futures
speculation in inflation?, How do financial futures affect monetary
policy? What role can futures play in aiding the development of third
world economies?, Should international cartels be allowed to use U.S.
futures markets for furthering their price policies?, and Do futures
have a place in pension and retirement portfolios?" They also focus on
practitioner interests such as price forecasting, modeling techniques,
and the development of hedge strategies. Some recent articles have
analyzed the economic effects of the new futures and options markets.
Articles are scholarly and usually quite technical in nature. The
majority of authors are academics at American departments of economics
or business.
    Most issues contain from seven to nine articles, "Legal Notes" and
"Futures Bibliography" sections. The latter is quite extensive, has a
separate editor, and is separated by topic. Occasionally a signed book
review is included.

279.   Journal of Health Economics. DATE FOUNDED: 1982. FREQUENCY:
3/yr. PRICE: $62/yr. institutions, $32.75/yr. personal. PUBLISHER:
Elsevier Science Publishers B.V. (North-Holland), P.O. Box 1991, 1000 BZ
Amsterdam, the Netherlands. EDITOR: Joseph P. Newhouse. ILLUSTRATIONS.
INDEX. ADVERTISEMENTS. MANUSCRIPT SELECTION: Editors. INDEXED/AB-
STRACTED: CREJ. DATABASES: EMBASE. TARGET AUDIENCE: AC, SP. SAMPLE
COPIES: Libraries and Individuals.

The Journal of Health Economics is an international publication covering
the economics of health and medical care. Its scope includes topics such
as demand and utilization of health services, financing of health
services, behavioral models of health care demanders and suppliers,

manpower planning and forecasting, cost-benefit and cost-effectiveness analyses, and efficiency and distributional aspects of health policy. The articles are scholarly with extensive references. Many present a theoretical model and demonstrate how empirical data validate the model. Others use data gathered from U.S. government surveys to prepare a statistical analysis of heatlh care problems. Most of the articles deal with situations in the U.S. but a few study other countries. Most of the authors are researchers affiliated with American universities, government agencies, or private research institutes. The Journal of Health Economics is more technical and emphasizes macro level economics more than Inquiry which focuses on the management of hospitals and other health care agencies.

Each issue includes three or four full length articles and two or three shorter notes. A special feature is the inclusion of two or three "Editorials" which are papers presenting a point of view on current health care problems. An annual index appears in the last issue of each volume.

280.   The Journal of Human Resources. DATE FOUNDED: 1966. FREQUENCY: 4/yr. PRICE: $32/yr. institutions, $16/yr. personal. PUBLISHER: The University of Wisconsin Press, Journals Department, 114 North Murray St., Madison, Wisconsin 53715. EDITOR: W. Lee Hansen. ILLUSTRATIONS. INDEX. ADVERTISEMENTS. CIRCULATION: 2,200. MANUSCRIPT SELECTION: Editor. MICROFORMS: MIM, UMI. INDEXED/ABSTRACTED: BPIA, Imed, InEcA, IntBibE, JEL, PersManageAbstr, SSI, WAERSA, WorkRelAbstr. DATABASES: CAB AB, ECONLIT, MC, MEDLINE, SSI. TARGET AUDIENCE: AC, SP. SAMPLE COPIES: Libraries.

The Journal of Human Resources is published under the auspices of the Industrial Relations Research Institute and the Institute for Research on Poverty at the University of Wisconsin. It publishes articles that analyze the "role of education and training in enhancing production skills, employment opportunities, and income, as well as of manpower, health, and welfare policies as they relate to the labor market and to economic and social development." Recent issues have included articles on mandatory retirement, occupational investment, on-the-job-training, the gender gap in earnings, quit rates, reverse discrimination, physician-induced demand, minimum wage effects, and teenage unemployment. Articles are technical in nature and make ample use of statistics and econometrics. Most present a model and have strong empirical content. A few concern themselves with a statistical or econometric technique rather than with a social issue. Most of the authors are economists associated with American universities. This publication resembles Journal of Labor Economics in subject coverage and level of scholarship.

Most issues contain six or seven articles plus from two to six "Communications." The latter cover both comments on previously published articles and brief articles or notes. An extensive "Books Received" list is included in each issue. An index is published in the Fall issue.

281.   The Journal of Industrial Economics. DATE FOUNDED: 1952. FREQUENCY: q. PRICE: $59.50/yr. institutions, $35/yr. personal. PUBLISHER: Basil Blackwell Publisher Ltd., 108 Cowley Road, Oxford OX4 1JF, England. EDITOR: Donald Hay. ILLUSTRATIONS. INDEX. ADVERTISEMENTS. CIRCULATION: 1,850. MANUSCRIPT SELECTION: Editors and Referees. MICRO-

FORMS: MIM, Publisher, UMI. REPRINTS: Publisher. SPECIAL ISSUES. INDEXED/ABSTRACTED: BPIA, BrithumI, InEcA, IntBibE, JEL, KeyEcS, PAIS, WorkRelAbstr. DATABASES: ECONAB, ECONLIT, MC, PAIS INT. TARGET AUDIENCE: AC, SP. SAMPLE COPIES: Libraries and Individuals.

The Journal of Industrial Economics is the leading analytical journal in the field of industrial organization. Articles analyze "modern industry, particularly the behavior of firms, and the functioning of markets" in industrial economies. Areas of special interest are: (1) the relationship between market structure and market behavior in the areas of pricing, product differentiation, advertising and the dissemination of research and development results, 2) the objectives, finance, investment, and growth of firms, and 3) the background environment within which industrial firms operate such as public policy on monopoly and restrictive trade practices, regulations, fiscal and monetary policy as they affect firms, and underlying changes in productivity and international competitiveness. Most articles blend theory and evidence. Many are case studies of industries or firms. The typical article is quite technical in nature and makes use of modern quantitative methodologies. Most articles are written by academic economists from industrial countries. The U.S. and England head the list, but other European countries as well as Canada and Australia are also represented. Occasionally an author will be associated with a government agency or a private firm. The Journal of Industrial Economics is more technical, contains more economic theory, and is less public policy oriented than The Antitrust Bulletin. Its subject coverage and technical level are similar to International Journal of Industrial Organization.

Most issues contain from six to eight articles. Some have an additional note or two, a comment on a previously published article, and possibly a reply.

282.   Journal of Industrial Relations. DATE FOUNDED: 1959. FREQUENCY: q. PRICE: $38/yr. PUBLISHER: Industrial Relations Society of Australia, G.J. Bennett Associates, P.O. Box 2260, Sydney, N.S.W. Z001, Australia. EDITOR: John Niland. INDEX. ADVERTISEMENTS. CIRCULATION: 4,000. MANUSCRIPT SELECTION: Editor. BOOK REVIEWS. INDEXED/ABSTRACTED: WorkRelAbstr. TARGET AUDIENCE: AC, SP.

The Journal of Industrial Relations deals primarily with labor and industrial relations in Australia. Recurring themes include union growth and concentration in Australia, Australian union structure, Australian labor law, the effects of specific wage policies, employment of women, and employment effects of technological change. Occasionally an article is not specifically concerned with Australian industrial relations such as those that survey some general theories of industrial relations and those that discuss industrial relations in another country. Recent issues contained articles on industrial relations in China, Japan, and Malaysia. Articles are non-technical and largely expository in nature. Most do not employ quantitative analysis. Almost all the articles are written by academic labor economists associated with Australian universities. The Journal covers the same subject area as Australian Bulletin of Labour.

A typical issue contains five or six articles averaging about fifteen pages in length. Many issues also include one or two addresses by Australian government labor officials. Some issues have a "Notes" section which may contain a short research paper, a comment on a previously published article, and/or a reply. The March issue of each volume contains an "Annual Review" section which has from four to six articles covering major Australian industrial relations happenings of the previous year. Some issues contain several signed book reviews.

283.   Journal of Institute of Economic Research. DATE FOUNDED: 1966. FREQUENCY: 2/yr. PRICE: $4/yr. PUBLISHER: Institute of Economic Research, Vidyagiri, Dharwad - 580 004, Karnatka State, India. EDITOR: N. Vajra kumar. ADVERTISEMENTS. MANUSCRIPT SELECTION: Editor. BOOK REVIEWS. INDEXED/ABSTRACTED: WAERSA. DATABASES: CAB AB. TARGET AUDIENCE: AC, GP, SP.

The Journal of Institute of Economic Research is published by a regional research institute in India. It includes "articles based on empirical research on socio-economic or demographic aspects" of specific regions on the entire country of India. The Journal's main emphasis is on family planning and population control. Recent issues have included articles on contraceptive practice surveys, birth and death rate estimation, population policy, family welfare programs, and mean age at marriage. Articles have also dealt with topics, such as employment, urbanization, health care services, assistance programs for small farmers, rural-urban migration, and public debt analysis. Most of the articles are descriptive in style and incorporate tables of data. A few employ quantitative methodologies. The authors are Indian scholars affiliated with universities, research institutes, or government agencies.
    A typical issue contains four to six articles, each varying in length from seven to thirty pages. Some issues have signed book reviews. A brief annual report of the Institute's activities is included in the last issue of each volume.

284.   Journal of International Business Studies. DATE FOUNDED: 1970. FREQUENCY: 3/yr. PRICE: $20/yr. PUBLISHER: University of South Carolina, Graduate School of Business, Columbia, South Carolina 29208. EDITOR: David A. Ricks. ILLUSTRATIONS. INDEX. CIRCULATION: 1,200. MANUSCRIPT SELECTION: Editors and Referees. MICROFORMS: UMI. REPRINTS: UMI. BOOK REVIEWS. SPECIAL ISSUES. INDEXED/ABSTRACTED: BPI, BPIA, InEcA, IntBibE, JEL, PAIS, Pred. DATABASES: ECONLIT, MC, PAIS INT, PF. TARGET AUDIENCE: AC, SP.

The Journal of International Business Studies, although published by a graduate school of business, is the membership journal of the Academy of International Business. The Academy is a professional association of individuals interested in international business education. JIBS publishes articles covering a broad range of topics relevant to international business. Both theoretical and applied studies are included. Recent issues covered topics such as international finance, multinational corporations in developing countries, studies of Korean and Japanese multinationals, international industries such as aluminum and coal, international political risk analysis, international technology transfer, and East-West industrial cooperation. There are also articles dealing with education in international business. The articles are scholarly and many employ sophisticated quantitative methodologies. The authors are professors of business and economics and are affiliated with universities all over the world. This publication covers the same subject area but provides a more technical approach than the Columbia Journal of World Business.

A typical issue includes ten to twelve full length articles. Occasionally a special issue with a guest editor is published such as the recent one devoted to "Cross-Cultural Management". Each issue has a "Dissertation Abstracts" section which announces recent dissertation titles with brief summaries. Six to eight signed book reviews appear in each issue.

285.   Journal of International Economics. DATE FOUNDED: 1971. FREQUENCY: q. PRICE: $166/yr. institutions, $57.70/yr. personal. PUBLISHER: Elsevier Science Publishers B.V. (North-Holland), P.O. Box 1991, 1000 BZ Amsterdam, The Netherlands. EDITORS: Richard A. Brecher, Jagdish N. Bhagwati, John S. Chipman. ILLUSTRATIONS. INDEX. ADVERTISEMENTS. MANUSCRIPT SELECTION: Editorial Board and Referees. MICROFORMS: Elsev., MIM. REPRINTS: Elsev. BOOK REVIEWS. INDEXED/ABSTRACTED: BPIA, CREJ, InEcA, IntBibE, JEL, KeyEcS, SSI. DATABASES: ABI, ECONAB, ECONLIT, MC, SSI. TARGET AUDIENCE: AC. SAMPLE COPIES: Libraries and Individuals.

The Journal of International Economics covers "analytical work in the pure theory of international trade and in balance-of-payments analysis." Articles employ econometric methodologies to analyze international trade problems. Recent issues have presented studies dealing with multinational enterprises, government intervention by establishing tariffs and cartels, the black market for foreign exchange, commodity trade, exchange rate instability, international migration flows, international capital transfer, and dumping in international markets. Each of the articles is very technical. Each one presents an econometric model of a hypothesis and then attempts to prove the validity of the hypothesis. The authors are economists from prestigious universities in the U.S. A few are from Canada, Western Europe, and Israel. The editorial board is composed of the same international mix. This Journal is quite comparable in complexity to Journal of Econometrics, Journal of Economic Theory, and International Economic Review.

Each issue includes ten to twelve articles, varying from twelve to twenty four pages in length. Six to eight books are reviewed in each issue. The reviews are substantial evaluations. Occasionally two titles on the same subject are reviewed on a comparative basis. All reviews are signed. Once a year, the editors acknowledge the assistance of the referees and list their names in the back of an issue.

286.   Journal of International Money and Finance. DATE FOUNDED: 1982. FREQUENCY: 3/yr. PRICE: $130/yr. institutions, $65/yr. personal. PUBLISHER: Butterworth Scientific Ltd., P.O. Box 63, Guildford, Surrey GU2 5BH England. EDITOR: Michale R. Darby. ILLUSTRATIONS. INDEX. MANUSCRIPT SELECTION: Editor. REPRINTS: Publisher and Authors. BOOK REVIEWS. INDEXED/ABSTRACTED: BPIA. DATABASES: MC. TARGET AUDIENCE: AC, SP. SAMPLE COPIES: Libraries and Individuals.

The Journal of International Money and Finance is a relatively new publication that presents research results in the following branches of international economics: foreign exchange markets; balance of payments; international monetary arrangements; international interactions of prices, incomes and money; finance of multinational corporations; foreign aid; and international economic institutions. The articles are scholarly in nature with extensive references. Most of them present an econometric model of the hypothesis and test the validity of the model with empirical data. Most of the authors are professors of business and economics affiliated with universities all over the world. A few are researchers with private institutes or banks. An international editorial board of academics provides policy leadership for this publication. The Journal overlaps the subject area of the Journal of International Business Studies. They are quite comparable in level of scholarship and technical expertise. The former concentrates on finance while the latter offers a broader range of topics.

A typical issue includes eight to ten articles of ten to fifteen pages each. Some issues include up to three signed book reviews. The last issue of each volume contains the annual index.

287.   Journal of Labor Economics. DATE FOUNDED: 1983. FREQUENCY: q. PRICE: $60/yr. institutions, $30/yr. personal. PUBLISHER: The University of Chicago Press, 5801 South Ellis Ave., Chicago, Illinois 60637. EDITOR: Edward P. Lazear. ILLUSTRATIONS. INDEX. ADVERTISEMENTS. MANU- SCRIPT SELECTION: Editors. MICROFORMS: UMI. SPECIAL ISSUES. TARGET AUDIENCE: AC, SP.

The Journal of Labor Economics is published in conjunction with the Economics Research Center of the National Opinion Research Center, the University of Chicago. It publishes articles reporting on "theoretical and empirical research in labor economics." Specifically, it is con- cerned with "the supply and demand for labor services, compensation, labor markets, the distribution of income, labor demographics, unions and collective bargaining, and applied and policy issues in labor economics." Recent issues have included articles dealing with right- to-work-laws, quit behavior, the earnings of different minority groups in the U.S., elderly workers, comparative reward schemes, retirement behavior, discouraged workers, and cost-of-living adjustment clauses. The Journal of Labor Economics is relatively new, but already a leading labor journal. It is a scholarly journal that publishes only technical articles in labor economics. The typical article presents a model and the empirical test results. It employs economic theory and quantitative methodologies. Most authors are academic economists associated with prestigious American universities. This publication is more analytical and technical than most labor journals. In level of scholarship and subject coverage it most closely resembles The Journal of Human Re- sources.

Most issues contain five or six articles ranging from twenty to thirty pages each. One special issue has been published to date, the April, 1984 issue of six essays in honor of Melvin W. Reder.

288.   Journal of Labor Research. DATE FOUNDED: 1980. FREQUENCY: q. PRICE: $47/yr. institutions, $25/yr. personal. PUBLISHER: Department of Economics, George Mason University, 4400 University Drive, Fairfax, Virginia 22030. EDITOR: James T. Bennett. ILLUSTRATIONS. INDEX. ADVER- TISEMENTS. CIRCULATION: 1,200. MANUSCRIPT SELECTION: Editor and Refer- ees. MICROFORMS: UMI. REPRINTS: Authors. BOOK REVIEWS. INDEXED/AB-

STRACTED: BPIA, HumRab, IntBibE, PAIS, WorkRelAbstr. DATABASES: MC, PAIS
INT. TARGET AUDIENCE: AC, SP. SAMPLE COPIES: Libraries.

The Journal of Labor Research seeks to "enhance understanding of the
political, economic, and social objectives and impacts of labor unions."
Its scope includes labor economics and labor relations in both the
private and public sectors of the United States. Compared to other labor
journals, it is the most ethnocentric as it only rarely publishes an
article dealing with a labor topic that is not concerned with a U.S.
situation. Within the U.S. context, articles run the gamut of the field.
Examples of recent topics include the effect of unions on relative
wages, right-to-work legislation, minimum-wage effects on nepotism,
union codetermination, union effects on employment stability, union
effects on productivity, compensation of union officials, and the
determinants of strikes. The majority of articles are theoretical and/or
empirical in nature. These may employ mathematical models and statistical methodologies. Occasionally expository articles are included. Most
authors are American academic economists. A few are economic researchers
at the U.S. Department of Labor, another U.S. Agency, or an American
research institute.

Issues contain from six to nine articles averaging about fifteen
pages in length. Each is preceded by a brief abstract. Most issues
include two signed book reviews.

289.   Journal of Law and Economics. DATE FOUNDED: 1958. FREQUENCY:
2/yr. PRICE: $28/yr. institutions, $20/yr. personal. PUBLISHER: The
University of Chicago Press, Journals Division, P.O. Box 37005, Chicago,
Illinois 60637. EDITORS: William M. Landes, Dennis W. Carlton, Frank H.
Easterbrook. ILLUSTRATIONS. INDEX. ADVERTISEMENTS. MANUSCRIPT SELECTION:
Editors. MICROFORMS: MIM, UMI. SPECIAL ISSUES. INDEXED/ABSTRACTED: BPIA,
ILP, InEcA, IntBibE, JEL, PAIS, SSI, WAERSA. DATABASES: CAB AB, ECONLIT,
MC, PAIS INT, SSI. TARGET AUDIENCE: AC, SP.

The Journal of Law and Economics is a publication associated with the
University of Chicago Law School, which to a considerable degree gave
birth to the field of law and economics. The field, as does the Journal,
deals with the economic analysis of law -- the interplay between
economic reasoning and legal analysis. The economic concepts of competition, efficiency, equity, and risk bearing are applied to legal dilem-
mas. Many articles cover the related fields of law and economics and
industrial organization. Articles might offer an economic analysis of a
particular antitrust law, the economic effects of various contractual
arrangements, the economic consequences of regulations and of deregulation, and the role played by laws and legal institutions in shaping
markets. The Journal of Law and Economics is a scholarly journal that
combines theory and evidence. Many articles have strong empirical
content. Some are technical and employ economic theory and mathematical
methodology. Most use statistical analysis. The authors are predominantly American academics who are associated with an economics department, a law school, or both.

A typical issue contains eight or nine articles. Occasionally a
special issue is published which contains the papers presented at a
conference such as recent ones on the "Intellectual Development of Law
and Economics" and "Corporations and Private Property."

290.   Journal of Macroeconomics. DATE FOUNDED: 1979. FREQUENCY: q.
PRICE: $26/yr. institutions, $20/yr. personal. PUBLISHER: Wayne State
University Press, 5959 Woodward Ave., Detroit, Michigan 48202. EDITOR:
David J. Smyth. ILLUSTRATIONS. INDEX. ADVERTISEMENTS. CIRCULATION: 800.
MANUSCRIPT SELECTION: Editor and Editorial Board. MICROFORMS: UMI.
REPRINTS: Authors. INDEXED/ABSTRACTED: InEcA, JEL. DATABASES: ECONLIT.
TARGET AUDIENCE: AC, SP. SAMPLE COPIES: Libraries and Individuals.

The Journal of Macroeconomics is a scholarly journal dealing with
aggregative economics. It emphasizes macroeconomic theory, but does
publish policy articles as well. It is international in scope, but more
articles relate to U.S. policies than to those of any other country. It
treats both fiscal and monetary theory and policy. Articles in recent
issues have dealt with topics such as the stability of the demand for
money, rational expectations, international transmission of inflation,
the natural rate of unemployment hypothesis, incomes policies, the
real-balance effect, the relationship between money growth and budget
deficits, and the dynamics of IS-LM models. Other articles focus on the
experience of specific nations such as the macroeconomic impact of
Federal Reserve behavior during a certain time period, the Nixon wage
and price controls, the Chinese hyperinflation in the late 1940s and the
Thatcher experiment in England. Articles are technical in nature and
make use of mathematics and statistics. Most present a model and
empirical test results. The editorial board includes some of the most
prominent macroeconomic economists in the world. The authors are a mix
of U.S. academics, European academics, and economists associated with
institutions such as the Federal Reserve System.
    A typical issue contains eight articles and from ten to twelve
annotations of "Recent Books in Macroeconomics". A title and author
index is published in the last issue of each volume.

291.   Journal of Mathematical Economics. DATE FOUNDED: 1974. FRE-
QUENCY: 3/yr. PRICE: $80/yr. PUBLISHER: Elsevier Science Publishers B.V.
(North-Holland), P.O. Box 1991, 1000 B2 Amsterdam, The Netherlands.
EDITOR: W. Hildenbrand. ILLUSTRATIONS. INDEX. ADVERTISEMENTS. MANUSCRIPT
SELECTION: Editorial Board. MICROFORMS: Elsev. REPRINTS: Authors.
INDEXED/ABSTRACTED: BPIA, CREJ, CurIS, InEcA, JEL, MathR. DATABASES:
ABI, ECONLIT, MC, MATHFILE. TARGET AUDIENCE: AC. SAMPLE COPIES: Li-
braries and Individuals.

The Journal of Mathematical Economics is a publication that serves as a
bridge between mathematics and economics. Its scope includes economic
theory that is of interest to mathematicians and contributions in
mathematics that can be used in economics. Recent issues have presented
papers dealing with competitive equilibria, core of an economy, equilibrium analysis, price adjustment and stability, preferences and utility,
game theory, demand theory, social choice and social welfare functions,
incentives and implementation, growth and optimal saving policy, and
miscellaneous mathematical topics. All of the articles present advanced
mathematical theories. The authors are academics from well known
universities in the U.S., Western Europe, and Israel. The editorial
board is composed of individuals from similar institutions. It is
comparable in scholarship and subject scope to International Journal of
Game Theory, Journal of Economic Dynamics and Control and Journal of
Economic Theory.

Each issue contains five full-length articles and some include a short note. An occasional special issue is devoted to a single topic with guest editors supervising the publication. A recent special issue focused on the "Implementation Problem."

292.   The Journal of Modern African Studies. DATE FOUNDED: 1963. FREQUENCY: q. PRICE: $90/yr. institutions, $44/yr. personal. PUBLISHER: Cambridge University Press, Box 110, Cambridge CB2 3RL, England. EDITOR: David Kimble. ILLUSTRATIONS. INDEX. ADVERTISEMENTS. CIRCULATION: 2,500. MANUSCRIPT SELECTION: Editor. MICROFORMS: UMI. BOOK REVIEWS: INDEXED/ ABSTRACTED: HistAb, IntBibE, SSI, WAERSA. DATABASES: CAB AB, HISTAB, SSI. TARGET AUDIENCE: AC, GP, SP.

The Journal of Modern African Studies is an interdisciplinary journal that surveys "politics, economics and related topics in contemporary Africa". It is intended for a wide audience; not only for academics, but for politicians, business people, diplomats, and civil servants. Articles in recent issues that have strong economic content have dealt with economic growth in Nigeria, economic problems in Lesotho, labor migration among African countries, agricultural policy and performance in sub-Saharan Africa, the Ivory Coast economic "miracle", and the role of the Arab Bank for African development. Many other articles have a political theme and still others focus on education and on social problems. Most articles are scholarly and avoid the adherence to a particular viewpoint or ideology. Articles are non-technical and while data are often introduced, they are not utilized in quantitative analysis. The authors are predominantly academics, the majority from England and the U.S.

Most issues contain six articles of about twenty pages each. An "Africana" section frequently adds from two to five shorter articles. The majority of issues contain a book review section in which as many as fifteen to twenty one-to-two page signed reviews are included. The December issue contains an author index which includes articles and reviews.

293.   Journal of Monetary Economics. DATE FOUNDED: 1975. FREQUENCY: 6/yr. PRICE: $153.85/yr. institutions, $46.90/yr. personal. PUBLISHER: Elsevier Science Publishers B.V. (North-Holland), P.O. Box 1991, 1000 BZ Amsterdam, The Netherlands. EDITOR: Karl Brunner. ILLUSTRATIONS. INDEX. ADVERTISEMENTS. MANUSCRIPT SELECTION: Editorial Board and Referees. MICROFORMS: Elsev. REPRINTS: Elsev. BOOK REVIEWS: INDEXED/ABSTRACTED: BPIA, CREJ, InEcA, IntBibE, JEL. DATABASES: ECONLIT, MC. TARGET AUDIENCE: AC, SP. SAMPLE COPIES: Libraries and Individuals.

The Journal of Monetary Economics is published in collaboration with the Graduate School of Management, University of Rochester. This publication serves as a forum for research studies in monetary economics. This field covers monetary analysis, structure of financial institutions, effects of changes in the banking structure, operation of credit markets, and various aspects of rates of return on assets. Recent issues dealt with topics such as exchange rate determination, government financing policies, interest rates and money demand, Federal Reserve policy, inflationary finance, long-term nominal wage contracts, and the role of inventories of finished goods in the business cycle. The articles are

technical and have both footnotes and references. The _Journal_ aims at prompt publication of manuscripts – a maximum period of one year from receipt to publication. It is highly selective and rejected close to 90% of submitted manuscripts in a recent ten month period. The authors are primarily academics at American universities but some are bank officers or academics from other countries. The _Journal_ overlaps the subject scope of _Journal_ of _Money,_ _Credit_ and _Banking._ The latter is somewhat less theoretical in its focus.
  A typical issue contains seven or eight full-length articles. An occasional signed in-depth book review is included.

294.   Journal of Money, Credit and Banking. DATE FOUNDED: 1969. FREQUENCY: q. PRICE: $28/yr. institutions, $22/yr. personal. PUBLISHER: Ohio State University Press, 2070 Neil Ave., Columbus, Ohio 43210. EDITORS: Stephen A. McCafferty, J. Huston McCulloch. ILLUSTRATIONS. INDEX. ADVERTISEMENTS. CIRCULATION: 3,700. MANUSCRIPT SELECTION: Editor and Referees. MICROFORMS: UMI. REPRINTS: UMI. BOOK REVIEWS. INDEXED/ ABSTRACTED: BPI, BPIA, InEcA, IntBibE, JEL, PAIS, SSI. DATABASES: ECONLIT, MC, PAIS INT, SSI. TARGET AUDIENCE: AC, SP. SAMPLE COPIES: Libraries.

The _Journal_ of _Money,_ _Credit_ and _Banking_ is published under the auspices of the Department of Economics of Ohio State University. A number of banks provide financial assistance. The _Journal_ covers a broad range of topics within the field of money, credit and banking. The major emphasis is on domestic conditions but a few articles deal with other countries. Recent issues include articles dealing with exchange rate determination, stock price movements, thrift institution deposits, state bonds, interest rates, monetary policy, inflation, and tax-exempt financing. Most of the articles are highly technical in nature and present an econometric analysis of the problem being studied. Occasionally a non-technical article presents an overview of an aspect of banking such as the role of clearinghouse associations or the role of Federal Reserve Banks. The authors are professors of finance or economics and economists with Federal Reserve Banks, private banks, or private research insti- tutes. The _Journal's_ Advisory Board is made up of internationally known economists. This publication is comparable in technical level to _Journal_ of _Banking_ and _Finance_ but the latter is more international in scope.
  A typical issue contains six full-length articles and four shorter "Notes, Comments, Replies". The "Money, Credit, and Banking Lecture" delivered at the Western Economic Association meeting appears in this journal. There is a substantial book review section. Signed reviews with references evaluate six to ten books per issue.

295.   The Journal of Peasant Studies. DATE FOUNDED: 1973. FREQUENCY: q. PRICE: ⌐ 46/yr. institutions, L 24/yr. personal. PUBLISHER: Frank Cass & Co. Ltd., Gainsborough House, 11 Gainsborough Road, London E11 IRS, England. EDITORS: T.J. Byres, C.A. Curwen. ILLUSTRATIONS. INDEX. ADVERTISEMENTS. CIRCULATION: 900. MANUSCRIPT SELECTION: Editors. BOOK REVIEWS. SPECIAL ISSUES. INDEXED/ABSTRACTED: IntBibE, PAIS, WAERSA. DATABASES: CAB AB, PAIS INT. TARGET AUDIENCE: AC, SP.

The _Journal_ of _Peasant_ _Studies_ is an interdisciplinary journal that focuses on peasant societies, both past and present. It is a scholarly

journal of essays and articles in the fields of economic history,
political history, economic development, social history, and anthropology. Most articles examine peasant societies in Asia, Africa, and
Latin America. They usually have a hypothesis or theme and do not merely
describe a situation. Many articles rely heavily on data but few are
technical in the sense that they present mathematical models or engage
in empirical testing using statistics or econometrics. The authors are
academics in departments of economics, history, political science,
anthropology, and sociology. The majority are British, but other
European countries, Australia, Canada, the U.S., and a few more are also
represented.
A typical issue is made up of three or four regular articles plus two
or three review articles. The latter are full-length essays that
critique one or more works on a particular theme. There is also a book
review section containing from six to twelve one-to-two page signed
reviews. About once a year a special issue is published such as the
recent ones on agrarian movements in India, sharecropping, and the
Agrarian Marxists.

296.   Journal of Philippine Development. DATE FOUNDED: 1974. TITLE
CHANGES: NEDA Journal of Philippine Development (1974-1980). FREQUENCY:
2/yr. PRICE: $18/yr. PUBLISHER: Philippine Institute for Development
Studies, NEDA Makati Bldg, 106 Amorsolo St., Legaspi Village, Makati,
Metro Manila, Philippines. EDITOR: Filologo L. Pante, Jr. ILLUSTRATIONS.
CIRCULATION: 300. MANUSCRIPT SELECTION: Editor and Editorial Board.
SPECIAL ISSUES. TARGET AUDIENCE: AC, SP. SAMPLE COPIES: Libraries and
Individuals.

The Journal of Philippine Development which was formerly published by
the Philippine National Economic and Development Authority is now
published by PIDS, a Philippine government research institute aimed at
conducting long-term policy oriented research. It is a scholarly journal
aimed at economic researchers and government policy makers and planners.
It concentrates on economic development planning in the Philippines.
Examples of development topics are Philippine population and development
planning, a comparative analysis of the administration of different
external agencies' official development assistance, the impact of
development loans to the Phillipines from 1956 to 1976, consumption
patterns of rural Philippine households, pricing port facilities and
services, and Philippine import flows. Some articles deal with topics
beyond the Philippine borders and discuss prospects for economic growth
in all of Southeast Asia. Articles vary greatly as to their technical
nature. Some are descriptive while others employ mathematics and
statistics. The authors are all Philippine economists associated with
the National Economic and Development Authority and/or the Philippine
Institute for Development Studies.
A typical issue contains five articles of varying lengths. The editor
of the journal intends to fill in the backlog of 1981 and 1982 issues
that were not published due to the change in publishers.

297.   Journal of Policy Modeling. DATE FOUNDED: 1979. FREQUENCY: q.
PRICE: $98/yr. institutions, $49/yr. personal. PUBLISHER: Elsevier
Science Publishing Co., Inc., 52 Vanderbilt Ave., New York, New York
10017. EDITOR: Antonio Maria Costa. ILLUSTRATIONS. INDEX. ADVERTISE-

MENTS. MANUSCRIPT SELECTION: Editor and Board of Editors. BOOK REVIEWS.
SPECIAL ISSUES. INDEXED/ABSTRACTED: BPIA, IntBibE. DATABASES: MC. TARGET
AUDIENCE: AC, SP. SAMPLE COPIES: Libraries and Individuals.

The Journal of Policy Modeling is the publication of the Society for
Policy Modeling. It is aimed at academics and decision makers who are
concerned with formal modeling techniques that aid in decision making.
"The Journal addresses questions of critical import to the world
community as a whole, and it focuses upon the economic, social, and
political interdependencies between national and regional systems." It
searches for improved methodological underpinnings of models for
decision making. Most articles present a model and then apply it to the
specific case of a nation or a region of the world. Recent examples are
agricultural investment in Peru, planning in Sri Lanka, policy responses
to external shocks in different groups of sub-Saharan African countries,
demand management policies in Asian countries, debt management in
Belgium, fiscal behavior in Canada, regulation policy in the U.S., and
investment policies in Hungary. Articles are technical and employ
economic theory, mathematics, and statistics. Many use simulation
techniques. The Board of Editors and Board of Advisers are made up of
well known scholars associated with prestigious universities and other
institutions from around the world. The authors reflect the Boards.
    Most issues include from six to eight articles. Some issues include
from one to three additional "survey" articles which have less original
content. Some issues have from one to three signed book reviews.
Occasionally a special issue is published such as a 1984 one which
contains six articles in honor of Jan Tinbergen.

298.   Journal of Political Economy. DATE FOUNDED: 1892. FREQUENCY:
6/yr. PRICE: $50/yr. institutions, $29/yr. personal. PUBLISHER: Univer-
sity of Chicago Press, 5801 Ellis Ave., Chicago, Illinois 60637. EDITOR:
Editorial Board. ILLUSTRATIONS. INDEX. ADVERTISEMENTS. CIRCULATION:
8,000. MANUSCRIPT SELECTION: Editorial Board and Referees. MICROFORMS:
Johnson, KR, MIM, UMI. REPRINTS: ISI, UMI. BOOK REVIEWS. SPECIAL ISSUES.
INDEXED/ABSTRACTED: ABC, AmerH, BPIA, InEcA, IntBibE, JEL, KeyEcS, SSI,
WAERSA, WorkRelAbstr. DATABASES: AMERH, CAB AB, ECONAB, ECONLIT, MC,
SSI. TARGET AUDIENCE: AC, SP.

The Journal of Political Economy is a publication associated with the
Department of Economics and the Graduate School of Business of the
University of Chicago. It is a scholarly journal that ranks among the
most prestigious in the discipline. It has a somewhat more micro than
macroeconomic orientation but publishes theoretical and empirical
research in virtually every field of economics. It, like the American
Economic Review, seeks high quality economic research articles without
restriction to field. JPE differs from the AER in that it will more
readily publish the "interesting idea" or the "interesting application"
such as the role of extrinsic uncertainty, how to elicit honest preferences for the assignment of a position, and a refutation of Marx's
hypothesis of the uniform length of the working day. Recurring areas of
interest include the economics of information, the effects of implicit
contracts, and welfare considerations in a variety of economic activities. Articles are technical in nature, many present a model and
empirical test results, and virtually all make significant use of
quantitative methodologies. The majority of authors are academic

economists associated with prestigious American universities. Others are
Canadian, Israeli, and European academics and economic researchers at
well-known economic research institutes.

Most issues contain about eight articles which range from ten to
sixty pages in length. Many issues include one or two brief comments
and/or a brief "Confirmations and Contradictions" article and/or a novel
note in a "Miscellany" section. All issues have a book review section
containing from two to five signed book reviews and a provocative
history of economic thought quote on the back cover.

299.   Journal of Post Keynesian Economics. DATE FOUNDED: 1978.
FREQUENCY: q. PRICE: $37.50/yr. institutions, $26/yr. personal. PUB-
LISHER: Myron E. Sharpe, Inc., 80 Business Park Drive, Armonk, New York
10504. EDITOR: Paul Davidson. ILLUSTRATIONS. INDEX. ADVERTISEMENTS.
CIRCULATION: 1,500. MANUSCRIPT SELECTION: Editors. INDEXED/ABSTRACTED:
BPIA, InEcA, IntBibE, JEL. DATABASES: ECONLIT, MC. TARGET AUDIENCE: AC,
SP. SAMPLE COPIES: Libraries and Individuals.

The Journal of Post Keynesian Economics is a scholarly and high quality
heterodox journal. It seeks to publish "innovative theoretical work that
can shed fresh light on contemporary economic problems" and to contest
the "conformist orthodoxy" that its editors believe "now suffuses
economic journals in the United States". The title of the Journal
reveals its great respect for John M. Keynes who it claims had the
vision of "the open-ended nature of economic study." JPKE's subject
scope is quite broad and not limited to macroeconomics. Articles cover
economic methodology, the history of economic thought, and market versus
government solutions to economic problems. Most articles do not introduce a formal model and/or the results of empirical testing, but are
rather critiques of others' works presented in an expository style. Some
articles employ quantitative methodologies but many do not. The authors
are predominantly academic economists associated with American and other
industrialized countries' universities.

Most issues include from twelve to fifteen articles plus two or three
brief comments. An "Editor's Corner" allows the Editor or his guest to
make some pronouncements. Articles critical of a contemporary economist's views are published together with an invited reply from that
economist. Portions of some issues are devoted to special symposia such
as recent ones honoring Nicholas Kaldor and John K. Galbraith.

300.   Journal of Public Economics. DATE FOUNDED: 1972. FREQUENCY:
9/yr. PRICE: $300/yr. institutions, $115/yr. personal. PUBLISHER:
Elsevier Science Publishers B.V. (North-Holland), P.O. Box 1991, 1000 BZ
Amsterdam, The Netherlands. EDITORS: A.B. Atkinson, N.H. Stern. ILLUS-
TRATIONS. INDEX. ADVERTISEMENTS. MANUSCRIPT SELECTION: Editorial Board.
MICROFORMS: Elsev. BOOK REVIEWS: SPECIAL ISSUES. INDEXED/ABSTRACTED:
BPIA, CREJ, InEcA, IntBibE, JEL, PAIS, PolSciAb. DATABASES: ABI,
ECONLIT, MC, PAIS INT. TARGET AUDIENCE: AC, SP. SAMPLE COPIES: Li-
braries.

The Journal of Public Economics is a publication that emphasizes "the
application of modern economic theory and methods of quantitative
analysis" to the problems of public sector economics. Articles concentrate on problems in the U.S. but other Western industrialized countries

are included. Recent issues have dealt with topics such as the effects of the property tax, financing of public education, public health insurance, income tax reforms, effects of unemployment insurance, theory of social choice, costs of environmental quality control, and social security reforms. The articles are scholarly in nature with extensive references. Each one presents a mathematical model of the problem under consideration. Some articles use empirical data to validate the model and others restrict themselves to mathematical proofs. The authors are economists from the U.S., Canada, the U.K., various Western European countries, and Israel. Half the Editorial Board is made up of professors from prestigious U.S. universities and the rest from comparable institutions in Canada, Western Europe, and Israel.

A typical issue contains five to seven full-length articles. Occasionally one or two short notes are included. Some special issues have been published. Two recent ones present the proceedings of international conferences.

301.   Journal of Regional Science. DATE FOUNDED: 1958. FREQUENCY: q. PRICE: $45/yr. institutions, $28/yr. personal. PUBLISHER: Regional Science Research Institute, 256 N. Pleasant St., Amherst, Massachusetts 01002. EDITOR: Ronald E. Miller. ILLUSTRATIONS. INDEX. CIRCULATION: 2,500. MANUSCRIPT SELECTION: Editor and Referees. MICROFORMS: UMI. REPRINTS: UMI. BOOK REVIEWS. SPECIAL ISSUES. INDEXED/ABSTRACTED: BPIA, CREJ, InEcA, IntBibE, JEL, SSI. DATABASES: ECONLIT, MC, SSI. TARGET AUDIENCE: AC, SP. SAMPLE COPIES: Libraries.

The Journal of Regional Science is published in cooperation with the Department of Regional Science of the University of Pennsylvania. The Journal covers an interdisciplinary field combining aspects of both economics and geography. The main focus of the Journal is the development and empirical testing of theory. Some typical topic areas include industrial location, spatial structure of urban areas, regional economic growth and development, interregional migration, housing, transportation, and employment. Most of the studies focus on the U.S. but occasionally an article will cover a study in another country such as Canada or Great Britain. The articles are highly technical in content. Most of them present an econometric model and test its validity with empirical data. Half of the authors are academics from American universities. The others are from universities in Japan, Canada, England, and other countries.

A typical issue includes nine full-length articles. Occasionally an issue includes the proceedings of a symposium in addition to other articles. Each issue includes an average of five signed book reviews. A regular feature is a bibliography of selected titles of articles from current journals that are of potential interest to readers.

302.   Journal of Reprints for Antitrust Law and Economics. DATE FOUNDED: 1969. FREQUENCY: 2/yr. PRICE: $45/yr. institutions, $30/yr. personal. PUBLISHER: Federal Legal Publications, Inc., 157 Chambers St., New York, New York 10007. EDITOR: James M. Clabault. ILLUSTRATIONS. INDEX. ADVERTISEMENTS. CIRCULATION: 900. MANUSCRIPT SELECTION: Guest Editors. REPRINTS: UMI. TARGET AUDIENCE: AC, SP.

The Journal of Reprints for Antitrust Law and Economics, as stated in
its title, reprints previously published articles in the field of
antitrust law and economics. The subject matter is the same as in The
Antitrust Bulletin, a journal by the same publisher, which contains
original articles. The editor of this reprint journal selects a topic
for each issue and one or more guest editors who is (are) given the task
of selecting the articles to be included in that issue. Examples of
topics are joint ventures, barriers to entry, the concept of relevant
market, conscious parallelism, conglomerate mergers, resale price
maintenance, predatory conduct, patents, and competition and regulation.
Occasionally issues have been devoted to an important report or conference concerning antitrust law and economics. The articles and reports
chosen for reprint vary greatly in type and source. A few are technical
economic research papers but most are expository in style. They were
originally published in economics journals, law reviews, books, and
government or private reports. The authors are predominantly academics
at law schools or departments of economics.
    The typical issue is from 500 to 600 pages and contains from ten to
twenty contributions.

303.   The Journal of Risk and Insurance. DATE FOUNDED: 1933. TITLE
CHANGES: Journal of Insurance (1957-1963). American Association of
University Teachers of Insurance Journal (1933-1957). FREQUENCY: q.
PRICE: $35/yr. PUBLISHER: American Risk and Insurance Association, Inc.,
Rm. 297 Brooks Hall, The University of Georgia, Athens, Georgia 30602.
EDITOR: C. Arthur Williams, Jr. ILLUSTRATIONS. INDEX. ADVERTISEMENTS.
CIRCULATION: 2,200. MANUSCRIPT SELECTION: Editors and Referees. MICRO-
FORMS: UMI. REPRINTS: ISI, UMI. BOOK REVIEWS. INDEXED/ABSTRACTED: BPI,
BPIA, InEcA, JEL, PAIS. DATABASES: ECONLIT, MC. PAIS INT. TARGET
AUDIENCE: AC, SP.

The Journal of Risk and Insurance is the publication of the foremost
professional association in the field of insurance and risk. This
scholarly journal is aimed at researchers interested in this field. The
journal covers a broad range of risk and insurance research topics
including risk management, pricing strategies, workers compensation,
pension plans, rate discrimination, portfolio analysis, regulation,
actuarial methods, efficiency and equity questions surrounding the
insurance industry, the effects of inflation on pension benefits and
retirement, and the degree of monopoly control in specific insurance
markets. Most articles are technical and make use of quantitative
methodologies. Some introduce mathematical models, while others employ
econometric or statistical analysis. The majority of authors are
academics at American business schools, but academics from other Western
Countries and researchers with private firms or government agencies are
also represented.
    A typical issue contains six feature articles and four or five
shorter notes. Some issues include an "Invited Paper". All issues have a
"From the Library Shelf" section that contains about twenty annotations
of recently published books or articles and some brief discussions of
recent court decisions. Some issues have a "Reviews" section with from
one to five signed book reviews. Information concerning the ARIA is
provided in an "Association Business" section.

304.   The Journal of Social, Political and Economic Studies. DATE
FOUNDED: 1976. TITLE CHANGES: The Journal of Social and Political
Affairs (1976). The Journal of Social and Political Studies (1977-1980).
FREQUENCY: q. PRICE: $40/yr. institutions, $20/yr. personal. PUBLISHER:
Council for Social and Economic Studies, Suite Comm 2, 1133 13th St.,
N.W., Washington D.C. 20005. EDITOR: Roger Pearson. INDEX. ADVERTISE-
MENTS. CIRCULATION: 1,100. MANUSCRIPT SELECTION: Editors. BOOK REVIEWS.
SPECIAL ISSUES. INDEXED/ABSTRACTED: ABC, HistAb, IntBibE, PAIS, SocAb.
DATABASES: HISTAB, PAIS INT, SOCAB. TARGET AUDIENCE: AC, GP, SP.

The Journal of Social, Political and Economic Studies is published in
cooperation with the Contemporary Economics and Business Association at
George Mason University. It is an interdisciplinary journal dealing with
contemporary public policy issues "in areas of social, political,
economic, and international concern." The Journal reflects its publisher's concern for individual freedom and the power of the market.
Topics covered vary widely. They include private eion and the law, U.S.
- Soviet relations, trade union power, inflation in the U.S. and other
countries, meeting the Soviet military challenge, regulatory policies in
the U.S., monetary policy, and the export of U.S. technology.
ArticlU.S., monetary policy, and the export of U.S. technology. Articles are written in a narrative style and are non-technical
in nature. Some articles include data presented in tables or charts, but
no quantitative analysis is engaged in. The authors are a mixed group
including academics, political figures, journalists, researchers, and
consultants. They are predominantly American and the majority are either
economists or political scientists.
    Most issues contain from five to seven articles varying greatly in
length. Some issues include one or two book reviews which are not always
signed. Occasionally an entire issue will be devoted to a single topic
under the guidance of a guest editor or will contain the papers presented at a conference.

305.   Journal of the American Planning Association. DATE FOUNDED:
1935. TITLE CHANGES: Journal of the American Institute of Planners
(1935-1978). FREQUENCY: q. PRICE: $20/yr., members, $30/yr., non-
members. PUBLISHER: American Planning Association, 1313 East 60th
Street, Chicago, Illinois 60637. EDITORS: Raymond J. Burby, Edward
Kaiser. ILLUSTRATIONS. INDEX. CIRCULATION: 13,000. MANUSCRIPT SELECTION:
Editors and Referees. MICROFORMS: UMI. BOOK REVIEWS. INDEXED/ABSTRACTED:
BPIA, IntBibE, SSI, UAA. DATABASES: MC, SSI. TARGET AUDIENCE: AC, GP.
SP.

The Journal of the American Planning Association is a professional
journal with a broad interdisciplinary outlook. It is intended to
provide a "key communications link among a diverse worldwide readership
of practicing planners, planning educators, and friends in related
fields." Economists, sociologists, urban affairs specialists, environ-
mentalists, and public policy officials are the "friends in related
fields" referred to by the editors. JAPA covers diverse topics in such
areas as housing, transportation, water usage, and demographics. The
articles are scholarly in nature with extensive references. Most of them
are descriptive in style and do not employ mathematical methodology. The
authors include practicing planners, academic economists, urban planning
officials, academic geographers, and civil engineers.

A typical issue contains five to eight articles, ranging from eight
to fifteen pages in length. Each issue has the following regular
features: "The Planner's Notebook" -- an article discussing new technology or methodology, "Commentary" — short opinion pieces on current
issues, "Conference Calendar" -- a schedule of meetings of interest to
Association members, "Letters to the Editor" -- letters from readers
commenting on previously published articles, and "Periodical Literature
in Urban Studies and Planning" -- citations of selected articles
arranged in subject categories. An extensive book review section is
included in each issue. Eighteen to twenty books covering a broad range
of economic and urban planning subjects are evaluated in one to two page
signed reviews. Many issues feature a "Symposium" which consists of a
group of articles addressing a specific theme. Recent themes included
"Canadian Planning", "High Technology and Economic Development," and
"Growth Management."

306.   The Journal of The Institute for Socioeconomic Studies. DATE
FOUNDED: 1976. FREQUENCY: q. PRICE: Free. PUBLISHER: The Institute for
Socioeconomic Studies, Airport Road, White Plains, New York 10604.
EDITOR: B.A. Rittersporn, Jr. ILLUSTRATIONS. INDEX. CIRCULATION: 17,500.
MANUSCRIPT SELECTION: Editor. BOOK REVIEWS. TARGET AUDIENCE: GP.

The Journal of The Institute for Socioeconomic Studies is published by a
non-profit, non-partisan research institute. The Journal serves as a
forum for discussions on "the quality of life, economic development,
social motivation, poverty, urban regeneration, and the problems of the
elderly." Conditions in the U.S. are emphasized but articles covering
Canada, West Germany, Jamaica, and other countries have appeared.
Examples of topics dealing with U.S. problems discussed in recent issues
are social security reforms, minimum wage laws, the federal budget,
welfare programs, and education. Articles dealing with other countries
focus either on economic development or social assistance programs. All
of the articles are written in a popular, non-technical style. Only some
of them incorporate data which is carefully documented. All of the
articles present a point of view but no one point of view dominates. The
authors are drawn from a wide variety of backgrounds. They include
members of congress, economists at research institutes, journalists,
academics, corporate executives, and staff members.
    A typical issue contains seven to nine full length articles. Some
articles are accompanied by photographs that illustrate the writer's
thesis. Each issue includes an average of six signed book reviews. A
cumulative subject and author index to the first seven volumes appears
in the first issue of volume eight.

307.   Journal of Transport Economics and Policy. DATE FOUNDED: 1967.
FREQUENCY: 3/yr. PRICE: $68/yr. institutions, $36/yr. personal. PUB-
LISHER: The London School of Economics and The University of Bath,
Claverton Down, Bath BA2 7AY, England. EDITOR: M.E. Beesley. ILLUSTRA-
TIONS. INDEX. ADVERTISEMENTS. CIRCULATION: 1,500. MANUSCRIPT SELECTION:
Editors and Referees. INDEXED/ABSTRACTED: BPIA, InEcA, JEL, PAIS.
DATABASES: ECONLIT, MC, PAIS, INT. TARGET AUDIENCE: AC, SP. SAMPLE
COPIES: Libraries.

The Journal of Transport Economics and Policy is jointly published by
two universities in England. It encompasses all forms of transportation
and all aspects of transportation economics and public policies on an
international scale. Articles do emphasize personal travel in the U.S.
Typical topics in that area include the impact of subsidies on cost of
urban public transport, economies of scale in the taxicab industry,
international air fares, labor problems in urban transit systems,
unlimited use transit passes, elasticity measures of travel options, and
cost-effectiveness of motor vehicle inspection. Other articles deal with
transportation of goods. Representative topics include deregulation of
freight rates in the European Community, coal rates on U.S. railroads,
Israeli investment in a shipping industry, and Canadian carriers on the
Great Lakes/St. Laurence Seaway System. The articles are written in a
scholarly style. Most of them employ econometric analysis of the problem
under investigation. About half the authors are academics at American
universities. The others are academics from the U.K., Israel, Canada,
and other countries or are government officials.

Each issue contains five or six articles ranging in length from
fifteen to twenty-five pages. Some issues include a few short notes. A
section of "Book Notes" features an annotated bibliography of new books
in the field. Each issue has abstracts of the articles in English,
French, and German.

308.   Journal of Urban Economics. DATE FOUNDED: 1974. FREQUENCY: 6/yr.
PRICE: $128/yr. PUBLISHER: Academic Press, Inc., 111 Fifth Avenue, New
York, New York 10003. EDITOR: Edwin S. Mills. ILLUSTRATIONS. INDEX.
ADVERTISEMENTS. MANUSCRIPT SELECTION: Editor. REPRINTS: Authors.
INDEXED/ABSTRACTED: BPI, BPIA, InEcA, JEL, PAIS. DATABASES: ECONLIT, MC,
PAIS INT. TARGET AUDIENCE: AC, SP.

The Journal of Urban Economics is a scholarly journal publishing
research papers on a wide range of topics related to urban economics.
The Journal emphasizes research studies of U.S. housing problems.
Typical topics include low-income government housing policies, rental
versus owner-occupied housing, urban housing stocks, rent control, urban
development grants, property taxes and the demand for housing, land
prices, land use policies, and effects of mortgage rates on home
ownership. Occasionally an article will deal with housing in another
country such as a recent one on the Korean housing market. Other
articles report the results of studies of demand for public education
and location theory of the firm. The articles are highly technical and
use quantitative analysis of the problem under consideration. Most of
the authors are American academics but a few are from Israeli or
Canadian universities or U.S. government research agencies. Many members
of the Editorial Board are faculty from distinguished American universities. The Journal is comparable in technical level and subject scope
to AREUEA Journal.

Each issue includes eight or nine articles of twelve to twenty pages
each. Some issues have short notes which may comment on previously
published papers.

309.   Journal of World Trade Law. DATE FOUNDED: 1967. FREQUENCY: 6/yr.
PRICE: $85/yr. PUBLISHER: Vincent Press, 10 Hill View Road, Twickenham,
TW1 1EB, England. EDITOR: Dennis Thompson. INDEX. ADVERTISEMENTS.

MANUSCRIPT SELECTION: Editor. BOOK REVIEWS. INDEXED/ABSTRACTED: BPIA,
InEcA, IntBibE, JEL, PAIS, WAERSA. DATABASES: CAB AB, ECONLIT, MC, PAIS
INT. TARGET AUDIENCE: AC, GP, SP.

The Journal of World Trade Law is a publication covering a number of
interrelated areas: economic development, world trade, trade agreements,
and trade laws. Recent articles dealing with the first two areas include
the following topics: rural industrialization in Italy, economic
analysis of Yugoslav joint ventures, Japan's direct investment in
California, international trade policies, and Latin American debt
crisis. The latter two areas are represented by topics such as the
international natural rubber agreement, export controls in GATT,
protectionism inside the EEC Treaty, and the Uruguayan-Argentinian Trade
Co-operation Agreement. The articles are expository in style and do not
use quantitative methodologies. Some of the articles cite court decisions, treaty provisions, or documented data. The authors have a variety
of backgrounds. Some of them are lawyers and others are economists. Some
are academics and others are researchers with various international
organizations such as EEC, OECD, UNCTAD, and other UN agencies. The
Journal concentrates on development and trade practices whereas Managing
International Development includes some policy and theoretical discussions.
    A typical issue includes three or four full-length articles and four
shorter notes. Each issue features an editorial on a current development
in world trade law. Some issues have up to three signed book reviews.

310.   Kajian Ekonomi Malaysia/Malaysian Economic Studies. DATE
FOUNDED: 1964. FREQUENCY: 2/yr. PRICE: M$24/yr. PUBLISHER: Persatuan
Ekonomi Malaysia, University of Malaya, Faculty of Economics and
Administration, Kuala Lumpur, Malaysia. EDITOR: Chee Peng Lim. ILLUSTRA-
TIONS. CIRCULATION: 1,500. MANUSCRIPT SELECTION: Editor and Editorial
Board. BOOK REVIEWS. TARGET AUDIENCE: AC, SP.

Kajian Ekonomi Malaysia/Malaysian Economic Studies is the publication of
the Malaysian Economics Association. This journal publishes empirical
studies on the economic conditions of countries in the Pacific region
but emphasizes studies relating to Malaysia. Recent issues have included
articles on demographic studies of peninsular Malaysia, commodities and
development of Malaysia, wealth distribution in Malaysia, Malaysia's
rice production, elasticities of export and domestic demand for Malaysian wood products, and petroleum products pricing in Malaysia. The
journal also accepted contributions dealing with Australia, Singapore,
and Japan. The articles vary in level of treatment from descriptive to
quantitative. About half of the authors are academics at the University
of Malaya. The rest are from universities in Australia, Singapore, the
U.S., the U.K., and other countries.
    A typical issue has five or six articles varying from fifteen to
twenty-five pages in length. Some issues include a signed book review.
As of 1985 there is a two year lag in the production schedule.

311.   Kansai University Review of Economics and Business. DATE
FOUNDED: 1972. FREQUENCY: 2/yr. PUBLISHER: Kansai University Press, P.O.
Box 50, Suita-shi, Osaka-fu, 564, Japan. EDITOR: Toshiya Kohdo. ILLU-

STRATIONS. INDEX. MANUSCRIPT SELECTION: Editor and Editorial Board.
TARGET AUDIENCE: AC, SP.

Kansai University Review of Economics and Business is a scholarly
journal featuring both theoretical and applied articles in economics and
business. The most recent issues, in contrast to those of the mid and
late 1970s, contain articles that are technical in nature and that
employ modern quantitative methodologies. Economics topics covered in
such articles include the theory of consumer behavior, monetary growth
models, interest-arbitrage theory, distribution of seigniorage in
international currency, and international trade. Technical papers with
more of a business orientation deal with topics such as management
organization, industrial relations, productivity management, and the
management of information systems. Other articles are non-technical such
as a description of overseas investment by Japan's Sogo-Shosha, and
articles that analyze English common-usage phrases used in business
letters. All of the authors are Japanese academics in departments of
economics or business administration. Most, if not all, are associated
with Kansai University. This journal is similar to KSU Economic and
Business Review.
     Each issue contains from two to six articles of varying lengths. A
very brief abstract precedes each article. Although most articles are in
English, occasionally one appears in German or Esperanto.

312.   Kansallis-Osake-Pankki Economic Review. DATE FOUNDED: 1948.
FREQUENCY: 2/yr. PRICE: $5/yr. PUBLISHER: Kansallis-Osake-Pankki,
Economic Research Department, Aleksanterinkatu 44, Box 10, SF-00101
Helsinki 10, Finland. EDITOR: Heikki Koivisto. ILLUSTRATIONS. INDEX.
CIRCULATION: 6,500. MANUSCRIPT SELECTION: Editor. MICROFORMS: UMI.
REPRINTS: UMI. INDEXED/ABSTRACTED: IntBibE, PAIS. DATABASES: PAIS INT.
TARGET AUDIENCE: AC, GP, SP.

Kansallis-Osake-Pankki Economic Review is the publication of the leading
commercial bank in Finland. It publishes articles dealing with the
Finnish economy and provides a detailed report on the current economic
situation in Finland. Occasionally an article deals with the Finnish
political scene. Topics discussed in recent issues include the following: the Finnish equities market, the rouble in Soviet-Finnish trade,
the Finnish exchange rate system, energy-saving methods in Finland, the
forest industry in Finland, the tourist industry in Finland, and the
structure and development of the Finnish economy. Articles are written
so as to communicate to business people. They are narrative in style,
but include tables of data, charts and graphs. The authors are Finnish
professionals from government, industry, and academe. Their affiliations
include the Kansallis-Osake-Pankki Bank, the Bank of Finland, the
Central Statistical Office, the Labor Institute for Economic Research ,
the Ministry of Trade and Industry, and several universities.
     Each issue contains from one to three articles, a report on the
economic situation of Finland, and a "Facts about Finland" section.
Usually more than half of each issue is devoted to the economic report
which is divided into the following seven sections: 1) Foreign trade and
the balance of payments, 2) Consumption and investment, 3) Production,
4) Employment, 5) Prices, incomes and costs, 6) Public finance, and 7)
Money and stock market. The second issue of the 1984 volume contains a
cumulative author index dating back to 1948.

313.   **Keio Economic Studies.** DATE FOUNDED: 1963. FREQUENCY: 2/yr.
PRICE: $25.70/yr. PUBLISHER: Keio Economic Society, Keio Univeristy,
2-15-45 Mita, Minato-ku, Tokyo, 108, Japan. EDITOR: Denzo Kamiya.
ILLUSTRATIONS. INDEX. CIRCULATION: 800. MANUSCRIPT SELECTION: Editorial
Committee. TARGET AUDIENCE: AC, SP.

Keio Economic Studies is the publication of a research group at a noted
Japanese university. Its scope and coverage is very broad. Recent issues
have concentrated on theoretical work but over the past several years a
greater variety of articles have appeared. Many articles present
theoretical models employing sophisticated mathematics to prove theorems. Others present models and the empirical results found in testing
the models. These may involve economic development, economic growth, or
pricing models. Some articles are basically empirical studies such as
one that reported on the liberalization of interest rates of Japanese
long-term national bonds. Surprisingly this journal also publishes
expository economic history and political economy articles such as ones
dealing with industrialization in Japan during the 18th and 19th
centuries and the French presence in Africa. The publication of articles
on Australian trade unions and on macropolicy innovations in Poland
further show the diversity of coverage. About half the articles are
written by economists teaching at Keio University. The rest are contributed by academic economists at other Japanese universites as well as
American, British, French, and Australian universities.
    Most issues contain from five to seven articles. Some issues also
include a shorter article in a "Notes" section. Occasionally a German
language article is included.

314.   **Kentucky Economy: Review & Perspective.** DATE FOUNDED: 1977.
FREQUENCY: q. PRICE: Free. PUBLISHER: University of Kentucky, Center for
Business & Economic Research, College of Business and Economics, 301
Mathews Building, Lexington, Kentucky 40506. EDITOR: Margaret O'Neill
Adams. ILLUSTRATIONS. INDEX. CIRCULATION: 2,500. MANUSCRIPT SELECTION:
Editor. INDEXED/ABSTRACTED: PAIS. DATABASES: PAIS INT. TARGET AUDIENCE:
GP. SAMPLE COPIES: Libraries and Individuals.

Kentucky Economy: Review & Perspective supersedes Kentucky Economic
Outlooks and Kentucky Council of Economic Advisors: Quarterly Report.
Its main objective is to provide "current information concerning the
Kentucky economy." It publishes "expository articles, analyses of some
aspect of the Kentucky economy, forecast of the Kentucky economy, and
tables of selected data chosen as indicators of developments in the
Kentucky and national economies." This title is among the most parochial
of the business school publications. Others that also concentrate on
their home states are Montana Business Quarterly, Georgia Business and
Economic conditions, and Arizona Business. Recent issues have included
articles on the following topics: equity versus adequacy in Kentucky
taxation, the Kentucky state budget, Kentucky's public infrastructure
needs, Kentucky educational finance, Kentucky's worker's compensation
program, and Kentucky's unemployment insurance program. Articles are
generally non-technical, but most rely on a great deal of data that is
presented in tables and charts. Many articles contain footnotes. The
majority of articles are written by academics associated with the Center
at the University of Kentucky. Some are contributed by economists
working for the state of Kentucky.

In addition to an overview of the state economy, a typical issue
contains from one to three articles, a "News and Notes" section, and
tables of data on the economic activity of the U.S. and Kentucky
economies.

315.   **Kidma**. DATE FOUNDED: 1973. FREQUENCY: 2/yr. PRICE: $18/volume.
PUBLISHER: Israel Chapter, Society for International Development, 3
Moshe Wallach St., Jerusalem, 94385, Israel. EDITOR: Artur Isenberg.
ILLUSTRATIONS. ADVERTISEMENTS. CIRCULATION: 6,000. MANUSCRIPT SELECTION:
Editor and Editorial Board. BOOK REVIEWS. SPECIAL ISSUES. INDEXED/
ABSTRACTED: IntBibE, WAERSA. DATABASES: CAB AB. TARGET AUDIENCE: AC, GP.
SP. SAMPLE COPIES: Libraries and Individuals.

Kidma is subtitled Israel journal of development. It is a publication
covering the latest trends and accomplishments in Israel's economic
development. Articles cover many aspects of development such as agriculture, housing, industry, the environment, energy, and education.
Articles cover development projects primarily in Israel but other
countries' progress is reported on occasionally. Recent issues include
articles on agriculture in Nigeria, the cattle industry in Turkey, solar
energy research in Japan, and handicrafts in Latin America. Most of the
articles are descriptive and occasionally include tables of data and/or
diagrams. The authors are predominantly academics or researchers with a
few being practioners, government employees, or journalists. Most of the
authors are Israeli, many of whom received their professional training
in the U.S. or the U.K.
     A typical issue includes six articles of five or six pages each.
Abstracts of these articles in both French and Spanish appear as inserts
in the front of the issue. Regular features of each issue include the
following: "Kidma Reviews" - two or three signed book reviews, "Kidma
Reports" - eight to ten brief accounts of innovations in technology or
science, "SID Bulletin Board" - news reports relating to the Society for
International Development, and "Calendar of Conferences and Training
Courses in Israel." Kidma includes many photographs that complement the
articles.

316.   **Kobe Economic and Business Review**. DATE FOUNDED: 1953. FRE-
QUENCY: a. PRICE: Exchange basis. PUBLISHER: Kobe University, Research
Institute for Economics and Business Administration, Rokko, Kobe, 657,
Japan. ILLUSTRATIONS. INDEX. CIRCULATION: 600. INDEXED/ABSTRACTED:
AcctInd, InEcA, IntBibE, JEL. DATABASES: ACCTIND, ECONLIT. TARGET
AUDIENCE: AC, SP. SAMPLE COPIES: Libraries.

The Kobe Economic and Business Review is published by a research
institute affiliated with Kobe University. The Review publishes articles
covering a wide range of topics in both economics and business. Some
articles deal with accounting practices such as recent studies of
current cost accounting and conventional accounting income information.
Others deal with international trade and flexible exchange rate systems.
Some offer historical accounts of Japanese commercial banking and U.S.
modern corporate financial reporting. Others present theoretical papers
on economic growth models or simultaneous equations estimates. Empirical
studies of input-output tables for the Japanese shipping industry and a
comparative evaluation of the U.S. and Japanese economies have appeared

recently. The nature of the articles vary as much as the topics. Some are purely descriptive while others are quite technical and employ econometric models. All of the authors are academics and most of them are staff members of the Institute.

Each issue contains three to five lengthy articles. A brief report of the history of the Institute appears in each issue. A listing of the professional staff is on the inside back cover.

317.   KSU Economic and Business Review. DATE FOUNDED: 1974. FREQUENCY: a. PRICE: Free. PUBLISHER: Society of Economics and Business Administration, Kyota Sangyo University, 36 Motoyama, Kamigamo, Kita-ku, Kyoto, Japan. EDITOR: Kazumi Kobayashi. ILLUSTRATIONS. MANUSCRIPT SELECTION: Editor. INDEXED/ABSTRACTED: WAERSA. DATABASES: CAB AB. TARGET AUDIENCE: AC, SP.

KSU Economic and Business Review is a scholarly journal containing articles in many different areas of economics and business. Articles range from the highly technical that employ modern quantitative methodologies to non-technical papers that are primarily descriptive. In scope, level, and diversity it resembles Kansai University Review of Economics and Business. Economics topics discussed in recent issues include the effectiveness of monetary and fiscal policy in the long run, the existence of an optimal income tax, a conflict model of inflation and income distribution, input-output analysis applied to Japanese-American trade, development planning, vertical disintegration under demand uncertainty, and growth and stability in the Indonesian economy. Business topics found in recent issues include a comparison of annual reports issued by companies from a number of different English speaking countries, how industrialization was introduced into the U.S., accounting theory and practice, and the systems approach and contingency view in management behavior and organization. The authors are predominantly academics in economics, management, business history, and accounting at Kyoto Sangyo and Aoyama Gakuin Universities. Occasionally articles are versions of papers given at conferences or Ph.D. dissertations.

A typical issue contains three articles plus one or two notes. Articles vary greatly in length as do notes. One note related to the work of J.B. Say exceeded 100 pages. It, as did one other note, appeared in French.

318.   Kyklos. DATE FOUNDED: 1948. FREQUENCY: q. PRICE: SFr. 70/yr. PUBLISHER: Kyklos-Verlag, Postfach 524, CH4002, Basel, Switzerland. EDITORS: Rene L. Frey, Bruno S. Frey. ILLUSTRATIONS. INDEX. ADVERTISEMENTS. CIRCULATION: 3,400. MANUSCRIPT SELECTION: Editors and Referees. MICROFORMS: MIM, UMI. BOOK REVIEWS. SPECIAL ISSUES. INDEXED/ABSTRACTED: InEcA, IntBibE, JEL, KeyEcS, PAIS, SSI. DATABASES: ECONAB, ECONLIT, PAIS INT, SSI. TARGET AUDIENCE: AC. SP.

Kyklos is subtitled the "International Review for Social Sciences". That is misleading since it publishes exclusively in economics. It is associated with the German-based List Society, "an international non-profit organization whose main purpose is to analyse socio-economic problems of our times." Kyklos is published in three languages with the following approximate breakdown: 80% English, 15% German, 5% French. Articles cover all fields in economics, both micro and macroeconomics.

Most analyze actual economic problems, but some concern themselves with
the history of economic thought. Articles vary in type and level. Some
are essays while others are research articles. Some are expository in
nature while others are technical papers that present models and
empirical results gained in testing the models. Few employ very sophisticated quantitative methodologies. The authors are predominantly
academic economists. The majority are associated with universities in
Western Europe, but American, Canadian, Israeli, Australian, and Eastern
European economists are also represented.

Most issues contain from four to six articles. Each article is
followed by summaries in English, German, and French. A "Notes" section
is found in most issues with from one to three comments and replies.
More than one-fourth of each issue is devoted to book reviews and books
received. Each issue includes about thirty one-to-two page signed
reviews.

319.   The Kyoto University Economic Review. DATE FOUNDED: 1926.
FREQUENCY: 2/yr. PUBLISHER: Economic Research Office, Faculty of
Economics, Kyoto University, Sakyo-ku Yoshida, Kyoto, Japan. ILLUSTRA-
TIONS. INDEX. MANUSCRIPT SELECTION: Editors. INDEXED/ABSTRACTED: InEcA,
IntBibE, JEL, PAIS. DATABASES: ECONLIT, PAIS INT. TARGET AUDIENCE: AC,
SP.

The Kyoto University Economic Review is subtitled "Memoirs of the
Faculty of Economics, Kyoto University." It publishes only articles
written by its own faculty and an occasional "guest scholar". Articles
appear in virtually all areas of economics and some areas of business.
Many relate to Japanese economic problems and issues, both present and
past, but others deal with situations in England, the U.S. or Germany.
Whatever faculty members are interested in, often related to where they
had recently studied and conducted research, is "fair game" for publication in this journal. Examples of topics discussed in recent issues are
real wage rates in Germany and the U.K., physician manpower allocation
in the U.S, U.K. and Japan, comparative accounting, organization theory,
Marx on "capital in process", motivation of employees in Japan, urbanization in Tokyo, and large scale farming in the U.S. Quality varies
considerably as does type and level. Some are technical research papers
while others are historical essays, and yet others exploratory expositions.

For the past ten years both issues of each volume have been published
together. Such a "double" issue typically contains three articles. The
1980 volume contains the table of contents of each issue published from
1926 to 1980.

320.   Labor History. DATE FOUNDED: 1960. FREQUENCY: q. PRICE: $25/yr.
institutions, $19.50/yr. personal. PUBLISHER: New York University,
Tamiment Institute, Bobst Library, 70 Washington Square South, New York,
New York 10012. EDITOR: Daniel J. Leab. INDEX. ADVERTISEMENTS. CIRCULA-
TION: 1,750. MANUSCRIPT SELECTION: Editorial Board. MICROFORMS: UMI.
REPRINTS: Publisher. BOOK REVIEWS. INDEXED/ABSTRACTED: API, HumI, InEcA,
JEL, WorkRelAbstr. DATABASES: ECONLIT. TARGET AUDIENCE: AC, GP, SP.
SAMPLE COPIES: Libraries.

Labor History supersedes Labor Historian's Bulletin published from 1953
to 1957. Its scope is "original research in labor history, studies of
specific unions and of the impact of labor problems upon ethnic and
minority groups, the nature of work and working class life, theories of
the labor movement, biographical portraits of important labor figures,
comparative studies and analyses of foreign labor movements that shed
light on American labor developments, and studies of radical groups or
of radical history as they relate to American Labor history." Articles
are written in a scholarly style with extensive footnotes. They are
expository in nature, no quantitative analysis is engaged in, and only
seldom does an author offer a table of data to lend support. The "new
economic history" technical methods used by modern economic historians
are not employed. Authors are mostly academics. Occasionally professional librarians and free-lance writers make contributions. The majority of
academics are professors of history, but some are economists, sociologists and political scientists. An Australian version of Labor
History is Labour History which is similar in style and scope except
that it is entirely concerned with Australian labor history.
    A typical issue contain three or four regular articles, two shorter
articles in a "Notes and Documents" section, and one or two essays in an
"Essay Review" section. Each issue also contains from five to thirty
one-to-two page signed book reviews. A brief biographical sketch about
each contributor appears at the front of each issue.

321.   Labor Law Journal. DATE FOUNDED: 1949. FREQUENCY: m. PRICE:
$60/yr. PUBLISHER: Commerce Clearing House, Inc., 4025 W. Peterson Ave.,
Chicago, Illinois 60646. EDITOR: David C. Hamilton. ILLUSTRATIONS.
INDEX. CIRCULATION: 3,000. MANUSCRIPT SELECTION: Editors. MICROFORMS:
UMI. SPECIAL ISSUES. INDEXED/ABSTRACTED: BPI, BPIA, CLI, ILP, LRI, PAIS,
WAERSA, WorkRelAbst. DATABASES: CAB AB, LRI, MC, PAIS INT. TARGET
AUDIENCE: AC, SP.

Labor Law Journal contains "a continuing survey of important legislative, administrative, and judicial developments and signed articles on
subjects pertaining to legal problems in the labor field." It concentrates on U.S. labor law whereas Industrial Law Journal focuses largely
on British labor law, and Comparative Labor Law features comparisons
among the labor laws of different countries. All three are scholarly
publications aimed at labor law practitioners and academics. Labor Law
Journal publishes articles which analyze labor laws, specific cases, and
major labor issues. Topics discussed in recent issues include arbitration in public sector labor agreements, employment discrimination
against resident aliens, contractual plant closings, employee dis-
missals, union removal efforts, unionism in Japanese-owned firms in the
U.S., anti-nepotism rules, union options in corporate chapter 11
proceedings, and the future of OSHA. About half of the articles are
written by academics at law schools and departments of management,
economics, and labor relations. The other half are by practicing
attorneys in the private and public sector and by administrators and
researchers at U.S. government agencies such as the U.S. Department of
Labor and OSHA.
    A typical issue contains six articles plus brief news sections
covering "Who's What in Labor", "Equal Employment Opportunity", "Job
Safety and Health", and "Labor-Management Relations". The August issue

of each volume is devoted to publishing the proceedings of the annual spring meeting of the Industrial Relations Research Association.

322.   **Labor Notes.** DATE FOUNDED: 1979. FREQUENCY: m. PRICE: $20/yr. institutions, $10/yr. personal. PUBLISHER: Labor Education & Research Project, Box 20001, Detroit, Michigan 48220. EDITOR: Jim Woodward. ILLUSTRATIONS. INDEX. CIRCULATION: 4,200. MANUSCRIPT SELECTION: Editor and Staff. BOOK REVIEWS. INDEXED/ABSTRACTED: API. TARGET AUDIENCE: GP. SAMPLE COPIES: Libraries and Individuals.

Labor Notes is a publication receiving financial assistance from a group of individuals who are officers of various American and Canadian labor unions. The publication covers all aspects of current events of interest to the members of labor unions. Although it focuses on American and Canadian unions, it occasionally includes articles dealing with unions in other countries. Articles present reports of current developments in particular strikes, business trends that may affect unions, summaries of labor conference proceedings, court decisions on collective bargaining cases, and descriptions of union activities in third world countries. All the articles are written in a narrative style and are non-technical in nature. They exhibit a strong pro-union viewpoint and frequently display a militant tendency. The authors are either staff writers or union officials. Labor Notes is similar in scope of coverage, viewpoint, and format to Economic Notes.

Each issue is sixteen pages in length. In addition to ten to twelve articles, several regular features appear in each issue. "Resources" lists new publications of interest to readers, "Stewards Corner" provides advice to union stewards, and "Newswatch" announces news events or reprints items from other sources that interest union activists.

323.   **Labor Studies Journal.** DATE FOUNDED: 1976. FREQUENCY: 3/yr. PRICE: $25/yr. institutions, $15/yr. personal. PUBLISHER: Transaction Periodicals Consortium, Rutgers University, New Brunswick, New Jersey 08903. EDITOR: Jacqueline Brophy. INDEX. ADVERTISEMENTS. CIRCULATION: 800.   MANUSCRIPT SELECTION: Editor and Referees. MICROFORMS: UMI. REPRINTS: Publisher, UMI. BOOK REVIEWS. SPECIAL ISSUES. INDEXED/ABSTRACTED: WorkRelAbstr. TARGET AUDIENCE: AC, GP, SP. SAMPLE COPIES: Libraries.

The Labor Studies Journal is published under the auspices of the University and College Labor Education Association. It is aimed at labor education extension faculty and administrators; faculty in labor studies; union educators, officers and rank and file members; and government labor officials. The purpose of the Journal is to provide a "professional source" of articles and discussions that deal with "labor education materials and resources, with teaching methods useful in labor education and labor studies, and with the philosophy and substance of labor education." It is not a scholarly journal. Most articles are informed discussions concerning labor education topics such as the stake of labor in enterprise zones, how media technology can be used, labor's image, the impact of union education, and how other countries' labor education programs compare to those in the U.S. Some articles describe particular case experiences in designing and teaching labor studies and labor education courses. Occasionally a research article with empirical content is published. Most are non-technical and devoid of quantitative analysis. Almost all of the authors are academics in the labor education and studies fields.

A typical issue contains four articles, a "Newsletter" section which includes association reports from committees such as the Committee on Programs for Union Women and the Occupational Safety and Health Task Force, an "Audio-Visual Reference Shelf" section which reviews movies and tapes, and a "Book Review" section which offers from twelve to twenty signed reviews. Occasionally a "Theme Issue" employing a guest editor is published such as recent ones on occupational safety and health and on worker participation programs.

324.   **Labour and Society.** DATE FOUNDED: 1976. FREQUENCY: 3/yr. PRICE: 45 SFr./yr. PUBLISHER: International Institute for Labour Studies, P.O. Box 6, CH-1211 Geneva 22, Switzerland. EDITOR: Rose Marie Greve. INDEX. ADVERTISEMENTS. CIRCULATION: 1,100. MANUSCRIPT SELECTION: Editors and referees. BOOK REVIEWS. INDEXED/ABSTRACTED: ANB, HumRAb, PAIS, WAERSA. DATABASES: CAB AB, LABORDOC, PAIS INT. TARGET AUDIENCE: AC, SP.

Labour and Society supersedes International Institute for Labour Studies Bulletin (1967-1975). It is a scholarly, but generally non-technical journal focusing on the welfare of human beings in their role as workers. It is international in scope featuring articles concerning trade unions, industrial relations, and the condition of laborers in many different industrial as well as developing countries in the world. Recent issues have included articles dealing with labor in Spain, Nigeria, New Zealand, Switzerland, England, China, Ethiopia, the Netherlands, Germany, and India. Not all articles are bound to a particular country, but instead deal with a general question of social policy or with a labor theory. Examples of such articles are "Sociological Aspects of Solitude in Advanced Industrial Societies", "The Social Classes", and "the Development and Scope of Economic and Social Rights." The majority of authors are academics in departments of economics, sociology, and history at universities all over the world. Many articles are invited by the editor "on the basis of a detailed plan."

Most issues contain from five to eight articles. Recent issues contain a separate "Social Policy-Theory and History" section which includes two or three articles "prepared under the responsibility" of two professors at the University of Geneva. Each issue has a brief "News of the Institute" section and some issues have up to six signed book reviews.

325.   **Labour History.** DATE FOUNDED: 1962. FREQUENCY: 2/yr. PRICE: $A20/yr. institutions, $A16/yr. personal. PUBLISHER: Australian Society for the Study of Labour History, P.O. Box 1577, Canberra City, A.C.T. 2601 Australia. EDITOR: John Merritt. ILLUSTRATIONS. ADVERTISEMENTS. CIRCULATION: 1,000. MANUSCRIPT SELECTION: Editor. BOOK REVIEWS. INDEXED/ABSTRACTED: AustPAIS, WorkRelAbst. TARGET AUDIENCE: AC, SP.

Labour History publishes articles dealing with labor history in Australia. It is a scholarly journal that reports on research done on such topics as the growth of the Australian labor movement, the Australian Labor Party's reaction to certain internal and external events, educa-

tion in Australia, how particular Australian labor groups were treated
in the past, and the effect of major strikes by Australian labor unions.
Articles are non-technical in nature and they seldom include data to
lend support. They are expository in style and most include extensive
footnotes. In a great many respects this journal is the Australian
version of the American journal, Labor History. Both are devoid of
quantitative analysis and do not include articles that employ modern
economic history techniques. Authors are predominantly academics in
departments of history at Australian universities. Some are economists
or labor relations experts.

Each issue begins with a brief editorial statement which includes an
introduction to the articles in that issue. This is followed by about
six articles averaging fifteen pages in length and about twenty one-page
signed book reviews. In addition, some issues include a full-length
review article, comments, reports and obituaries.

326.   Land Economics. DATE FOUNDED: 1925. TITLE CHANGES: Journal of
Land and Public Utility Economics (1925-1947). FREQUENCY: q. PRICE:
$36/yr. institutions, $20/yr. personal. PUBLISHER: University of
Wisconsin Press, 114 North Murray Street, Madison, Wisconsin 53715.
EDITOR: Daniel Bromley. ILLUSTRATIONS. INDEX. ADVERTISEMENTS. CIRCULA-
TION: 2,600. MANUSCRIPT SELECTION: Editorial Board and Referees.
MICROFORMS: UMI. REPRINTS: UMI. BOOK REVIEWS. INDEXED/ABSTRACTED: BPI,
BPIA, InEcA, IntBibE, JEL, KeyEcS, PAIS, SSI, WAERSA. DATABASES: CAB AB,
ECONAB, ECONLIT, MC, PAIS INT, SSI. TARGET AUDIENCE: AC, SP. SAMPLE
COPIES: Libraries.

Land Economics is a publication that "explores the relationship between
economics and natural and environmental resources." Subjects covered in
this journal include wilderness development projects, natural resource
conservation, utility regulation, energy, housing markets, pollution
control, transportation, industry studies, and agriculture. Most of the
articles present empirical studies pertaining to these subjects in the
U.S., but a few articles use data from Canada, Mexico, and other
countries. Some articles present theoretical or philosophical treatments
of topics such as the concept of value, co-evolutionary development, and
option value. The writing is scholarly and is carefully documented. More
than half the articles use some quantitative methodologies. Most of the
authors are professors of economics from American universities. An
occasional contribution is made by a professor of urban studies or
business administration or a government economist.

A typical issue includes seven to nine full-length articles. Some
issues also have three or four shorter papers or a number of comments on
previously published papers and the authors' replies. A two or three
page signed book review appears in some issues.

327.   Leumi Review. DATE FOUNDED: 1955. TITLE CHANGES: Bank Leumi
Economic Review (1969-1983) Review of Economic Conditions in Israel
(1955-1968). FREQUENCY: ir. PRICE: Free. PUBLISHER: Bank Leumi, Economic
Research Department, P.O. Box 2, 61000 Tel Aviv, Israel. EDITOR: G.
Shifron. ILLUSTRATIONS. CIRCULATION: 9,000. MANUSCRIPT SELECTION:
Editor. TARGET AUDIENCE: GP. SAMPLE COPIES: Libraries and Individuals.

The Leumi Review is published by one of the largest banks in Israel. It presents an overview of economic conditions in Israel. Articles report on current economic developments, the outlook for the future, external debt, public sector expenditure, private consumption, balance of trade, employment and wages, inflation, industry, agriculture, construction, tourism, and the capital market. The articles are descriptive in nature and incorporate charts, graphs, and tables of data. The articles are not signed but the contributors names and educational credentials are listed on the cover. Leumi Review is quite different from the Bank of Israel Economic Review. The former is designed for the general public while the latter is aimed at professional economists.

The format of this serial varies from issue to issue. Some issues are eight page newsletters while others are pamphlets three times that length. Some issues contain as many as seventeen one or two page articles while other issues consist of a single essay that comprises the entire publication. Due to a recent title change, it is difficult to forecast whether this format will be maintained.

328.   Liiketaloudellinen Aikakauskirja/The Finnish Journal of Business Economics. DATE FOUNDED: 1952. FREQUENCY: q. PRICE: FIM70/yr. PUBLISHER: Helsinki School of Economics, Runeberginkatu 22-24, 00100 Helsinki 10, Finland. EDITOR: Mika Kasikimies. ILLUSTRATIONS. INDEX. ADVERTISEMENTS. CIRCULATION: 1,500. MANUSCRIPT SELECTION: Editorial Board. MICROFORMS: UMI. REPRINTS: Publisher. INDEXED/ABSTRACTED: InEcA, IntBibE, JEL. DATABASES: ECONLIT. TARGET AUDIENCE: AC, SP. SAMPLE COPIES: Libraries and Individuals.

Liiketaloudellinen Aikakauskirja/The Finnish Journal of Business Economics is published by one of the leading universities in Finland. It covers a broad range of topics in economics and business management. Some of the articles deal with economic theory. Representative titles include "Conjoint Analysis Models in Explaining Consumer Price Utility Structures", "On Investment Incentives and Allocational Implications of Corporate Income Taxation", and "A Simulation Model of the Investment Behavior of the Firm." Other articles deal with applied economics. These emphasize business conditions in Finland. Examples of titles of this type are "Testing the Efficiency of the Finnish Bond Market", "Empirical Evidence on the Measurement of the Performance of the Firm", and "An evaluation of Experimental Research: A Case Study Concerning the Effects of Marketing Mix on Retail Level." The articles are scholarly in nature. Most of them employ mathematical models and/or statistical analyses. The authors are predominantly academics at various Finnish universities. A few are American professors of Finnish background.

A typical issue contains six or seven full-length articles. Approximately half are in English with the remainder in Finnish. Finnish articles are accompanied by English summaries.

329.   Lloyds Bank Review. DATE FOUNDED: 1946. FREQUENCY: q. PRICE: Free. PUBLISHER: Lloyds Bank Group, Economics Department, P.O. Box 215, 71 Lombard St., London EC3P 3BS, England. EDITOR: Christopher Johnson. ILLUSTRATIONS. CIRCULATION: 65,000. MANUSCRIPT SELECTION: Editor. MICROFORMS: UMI. REPRINTS: UMI. INDEXED/ABSTRACTED: BPIA, InEcA, IntBibE, JEL, PAIS. DATABASES: ECONLIT, MC, PAIS INT. TARGET AUDIENCE: AC, GP, SP. SAMPLE COPIES: Libraries and Individuals.

Lloyds Bank Review is a publication covering current economic developments and thought. The overall emphasis is on modern economic theory and
economic problems of the industrialized nations. Empirical studies
concentrate on conditions in the U.K. Recent articles deal with farm
incomes, tax reform proposals, the automobile industry, privatization of
nationalized industries, and multilateral trade policies. Theoretical
studies cover topics such as monopoly theory, monetary theory, the
Keynesian approach to full employment, and the role of commodity prices
in an economic recovery. A few of the articles were originally delivered
as addresses at various conferences. The articles are expository in
style and devoid of quantitative analysis. Many of them offer specific
proposals or viewpoints. They are aimed at a general audience but
elementary training in economies is required for comprehension. Most of
the authors are British academics but occasionally an American, a
German, or a Canadian writer makes a contribution.
    Each issue has three full-length articles. Some issues have a
"Letters to the Editor" section which presents comments on previously
published articles and the author's reply to the comments.

330.   The Logistics and Transportation Review. DATE FOUNDED: 1965.
TITLE CHANGES: Logistics Review and Military Logistics Journal (1965-
1966) Logistics Review (1967-1971). FREQUENCY: q. PRICE: $28/yr.
PUBLISHER: University of British Columbia, Faculty of Commerce and
Business Administration, Vancouver, B.C., V6T 1W5, Canada. EDITOR: Karl
M. Ruppenthal. INDEX. ADVERTISEMENTS. CIRCULATION: 1,300. MANUSCRIPT
SELECTION: Editor. MICROFORMS: UMI. REPRINTS: UMI. BOOK REVIEWS. SPECIAL
ISSUES. INDEXED/ABSTRACTED: BPIA, GeoAb. DATABASES: MC. TARGET AUDIENCE:
AC, SP.

The Logistics and Transportation Review is an international journal
emphasizing various aspects of transportation of both goods and people.
Articles deal with economic evaluation of railroads, the trucking
industry, urban transportation systems, airlines, postal services,
travel safety, transport of agricultural commodities, and private
automobiles. Most of these articles offer empirical studies of specific
aspects of these topics in either the U.S. or Canada. An occasional
study, based on data from England or Australia, is included. Some issues
offer a "point of view" article which discusses implications of government policies related to regulation of transportation modes. The
majority of articles utilize some type of quantitative methodology. Some
of the articles are based on papers presented at conferences. The
authors are predominantly American or Canadian and come from academe,
business, and government. Several authors are also on the editorial
board of the Review.
    A typical issue includes six articles from ten to twenty pages in
length each. The book review section varies in both the number and
length of reviews. Up to six reviews are included and the length may
range from a brief annotation to a two page evaluation. Some of the
reviews are signed.

331.   Louisiana Business Review. DATE FOUNDED: 1937. FREQUENCY: q.
PRICE: Free. PUBLISHER: Louisiana State University, Division of Research, College Of Business Administration, Baton Rouge, Louisiana
70803. EDITOR: Joseph H. Wagner. ILLUSTRATIONS. ADVERTISEMENTS. CIRCULA-

TION: 7,500. MANUSCRIPT SELECTION: Editorial Board. BOOK REVIEWS.
INDEXED/ABSTRACTED: PAIS. DATABASES: PAIS INT. TARGET AUDIENCE: GP, SP.
SAMPLE COPIES: Libraries and Individuals.

Louisiana Business Review is provided as an educational service to a
primarily Louisiana readership. It provides current information on
local, state, and national economic developments of interest to members
of the Louisiana business and government communities. Compared to other
business school publications, it is somewhat more parochial than Arizona
Review, Arkansas Business and Economic Review, and Colorado Business
Review, but a little less so than Montana Business Quarterly, Kentucky
Economy: Review and Perspective, and Georgia Business and Economic
Conditions. Examples of strictly Louisiana topics discussed in recent
issues of LBR are the finances of the 1984 Louisiana World's Fair, water
in Louisiana, port development in Louisiana, residential construction in
Louisiana, financial assistance in Louisiana, and conditions of the
Louisiana economy. Examples of topics that reached beyond Louisiana's
borders include tax planning, the U.S. trade position, and alternative
mortgage instruments. Articles are non-technical, but are often accompanied by tables and charts. Many have extensive endnotes. Articles are
written by staff economists, academics at Louisiana State University and
elsewhere, representatives from business, and government economists.
      Most issues contain four articles, a letter from the Editorial Board,
economic news items separated into "Louisiana Bulletin" and "National
News" sections, a section providing news about the Business College, a
section announcing research opportunities, and four or five brief signed
book reviews.

Malaysian Economic Studies. see Kajian Ekonomi Malaysia/Malaysian
Economic Studies.

332.   Management Science. DATE FOUNDED: 1954. FREQUENCY: m. PRICE:
$76/yr. institutions, $45/yr. personal. PUBLISHER: The Institute of
Management Sciences, 290 Westminister Street, Providence, Rhode Island
02903. EDITOR: Donald G. Morrison. ILLUSTRATIONS. INDEX. ADVERTISEMENTS.
CIRCULATION: 11,000. MANUSCRIPT SELECTION: Editor and Referees. MICRO-
FORMS: MIM, UMI. REPRINTS: UMI. SPECIAL ISSUES. INDEXED/ABSTRACTED:
AcctInd, BPI, BPIA, IntBibE, KeyEcS. DATABASES: ACCTIND, ECONAB, MC.
TARGET AUDIENCE: AC, SP.

Management Science is published by a professional association of
individuals in the fields of management, industrial engineering,
operations research, and economics. The articles in this publication
reflect the inter-relationship of these fields. This journal presents
theoretical studies of problems in the following areas: applied stochastic models; decision analysis; finance, information systems and accounting; logistics, distribution and inventory; marketing; mathematical
programming and networks; organization analysis, performance and design;
planning, forecasting and applied game theory; production and operations
management; public sector applications; research and development and
innovation; and simulation. Each of these subject areas is directed by
its own editor. Articles emphasize methodology rather than empirical
findings and most of them employ econometric models or statistical
techniques. Most of the authors are American academics or consultants.

Management Science concentrates more on theoretical studies in management than does Managerial and Decision Economics which covers both empirical and theoretical studies of a broader range of topics.

A typical issue contains eight or nine full-length articles. Short biographical sketches of the authors are provided. Special issues devoted to a single topic under the guidance of a guest editor appear occasionally. A recent one was devoted to state-of-the art techniques in risk analysis.

333.   Managerial and Decision Economics. DATE FOUNDED: 1980. FREQUENCY: q. PRICE: $100/yr. institutions, $40/yr. personal. PUBLISHER: John Wiley & Sons Ltd., Baffins Lane, Chichester, Sussex PO19 1UD, England. EDITOR: W. Duncan Reekie. ILLUSTRATIONS. INDEX. ADVERTISEMENTS. CIRCULATION: 250. MANUSCRIPT SELECTION: Editor and Referees. MICROFORMS: UMI. REPRINTS: UMI. BOOK REVIEWS. INDEXED/ABSTRACTED: PAIS. DATABASES: PAIS INT. TARGET AUDIENCE: AC, SP. SAMPLE COPIES: Libraries and Individuals.

Managerial and Decision Economics, subtitled the international journal of research and progress in management economics, is the official publication of the Association of Managerial Economists, an international organization devoted to the study of managerial and decision economics. MDE also receives support from the Business Economics Research Group of the University of the Witwatersrand, South Africa. MDE emphasizes both theoretical and empirical analyses of economic models "used in forecasting, pricing, advertising, diversification, competitive strategy, innovation, financial and location decisions." Articles relating to government regulation and antitrust policy are also included. The articles are scholarly, provide extensive references, and frequently use econometric models. The authors are professors of economics or business administration. The majority of authors are from the U.S., the U.K., and Canada with a few from Australia, Israel, and Western Europe. The editorial board is international in composition. MDE somewhat overlaps with the subject content of Management Science and has much more economic content.

A typical issue contains seven to nine articles of varying length. Most issues have up to four signed book reviews. Forthcoming conferences and meetings in this area of specialization are listed in the back of each issue.

334.   Managing International Development: MID. DATE FOUNDED: 1984. FREQUENCY: 6/yr. PRICE: $100/yr. PUBLISHER: M.E. Sharpe, Inc., 80 Business Park Drive, Armonk, New York, 10504. EDITOR: Joel Kurtzman. ILLUSTRATIONS. ADVERTISEMENTS. MANUSCRIPT SELECTION: Editor. SPECIAL ISSUES. TARGET AUDIENCE: AC, SP.

Managing International Development: MID is a new journal that covers a broad spectrum of interests. MID deals with many aspects of development although it emphasizes the pragmatic approach. Empirical studies have focused on topics such as trade between Brazil and Black Africa, multinational investment, land reform in Costa Rica, natural versus synthetic products, national development legislation, the debt crisis, and foreign investment in Iran. Other articles have presented policy discussions or theoretical analyses of development issues such as rural development planning, peripheral capitalism, resource allocation models, and assessing risk in planning. The articles are scholarly in nature. Most of them are expository and contain references and documented data. A few use mathematical analysis in their treatment. The authors are academics from American and Canadian universities, consultants to private development foundations, officials with UN agencies, and planning experts with national development agencies. MID includes more policy discussions of development issues than Journal of World Trade Law.

Each issue includes five or six full-length articles. The editor introduces the articles in a two page "About This Issue" essay. "Reports From The Field" documents activities of various organizations, announces new publications, and reports on new development projects. "Dataline" lists international projects open for bid by consultants and business firms. Occasional special issues are planned. The first one was devoted to the world population problem.

335.   The Manchester School of Economic and Social Studies. DATE FOUNDED: 1930. FREQUENCY: q. PRICE: $40/yr. institutions, $25/yr. personal. PUBLISHER: The Manchester School, Economics Department, The University, Manchester M13 9PL, England. EDITOR: M.J. Artis. ILLUSTRA-TIONS. INDEX. CIRCULATION: 1,500. MANUSCRIPT SELECTION: Editor and Referees. MICROFORMS: KR. REPRINTS: Publisher. BOOK REVIEWS. INDEXED/ ABSTRACTED: InEcA, IntBibE, JEL, KeyEcS, PAIS, SSI, WorkRelAbstr. DATABASES: ECONAB, ECONLIT, PAIS INT, SSI. TARGET AUDIENCE: AC, SP.

The Manchester School of Economic and Social Studies is a scholarly publication covering a broad range of topics in economics. Articles present both theoretical and empirical studies on a variety of economic problems. Empirical studies emphasize conditions in the U.K. as illus-trated by the two recent articles on the demand for money in the U.K. from 1963-1978 and house price indices for the U.K., 1975-1981. Examples of recent theoretical studies include the following articles: "Unemploy-ment, Bankrupty, and Asymmetric Information", "The Modified Fisher Hypothesis and the Steady State Demand for Money," and "Natural Prices, Differential Profit Rates and the Classical Competitive Process." Most of the articles employ modern econometric or statistical methodologies. The authors are predominantly British academics although a few contri-butors are from Australia and Western Europe. This publication is comparable in subject coverage and authorship to the Bulletin of Eco-nomic Research and the British Review of Economic Issues.

A typical issue contains five full-length articles and up to four short comments and replies to comments on previously published papers. An extensive book review section includes an average of fifteen signed reviews. A list of "Other Books Received" appears in each issue.

336.   Manpower Journal. DATE FOUNDED: 1965. FREQUENCY: q. PRICE: $10/yr. PUBLISHER: Institute of Applied Manpower Research, Indraprastha Estate, Ring Road, New Delhi-110002, India. EDITOR: M.L. Nakhasi. ILLUSTRATIONS. INDEX. ADVERTISEMENTS. CIRCULATION: 500. MANUSCRIPT SELECTION: Editor and Referees. BOOK REVIEWS. INDEXED/ABSTRACTED: WAERSA. DATABASES: CAB AB. TARGET AUDIENCE: AC, SP. SAMPLE COPIES: Individuals.

Manpower Journal is an Indian publication in the labor field that
concentrates on training and employment of workers. It differs from the
Indian Journal of Labour Economics and the Indian Journal of Industrial
Relations in that it excludes subjects such as unions, collective
bargaining, industrial psychology, and labor management relations. Most
of the articles deal with labor situations in India but a few concern
themselves with the Nigerian situation. Some representative topics
include employment in the fertilizer industry, employment potential in
the Post and Telegraph Service, urban underemployment, cost of engineering education, worker emigration, and child labor participation. Most of
the articles present empirical research. They incorporate extensive
tables of data in an expository narrative. A few articles present a
mathematical model and test it with empirical data. The authors are
predominantly economists affiliated with universities, research institutes, or government agencies in India. Occasionally, contributions are
made by Nigerian scholars.
    A typical issue includes four or five full-length articles. A "Notes
and Comments" section has one shorter article. One signed book review
and several book annotations appear in each issue. A list of reports
published by the Institute appears in the back of each issue.

337.   Margin. DATE FOUNDED: 1968. FREQUENCY: q. PRICE: $10/yr.
PUBLISHER: National Council of Applied Economic Research, Parisila
Bhawan, 11, I.P. Estate, New Delhi - 110002, India. EDITOR: I.Z. Bhatty.
ILLUSTRATIONS. ADVERTISEMENTS. CIRCULATION: 1,000. MANUSCRIPT SELECTION:
Editor. REPRINTS: Authors. BOOK REVIEWS. INDEXED/ABSTRACTED: WAERSA.
DATABASES: CAB AB. TARGET AUDIENCE: AC, SP.

Margin is a government publication presenting articles on the Indian
economy. The articles cover a broad range of economic topics, many of
them offering the results of applied economic research. Recent issues
have dealt with topics such as evaluation of large scale irrigation
projects, study of fertilizer use, regional rice productivity, poverty
levels, regional legume productivity, inter-regional disparities in
industrialization, education planning, demand for money, birth rate and
economic development, exports, the sugar industry of a region, and
reclamation of soil. A few articles are more theoretical such as those
dealing with tax elasticity estimation and measurement of income
inequality. Most of the articles use quantitative analyses and some of
them have extensive tables of data. The authors are Indian academics,
staff members, or other government researchers.
    A typical issue contains five or six full-length articles. Each issue
includes two to five signed book reviews. A regular feature is "The
Indian Economy" which presents selected economic indicators and a review
of the economy for the previous quarter. This review provides data on
agriculture, industry, money and credit, prices, and balance of payments. A list of research in progress at the National Council is
included in each issue.

338.   Matekon. DATE FOUNDED: 1964. TITLE CHANGES: Mathematical Studies
in Economics and Statistics in the USSR and Eastern Europe (1964-1969).
FREQUENCY: q. PRICE: $170/yr. institutions, $44/yr. personal. PUBLISHER:
Myron E. Sharpe, Inc., 80 Business Park Drive, Armonk, New York 10504.
EDITOR: Martin Cave. INDEX. ADVERTISEMENTS. MANUSCRIPT SELECTION:

Editor. SPECIAL ISSUES. INDEXED/ABSTRACTED: InEcA, IntBibE, JEL, KeyEcS.
DATABASES: ECONAB, ECONLIT. TARGET AUDIENCE: AC, SP. SAMPLE COPIES:
Libraries and Individuals.

Matekon is subtitled Translations of Russian and East European mathematical economics. It contains translations of articles from scholarly
journals or collections of articles published in book form. The purpose
of this journal is to make available the more important works to
scholars not able to read Russian or other East European languages. Most
articles deal with theoretical economic studies on topics such as
consumer preference functions, labor force structure, world economic
relationships, population mobility, location planning, wage regulation,
economic growth, and long-term national planning. A few articles present
pure mathematical theory such as those dealing with mathematical
programming problems and applications of Lagrange functions. A few offer
empirical studies such as the development of the Hungarian aluminum
industry or family consumption in Czechoslavakia. All of the articles
utilize advanced mathematical methodologies. Most of the authors are
from the U.S.S.R. but no professional affiliation is provided.
     A typical issue includes four or five full-length articles. The
bibliographic citation for the original article is given. A recent
"Special Issue" on natural resource economics in the U.S.S.R. was under
the direction of a guest editor.

339.   Mathematical Social Sciences. DATE FOUNDED: 1980. FREQUENCY:
6/yr. PRICE: Dfl 422/yr. PUBLISHER: Elsevier Science Publishers B.V.
(North-Holland), P.O. Box 1991, 1000 BZ Amsterdam, The Netherlands.
EDITOR: Ki Hang Kim. ILLUSTRATIONS. INDEX. ADVERTISEMENTS. MANUSCRIPT
SELECTION: Editorial Board. REPRINTS: Author. BOOK REVIEWS. SPECIAL
ISSUES. INDEXED/ABSTRACTED: SocAb. DATABASES: SOCAB. TARGET AUDIENCE:
AC, SP.

Mathematical Social Sciences is an international journal covering the
mathematical treatment of various social science topics. It is interdisciplinary in scope and includes economics, political science,
psychology, and sociology. Most of the articles present a study of
theoretical concepts. Recent examples include articles on expected
utility theory, allocation of incentives in hierarchies, game theory,
election strategies, index of poverty, inequality of the market system,
oligopolistic markets, and the Pareto-satisfactory mechanism. A few
articles present empirical research. Recent examples include articles on
medical care demand, behavior settings and eco-behavioral science, and
intercounty migration in the U.S. All of the articles are scholarly in
style and employ advanced mathematical techniques. The authors are
academics and researchers from institutions all over the world. A
preponderance of them are economists. The Editorial Board is large and
international in scope. Board members' addresses and areas of specialization are listed in each issue.
     Each issue varies in format. An issue may consist only of three
lengthy articles or may contain six short articles, four short notes,
and up to six signed book reviews. Some issues include abstracts of
papers presented to the Jacob Marschak Interdisciplinary Colloquium on
Mathematics in the Behavioral Sciences. Special issues feature invited
papers such as a recent one on the theme of structure in socio-economic
systems.

340.   MEED; Middle East Economic Digest. DATE FOUNDED: 1957. FRE-
QUENCY: w. PRICE: $295/yr. PUBLISHER: Middle East Economic Digest Ltd.,
21 John St., London WC IN 2BP, England. EDITOR: Richard Purdy. ILLUSTRA-
TIONS. INDEX. ADVERTISEMENTS. CIRCULATION: 10,000. MANUSCRIPT SELECTION:
Editor. BOOK REVIEWS. SPECIAL ISSUES. TARGET AUDIENCE: GP, SP.

MEED; Middle East Economic Digest is a news magazine covering new
developments in business, economics, and politics in the Arab World.
Articles deal with industrial development, finance, trade, agriculture,
health care, education, and political changes. The articles are descriptive with accompanying statistics and photographs. Most of the articles
are written by staff journalists. Occasionally a feature story will be
written by a non-staff writer. MEED provides similar coverage of the
Arab World as Business Week provides for the U.S.
    A typical issue includes five or six short articles and one in-depth
feature story of ten to fifteen pages. Some issues have two or three
signed book reviews. A regular section is "News" which presents brief
reports of new developments covering the region as a whole as well as
national developments in twenty individual Middle Eastern and North
African countries. A section named "Tenders" invites inquires about a
variety of business opportunities available. MEED publishes frequent
special reports that are included as part of the subscription. Each
special report focuses on a national economy.

341.   Mergers & Acquisitions. DATE FOUNDED: 1965. MERGER: Mergers and
Acquisitions Quarterly and Mergers and Acquisitions Monthly. FREQUENCY:
5/yr. PRICE: $129/yr. PUBLISHER: Information for Industry, 229 S. 18th
St., Philadephia, Pennsylvania 19103. EDITOR: Leonard Zweig. ILLUSTRA-
TIONS. INDEX. ADVERTISEMENTS. CIRCULATION: 4,000. MANUSCRIPT SELECTION:
Editors and Technical Advisors. MICROFORMS: UMI. REPRINTS: Publisher,
UMI. SPECIAL ISSUES. INDEXED/ABSTRACTED: AcctInd, BPI, BPIA, FedTaxArt,
PAIS, Pred. DATABASES: ABI, ACCTIND, MC, PAIS INT, PF. TARGET AUDIENCE:
AC, SP. SAMPLE COPIES: Libraries and Individuals.

Mergers & Acquisitions is subtitled The Journal of Corporate Venture. It
is a specialized publication aimed at corporate development directors;
accountants, lawyers, investment bankers, and brokers associated with
merger transactions; and academics in finance and industrial organization economics. It contains reports, articles, interviews and a complete
detailed listing of all mergers involving U.S. companies. The journal
offers the viewpoint that mergers can add value to enterprises and to
the economy if they are well-conceived, well-structured, and well-
managed. Most articles are "how to" expositions which share the writer's
experience such as how to choose a depository in tender offers, how to
value closely held businessses, how to deal with labor after a merger,
and how to handle employee benefit plans in merger negotiations. Other
articles provide summaries of research done in the merger field, but
scholarly research articles are not published. Not all articles are
signed. Authors that are identified are professionals with financial
consulting firms, banks, law firms, economic research institutes and
universities.
    A typical issue contains four articles, a letter from the publisher,
six reports, interviews, and a roster of mergers. Reports include a
merger review, a Washington update, joint ventures that took place,
mergers that were cancelled, and mergers in other countries. The roster

of mergers takes up about half of each issue and involves about 2,000 companies per year. An "Almanac and Index" summary issue is published in April of each year.

342.   MERI's Monthly Circular: Survey of Economic Conditions in Japan. DATE FOUNDED: 1923. TITLE CHANGES: Monthly Circular: Survey of Economic Conditions in Japan. (1923-1969). FREQUENCY: m. PRICE: $27/yr. PUB-LISHER: The Mitsubishi Economic Research Institute, 3-1 Marunoucki, 3-chome, Chiyoda-Ku, Tokyo, Japan. EDITOR: Kaoru Inoue. ILLUSTRATIONS. ADVERTISEMENTS. CIRCULATION: 3,170. MANUSCRIPT SELECTION: Editor. TARGET AUDIENCE: GP.

MERI's Monthly Circular: Survey of Economic Conditions in Japan is the oldest English language monthly economic review published in Japan. This publication focuses on describing economic conditions in Japan but also discusses the world economic outlook and the U.S. economy. Examples of articles reviewing the world economy include "Uneasy International Oil Situation," "The Trend of World Economy and Trade," and "The Duty of the Advanced Nations." Examples of articles reviewing the U.S. economy includes "Can the U.S. Economy Be Revitalized?", "The State of the American Defense Industry", and "American Financial Revolution Moves Ahead." Articles dealing with the Japanese economy cover topics such as government policies, overseas production, agricultural production, wages, retail sales, and exports. Occasionally, articles describe technological innovations such as development of the fifth-generation computer, factory automation, hybrid materials, and fiber optics. The articles are expository in style with some numerical data and are unsigned.
    Each issue includes four short articles and two regular features. One regular feature, "Industry and Trade Topics", presents reports on specific industries. The other regular feature, "Economic Statistics", lists data for economic factors such as consumer price index, department store sales, unemployment, wages, industrial production, new housing construction, and gross national expenditure.

343.   Metroeconomica. DATE FOUNDED: 1949. FREQUENCY: 3/yr. PRICE: $50/yr. PUBLISHER: Nuova Casa Editrice L. Cappelli, Via Marsili 9, 40124 Bologna, Italy. EDITOR: Sergio Parrinello. ILLUSTRATIONS. INDEX. ADVERTISEMENTS. CIRCULATION: 2,000. MANUSCRIPT SELECTION: Editor. REPRINTS: Authors. TARGET AUDIENCE: AC, SP. SAMPLE COPIES: Libraries and Individuals.

Metroeconomica, subtitled International Review of Economics, is an English language periodical published in Italy. Its main area of concentration is economic theory. Only rarely are other types of articles included. Recent articles have dealt with topics such as the determinants of international competitiveness, the measurement of productivity increase, the analysis of the process of innovation, choice in the theory of consumption, analysis of international investment, and optimal economic behavior under uncertainty. Examples of other topics included in this journal are the development of cable TV in the U.K., comparison of productivity in capitalism and socialism, and a case study of the Australian labor market. The articles are scholarly in style and most of them utilize advanced mathematical methodology either in the body of the text or in an appendix. The authors are academic economists from an international roster of universities. The majority are European. A typical issue includes five full-length articles. Recent issues have been published together in one combined volume. Current volumes have exhibited a fourteen to eighteen month lag in publication schedule.

344.   The Mid-Atlantic Journal of Business. DATE FOUNDED: 1963. TITLE CHANGES: The Journal of Business (1963-1980). FREQUENCY: 2/yr. PRICE: $4/yr. PUBLISHER: Seton Hall University, Division of Research, The W. Paul Stillman School of Business, South Orange, New Jersey 07079. EDITOR: Nicholas J. Beutell. ILLUSTRATIONS. INDEX. CIRCULATION: 1,400. MANUSCRIPT SELECTION: Editor and Editorial Board. MICROFORMS: UMI. REPRINTS: UMI. BOOK REVIEWS. INDEXED/ABSTRACTED: AcctArt, AcctInd, BPIA. DATABASES: ACCTIND, MC. TARGET AUDIENCE: AC, SP. SAMPLE COPIES: Libraries and Individuals.

The Mid-Atlantic Journal of Business publishes articles "in all fields of business and economics". Articles are scholarly in nature. Most are technical research papers which introduce a model and report empirical results derived from testing the model. Articles employ quantitative methodologies. The Journal is not aimed primarily at business people as are most business school publications. It offers no account of the New Jersey economy and is of national and international interest. Compared to other business school publications, it most resembles the Akron Business and Economic Review. Articles are published in economics, finance, management, and marketing. Topics dealt with most in recent issues include market power, firm entry, multinational corporations, efficient markets, employee performance, demarketing strategies, standardization in international marketing, and the relationship between business forms and x-inefficiency. Most authors are American academics in departments of accounting, economics, finance, management, or marketing.

An issue contains from three to five articles plus one or two shorter narrative style papers in a "other contributions" section. Brief biographical sketches of the authors appear in the front of each issue. Some issues contain one or two signed book reviews.

345.   Mid-South Business Journal. DATE FOUNDED: 1981. FREQUENCY: q. PRICE: Free. PUBLISHER: Memphis State University, Bureau of Business and Economic Research, The Fogelman College of Business and Economics, Memphis, Tennessee 38152. EDITOR: James McFadyen. ILLUSTRATIONS. CIRCULATION: 3,300. MANUSCRIPT SELECTION: Editors. INDEXED/ABSTRACTED: BPIA. DATABASES: MC. TARGET AUDIENCE: AC, GP, SP. SAMPLE COPIES: Libraries and Individuals.

The Mid-South Business Journal supersedes the Mid-South Quarterly Business Review published from 1963 to 1980. It publishes articles oriented to the business reader on accounting, banking, economics, finance, marketing, labor/management, and personnel. While some articles are aimed specifically at Mid-South readers, most are of national and international interest. It is less parochial than most business school publications and in this regard most like Akron Business and Economic Review and Indiana University's Business Horizons. Articles in recent issues have dealt with topics such as information processing, a simpli-

fied approach to the alternative minimum tax, deregulation, managing an
R&D unit, exporting the federal deficit, international licensing, and
human life value calculations. Articles are written in a narrative style
and are generally non-technical in nature. But they are more scholarly
than those found in the average business school publication. Most
include some supporting data, a few footnotes, and several references.
The majority of authors are academics, less than half of them at Memphis
State University. Others are professionals in private business or
government such as the publisher of The Janeway Letter and the Chief
Economist of the Tennessee Valley Authority.

An issue contains from five to seven articles and a four to eight
page statistical supplement on the Mid-South economy.

Middle East Economic Digest. see MEED; Middle East Economic Digest.

346.   Mississippi Business Review. DATE FOUNDED: 1939. FREQUENCY: m.
PRICE: $3.50/yr. PUBLISHER: Mississippi State University, Division of
Business Research, College of Business and Industry, Mississippi State,
Mississippi 39762. EDITOR: J. William Rush. ILLUSTRATIONS. CIRCULATION:
1,900. MANUSCRIPT SELECTION: Editor and Editorial Advisors. INDEXED/
ABSTRACTED: PAIS. DATABASES: PAIS INT. TARGET AUDIENCE: GP, SP.

The Mississippi Business Review covers a broad range of business and
economics topics as well as economic data pertaining to the Southeastern
region of the U.S., the State of Mississippi and many Mississippi
cities, counties and SMSAs. The articles published in this title are of
national interest and not specifically aimed at Mississippi readers. It
differs in this respect from the majority of business school publications. It most closely resembles Akron Business and Economic Review,
Mid-South Business Journal, and Indiana University's Business Horizons.
Recent issues have contained articles on the following topics: the
Japanese production system, job satisfaction and change, investment in
precious metals, tax aspects of bankruptcy, mergers in the savings and
loan association industry, how to structure a national economic policy,
interest rates, and the theories of organizational design. Articles are
generally non-technical in nature but do rely on data presented in
tables and charts. Most of the authors are American academics associated
with departments of economics, finance, management or marketing. The
majority teach outside of the state of Mississippi.

Most issues contain only a single article, usually under ten pages in
length. A photograph and a short biographical sketch of the author
accompanies each article. The remaining ten to fifteen pages of each
issue are devoted to statistical tables and charts.

Monetary Trends. see Federal Reserve Bank of St. Louis. Monetary Trends.

347.   Montana Business Quarterly. DATE FOUNDED: 1962. FREQUENCY: q.
PRICE: $10/yr. PUBLISHER: University of Montana, Bureau of Business and
Economic Research, School of Business Administration, Missoula, Montana
59812. EDITOR: Mary Logan Lenihan. ILLUSTRATIONS. INDEX. CIRCULATION:
1,400. MANUSCRIPT SELECTION: Editorial Review Board. MICROFORMS: UMI.
REPRINTS: Publisher. SPECIAL ISSUES. INDEXED/ABSTRACTED: BPIA, PAIS.

DATABASES: MC, PAIS INT. TARGET AUDIENCE: GP. SAMPLE COPIES: Libraries and Individuals.

The Montana Business Quarterly is a publication almost entirely devoted to discussions concerning the Montana economy. It is aimed to serve "the general public, as well as business, labor, and government" in the state of Montana. Of the many business school publications, only Kentucky Economy: Review and Perspective, Georgia Business and Economic Conditions, and Arizona Business concentrate as much on their home state. Articles deal with such topics as Montana's forest products industry, Montana's travel and recreation industry, the Montana employment situation, economic development in Montana, and education issues in the state. Some articles focus on a region of the state such as the Bozeman area and the Butte-Anaconda area or a city such as Billings, Great Falls, Helena, and Missoula. Articles are non-technical in nature but most rely on data presented in tables, charts, and graphs. Most authors are associated with the University of Montana, either as Bureau research staff or Business School faculty.

A typical issue contains five or six articles. One or two of these are usually based on the responses received from "the Montana Poll", a quarterly statewide public opinion survey developed by the Bureau and co-sponsored by the Great Falls Tribune. The Spring issue of each volume is a special issue devoted to the economic outlook for Montana. It contains the proceedings of the annual series of Economic Outlook Seminars held in four Montana cities.

348.   Monthly Commentary on Indian Economic Conditions. DATE FOUNDED: 1959. TITLE CHANGES: Monthly Statistical Commentary on Indian Economic Conditions (1959-1964). FREQUENCY: m. PRICE: $40/yr. PUBLISHER: Indian Institute of Public Opinion Ltd., 2-A National Insurance Bldg, Parliament St., Box 288, New Delhi, 110001, India. EDITOR: E.P.W. da Costa. ILLUSTRATIONS. ADVERTISEMENTS. MANUSCRIPT SELECTION: Editor. BOOK REVIEWS. SPECIAL ISSUES. TARGET AUDIENCE: AC, GP, SP.

Monthly Commentary on Indian Economic Conditions is a publication that provides perspectives on the Indian economy and on world business, as well as current economic statistics for the Indian economy. Articles are written in a narrative style and rather than being based on the writer's research they usually reflect the writer's opinion. Some are written specifically for this title while others are reprinted from newspapers and magazines. Many articles are unsigned and when signed no affiliation of the author is provided. Articles deal with a great variety of topics. Examples that pertain to the Indian economy are the national milk grid, coal prices, the national budget, revenues and costs of railways, a new approach to government finance, the takeover of textile mills in Bombay, and foreign trade policy. Others deal with Indian politics and Indian alliances with other countries. A third category focuses on economic conditions in other parts of the world such as North America, Europe, Latin America, and Africa.

A typical issue is divided into four main sections: 1) "Leading Articles", three or four one-page articles, 2) "Special Articles". two or three somewhat longer articles, 3) "Business World", one to four brief articles, and 4) "Economic Indicators", tables and charts of price, industrial production, monetary, and consumption data. Each issue also contains an in-depth "Blue Supplement" on a topic of current interest, and news items in brief "Highlights", "Business Notes", and "Company Affairs" sections. An "Annual Number", five times the length of a regular issue, and providing a political prologue and an economic assessment is published in December.

349.   **Monthly Labor Review.** DATE FOUNDED: 1915. FREQUENCY: m. PRICE: $24/yr. PUBLISHER: U.S. Department of Labor, Bureau of Labor Statistics, 441 G. ST., N.W., Washington, D.C. 20212. EDITOR: Henry Lowenstern. ILLUSTRATIONS. INDEX. ADVERTISEMENTS. CIRCULATION: 14,000. MANUSCRIPT SELECTION: Editor. BOOK REVIEWS. SPECIAL ISSUES. INDEXED/ABSTRACTED: AcctInd, BPI, BPIA, InEcA, IntBibE, JEL, KeyEcS, PAIS, Pred, SSI, WAERSA, WorkRelAbstr. DATABASES: ACCTIND, CAB AB, ECONAB, ECONLIT, MC, PAIS INT, PF, SSI. TARGET AUDIENCE: AC, GP, SP.

The Monthly Labor Review is "the oldest, most authoritative Government journal in its field." It presents articles on employment, wages, productivity, job safety, and economic growth in the U.S. It also includes articles on foreign labor developments. Recent articles have dealt with the following topics: inflation and the business cycle, female-male earnings differentials, the retirement process, private pension plans, productivity in the meatpacking industry, and employment conditions in Japan. The articles are scholarly in style with extensive footnotes, documented data, and many diagrams. Most of them are descriptive but a few develop an econometric model or provide a mathematical appendix. The authors are academics at U.S. universities or government economists.

A typical issue contains four or five full-length articles and three or four shorter reports. Regular features that appear in most issues are: "Major Agreements Expiring Next Month" - a list of collective bargaining agreements expiring next month, "Developments in Industrial Relations": - a report of agreements reached and rulings of the National Labor Relations Board, and "Book Reviews" - one or two signed reviews plus a list of publications received. Each issue includes a thirty-five to forty page section of "Current Labor Statistics". This section provides the "principal statistical series collected and calculated by the Bureau of Labor Statistics" on employment, prices, wages, and productivity.

350.   **Multinational Business.** DATE FOUNDED: 1972. FREQUENCY: q. PRICE: $220/yr. PUBLISHER: The Economist Intelligence Unit, Spencer House, 27 St. James's Place, London SWIA INT, England. EDITOR: Sarah Child. INDEX. ADVERTISEMENTS. CIRCULATION: 500. MANUSCRIPT SELECTION: BOOK REVIEWS. INDEXED/ABSTRACTED: BPIA, KeyEcS, PAIS. DATABASES: ECONAB, MC, PAIS INT. TARGET AUDIENCE: AC, GP, SP.

Multinational Business is a publication that reviews "news and analysis of multinational corporate enterprise". It claims to "provide essential information and analysis for decision makers worldwide." Each issue contains "reports ranging from analysis of economic and political conditions to aspects of government policies specifically relevant to multinational corporations." Articles in recent issues have dealt with topics such as why Japan appears to have a competitive edge in manufacturing, U.S. private bank flow to African countries, how to deal with exchange rate volatility, the multinational reinsurance market, the role played by multinational corporations in economic development, the international labor market, the international transfer of technology, the characteristics of specific countries' multinational firms, and the prospects for the economy and foreign involvement in specific nations. Articles are non-technical in nature. They are concisely written and usually contain a great deal of information. Many include data presented in tables and charts. They are written by economic and financial researchers in the U.S., Britain, and other European countries. Many are academics, but others are international business consultants, analysts with research institutes or business executives.

Each issue is divided into two parts, 1) "In Depth" which contains three approximately ten page articles and 2) "Multinational Report" which contains from three to six shorter articles plus reports and data. A "Research Review" provides several unsigned book reviews. Newsworthy items are presented in "Round Up". Important acquisitions and mergers are listed and "Currency Focus" discusses the relative strength and weaknesses of different currencies.

National Economic Trends. see Federal Reserve Bank of St. Louis. National Economic Trends.

351.   National Food Review. DATE FOUNDED: 1978. FREQUENCY: q. PRICE: $11/yr. PUBLISHER: U.S. Department of Agriculture, Economic research Service, 500 12th Street, S.W., Room 246, Washington, D.C. 20250. EDITOR: Kathryn Longen Lipton. ILLUSTRATIONS. INDEX. ADVERTISEMENTS. CIRCULATION: 4,000. MANUSCRIPT SELECTION: Editor. MICROFORMS: UMI. REPRINTS: UMI. INDEXED/ABSTRACTED: BPI, PAIS. DATABASES: PAIS INT. TARGET AUDIENCE: GP.

The National Food Review which supersedes National Food Situation, is a government publication that covers a wide range of topics related to food. Recent issues have dealt with food consumption and demand, food preservation and manufacturing, food quality and safety, and nutrition. Many articles cover the economic aspect of food such as food expenditures, food prices, the food stamp program, the national school breakfast and lunch programs and special supplemental programs for women, infants, and children (WIC). Other articles report on a specific type of food or food industry such as fish farms, the poultry industry, and frankfurters. The articles are descriptive and incorporate charts, graphs, and tables of data. The authors are staff members of the Economic Research Service.

The format varies somewhat from issue to issue. Some issues have a theme and present four to six articles relating to that theme. Regular sections, which however, do not necessarily appear in every issue, include "Legislation", "Food Situation and Review", "Consumer Research", "Marketing" and "Perspectives." A total of ten to twelve short two or three page articles distributed among various sections appear in each issue.

352.   National Institute Economic Review. DATE FOUNDED: 1959. FREQUENCY: q. PRICE: $80/yr. PUBLISHER: National Institute of Economic and Social Research, 2 Dean Trench St., Smith Square, London SW1P 3HE England. EDITOR: David Savage. ILLUSTRATIONS. INDEX. CIRCULATION: 4,000. MANUSCRIPT SELECTION: Editorial Board. MICROFORMS: EPML. REPRINTS: DAW.

SPECIAL ISSUES: INDEXED/ABSTRACTED: BPI, BPIA, InEcA, IntBibE, JEL, KeyEcS, PAIS, Pred, WAERSA. DATABASES: CAB AB, ECONAB, ECONLIT, MC, PAIS INT, PF. TARGET AUDIENCE: AC, SP.

The National Institute Economic Review is the publication of an independent, non-profit research institute in the U.K. Its primary emphasis is on "current economic developments and a coherent view of likely trends..." The Review concentrates on the economic situation in the U.K. Articles generally present current empirical data and future projections on a variety of economic concerns. Recent issues have included articles on topics such as Treasury Bill interest rates, protectionism in Europe, unemployment, government expenditure, and labor productivity. The articles are scholarly in style and sometimes use statistical methodologies. The source for data used is always given. The authors are economists with various universities in the U.K., the Institute, or other research institutes. The Review deals with the same subject area as Economic Review and Cambridge Economic Policy Review.
Each issue begins with an in-depth section on the economic situation which is divided into the home economy and the world economy. Three or four regular articles follow this section. A "Calendar of Economic Events" lists business and government happenings for the previous three months. Another in-depth section is the "Statistical Appendix" which lists data for economic factors such as gross domestic product, production in industry, prices, incomes, imports and exports, balance of payments, and others.

353.   National Tax Journal. DATE FOUNDED: 1948. FREQUENCY: q. PRICE: $30/yr. PUBLISHER: National Tax Association-Tax Institute of America, 21 East State Street, Columbus, Ohio 43215. EDITOR: Daniel M. Holland. ILLUSTRATIONS. INDEX. CIRCULATION: 4,000. MANUSCRIPT SELECTION: Editor and Referees. MICROFORMS: UMI. REPRINTS: UMI. SPECIAL ISSUES: INDEXED/ABSTRACTED: AcctInd, BPI, BPIA, InEcA, IntBibE, JEL, PAIS. DATABASES: ACCTIND, ECONLIT, MC, PAIS INT. TARGET AUDIENCE: AC, SP.

The National Tax Journal is the publication of a professional association of accountants, lawyers, business managers, government administrators, and academics. It presents "a broad spectrum of professional subject matter dealing with government finance and taxation...to all concerned with public sector finance and policy." Recent issues deal with topics such as the regional distribution of federal expenditures, educational finance reforms, the social security system, tax-exempt bonds, state gasoline taxation, a flat rate income tax system, corporate taxation, state tax revenues, and tax-sheltered individual retirement savings plans. The articles are scholarly and vary in their degree of technicality. Some articles include methodological discussions in an appendix. Most of the authors are academics at American universities. The National Tax Journal's scope is similar to that of Public Finance Quarterly, but offers fewer theoretical analyses.
A typical issue includes six to eight articles ranging from ten to thirty pages each. A "Notes and Comments" section includes from two to nine short papers. The September issue contains the papers read at the Spring Symposium. Recent symposia were devoted to government budget deficits. The December issue announces the winners of the annual competition for outstanding Doctoral dissertations.

354.   National Westminster Bank Quarterly Review. DATE FOUNDED: 1968.
FREQUENCY: q. MERGER: Westminster Bank Review, National Provincial Bank
Review and District Bank Review (1968). PRICE: Free. PUBLISHER: National
Westminster Bank PLC, 41 Lothbury, London EC2P 2BP England. EDITOR:
David F. Lomax. ILLUSTRATIONS. CIRCULATION: 45,000. MANUSCRIPT SELEC-
TION: Editor. MICROFORMS: UMI. REPRINTS: UMI. INDEXED/ABSTRACTED: InEcA,
IntBibE, JEL, PAIS, Pred, WAERSA. DATABASES: CAB AB, ECONLIT, PAIS INT,
PF. TARGET AUDIENCE: AC, GP, SP. SAMPLE COPIES: Libraries.

The National Westminster Bank Quarterly Review publishes a broad array
of articles dealing with applied economics, business conditions, and
public policies. Many of them are concerned with conditions in the U.K.
but industrialized countries in Continental Europe, the U.S., and Japan
are also included. Articles are descriptive, didactic, or evaluative.
Descriptive articles cover topics such as the U.K. financial system,
enterprise zones, the Japanese economy in the 1980's, capital spending
on roads, the truck manufacture industry, and comparison of national
health service policies. Examples of topics that have received a
critical evaluation by the author are French macro-economic policies,
regulation of business rates in the U.K., OPEC pricing policies, and the
"right to work" concept. Articles that explain basic economic concepts
to readers have covered GNP, monetary exchange rates, and the economic
costs of inflation. The articles are expository in style and occasionally include statistical data. Most of the authors are economists
associated with universities in the U.K. Some are affiliated with
consulting firms, banks, or investment firms.
    Each issue contains from four to five articles varying in length from
ten to fifteen pages each.

355.   Natural Resources Forum. DATE FOUNDED: 1977. FREQUENCY: q.
PRICE: $74/yr. PUBLISHER: Graham & Trotman Ltd., Sterling House, 66
Wilton Road, London SW1V IDE, England. EDITOR: Raymond R. Knowles.
ILLUSTRATIONS. INDEX. MANUSCRIPT SELECTION: Editor. REPRINTS. Authors.
BOOK REVIEWS. INDEXED/ABSTRACTED: WAERSA. DATABASES: CAB AB. TARGET
AUDIENCE: AC, SP.

Natural Resources Forum is published for the United Nations Department
of Technical Cooperation for Development. It presents "analyses of the
major economic, technological and policy issues associated with energy,
mineral and water resources exploration, development and management."
The journal is international in scope but emphasizes natural resources
utilization in the developing countries. Recent issues have included
economic articles dealing with topics such as prospects of the world oil
market, effects of state versus private ownership on the base metals
industry, non-OPEC production of oil, limitations of econometric models
of minerals markets, and World Bank financing of energy projects in
developing countries. The articles are scholarly and employ charts,
graphs, and data but do not use mathematical methodology in their
discussions. The authors are from the international community of
economists, engineers, geologists, and financiers. Natural Resources
Forum has an international and technological orientation whereas Natural
Resources Journal focuses on the U.S. and legal decisions of U.S.
courts.

A typical issue includes six to seven full-length articles and up to four short notes. An average of three signed book reviews appear in each issue.

356.   **Natural Resources Journal.** DATE FOUNDED: 1961. FREQUENCY: q. PRICE: $20/yr. PUBLISHER: The University of New Mexico, School of Law, 1117 Albuquerque, New Mexico, 98731. EDITOR: Albert E. Utton. ILLUSTRA-TIONS. INDEX. ADVERTISEMENTS. CIRCULATION: 2,000. MANUSCRIPT SELECTION: Editor. BOOK REVIEWS. SPECIAL ISSUES: INDEXED/ABSTRACTED: InEcA, IntBibE, JEL, PAIS. DATABASES: ECONLIT, PAIS INT. TARGET AUDIENCE: AC, SP.

The Natural Resources Journal emphasizes research studies on the utilization of natural and environmental resources and its relationship to public policy. This journal offers a mix of economic and legal analyses of current concerns about the preservation of the environment and natural resources. Recent issues have dealt with topics such as fisheries management, water rights, restoration of surface mines, taxation of mineral resources, land use planning, and energy policy. Most of these studies focus on the U.S., but occasionally an article such as "International Steam Coal Markets" is included. Most of the articles are expository in style but those articles offering economic analysis may use a quantitative approach. The authors of the "lead" articles are American academics in the fields of economics, geography, agricultural economics, and law. Occasional contributions from re-searchers at the National Park Service are included. The "notes" which present analyses of court decisions are written by law students at the University of New Mexico. Natural Resources Journal occasionally overlaps the subject area of Natural Resources Forum but differs in its focus on resources and legal decisions relating to resources in the U.S. while Forum is international in scope and includes articles dealing with technological innovations.

A typical issue includes six or seven full-length "lead" articles and six or seven shorter "notes." Four signed book reviews and a list of books received appear in each issue. Occasionally, issues are devoted to a symposium on a specific topic such as structural changes in energy demand and supply or environmental management policies.

357.   **Nevada Review of Business and Economics.** DATE FOUNDED: 1977. FREQUENCY: q. PRICE: Free. PUBLISHER: University of Nevada, Bureau of Business and Economic Research, College of Business Administration, Reno, Nevada 89557. EDITOR: Albin J. Dahl. ILLUSTRATIONS. CIRCULATION: 2,000. MANUSCRIPT SELECTION: Editorial Review Board. INDEXED/ABSTRACTED: PAIS. DATABASES: PAIS INT. TARGET AUDIENCE: AC, GP, SP. SAMPLE COPIES: Libraries and Individuals.

The Nevada Review of Business and Economics supersedes Nevada Business Review published since 1957. It concentrates on the "business and economic environment of Nevada," with occasional articles pertaining to the American economy. Compared to other business school publications, it is closest to Georgia Business and Economic Conditions, Montana Business Quarterly, and Arkansas Business and Economic Review in the degree of focus on its home state. Examples of topics covered in recent issues are economic conditions in Nevada, population projections for Nevada,

Nevada's business climate, computer usage in the State, managing
accounts receivable, ethical premises in business, Nevada's gambling
industry, Nevada's barite industry, casino gambling in Alberta, Canada,
and public sector collective bargaining in right-to-work states.
Articles are non-technical, but frequently include tables of data and
charts. Occasionally a somewhat technical article with diagrams is
published. Most authors are academics in departments of economics or
business administration. The majority teach at Nevada institutions.
     A typical issue contains four articles. About one-third of an issue
is devoted to statistical tables providing Nevada economic indicators,
Las Vegas and Reno SMSA data, Nevada data by county, and selected U.S.
economic indicators.

New England Economic Indicators. see Federal Reserve Bank of Boston. New
England Economic Indicators.

New England Economic Review. see Federal Reserve Bank of Boston. New
England Economic Review.

358.   The New England Journal of Business and Economics. DATE FOUNDED:
1974. FREQUENCY: 2/yr. PRICE: Free. PUBLISHER: University of Rhode
Island, College of Business Admininstration, Research Center in Business
and Economics, Kingston, Rhode Island 02881. EDITORS: Peter E. Kaveos,
Blair M. Lord. ILLUSTRATIONS. INDEX. ADVERTISEMENTS. CIRCULATION: 2,200.
MANUSCRIPT SELECTION: Editors and Reviewers. SPECIAL ISSUES: INDEXED/
ABSTRACTED: PAIS. DATABASES: PAIS INT. TARGET AUDIENCE: AC, SP. SAMPLE
COPIES: Libraries and Individuals.

The New England Journal of Business and Economics supersedes Rhode
Island Business Quarterly published since 1965. Since 1978 it is the
official publication of the New England Business and Economic Association. It publishes research articles "of regional interest with particular focus on New England." In contrast to most business school
publications, it is a technical journal aimed at professional economists
and business administration specialists. It does not, however, publish
articles that have a national focus such as Akron Business & Economic
Review or Indiana's Business Horizons. Topics covered in recent issues
include migration and economic change in New England, regional business
cycles, hospital output costs in Rhode Island, residential demand for
fuels in New England, high technology industry in New Hampshire,
inequities in public education, hydroelectric power in New England, and
competitive tax exportation across states. Articles are often as
concerned with the theoretical models and methodologies employed as with
the empirical results which are invariably drawn from New England data.
Most articles use mathematics and statistics. The authors are predominantly academics at universities located in New England, but some
are from other universities and a few are corporate or government agency
researchers.
     A typical issue contains six articles, each about twelve pages in
length. Occasionally a comment on a previously published article and a
reply is included.

359.   **New Labor Review.** DATE FOUNDED: 1978. FREQUENCY: a. PRICE: Free. PUBLISHER: San Francisco State University, Labor Studies Forum, Division of Cross Disciplinary Programs in the Behavioral and Social Sciences, 1600 Holloway Avenue, San Francisco, California 94132. EDITOR: Melvin H. Pritchard. ADVERTISEMENTS. CIRCULATION: 1,000. MANUSCRIPT SELECTION: Editors. MICROFORMS: UMI. BOOK REVIEWS. TARGET AUDIENCE: AC, GP, SP. SAMPLE COPIES: Libraries and Individuals.

New Labor Review is an interdisciplinary journal in the labor field. It is subtitled "A journal of the labor movement past and present." It focuses on labor economics, labor law, industrial sociology, and labor history. Representative topics written about in recent issues include industrial policy and how it impacts the labor movement, worker participation schemes at the point of production, economic evaluation of comparable worth, OSHA reproductive-health protection in the work place, Samuel Gomper's views on social insurance and workmen's compensation, non-compliance with the Landrum Griffin Act, British and U.S. response to the Industrial Workers of the World, strike tactics, and union busting. Occasionally an article presents a point of view, but most are scholarly in nature and positive in approach. The typical article is expository and written in a narrative style. Quantitative methodologies are not employed. The authors include academics in economics, history or law, graduate students in economics or history, labor leaders, and researchers.

Each issue begins with "From the Editors", a one to three page introduction to the articles in the issue. This is followed by four to seven page articles of various lengths. Each issue also contains from four to seven signed book reviews varying from one to nine pages each.

360.   **New Zealand Economic Papers.** DATE FOUNDED: 1966. FREQUENCY: a. PRICE: $15/yr. PUBLISHER: New Zealand Association of Economists, P.O. Box 568, Wellington, New Zealand. EDITOR: P. A. Wooding. ILLUSTRATIONS. INDEX. CIRCULATION: 800. MANUSCRIPT SELECTION: Editors and Referees. BOOK REVIEWS. INDEXED/ABSTRACTED: WAERSA. DATABASES: CAB AB. TARGET AUDIENCE: AC, SP.

New Zealand Economic Papers is the journal of the association of professional economists in New Zealand. It emphasizes "economics and economic history relevant to New Zealand." The majority of articles present the results of empirical research on a particular aspect of New Zealand's economy although a few articles present a theoretical discussion. Examples of topics covered in recent issues are labor productivity growth rates, subsidies of forest exports, costs of capital in agriculture, occupational segregation among white-collar workers, tax evasion by sheep owners, economies of scale in the life insurance industry, and market concentration. Some examples of theoretical articles are "The Inflationary/Unemployment Dynamic in New Zealand" and "Reflections on Fiscal Policy." The articles are scholarly in style and make use of references, data, and mathematical methodologies. The authors, all of them New Zealanders, are academics, government economists, or researchers with private organizations.

A typical issue contains from eight to eleven regular articles. Recent issues have contained as many as four shorter notes or comments. There is an extensive book review section containing eight to ten signed reviews as well as one to two review articles. A section "Discussion/Working Papers" lists work-in-progress reports issued by universities, government agencies and research institutes.

361.   The Nigerian Journal of Economics and Social Studies. DATE
FOUNDED: 1959. FREQUENCY: 3/yr. PRICE: $30/yr. PUBLISHER: Nigerian
Economic Society, Department of Economics, University of Ibadan, Ibadan,
Nigeria. EDITOR: Ibi Ajayi. ILLUSTRATIONS. INDEX. CIRCULATION: 1,800.
MANUSCRIPT SELECTION: Editorial Board. BOOK REVIEWS. INDEXED/ABSTRACTED:
WAERSA. DATABASES: CAB AB. TARGET AUDIENCE: AC, SP. SAMPLE COPIES:
Libraries.

The Nigerian Journal of Economic and Social Studies is the official
publication of a professional association of economists in Nigeria. The
publication concentrates on empirical research on the Nigerian economy
but purely theoretical papers are included occasionally. Some papers
deal with other West African countries or with general economic development topics. Occasionally, papers dealing with public policy relating to
economic planning are included. Empirical studies have appeared on
topics such as electricity costs in Nigeria, low cost housing in
Nigeria, and automobile assembly plants in Nigeria. Recent theoretical
studies have dealt with a macroeconomic model of Togo, multicriteria
decision making, input-output analysis, and production functions. The
articles vary from being descriptive to being almost entirely mathematical. Much use is made of statistical data. Most of the authors are
professors of economics at Nigerian universities. This publication
concentrates on economics whereas The Journal of Business and Social
Studies is interdisciplinary in scope.
    A typical issue includes six to eight articles, varying in length
from ten to thirty pages each. Most issues have one or two signed book
reviews. As of 1984 there is a one to two year lag in the publication
schedule.

362.   North Carolina Review of Business and Economics. DATE FOUNDED:
1974. FREQUENCY: q. PRICE: Free. PUBLISHER: University of North Carolina
at Greensboro, Center for Applied Research, School of Business and
Economics, 301 Business and Economics Building, Greensboro, North
Carolina 27412. EDITORS: G. Donald Jud, George B. Franigan, Robert D.
Norton. ILLUSTRATIONS. INDEX. ADVERTISEMENTS. CIRCULATION: 3,000.
MANUSCRIPT SELECTION: Editors and Editorial Board. BOOK REVIEWS. TARGET
AUDIENCE: GP. SAMPLE COPIES: Libraries and Individuals.

The North Carolina Review of Business and Economics is a business school
publication aimed at citizens interested in economics and finance. The
articles are non-technical yet presented on a fairly high level. Each
issue includes some material of special interest to North Carolinians,
but the majority of articles deal with topics of national interest.
Representative topics from recent issues include risk management, labor
relations, the health maintenance organization alternative, forecasting
the value of the dollar, tax shelters, and the money market. The authors
are predominantly academics in the School of Business and Economics at
the University of North Carolina-Greensboro. This title is less technical than business school journals such as the Quarterly Journal of
Business and Economics or the Review of Business and Economic Research.
It is far less parochial than many business school publications such as

South Dakota Business Review or the Montana Business Quarterly and is
most like Business Horizons and Mississippi Business Review.
A typical issue contains four or five articles. Features found in
most issues include a column on computer usage, one signed book review,
tables and charts that express recent trends in business activity in
North Carolina, and a School of Business and Economics section with a
message from the Dean.

363.   North Central Journal of Agricultural Economics. DATE FOUNDED:
1979. FREQUENCY: 2/yr. PRICE: $10/yr. PUBLISHER: North Central Adminis-
trative Committee, c/o North Dakota State University, Department of
Agricultural Economics, 203 Morrill Hall, Fargo, North Dakota, 58105.
EDITOR: Lee F. Schrader. ILLUSTRATIONS. CIRCULATION: 350.MANUSCRIPT
SELECTION: Editors and Referees. TARGET AUDIENCE: AC, SP.

The North Central Journal of Agricultural Economics is published by a
committee comprised of heads of agricultural economics departments at
land grant universities in thirteen states in the north central region
of the U.S. Its purpose is "to serve as a medium for communicating to
professionals in extension, teaching, and research, information about
empirical works in agricultural economics." NCJAE focuses on applied
research studies of problems related to agricultural development. Much
of the empirical data is derived from the north central region of the
U.S. Representative titles of recently published articles include "The
Economic Impact of Recent Tax Law Changes on Machinery Purchase Alternatives", "Tariffs and Transport Costs on U.S. Wheat Exports", and "The
Impact of Property Tax Relief on Education in Rural Areas." The articles
are scholarly in style and utilize modern quantitative methodologies.
The authors are predominantly professors of agricultural economics at
universities in the north central region, although economists from other
states also make contributions. NCJAE complements the American Journal
of Agricultural Economics by offering a regional focus as does the
Northeastern Journal of Agricultural and Resource Economics.
    Each issue contains from fifteen to eighteen articles. Some of the
articles are designated as being part of an agricultural experiment
station report series.

364.   Northeastern Journal of Agricultural and Resource Economics.
DATE FOUNDED: 1972. TITLE CHANGES: Journal of the Northeastern Agricul-
tural Economics Council (1972-1984). FREQUENCY: 2/yr. PRICE: $10/yr.
PUBLISHER: Northeastern Agricultural and Resource Economics Association,
University of Massachusetts, Department of Agricultural and Resource
Economics, 221 Draper Hall, Amherst, Massachusetts 01003. EDITOR: Cleve
Willis. CIRCULATION: 450. MANUSCRIPT SELECTION: Editor and Referees.
REPRINTS: Authors. TARGET AUDIENCE: AC, SP.

The Northeastern Journal of Agricultural and Resource Economics is
published by a regional association of professional agricultural
economists. It covers a wide range of topics related to agricultural and
resource economics. Most of the articles are empirical studies of
economic conditions existing in the Northeastern U.S. Recent issues have
included articles on topics such as measurement of the value of agricultural land, economics of milk and dairy farms, fresh vegetable production in the Northeastern U.S., pricing of hard blue crabs in the

Chesapeake Bay, the crop yield insurance program, agricultural pollution control policies, and hazardous waste accident liability. The articles are scholarly in nature and most of them use modern mathematical methodology. Most of the authors are academics at universities in the Northeastern U.S. A few graduate students are co-authors. At least one of the authors must be a member of the Association in order to have a paper accepted for publication. NJARE covers the same subject area and is on the same technical level as the American Journal of Agricultural Economics. The difference lies in NJARE's regional emphasis.

A typical issue includes fifteen to eighteen papers, ranging from five to ten pages each in length. The October issue includes invited papers read at the annual Association meeting, abstracts of Masters Theses receiving awards, and the minutes of the annual business meeting.

365.   Northern California Review of Business and Economics. DATE FOUNDED: 1974. FREQUENCY: q. PRICE: $10/yr. PUBLISHER: California State University, Chico, Center for Business and Economic Research, Chico, California 95926. EDITOR: Daniel Sullivan. ILLUSTRATIONS. CIRCULATION: 500. MANUSCRIPT SELECTION: Editors. REPRINTS: Publisher. SPECIAL ISSUES: INDEXED/ABSTRACTED: PAIS. DATABASES: PAIS INT. TARGET AUDIENCE: GP. SAMPLE COPIES: Libraries and Individuals.

The Northern California Review of Business and Economics is a business school publication that concentrates on business and economics pertaining to Northeastern California. In this parochial aspect it is similar to titles published by some other business schools such as those at the University of Montana, Arizona State, the University of Kentucky, and the University of Nevada. Since the Northeastern portion of California is an agricultural region, many of the articles focus on that sector. Topics discussed in recent issues include the use of the computer in agriculture, the almond industries in Spain and in Northern California, farm size, and kiwifruit production. Other topics that receive attention include the state of small business, the California water system, railroads of the region, regional population trends, the employment picture, advertising, and California's exports. Articles are non-technical in nature and descriptive in style. Many contain data which is presented in tables and charts. Photographs are used. The authors are predominantly academics and business writers. Some are Center staff or academics at CSU-Chico, but many are associated with other universities or business organizations.

An issue contains from three to eight articles of varying lengths. Most issues include a section, "Economic Indicators", which provides current Northeastern California data on a by-county basis. In 1983 a special issue appeared on regional "Economic Development."

Note Economiche; Revista Economica del Monte dei Paschi di Seina. see Economic Notes by Monte dei Paschi di Siena.

366.   OECD Economic Outlook. DATE FOUNDED: 1967. FREQUENCY: 2/yr. PRICE: $25/yr. PUBLISHER: OECD Information Sevice, Chateau de la Muette, 2, rue Andre-Pascal, F75775 Paris, Cedex 16, France. EDITOR: OECD Department of Economics and Statistics. ILLUSTRATIONS. ADVERTISEMENTS. MANUSCRIPT SELECTION: Department of Economics and Statistics. MICRO-

FORMS: Publisher. INDEXED/ABSTRACTED: Pred. DATABASES: PF. TARGET
AUDIENCE: AC, GP, SP.

OECD Economic Outlook is published in both English and French by the
Organisation for Economic Co-operation and Development, an international
organization of twenty-four member countries. The Outlook "provides a
periodic assessment of economic trends and prospects in OECD countries,
developments which largely determine the course of the world economy."
Articles report on both national and international developments with
respect to monetary and fiscal policies; labor markets; wages, costs,
and prices; foreign trade and current balances; and monetary exchange
rates. The articles are expository in style and utilize charts, graphs,
and tables of data. Names of authors are not provided. The Outlook is
"the joint work of members of the Secretariat of the Department of
Economics and Statistics." This publication provides statistical data
and forecasts while The OECD Observer provides articles for the general
public and OECD Economic Studies presents scholarly research articles.
    Each issue begins with a seven or eight page overview of the world
economy. A section "Domestic and International Developments" reports on
general economic indicators for various countries. A section "Development in Individual Countries" reports on the current and projected
economy of each of the twenty-four member countries. A "Technical Annex"
includes additional detailed tables and charts.

367.   OECD Economic Studies. DATE FOUNDED: 1983. FREQUENCY: ir. PRICE:
$25/yr. PUBLISHER: OECD Information Service, Chateau de la Muette, 2,
rue Andre-Pascal, F75775 Paris, Cedex 16, France. EDITOR: Stephen J.
Porter. ILLUSTRATIONS. ADVERTISEMENTS. MANUSCRIPT SELECTION: Editor.
MICROFORMS: Publisher. TARGET AUDIENCE: AC, SP.

OECD Economic Studies is published in both English and French by the
Organisation for Economic Co-operation and Development, an international
organization of twenty-four member countries. This publication supersedes OECD Economic Outlook Occasional Studies (1970-1983). Most of the
articles are "in the area of applied macroeconomic and statistical
analysis, generally with an international or cross-country dimension."
Recent issues included articles on Eurocurrency banking, international
economic linkages, output responsiveness and inflation, national saving
studies, effects of oil price changes, public sector deficits, and
effects of the minimum wage on the youth labor market. The articles are
scholarly and may utilize quantitative methodologies. Most of the
authors are economists with OECD but occasional contributions by
academics or researchers from private institutions are included. This
publication is aimed at a professional readership while The OECD Observer is for the general public and OECD Economic Outlook is for academics,
practitioners, and public policy officials.
    A typical issue includes four or five in-depth articles, each of
which may be as long as fifty pages. Each of the papers may include
notes, a bibliography, or a mathematical appendix.

368.   The OECD Observer. DATE FOUNDED: 1962. FREQUENCY: 6/yr. PRICE:
$11/yr. PUBLISHER: OECD Information Service, Chateau de la Muette, 2,
rue Andre-Pascal, F75775 Paris, Cedex 16, France. EDITOR: Jane Bussiere
ILLUSTRATIONS. INDEX. ADVERTISEMENTS. CIRCULATION: 25,000. MANUSCRIPT

SELECTION: Editor. MICROFORMS: BHW, UMI, MEd,. REPRINTS: UMI. INDEXED/
ABSTRACTED: BPI, PAIS, Pred, WAERSA, WorkRelAbstr. DATABASES: CAB AB,
PAIS INT, PF. TARGET AUDIENCE: GP.

The OECD Observer is published in both English and French by The
Organisation for Economic Co-operation and Development, an international
organization of twenty-four industrialized countries. The focus of the
Observer is to provide information to the public on the world economy.
Articles discuss a broad spectrum of topics such as economic policy,
energy needs, the environment, trade, economic development, financial
affairs, agriculture and fisheries, industry, science and technology,
education, manpower, and transportation. Articles deal with these topics
on both a national and an international basis. The articles are descriptive and incorporate charts, graphs, tables of data, and photographs.
Both signed and unsigned articles are included. The authors are staff
members of OECD. The OECD Observer is the popular "newsmagazine"
published by this organization while the OECD Economic Outlook provides
economic statistics and forecasts and OECD Economic Studies presents
scholarly research studies.
   A typical issue includes six to twelve articles of three to six pages
each. Some issues have a section on "Country Problems and Strategies"
which focuses on specific countries. New OECD publications are listed in
the back of each issue.

369.   Oeconomica Polona. DATE FOUNDED: 1974. FREQUENCY: q. PRICE:
$48/yr. PUBLISHER: Panstwowe Wydawnictwo Ekonomiczne, ul. Niecala 4a,
Warsaw, Poland. EDITOR: Aleksander Lukaszewicz. ILLUSTRATIONS. INDEX.
CIRCULATION: 2,000. MANUSCRIPT SELECTION: Editorial Committe. BOOK
REVIEWS. INDEXED/ABSTRACTED: IntBibE, PAIS. DATABASES: PAIS INT. TARGET
AUDIENCE: AC, SP. SAMPLE COPIES: Libraries and Individuals.

Oeconomica Polona is issued under the auspices of the Economic Committee
of the Polish Academy of Sciences, the Polish Economic Society and the
Institute of Economic Sciences. It is the only Polish economic journal
published in the English language. The articles are "translations or
revised and enlarged versions of the most significant papers and
excerpts from books that were published in Poland." Oeconomica Polona
includes views, discussions, and research results of Polish economists.
It is primarily a theoretical periodical; but empirical studies are also
published. Emphasis is placed on studies dealing with the problems of
socialist economies such as their growth and functioning patterns, their
objectives and measures of implementation, and their evolution of
concepts and methods of planned development. Occasionally papers on
issues of "the world economy", i.e: the capitalist system and the
problems of developing countries, are also published as are articles on
the history of economic thought. Articles vary as to technical content
with approximately half employing quantitative methodologies. The
authors are Polish professional economists, predominantly at Warsaw
University, the Central School of Planning and Statistics, the Foreign
Trade Institute, and various institutes associated with the Polish
Academy of Sciences.
   Each issue contains from four to eight articles of various lengths.
Some issues have a "Miscellania" section which may include excerpts from
or summaries of major documents concerning economic reform in Poland.

Most issues have a "Notes on Books" section with from one to three
signed book reviews.

370.   OPEC Review. DATE FOUNDED: 1976. FREQUENCY: q. PRICE: $40/yr.
PUBLISHER: Pergamon Press Inc., Maxwell House, Fairview Park, Elmsford,
New York 10523. EDITOR: Fadhil J. Al-Chalabi. ILLUSTRATIONS. INDEX.
CIRCULATION: 2,000. MANUSCRIPT SELECTION: Editorial Board. MICROFORMS:
Publisher. REPRINTS: OPEC. TARGET AUDIENCE: AC, GP, SP.

OPEC REVIEW, subtitled an energy and economic forum, is published on
behalf of the Organization of the Petroleum Exporting Countries. It's
aim is "to serve as an academic forum for observers of energy, development, and general economic matters affecting oil-producing and oil-
consuming nations." OPEC REVIEW presents articles that relate to energy
consumption and production on an international scale. It emphasizes
petroleum although other sources of energy such as natural gas and
hydro-power are also discussed. Articles in recent issues deal with
topics such as international finance, forecasts of energy demand and
supply, pricing policies and strategies, oil industries of Venezuela,
Nigeria, and Iraq, stability of OPEC, and development needs in the Third
World. There is a wide variation in the technical level of the articles.
Some use mathematical models while others offer a descriptive essay
devoid of mathematical analysis. There is also a broad spectrum of
authors. Many are economists with the OPEC Secretariat. Some are
academics at European universities, executives with banks or engineers
with energy companies. Occasionally an American academic makes a
contribution.
    Each issue includes from four to seven full-length articles. The
Winter issue features an "Energy Indicators" section which presents
retrospective data on energy demand and prices by region.

371.   The Oriental Economist. DATE FOUNDED: 1934. FREQUENCY: m. PRICE:
$90/yr. PUBLISHER: Toyo Keizai Shinposha, 1-4 Nihonbashi-Hongokucho,
Chuoku, Tokyo, Japan. EDITOR: Atsuo Tsuruoka. ILLUSTRATIONS. INDEX.
ADVERTISEMENTS. CIRCULATION: 9,000. MANUSCRIPT SELECTION: Editor and
Editorial Board. BOOK REVIEWS. INDEXED/ABSTRACTED: KeyEcS, PAIS, WAERSA.
DATABASES: CAB AB, ECONAB, PAIS INT. TARGET AUDIENCE: GP. SAMPLE COPIES:
Libraries and Individuals.

The Oriental Economist is one of the oldest English language serials
published in Japan. It reports on current business and economic conditions in Japan as well as other parts of Asia and in the U.S. Articles
in recent issues present reports on specific Japanese companies, Korean
conglomerates, business trends, yen/dollar exchange rates, export
processing zones, and agricultural import quotas. The articles are
non-techincal and expository in style. More than half of the articles
are signed and when signed no professional affiliation is provided for
the author. The Oriental Economist is comparable in style to Business
Week and other popular business periodicals.
    Each issue, in addition to ten short articles, has several regular
feature sections. Sections on "Banking", "Business Trends" "Frontiers of
Japanese Technology", and "Stock Market" appear in each issue. "Man in
the News" presents an interview with a president of a large corporation.
"Data Files" present data on a variety of economic factors such as

personal savings, equipment investment plans, skilled worker shortages, automobile production, and export/import trends. Other data is included in the "Statistics" section such as GNP, banking accounts, prices, wages, production, sales, and inventory. Short signed book reviews appear on an irregular basis.

372.   Oxford Bulletin of Economics and Statistics. DATE FOUNDED: 1939. FREQUENCY: q. PRICE: $75/yr. institutions, $39.95/yr. personal. PUBLISHER: Basil Blackwell Publisher Ltd., 108 Cowley Road, Oxford OX4 1JF, England. EDITOR: Editorial Board. ILLUSTRATIONS. INDEX. ADVERTISEMENTS. CIRCULATION: 1,200. MANUSCRIPT SELECTION: Editorial Board and Referees. REPRINTS: KR. SPECIAL ISSUES: INDEXED/ABSTRACTED: InEcA, IntBibE, JEL, KeyEcS, PAIS, WAERSA. DATABASES: CAB AB, ECONAB, ECONLIT, PAIS INT. TARGET AUDIENCE: AC, SP. SAMPLE COPIES: Libraries.

The Oxford Bulletin of Economics and Statistics is a scholarly journal that publishes articles in applied economics. It touches virtually all fields of the discipline. Its editors state that "particular stress is placed on publishing results useful to policy makers." It is a technical journal with heavy emphasis on the mathematical, econometric, and statistical methodologies employed. Almost all articles have empirical content. In the majority of cases British data are used, but recent issues have also included articles that utilized data from Japan, India, China, Kenya, and the U.S. Articles typically have a substantial number of references and more than half are accompanied by an appendix. The majority of authors are British academic economists, but U.S., Canadian, and other European researchers also make contributions. The Oxford Bulletin's scope and level are similar to the Review of Economics and Statistics. The latter, which is a more voluminous publication, also includes theoretical articles.

A typical issue contains from four to six regular articles varying greatly in length. Thirty to forty page articles are not uncommon. some issues also include a comment and a reply. Almost all issues have a "Practitioner's Corner" section, usually containing one "how-to" article concerning a statistical or econometric method. A special issue is published about once in two years. The most recent one, directed by two guest editors, contained eight articles on "Pay Policies for the Future."

373.   Oxford Economic Papers. DATE FOUNDED: 1938. FREQUENCY: 3/yr. PRICE: $60/yr. PUBLISHER: Oxford University Press, Walton Street, Oxford, OX2 6DP England. EDITORS: N.H. Dimsdale, C.L. Gilbert, PJN Sinclair. ILLUSTRATIONS. INDEX. ADVERTISEMENTS. CIRCULATION: 2,500. MANUSCRIPT SELECTION: Editors and Referees. MICROFORMS: UMI. REPRINTS: Publisher. SPECIAL ISSUES: INDEXED/ABSTRACTED: BritHumI, InEcA, IntBibE, JEL, KeyEcS, PAIS, SSI, WAERSA. DATABASES: CAB AB, ECONAB, ECONLIT, PAIS INT, SSI. TARGET AUDIENCE: AC, SP. SAMPLE COPIES: Libraries.

Oxford Economic Papers is a publication associated with one of the most prestigious universities in the world. It publishes articles in a wide variety of fields in economics. Its policy is to "accept contributions in economic theory, applied economics, econometrics, economic development, economic history, and the history of economic thought." Articles in the latter two fields are found more frequently than in other leading

212   Economics Journals and Serials

general economic journals such as the American Economic Review or the Journal of Political Economy. Occcasionally a survey article as distinguished from an original research paper is published. Most articles are technical in nature and employ modern quantitative methodologies. Articles are scholarly in style with long lists of references. Many are accompanied by mathematical and/or statistical appendices. Oxford Economic Papers, which was originally intended for publishing only contributions from members of Oxford University, now accepts articles from economists throughout the world. Perhaps twenty-five percent of the authors are associated with Oxford and other British universities. The rest are academics at other European universities as well as American, Australian, Canadian and Japanese universities.

A typical issue contains about ten full-length articles plus some short notes, comments and replies. Approximately once every two years a special "Supplement" issue is published such as a recent one that contained ten articles on "Economic Theory and Hicksian Themes."

374.   Pakistan & Gulf Economist. DATE FOUNDED: 1962. TITLE CHANGES: Pakistan Economist (1962-1982) MERGER: Finance and Industry (1969). FREQUENCY: w. PRICE: $85/yr. institutions, $100/yr. personal. PUBLISHER: Kaneez Sajjad, 9 Shafi Court (2nd Floor), Mereweather Road, P.O. Box 10449, Karachi, Pakistan. EDITOR: Muzaffar Hasan. ILLUSTRATIONS. INDEX. ADVERTISEMENTS. CIRCULATION: 20,000. MANUSCRIPT·SELECTION: Editors. BOOK REVIEWS. SPECIAL ISSUES: TARGET AUDIENCE: GP. SAMPLE COPIES: Libraries and Individuals.

Pakistan & Gulf Economist is a magazine aimed at business people and government agency policymakers in English speaking countries the world over. It provides "evaluation and comment on the changing economic milieu in Pakistan." Lead articles take the form of editorials and special reports. A viewpoint favoring free enterprise and faith in the market mechanism is frequently in evidence. Editorials and other articles deal with such economic topics as import policy, export policy, the Pakistan budget, the Pakistan economic plan, business-government relations, investment policy, and economic cooperation with different countries including Gulf countries, the U.K. and the U.S. Others focus on particular industries in Pakistan, management issues, genetic engineering, and the need for more scientific research. Articles are expository and non-technical. Some tables of data are provided. The authors are editors and writers of the journal plus government officials, academics, and business managers. Some are introduced on page one, but no affiliation is provided for the majority of them.

A typical issue is sixty pages in length and contains seven to eight articles, two to three editorials, four columns, nine features, and five reports and news digests. Most issues include sections on "Science and Technology", "the Gulf", "International", "Management", "Corporate Affairs", "Market Intelligence", and "Statistics."

375.   The Pakistan Development Review. DATE FOUNDED: 1961. FREQUENCY: q. PRICE: $50/yr. PUBLISHER: Pakistan Institute of Development Economics, Quaid-i-Azam University Campus, Post Box 1091, Islamabad, Pakistan. EDITOR: Syed Nawab Haider Naqvi. INDEX. ADVERTISEMENTS. MANUSCRIPT SELECTION. Editor and Editorial Board. REPRINTS: Author. BOOK

REVIEWS. SPECIAL ISSUES: INDEXED/ABSTRACTED: InEcA, IntBibE, JEL, WAERSA. DATABASES: CAB AB, ECONLIT. TARGET AUDIENCE: AC, SP.

The Pakistan Development Review, subtitled an international journal of development economics, concentrates on publishing the results of empirical research on Pakistan's socio-economic problems. Occasionally a theoretical discussion or a study of another developing country is included. Articles in recent issues deal with Pakistan's problems such as wheat production, wages and employment, redistribution of rural income, rural electrification projects, pricing of petroleum products, consumption patterns, and factors influencing fertility. Theoretical articles have dealt with topics such as human capital, distortions in factor markets, and optimal social order. The articles are scholarly in nature. Some are quite technical and employ various mathematical or statistical methodologies. The authors are research economists with the Institute, government researchers at various Pakistani agencies, or academics at European or American universities. The Review covers the same subject areas but is more technical than Government College Economic Journal and Pakistan Journal of Applied Economics.
   A typical issue includes three to five regular articles. Some issues also have one or two short notes and communications. Each issue has at least one in-depth signed book review and occasionally some annotations in a "Book Notes" section.

376.   Pakistan Economic and Social Review. DATE FOUNDED: 1959. TITLE CHANGES: Punjab University Economist (1959-1970). FREQUENCY: 2/yr. PRICE: $30/yr. PUBLISHER: University of the Punjab, Faculty of Economics, New Campus, Lahore, Pakistan. EDITOR: Rafig Ahmad. INDEX. CIRCULATION: 2,500. MANUSCRIPT SELECTION: Editors and Editorial Advisory Board. BOOK REVIEWS. INDEXED/ABSTRACTED: InEcA, JEL. DATABASES: ECONLIT. TARGET AUDIENCE: AC, SP.

Pakistan Economic and Social Review "is devoted to the publication of articles concerned with the economic and social problems facing Pakistan as well as other emergent nations of the World." It is aimed at academics, researchers, planners, and administrators interested in economic development problems. Representative topics include productivity changes in Pakistan's agriculture, rural versus urban consumption patterns in Pakistan, the relationship among farm size, tenancy and wheat produced with modern technology in the Punjab region, and characteristics of economic planning in developing countries. Some articles deal with Pakistan's industrial growth and with growth models for the nation. Occasionally an article dealing with a social issue is included such as recent ones on corruption in Pakistan and drug addiction in Pakistan. This scholarly journal publishes primarily technical articles. They incorporate economic theory and frequently have strong empirical content. Most make use of econometric methodologies. The authors are predominantly economists associated with Pakistan's universities, research institutes, or government agencies. A few are sociologists. Occasionally, the author is with a Russian research institute, an American government agency, or the World Bank. The Review covers the same subject area but is more technical than Government College Economic Journal and Pakistan Journal of Applied Economics.

Each issue contains from four to six articles averaging about twelve pages in length. Some issues have a note or comment and others a signed book review.

377.   **Pakistan Journal of Applied Economics.** DATE FOUNDED: 1982. FREQUENCY: 2/yr. PRICE: $30/yr. institutions, $22/yr. personal. PUB-LISHER: Applied Economics Research Centre, P.O. Box 8403, University of Karachi - 32, Pakistan. EDITOR: M. Shahid Alam. ILLUSTRATIONS. INDEX. ADVERTISEMENTS. CIRCULATION: 1,000. MANUSCRIPT SELECTION: International Board of Editors. REPRINTS: Publisher. BOOK REVIEWS. TARGET AUDIENCE: AC, SP. SAMPLE COPIES: Libraries and Individuals.

Pakistan Journal of Applied Economics is a new scholarly journal published by an active university research center in Pakistan. It publishes articles in the area of development economics with special emphasis on development problems in Pakistan. Most articles are in applied economic research but occasionally more expository papers are published such as a recent one which argued that a new international economic order can be achieved through reforms that include "correcting biases in the international system, concessional transfers and more voice." More representative of what the journal intends to publish in future years is exemplified by articles such as "the Economics of Private Medical Practice in Karachi," The Determinants of Mortality in a Low Income Area of Karachi" and "Development Ranking of Districts of Pakistan." Review articles are also published. Articles are technical in nature and usually make use of some quantitative analysis. More statistics than mathematics is employed. The authors are either American or other foreign academics or they are associated with the Karachi Applied Research Centre. The Journal covers the same subject area but is less technical than The Pakistan Development Review and Pakistan Economic and Social Review.
A typical issue contains six articles, ranging from ten to twenty-five pages in length. Occasionally a shorter "Note" is included. From one to three signed book reviews are found in most issues.

378.   **Pennsylvania Business Survey.** DATE FOUNDED: 1938. FREQUENCY: m. PRICE: $6/yr. PUBLISHER: The Pennsylvania State University, Center for Research of the College of Business Administration, 103 BAB11, University Park, Pennsylvania 16802. EDITOR: Norma I. Gavin. ILLUSTRATIONS. CIRCULATION: 1,500. MANUSCRIPT SELECTION: Editor. SPECIAL ISSUES: TARGET AUDIENCE: GP. SAMPLE COPIES: Libraries and Individuals.

The Pennsylvania Business Survey is a business school publication "designed to give a quick picture of current economic conditions in Pennsylvania and its major metropolitan areas." It publishes only articles relevant to the economy of the state of Pennsylvania. It views its role much like Montana Business, Georgia Business and Economic Conditions, and Arizona Business. Being a monthly, allows Pennsylvania Business Survey to be more up-to-date than its quarterly counterparts. In addition to a general survey of the current economic condition of the State, articles appear on such topics as personal income changes, spatial variations in type of employment, the development and perfor-mance of the Pennsylvania Index of Leading Indicators, the competitive position of the State, and population trends. Occasionally excerpts of

speeches given by business leaders or economists at Pennsylvania State
University conferences are published. Articles are non-technical, but
usually include a substantial amount of data. Most of the material in
each issue is prepared by the editor or members of her staff. Some
articles are written by faculty members at Pennsylvania State University.
     Issues range from four to sixteen pages in length. Each issue
contains an economic update for the State and an employment report.
Every third issue includes "Around the State", a survey of the economic
condition of each of the major metropolitan areas in the four regions of
the State. The February issue contains a "Year End Review."

379.   The Philippine Economic Journal. DATE FOUNDED: 1962. FREQUENCY:
q. PRICE: $20/yr. PUBLISHER: The Philippine Economic Society, P.O. Box
1764, Manila, Philippines. EDITOR: Mahar Mangahas. CIRCULATION: 1,000.
MANUSCRIPT SELECTION: Editor. SPECIAL ISSUES: INDEXED/ABSTRACTED: InEcA,
JEL, WAERSA. DATABASES: CAB AB, ECONLIT. TARGET AUDIENCE: AC, SP.

The Philippine Economic Journal is the publication of the professional
association of economists in the Philippines. It concentrates on all
aspects of the Philippine economy. Articles in recent issues deal with
such diverse topics as agrarian reform policies, progress in population
control, income distribution among farmers, performance of the steel and
cement industries, commercial banking policies, health care demand,
energy policy simulation models, pesonal savings, agricultural production development, foreign exchange rates' impact on less developed
countries, efficiency of rice production, construction cycles in Manila,
and the impact of oil prices on the economy. Occasionally, an article
deals with other Southeast Asia countries. The articles are scholarly in
style and frequently employ mathematical methodologies. Many of the
authors are academics from Philippine, American, or Australian universities. Others are researchers from Philippine government agencies or
international agencies such as the World Bank.
     A typical issue includes four or five articles, ranging from ten to
twenty pages in length. Recently, a special issue was devoted to
publications of papers based on the theses and dissertations of winners
of the Philippine Economic Spociety's competition for the best Master's
theses and Doctoral dissertations.

380.   Philippine Economy and Industrial Journal. DATE FOUNDED: 1964.
FREQUENCY: q. PRICE: 100pesos/yr. PUBLISHER: Sanve Publishing, Inc., May
Building, Suite 308, 834 Rizal Avenue, Manila, Philippines. EDITOR:
Santos Z. Concepcion. ILLUSTRATIONS. ADVERTISEMENTS. CIRCULATION:
10,000. MANUSCRIPT SELECTION: Editor. INDEXED/ABSTRACTED: WAERSA.
DATABASES: CAB AB. TARGET AUDIENCE: GP.

The Philippine Economy and Industrial Journal reports on the economy,
business activities, and civic activities of the Philippines. Articles
in recent issues deal with topics such as natural resources development,
land use policies, agricultural growth forecasts, the Bureau of Mines,
the government employees insurance system, employment problems of
Filipino workers, the patent office, pollution control, and the development of Quezon City. These articles are descriptive in style and
incorporate some numerical data. Most of the authors are government

officials or directors of corporations. The Philippine Economy and Industrial Journal covers the same subject area as Journal of Agricultural Economics and Development. The latter is more scholarly and occasionally includes an article dealing with other Asian countries. Each issue begins with an editorial that focuses on a specific aspect of the Philippine economy. A typical issue includes five full-length articles and up to ten shorter articles and notes. The full-length articles are accompanied by photographs. Many of the notes are news releases from government agencies or messages from President Marcos.

381.   **The Philippine Review of Economics and Business.** DATE FOUNDED: 1964. TITLE CHANGES: The Philippine Review of Business and Economics (1964-1979) FREQUENCY: q. PRICE: $20/yr. PUBLISHER: University of the Philippines, the School of Economics and the College of Business Administration, Diliman, Quezon City, 3004, Philippines. EDITORS: Ernesto M. Pernia, Cesar G. Saldana. ILLUSTRATIONS. INDEX. CIRCULATION: 1,000. MANUSCRIPT SELECTION: Editors. SPECIAL ISSUES: INDEXED/ABSTRACTED: WAERSA. DATABASES: CAB AB. TARGET AUDIENCE: AC, SP.

The Philippine Review of Economics and Business is a scholarly journal that publishes a wide variety of economics and business articles. Articles may be theoretical as recent ones on maximum - speed development and on management control or methodological as those on perfect multicollinearity and on truncation bias in household money demand tests. Many are empirical dealing with an aspect of the Philippine economy, the ASEAN countries of Indonesia, Malaysia, Philippines, Singapore, and Thailand, or with all of Asia. Examples include recent articles on the effective protection of the Philippine chemical industry, demographic development in ASEAN, farming systems development in small Southeast Asian farms, and problems of heavy industrialization in Asian development. The majority of articles are technical in nature and employ modern quantitative methodologies. Since the Review "serves primarily as a vehicle for the publication of research work done at the School of Economics and the College of Business Administration" (University of the Philippines) few authors have other affiliations. Most are professors, but a few are students or recent graduates. Occasionally articles are published by academics at other universities. By contrast, The Philippine Economic Journal, the scholarly journal of the Philippine Economic Society, offers contributions by economists representing a much wider geographic area.
A typical issue contains five or six articles plus a few abstracts of dissertations and theses recently completed at the University of the Philippines. In 1982 the Review published a special issue containing twenty-one essays in development economics in honor of Harry T. Oshima.

382.   **Population and Development Review.** DATE FOUNDED: 1975. FREQUENCY: q. PRICE: $141/yr. PUBLISHER: The Population Council, Center for Policy Studies, One Dag Hammarskjold Plaza, New York, New York 10017. EDITOR: Ethel P. Churchill. ILLUSTRATIONS. INDEX. CIRCULATION: 7,000. MANUSCRIPT SELECTION: Editor. MICROFORMS: UMI. REPRINTS: UMI. BOOK REVIEWS. INDEXED/ABSTRACTED: InEcA, IntBibE, JEL, PAIS, WAERSA. DATABASES: CAB AB, ECONLIT, PAIS INT. TARGET AUDIENCE: AC, GP, SP.

Population and Development Review is a journal that deals with "the
interrelationships between population and socioeconomic development" and
presents discussions of "related issues of public policy." The Review
focuses on two broad areas and their economic implications -demographic
studies of industrialized countries and fertility trends in developing
countries. Examples of articles dealing with the former are "Modern
fertility patterns in the United States and Japan" and "Immigrants,
Taxes, and Welfare in the United States." Articles dealing with the
latter areas are "Analysis of Recent Data on the Population of China"
and "Factors Affecting Fertility Control in India." The articles are
scholarly and make use of charts, graphs, numerical data, and references. The authors, from both the U.S. and other countries, are academics at universities, researchers at population research institutes,
or staff members at government agencies. This journal provides more of
an economic perspective yet is less technical than Population Studies.
    Each issue contains seven sections. The "Articles" section contains
four or five full-length papers. The "Notes and Commentary" section
contains one or two short notes and comments on papers appearing in
previous issues. A "Data and Perspectives" section features an in-depth
analysis of population growth of a specific country or region. "Archives" presents a retrospective glimpse of an early writer on population growth. "Book Reviews" provides up to six lengthy signed reviews
and up to eight brief reviews. The "Documents" section presents excerpts
from official documents concerning population problems. "Abstracts"
provides summaries of the articles in English, French, and Spanish.

383.   Population Studies. DATE FOUNDED: 1947. FREQUENCY: 3/yr.PRICE:
$60/yr. PUBLISHER: London School of Economics, Population Investigation
Committee, Houghton Street, Aldwych, London WC2A 2AE, England. EDITOR:
E. Grebenik. ILLUSTRATIONS. INDEX. ADVERTISEMENTS. CIRCULATION: 3,000.
MANUSCRIPT SELECTION: Editor and Referees. MICROFORMS: KTO. REPRINTS:
Author. BOOK REVIEWS. SPECIAL ISSUES. INDEXED/ABSTRACTED: InEcA,
IntBibE, JEL, PAIS. DATABASES: ECONLIT, PAIS INT. TARGET AUDIENCE: AC,
SP. SAMPLE COPIES: Libraries and Individuals.

Population Studies, subtitled a Journal of Demography covers empirical
research in demographic studies. Articles concentrate on studies
undertaken in Great Britain and other industrialized countries as well
as in developing countries. Articles deal with topics such as fertility
patterns, infant and child mortality, remarriage of widows/ers,
contraceptive   usage,   child-timing   decisions,   old   age
expectations, divorce, and adult mortality. Some articles present a
historical analysis of one or more of these topics. The articles are
of a scholarly nature and frequently employ statistical methodologies.
The authors are primarily academics at American and British
universities although some are researchers with private research
institutes or government agencies. Population Studies tends to
approach demographic studies from a sociological perspective while
Population and Development Review emphasizes the economic implications
of population growth. Population Studies is the more quantitative of
the two.
    A typical issue includes eight to ten full-length articles plus an
occasional comment on a previously published paper. Eight to twelve
signed book reviews appear in each issue. An extensive bibliography of
books received is also included.

384.   Problems of Economics. DATE FOUNDED: 1958. FREQUENCY: m.
PRICE: $270/yr. institutions, $76/yr. personal. PUBLISHER: Myron
Sharpe, Inc., 80 Business Park Drive, Armonk, New York 10504. EDITOR:
Murray Yanowitch. INDEX. ADVERTISEMENTS. MANUSCRIPT SELECTION: Editor.
INDEXED/ABSTRACTED: InEcA, JEL, KeyEcS, PAIS, WAERSA. DATABASES: CAB
AB, ECONAB, ECONLIT, PAIS INT. TARGET AUDIENCE: AC, SP. SAMPLE COPIES:
Libraries and Individuals.

Problems of Economics is a journal containing translations of
articles from Soviet economics journals. The articles selected "are
intended to reflect developments in Soviet economic theory and practice
and to be of interest to those professionally concerned with this
field." The main thrust of the articles is the formulation of proposals
to improve the economic situation of the U.S.S.R. Most of the articles
begin with a reminder of socialist ideology and a reference to a
particular government decree or established plan. The remainder of such
articles discuss methods of reaching or exceeding the goals and explanations of why the goals have not been reached in the past. Examples of
topics included in recent issues are utilization of technological
advances, pricing policies for new products, economic stimulation to
increase production, land utilization, increased capital investment, and
raising the people's living standard. The articles are expository in
style with occasional inclusion of numerical data. All of the authors
are Soviet writers but their professional affiliation is provided
infrequently. The bibliographical citation of the original article is
given.
     Each issue has five or six full-length articles. A glossary which
defines the terms used in the text appears in each issue.

385.   Process Economics International. DATE FOUNDED: 1979. FREQUENCY:
q. PRICE: ₺56/yr. PUBLISHER: Chemecon Publishing Ltd. Parnell House, 25
Wilton Road, London SW1V 1NH, England. EDITOR: A.V. Bridgewater.
ILLUSTRATIONS. ADVERTISEMENTS. CIRCULATION: 2,500. MANUSCRIPT SELECTION:
Editor. REPRINTS: Publisher. BOOK REVIEWS. TARGET AUDIENCE: AC, SP.
SAMPLE COPIES: Libraries and Individuals.

Process Economics International is an interdisciplinary journal covering
the three broad areas of chemical engineering, finance, and applied
economics. It provides information on management and economic factors
such as corporate planning, cost analysis, forecasting, inflation,
labor, location, market analysis, pricing, productivity, and taxation,
as well as information on new technology. Articles encompass industries
on an international scale. Examples of articles focusing on economic
factors are "Compensatory Arrangements in East-West Trade," "Life Cycle
Costing: An Alternative Approach to Economic Evaluation," and "The
Australian Chemical Industry in the 1980s." The articles are descriptive
in style and incorporate extensive data in the form of charts, graphs,
and tables. Quantitative analysis is used infrequently. The authors are
from a variety of backgrounds. They are generally engineers, economists,
or management executives and are associated with academia, industry, or
government agencies.
     A typical issue contains from five to eight articles, ranging from
two to ten pages in length. A large part of each issue is devoted to the
regular feature sections, which include 1) PEI Plant Cost Indices --
inflation indicators for capital plant equipment for thirty countries,

2) International Prices -- prices of forty basic industrial materials,
3) PEI Calendar of Events -- a list of future technical and techno-
economic conferences, 4) Money and Finance -- a report on a specific
financial topic, 5) Book Reviews -- two to eight short signed reviews,
and 6) Annotated Bibliography -- a classified list of current periodical
articles in relevant fields. This periodical is produced on glossy, high
quality paper and illustrates some of its articles with photographs.

386.   Public Choice. DATE FOUNDED: 1966. TITLE CHANGES: Papers on
Non-Market Decision Making (1966-1968). FREQUENCY: 9/yr. PRICE: $88/yr.
institutions, $29/yr. personal. PUBLISHER: Martinus Nijhoff Publishers,
P.O. Box 163, 3300 AD Dordrecht, The Netherlands. EDITOR: Gordon
Tullock. ILLUSTRATIONS. INDEX. ADVERTISEMENTS. CIRCULATION: 2,000.
MANUSCRIPT SELECTION: Editors and Referees. MICROFORMS: UMI. REPRINTS:
CCS. BOOK REVIEWS. SPECIAL ISSUES. INDEXED/ABSTRACTED: InEcA, IntBibE,
JEL. DATABASES: ECONLIT. TARGET AUDIENCE: AC, SP. SAMPLE COPIES:
Libraries and Individuals.

Public Choice is associated with the Center for Study of Public Choice
at George Mason University. It deals with "the intersection between
economics and political science." It applies "essentially economic
methods to problems normally dealt with by political scientists." Public
Choice publishes articles in "a field of interest to both economists and
political scientists who are interested in theoretical rigor, statistical testing, and applications to real world problems." Topics covered
in recent issues include intergovernmental grants, judicial systems,
sunset laws, election forecasting, free riding, interest group behavior,
local school spending, government regulation, and various issues in
public administration. The articles are scholarly and usually technical
in nature. Modern quantitative methodologies are employed. The majority
of authors are academic economists but some political scientists also
make contributions. Most are associated with American universities, the
rest with universities in Western Europe, Israel, and Canada.
    Most issues contain about six articles plus four or five signed book
reviews. Some issues also include a comment on a previously published
article and a reply. Articles are preceeded by brief abstracts. Each
year a special issue is published that contains the papers and comments
which comprise the proceedings of the Carnegie Conference on Political
Economy held annually at Carnegie-Mellon University.

387.   Public Finance/Finances Publiques. DATE FOUNDED: 1946. TITLE
CHANGES: Openbare Financien (1946-1947). FREQUENCY: 3/yr. PRICE: $45/yr.
PUBLISHER: Foundation Journal Public Finance, Goethestrasse 13, D-6240
Konigstein, West Germany. EDITOR: Dieter Biehl. ILLUSTRATIONS. INDEX.
CIRCULATION: 1,700. MANUSCRIPT SELECTION: Editor and Editorial Board.
SPECIAL ISSUES. INDEXED/ABSTRACTED: InEcA, IntBibE, JEL, KeyEcS, PAIS,
WAERSA. DATABASES: CAB AB, ECONAB, ECONLIT, PAIS INT. TARGET AUDIENCE:
AC, SP. SAMPLE COPIES: Libraries and Individuals.

Public Finance/Finances Publiques is an international journal devoted to
all aspects of public finance. The articles include empirical studies of
public finance problems as well as discussions of established theories
and public policy choices. Examples of empirical studies reported in
recent issues include corporate tax reform in Greece, income tax

progressivity in Australia, state pension expenditures in Illinois, and public expenditures in a variety of industrialized countries. Articles presenting theoretical discussions have dealt with topics such as measures of consumer surplus, indexation schemes, and utility analysis of choices involving risk. Articles dealing with public policy choices have covered topics such as adoption of a progressive personal expenditure tax, relevance of revenue tariffs for commercial policy, and industrial policy in market-oriented economies. Most of the articles are highly technical and employ mathematical models in either the text or in an appendix. The authors are academics from universities all over the world. This journal covers public finance on an international scope whereas Public Finance Quarterly concentrates on public finance concerns in the U.S.

A typical issue has eight full-length articles and up to five shorter "Communications". A summary of each article is provided in English, French, and German.

388.   Public Finance Quarterly. DATE FOUNDED: 1973. FREQUENCY: q. PRICE: $62/yr. institutions, $28/yr. personal. PUBLISHER: Sage Publication, Inc., 275 S. Beverly Drive, Beverly Hills, California 90212. EDITOR: J. Ronnie Davis. INDEX. ADVERTISEMENTS. CIRCULATION: 900. MANUSCRIPT SELECTION: Editor and Referees. MICROFORMS: UMI. REPRINTS: UMI. BOOK REVIEWS. INDEXED/ABSTRACTED: BPIA, InEcA, IntBibE, JEL, PAIS. DATABASES: ECONLIT, MC, PAIS INT. TARGET AUDIENCE: AC, SP.

Public Finance Quarterly is a journal devoted to "the study of the public sector of the economy." Papers deal with "both theoretical and empirical studies" and deal with "government policies at the federal, state, or local level." Articles in recent issues reported on empirical studies such as marginal tax rates for 1964-1984, effect of federal income tax rates on investment, income tax progressivity among the states, and effects of Michigan property tax credits. Theoretical studies covered topics such as the efficacy of fiscal policy, an optimal income tax system, welfare economics of taxes, and analysis of duopoly behavior among public good producers. The articles are scholarly in nature and generally employ sophisticated quantitative methodologies. The authors are predominantly American academic economists. A few are researchers with U.S. government agencies, bank executives, or academics from other countries. Public Finance Quarterly concentrates on public sector finance in the U.S. while Public Finance/Finances Publiques emphasizes international public finance concerns.

Each issue contains six or seven full-length articles. Some issues include two or three short comments or an in-depth signed book review.

389.   Public Utilities Fortnightly. DATE FOUNDED: 1929. FREQUENCY: bw. PRICE: $72/yr. PUBLISHER: Public Utilities Reports, Inc., Suite 2100, 1700 North Moore St., Arlington, Virginia 22209. EDITOR: Lucien E. Smartt. ILLUSTRATIONS. INDEX. ADVERTISEMENTS. CIRCULATION: 8,000. MANUSCRIPT SELECTION: Editors. MICROFORMS: UMI. BOOK REVIEWS. SPECIAL ISSUES. INDEXED/ABSTRACTED: AcctArt, AcctInd, BPI, BPIA, FedTaxArt, PAIS. DATABASES: ACCTIND, MC, PAIS INT. TARGET AUDIENCE: AC, GP, SP.

Public Utilities Fortnightly is subtitled "the magazine presenting information and views on major utility issues affecting utilities." This

title offers a mix of articles ranging from somewhat technical dicus-
sions to descriptive narrative. It deals with a great variety of public
utility subjects. Topics discussed in recent issues include telecommuni-
cation policies, offshore oil and gas drilling, public utility bankruptcy, rate adjustment mechanisms, surviving acid rain, residential
conservation programs, competition in various public utility industries,
optimal capitalization structure, natural gas deregulation, hydropower
relicensing, coal conversions by electric utilities, pricing telephone
services, life-cycle cost analysis, and future energy needs. The authors
are academics in finance or economics; public utility commissioners or
staff members; economic or management consultants; business executives;
and representatives of trade associations.

Most issues contain from three to five full-length articles. Additional short articles appear in six regular features: 1-Washington and
the Utilities, 2- Financial News and Comment, 3 - What Others Think, 4 -
The March of Events, 5 - Progress of Regulation, and 6-Industrial
Progress. Each issue also contains an editor's statement, readers'
letters concerning previously published articles, and a calendar of
utility events. About six special issues are published each year on
topics such as nuclear power, energy, and finance.

390.   **Quarterly Economic Commentary.** DATE FOUNDED: 1965. TITLE
CHANGES: Joint Quarterly Industrial Survey (1967-1968), Quarterly
Industrial Survey (1965-1967). FREQUENCY: q. PRICE: L30/yr. PUBLISHER:
The Economic and Social Research Institute, 4 Burlington Rd., Dublin 4,
Ireland. ILLUSTRATIONS. MANUSCRIPT SELECTION: Editors. TARGET AUDIENCE:
AC, GP, SP.

The Quarterly Economic Commentary is the publication of a major Irish
economic research institute. In addition to publishing the Commentary,
ESRI publishes books and several extensive research series. Commentary
has a dual purpose: 1) to provide data and analyses with respect to the
current economic condition of Ireland and 2) to publish scholarly
articles pertaining to the Irish economy. The former is prepared
exclusively by ESRI economists while the latter are written by academic
economists at Irish universities, economists at Irish government
agencies, researchers at the Central Bank of Ireland, as well as staff
economists at ESRI. Articles vary in their technical content, but all
are scholarly in nature.

A typical issue is from fifty to seventy pages in length. Each issue
begins with an unsigned summary of the state of the economic condition
of Ireland. This is followed by several tables showing current Irish
national accounts and a fairly detailed fifteen to thirty page "Commentary" on the condition of the Irish economy. The latter is separated
into segments on the international economy and on the domestic economy.
Most issues contain one or two additional articles, each from ten to
twenty pages in length. Each issue includes a statistical appendix that
provides data for a number of Irish economic indicators. In excess of
100 available ESRI books and monographs are listed in each issue.

391.   **Quarterly Economic Reviews.** DATE FOUNDED: 1952. FREQUENCY: q.
PRICE: $64/yr. per Review, institutions, $88/yr. per Review, personal.
(A progressive discount is available for 1-92 Reviews). PUBLISHER: The
Economist Intelligence Unit, Spencer House, 27, St. James's Place,

London SW1A INT, England. ADVERTISEMENTS. CIRCULATION: 40,000. MICRO-
FORMS: WMI. SPECIAL ISSUES. TARGET AUDIENCE: AC, GP, SP. SAMPLE COPIES:
Libraries and Individuals.

The Quarterly Economic Reviews are ninety-two separate publications that
together cover over 160 countries throughout the world. The publisher,
EIU, is an international economic research and management consulting
firm founded in 1946. QER's are aimed at business executives, government
policy makers, academics, and the general public. They provide "a
concise service of business oriented analysis of the latest economic
indicators in almost all countries of the world." They are prepared by
EIU staff and no authors are named.
    Each issue of each of the ninety-two QER's begins with a 300 word
"Summary" of the contents. This is followed by an "Economic Structure"
page that offers a succinct display of the latest gross domestic
production, exports, imports, balance of payments, and foreign debt
figures. Next is an "Outlook" section that provides a 1,000 to 3,000
word forecast of the economy's prospects in the next year. The heart of
each issue is the "Review" section which is a 5,000 to 10,000 word
analysis of the news and data releases of the latest three months.
Economic trends in graphic form are provided as a center spread in each
issue. The last few pages of each issue are given to statistical
appendices tabulating key economic data and detailed foreign trade
figures. A separate annual supplement is published for each QER. This
describes economic structure, places economic data in their setting and
outlines political conditions, planning policies, foreign investment
rules and exchange restrictions.

392.   Quarterly Journal of Business and Economics. DATE FOUNDED: 1962.
TITLE CHANGES: Nebraska Journal of Economics and Business (1962-1983).
FREQUENCY: q. PRICE: $10/yr. PUBLISHER: University of Nebraska-Lincoln,
College of Business Administration, Lincoln, Nebraska 68588. EDITOR:
George McCabe. ILLUSTRATIONS. INDEX. CIRCULATION: 1,000. MANUSCRIPT
SELECTION: Editor and Board of Editors. MICROFORMS: UMI. REPRINTS: UMI.
INDEXED/ABSTRACTED: BPIA, JEL, PAIS. DATABASES: ECONLIT, MC, PAIS INT.
TARGET AUDIENCE: AC, SP. SAMPLE COPIES: Libraries and Individuals.

The Quarterly Journal of Business and Economics is not a typical
business school publication. It is a scholarly journal which does not
deal with the business and economics of the state of Nebraska. Its
editorial policy is to publish articles which 1) "re-examine important
empirical works, using either a different set of data or an alternative
empirical or theoretical framework", 2) "test important theoretical
works and shed additional light on the issue", and 3) "review and
critically evaluate the literature." Articles are published in virtually
all fields of business and economics. Examples of topics covered in
recent issues are investment in human capital, econometric replication,
treasury bill futures, marginal tax rates and aggregate labor supply,
electric utility equities, the acquisition of motor carriers, natural
monopolies and regulation, the inventory theory of money demand, capital
budgeting, water transferring, and the relationship between concentration, advertising and profitability. Most articles are technical in
nature and make use of quantitative methodologies. Many have substantial
empirical content. The authors are predominantly academics in departments of economics or finance at American universities. Only rarely is

an article written by a Nebraska faculty member. This journal is comparable in level of scholarship and in scope of coverage to The Quarterly Review of Economics and Business.
A typical issue contains from five to seven articles averaging about twelve pages in length.

393.   Quarterly Journal of Economics. DATE FOUNDED: 1886. FREQUENCY: q. PRICE: $48/yr. PUBLISHER: John Wiley & Sons, Inc., 605 Third Avenue, New York, New York 10158. EDITOR: Editorial Board. ILLUSTRATIONS. INDEX. ADVERTISEMENTS. CIRCULATION: 5,000. MANUSCRIPT SELECTION: Editorial Board and Referees. MICROFORMS: MIM, UMI. INDEXED/ABSTRACTED: BPI, BPIA, HistAb, InEcA, IntBibE, JEL, KeyEcS, MathR, PubAdAb, SSI, UrStAb, WAERSA, WorkRelAbstr. DATABASES: CAB AB, ECONAB, ECONLIT, HISTAB, MATHFILE, MC, SSI. TARGET AUDIENCE: AC, SP. SAMPLE COPIES: Libraries.

The Quarterly Journal of Economics is published under the auspices of the Department of Economics, Harvard University. It is among the most prestigious general economics journals. It publishes research articles in all fields of economics, both micro and macro. In recent years a great many articles have appeared in the area of pricing in product and in factor markets. Occasionally articles in economic development and economic history are published. All articles are technical in nature and most employ modern quantitative methodologies. Mathematical models and empirical test results are common to most articles. Footnotes and references are provided in all articles and some are accompanied by appendices. The authors are predominantly American academic economists. Some economic researchers from other countries such as Canada, Australia and Israel also contribute. Occasionally an article is written by a research economist with the World Bank, the International Monetary Fund, or the Federal Reserve System. QJE's scope and level approximate the American Economic Review and the Journal of Political Economy.
Most issues contain from eight to ten full-length articles plus from two to six shorter papers, comments, and replies in a "Notes" section. Each article is preceded by a brief abstract.

394.   The Quarterly Review of Economics and Business. DATE FOUNDED: 1961. FREQUENCY: q. PRICE: $27/yr. institutions, $15/yr. personal. PUBLISHER: University of Illinois, Bureau of Economic And Business Research, College of Commerce and Business Administration, 428 Commerce West, 1206 S. Sixth Street, Champaign, Illinois 61820. EDITOR: Paul Uselding. ILLUSTRATIONS. INDEX. ADVERTISEMENTS. CIRCULATION: 2,000. MANUSCRIPT SELECTION: Editor and Editorial Board. MICROFORMS: MIM, UMI. REPRINTS: UMI. INDEXED/ABSTRACTED: AcctInd, BPI, BPIA, InEcA, IntBibE, JEL, PAIS, PersManageAbstr, WorkRelAbstr. DATABASES: ACCTIND, ECONLIT, MC, PAIS INT. TARGET AUDIENCE: AC, SP.

The Quarterly Review of Economics and Business supersedes Current Economic Comment (1949-1960). It is the official publication of the Midwest Economics Association. In contrast to other regional economic association journals, QREB publishes research articles in business as well as economics. It covers all fields, but more articles appear in micro than in macroeconomics. Articles are technical in nature and many employ mathematical and statistical methodologies. A few are theoretical, but most have substantial empirical content. QREB is not a typical business school publication. It is intended for professionals in economics and finance. Of the many business school publications, it comes closest to Quarterly Journal of Business and Economics published by the University of Nebraska. The authors are predominantly academics in departments of economics or finance at American universities. Only about half are associated with universities in the Midwest.

A typical issue contains seven or eight articles of varying lengths. Most issues also include one or two "Notes", short articles which may or may not refer to a previously published article. A brief description of each article and of the author(s) background(s) appears after the table of contents of each issue. An extensive list of "Books Received" appears at the end of each issue.

395. **Quarterly Review of the Rural Economy.** DATE FOUNDED: 1979. FREQUENCY: q. PRICE: Free. PUBLISHER: Bureau of Agricultural Economics, GPO Box 1563, Canberra, A.C.T., 2601, Australia. EDITOR: Judith Fenelon. ILLUSTRATIONS. MANUSCRIPT SELECTION: Editor. SPECIAL ISSUES. INDEXED/ABSTRACTED: InEcA, JEL, PAIS, WAERSA. DATABASES: CAB AB, ECONLIT, PAIS INT. TARGET AUDIENCE: GP, SP. SAMPLE COPIES: Libraries and Individuals.

The Quarterly Review of the Rural Economy supersedes the Quarterly Review of Agricultural Economics. It is published by the Australian equivalent of the U.S. Department of Agriculture. The Review offers detailed accounts of agricultural industries in Australia and how they are affected by developments in the U.S. and other countries. Recent issues have included articles on topics such as world agricultural trade, Australian farm output and income, the U.S. "payment in kind" (PIK) program, world tobacco prices, the U.S. dollar and the Australian rural sector, and factors affecting the Australian lamb industry. The articles are non-technical in style but incorporate data in the form of tables, charts, and graphs. The authors are predominantly Australian researchers with the Bureau of Agricultural Economics or chief executives of agricultural trade associations or commercial firms. Occasionally contributions are made by staff members of the U.S. Department of Agriculture. The Review publishes less technical articles on Australian agriculture than The Australian Journal of Agricultural Economics.

Regular features make up most of the content of each issue. These are "Overview", a report on the Australian agricultual sector; "Australian Economy", a report on national economic activity; "World Economy", a report on world economic activity; "Commodity Notes", reports on each of eleven agricultural products; and "Statistics", data on economic factors such as value of rural production, exports, prices, rural workforce, livestock numbers, rural credit, and others. In addition to these features, from two to five signed articles appear in each issue. The first issue of each volume includes the proceedings of the National Agricultural Outlook conference. A supplement accompanying the conference issue provides the results of annual surveys of the dairy, livestock, and horticultural industries.

396. **The Rand Journal of Economics.** DATE FOUNDED: 1970. TITLE CHANGES: Bell Journal of Economics (1970-1983). FREQUENCY: q. PRICE: $70/yr. institutions, $25/yr. personal. PUBLISHER: The Rand Corporation, 2100 M. Street, N.W. Washington, D.C. 20037. EDITORS: Alvin K. Klevorick, Stephen W. Salant. ILLUSTRATIONS. INDEX. MANUSCRIPT SELECTION: Editors. MICROFORMS: UMI. BOOK REVIEWS. INDEXED/ABSTRACTED: AcctInd,

BPIA, ComRev, InEcA, IntBibE, JEL, SSI, WAERSA. DATABASES: ACCTIND, CAB AB, ECONLIT, MC, SSI. TARGET AUDIENCE: AC, SP.

The Rand Journal of Economics is a scholarly journal that publishes research articles on "the behavior of regulated industries, the economic analysis of organizations, and more generally, applied microeconomics." This prestigious journal publishes articles that are technical in nature and that make heavy use of quantitative methodologies. Both theoretical and empirical works are published. Most articles present a mathematical model. Topics covered in articles of recent issues include peak load pricing, cartel stability, contracts and moral hazard, resale price maintenance, market contestability, natural monopoly, economic concentration, reputation and product quality, technology adoption, the economics of information, optimal pricing, potential entry, liability and safety regulation, research and development, vertical integration, advertising, merger, collusive behavior, and competition in oligopoly industries. The authors are predominantly academic economists at prestigious American universities. Occasionally economists at research institutes, government agencies, and corporations make contributions.

Most issues contain about seven regular articles that average about fifteen pages in length plus from three to seven "short" articles that are usually less than ten pages in length. Some issues contain an in-depth signed book review.

397.   Regional Science & Urban Economics. DATE FOUNDED: 1971. TITLE CHANGES: Regional and Urban Economics (1971-1974). FREQUENCY: q. PRICE: $120/yr. PUBLISHER: Elsevier Science Publishers B.V. (North-Holland), P.O. Box 1991, 1000 BZ Amsterdam, The Netherlands. EDITOR: Urs Schweizer. ILLUSTRATIONS. INDEX. ADVERTISEMENTS. MANUSCRIPT SELECTION: Editorial Board. MICROFORMS: Elsev. REPRINTS: Elsev. SPECIAL ISSUES. INDEXED/ABSTRACTED: BPIA, CREJ, GeoAb, InEcA, JEL. DATABASES: ECONLIT, MC. TARGET AUDIENCE: AC, SP. SAMPLE COPIES: Libraries and Individuals.

Regional Science and Urban Economics is a highly technical journal offering papers that meet the criteria of being theoretical analyses employing "formal methods from mathematics, econometric, operations research and related fields" and focusing on "immediate or potential uses for regional and urban forecasting, planning and policy." Articles in recent issues have dealt with topics such as the deterrence effect of police expenditures upon crime, location decisions for energy facilities, forecasting models for construction activity, and the economic impact of a proposed transportation system. The articles employ advanced quantitative methodologies. Most construct a model and demonstrate its validity with empirical evidence. Others are purely theoretical. The authors are academics associated with universities in the U.S., Canada, and many European countries. The editorial board is comprised of international scholars from top ranked universities. This publication includes considerably more quantitative analysis than does Regional Studies.

Each issue contains from eight to ten articles ranging from ten to twenty pages each. Special issues, which appear on an irregular basis, are devoted to a specific topic and sometimes have guest editors.

398.   **Regional Science Perspectives.** DATE FOUNDED: 1971. FREQUENCY: 2/yr. PRICE: $25/yr. institutions, $15/yr. personal. PUBLISHER: The Mid-Continent Regional Science Association c/o Kansas State University, Economics Department, Manhattan, Kansas 66506. EDITOR: M. Jarvin Emerson. ILLUSTRATIONS. CIRCULATION: 400. MANUSCRIPT SELECTION: Editor and Referees. REPRINTS: Editor. INDEXED/ABSTRACTED: InEcA, JEL. DATABASES: ECONLIT. TARGET AUDIENCE: AC, SP. SAMPLE COPIES: Libraries.

Regional Science Perspectives is published by a professional association with the assistance of the Economics Department of Kansas State University. It covers a broad range of applied and theoretical regional economic studies. Most of the studies emphasize American conditions but occasionally a Canadian study is included. Representative examples of topics covered in empirical studies include forecasts of economic growth in Minnesota, relationships between income inequality and social inequality in U.S. states, and spatial distribution of development funds in West Virginia. Examples of topics receiving theoretical treatment include equilibrium models of exhaustible natural resources, optimal public investment in pollution control, and a model of regional economic change. The articles are scholarly in nature. Most of them utilize quantitative methodologies. Most of the authors are professors of economics, geography, or management at American universities. Occasional contributions are made by graduate students. Regional Science Perspectives somewhat overlaps in subject content with The Annals of Regional Science, but the latter is more international in scope. They are comparable in technical level.

A typical issue contains six articles, ranging from five to twenty-five pages in length.

399.   **Regional Studies.** DATE FOUNDED: 1966. FREQUENCY: 6/yr. PRICE: $125/yr. institutions, $63/yr. personal. PUBLISHER: Cambridge University Press, The Edinburgh Building, Shaftesbury Road, Cambridge CB2 2RU, England. EDITOR: J.B. Goddard. ILLUSTRATIONS. INDEX. ADVERTISEMENTS. CIRCULATION: 1,300. MANUSCRIPT SELECTION: Editor. MICROFORMS: UMI. REPRINTS: UMI. BOOK REVIEWS. SPECIAL ISSUES. INDEXED/ABSTRACTED: InEcA, IntBibE, JEL, PAIS, WAERSA. DATABASES: CAB AB, ECONLIT, PAIS INT. TARGET AUDIENCE: AC, SP.

Regional Studies is the professional journal of the Regional Studies Association, an organization established in the United Kingdom to study urban and regional problems and policies. This journal publishes the results of "original research on such topics as industrial, retail and office location, labour markets, housing, migration, recreation, transport, communications and the evaluation of public policy..." Articles are international in scope and deal with both developed and less-developed countries. Articles in recent issues have dealt with regional variations in the underground economy, optimum location of shopping centers, manufacturing plants in Austria, and recreational sites in Chicago. The articles are scholarly and incorporate numerical data, graphs and charts. Some employ mathematical techniques. The authors are academics in departments of economics, geography, sociology, regional planning, or management at universities all over the world. This publication offers less sophisticated quantitative analysis than Regional Science and Urban Economics.

Each issue contains five full-length articles. A "Policy Review Section" features articles describing or evaluating public policies concerning economic development in the U.K. An average of ten substantial signed book reviews appear in each issue. An occasional special issue focuses on a particular theme under the guidance of a guest editor.

400.   Relations Industrielles/Industrial Relations. DATE FOUNDED: 1945. FREQUENCY: q. PRICE: Can. $40/yr. institutions, Can. $20/yr. personal. PUBLISHER: Laval University, Department of Industrial Relations, C.P. 2477, Quebec, G1K 7R4, Canada. EDITOR: Gerard Dion. INDEX. ADVERTISEMENTS. CIRCULATION: 2,800. MANUSCRIPT SELECTION: Editor and Referees. MICROFORMS: MIC, UMI. REPRINTS: MIC, UMI. BOOK REVIEWS. INDEXED/ABSTRACTED: BPIA, CBI, IntBibE, PAIS, WorkRelAbstr. DATABASES: CBI, MC, PAIS INT. TARGET AUDIENCE: AC, SP. SAMPLE COPIES: Libraries.

Relations Industrielles/Industrial Relations is a Canadian journal that presents articles in many areas of industrial relations such as labor relations, organizational behavior, human resources management, labor law, and labor economics. The publication emphasizes the situation in Canada but occasional contributions report on situations in other places such as Europe or Israel. Recent issues included articles on topics such as collective bargaining in Canada, youth unemployment in Quebec, industrial retraining programs, managerial rights in Canadian judicial decisions, and job satisfaction. Most of the articles are descriptive in nature. A few employ statistical analyses of numerical data or construct a model to represent a hypothesis. The authors are predominantly Canadian academics from the fields of economics, business, or law.

A typical issue includes nine full-length articles. The journal is in French and English and each article includes a summary in the other language. Regular features include a section on recent court decisions, on labor relations and on changes in labor legislation. A book review section contains eight to twelve signed reviews. A bibliography of recent publications in industrial relations appears in each issue.

401.   Resources and Energy. DATE FOUNDED: 1978. FREQUENCY: q. PRICE: DFL 24/yr. PUBLISHER: Elsevier Science Publishers B.V. (North-Holland) P.O. Box 1991, 1000 BZ Amsterdam, The Netherlands. EDITORS: George S. Tolley, James L. Sweeney. ILLUSTRATIONS. INDEX. ADVERTISEMENTS. MANUSCRIPT SELECTION: Editors and Referees. TARGET AUDIENCE: AC, SP.

Resources and Energy, subtitled a journal devoted to interdisciplinary studies in the allocation of natural resources, is a publication covering an area of interest to both economists and engineers. It encompasses the study of optimum use of natural resources on an international scale. Articles may provide empirical studies, theoretical models, or applications of specific techniques or methods. Examples of recent articles presenting theoretical models are "A Depletable Resource Under International Uncertainty", "Optimal Development of an Economy with a Bounded Inflow of One Essential Resource Input", and "On the Specification of Neoclassical Energy Demand Functions." Representative articles presenting empirical studies are "World Oil Prices and Equity Returns of Major Oil and Auto Companies", "Water Needs of Future Coal Development in the Soviet Union and The United States", and "Alternative

Electricity Supply Plans." Articles discussing applications of specific
methods includes "Energy Input-Output Analysis", "Future Conditions and
Present Extraction", and "Some Pitfalls in the Application of the
Incremental Cost Approach to Formulating U.S. Energy Policy." The
articles are scholarly and generally very technical. The authors, about
half of whom are American, are predominantly academics. A few are
researchers with government agencies or private research institutes.

Each issue contains five full-length articles. Some issues include
announcements of forthcoming conferences and seminars.

402.   Review. DATE FOUNDED: 1977. FREQUENCY: q. PRICE: $60/yr.
institutions, $25/yr. personal. PUBLISHER: Sage Publications, Inc., 275
S. Beverly Drive, Beverly Hills, California 90212. EDITOR: Immanuel
Wallerstein. ILLUSTRATIONS. INDEX. ADVERTISEMENTS. CIRCULATION: 1,000.
MANUSCRIPT SELECTION: Editor. SPECIAL ISSUES. TARGET AUDIENCE: AC.

The Review is published by the Fernand Braudel Center for the Study of
Economies, Historical Systems, and Civilizations. This Center is
associated with the State University of New York at Binghamton. The
Review presents "a perspective which recognizes the primacy of analyses
of economies over long historical time and large space, the holism of
the socio-historical process, and the transitory (heuristic) nature of
theories." The articles in this publication present a Marxist-Socialist
analysis of economic conditions, political systems, and economic history
on an international scale. Both industrialized and developing countries
are studied. Recent issues have included articles on topics such as
income distribution in capitalist countries, Marx's theory of rent as
applied to mineral resources, China's economic relationship with the
Western world in the nineteenth century, and worker's movements in
Africa in the 1930's. The articles are expository in nature. All of them
include extensive references and some include numerical data and graphs.
The authors are predominantly professors of economics or sociology and
are affiliated with universities all over the world.

A typical issue includes four or five articles, each from twelve to
fifty pages in length. Many of the quarterly issues are special issues
that publish papers presented at various colloquia and conferences.

403.   The Review of Black Political Economy. DATE FOUNDED: 1970.
FREQUENCY: q. PRICE: $30/yr. institutions, $15/yr. personal. PUBLISHER:
National Economic Association and the Southern Center for Studies in
Public Policy of Clark College, 240 Chestnut St. S.W. Atlanta, Georgia
30314. EDITOR: Margaret C. Simms. INDEX. ADVERTISEMENTS. CIRCULATION:
1,200. MANUSCRIPT SELECTION: Editor and Board of Editorial Advisors.
MICROFORMS: MIM, UMI. REPRINTS: UMI. BOOK REVIEWS. SPECIAL ISSUES.
INDEXED/ABSTRACTED: InEcA, JEL, PAIS, WorkRelAbstr. DATABASES: ECONLIT,
PAIS INT. TARGET AUDIENCE: AC, GP. SP.

The Review of Black Political Economy "is a scholarly journal devoted to
the examination of issues related to the economic status of black and
Third World peoples." It aims to promote "the analysis and empirical
study of inequality in economic status and opportunity based on race and
ethnic origin." Topics discussed in recent issues include the changes in
income of black versus white females, minority business formation and
failure, the race variable in social security pay outs, the impact of

black political participation, the effect of race on property tax assessment practices, and the impact of multinational firms on power relations in South Africa. Articles vary greatly as to technical content. Many are empirical in nature and employ quantitative method-ologies. But RBPE "does not emphasize methodological and theoretical elaboration for their own sake. The journal is devoted to appraising policy prescriptions for the attainment of economic opportunity on their merits..." The majority of authors are economists at American univer-sities. Academics in other disciplines such as political science, finance, history and geography also contribute. Some writers are economists with consulting firms, research institutes or government agencies such as the Federal Reserve System and the Department of Labor.

Most issues contain from six to eight articles plus one or two in-depth signed book reviews. Occasionally a special issue is published on a particular theme such as "Election Year 1984: Policies Affecting Black People" and "New Perspectives on Unemployment" or the proceedings of a National Economic Association meeting.

404.   Review of Business. DATE FOUNDED: 1964. FREQUENCY: q. PRICE: Free. PUBLISHER: St. John's University, Business Research Institute, College of Business Administration. St. John Hall, Jamaica, New York 11439. EDITOR: Christine Rider. ILLUSTRATIONS. CIRCULATION: 5,300. MANUSCRIPT SELECTION: Issue Editor. BOOK REVIEWS. INDEXED/ABSTRACTED: BPIA, PAIS. DATABASES: MC, PAIS INT. TARGET AUDIENCE: GP. SAMPLE COPIES: Libraries and Individuals.

Review of Business is a business school publication that presents articles in many different areas of business and economics. It is aimed primarily at MBA graduates and other alumni of St. John's University but is appropriate for all persons interested in economics and business subjects. The majority of the articles are non-technical yet presented on a fairly high level. Review of Business does not focus on local, state, or regional topics as do the majority of business school publica-tions. Articles deal with topics of national interest such as economic forecasting, interest rates, federal budget deficits, economic growth, economic development, marketing decision making, management information systems, accounting information systems, and econometric modelling. Each issue, under the direction of a different "issue editor", has a central theme. The authors are predominantly academics in departments of economics or business. A disproportionate number are from St. John's University. Occasionally, articles are contributed by business execu-tives. Review of Business is a little more technical and sophisticated than the average business school publication. It is most like Indiana University's Business Horizons, Akron Business and Economic Review and North Carolina Review of Business and Economics.

A typical issue contains from six to eight articles, each from three to six pages in length. Occasionally an issue contains one or two book reviews which are usually, but not always, signed.

405.   Review of Business and Economic Research. DATE FOUNDED: 1965. TITLE CHANGES: Mississippi Valley Journal of Business and Economics (1965-1975). FREQUENCY: 2/yr. PRICE: $10/yr. PUBLISHER: University of New Orleans, College of Business Administration, Division of Business and Economic Research, New Orleans, Louisiana 70148. EDITOR: Jerry P.

Simpson. ILLUSTRATIONS. INDEX. ADVERTISEMENTS. CIRCULATION: 1,000.
MANUSCRIPT SELECTION: Editor and Board of Editors. MICROFORMS: UMI.
INDEXED/ABSTRACTED: AcctInd, BPI, BPIA, InEcA, JEL, PAIS. DATABASES:
ACCTIND, ECONLIT, MC, PAIS INT. TARGET AUDIENCE: AC, SP.

The Review of Business and Economic Research is a breed apart from the
typical business school publication. It has no parochial interest and is
not aimed at the business community of Louisiana. Instead, it is a
scholarly journal which concentrates on publishing research results in
the fields of finance, accounting, management, marketing, and economics.
Topics discussed in recent issues include corporate bankrupcy, corporate
spin offs, bank holding companies, the velocity of money, the financial
profile of merged firms, capital budgeting, bond rating, risk and return
of options, inflation adjusted accounting data, tender offers, and
exchange rates. Articles are technical in nature and employ both
mathematics and statistics. Most have substantial empirical content. The
authors are academics, predominantly in departments of finance or
accounting, at American universities. Only rarely is an article written
by a faculty member at the University of New Orleans.
    A typical issue contains from seven to ten articles averaging about
twelve pages in length. Some issues include one or two shorter articles
in a "Notes" section. A list of "Books Received" appears in each issue.

406.   The Review of Economic Studies. DATE FOUNDED: 1933. FREQUENCY:
q. PRICE: $65/yr. institutions, $25/yr. personal. PUBLISHER: Society for
Economic Analysis Ltd., c/o Tieto Ltd., Bank House, 8A Hill Road,
Clevedon, Avon B521 7HH, England. EDITORS: G.E. Mizon, K.W.S. Roberts.
ILLUSTRATIONS. INDEX. CIRCULATION: 3,500. MANUSCRIPT SELECTION: Editors
and Referees. INDEXED/ABSTRACTED: InEcA, IntBibE, JEL, KeyEcS, SSI,
WAERSA. DATABASES: CAB AB, ECONAB, ECONLIT, SSI. TARGET AUDIENCE: AC,
SP. SAMPLE COPIES: Libraries and Individuals.

The Review of Economic Studies is a journal published by a professional
association of economists "to encourage research by young economists".
The journal covers economic theory, econometrics, and applied economics.
It emphasizes microeconomic topics. Recent issues have included articles
dealing with consumer behavior, resource allocation mechanisms, futures
markets, workers and wage distribution, balance of payments, competitive
commuter railways, the theory of perfect competition, monetary policy,
female fertility and labor-supply decisions, social choice probabili-
ties, and the economics of information. All articles use sophisticated
quantitative techniques. Many of them construct an econometric model and
test its validity with empirical findings. The articles are scholarly in
nature and employ extensive footnotes and references. The authors are
predominantly American academic economists from prestigious institutions, although contributions from academics from Canada, Great Britain,
and other countries are included. The Review compares favorably to top
quality journals such as the American Economic Review, Econometrica,
Journal of Economic Theory, and Rand Journal of Economics.
    Each issue includes ten to twelve full-length articles. Some issues
contain short comments on previously published papers.

407.   The Review of Economics and Statistics. DATE FOUNDED: 1919.
TITLE CHANGES: Review of Economic Statistics (1919-1948). FREQUENCY: q.

PRICE: $68/yr. institutions, $34/yr. personal. PUBLISHER: Elsevier
Science Publishers B.V. (North-Holland), P.O. Box 1991, 1000 BZ Amster-
dam, The Netherlands. EDITOR: Hendrik S. Houthakker. ILLUSTRATIONS.
INDEX. ADVERTISEMENTS. CIRCULATION: 5,400. MANUSCRIPT SELECTION:
Editors. MICROFORMS: MIM, Publisher. REPRINTS: Publisher. INDEXED/
ABSTRACTED: BPI, BPIA, InEcA, IntBibE, JEL, KeyEcS, PAIS, PubAdAb, SSI,
WAERSA, WorkRelAbstr. DATABASES: CAB AB, ECONAB, ECONLIT, MC, PAIS, INT,
SSI. TARGET AUDIENCE: AC. SP. SAMPLE COPIES.: Libraries and Individuals.

The Review of Economics and Statistics is published under the auspices
of the Department of Economics, Harvard University. It is a scholarly
journal that publishes both theoretical and empirical articles in
economics and statistics. The majority of articles are in applied
economics. Virtually all fields of economics are dealt with but a
preponderance of articles appear in the areas of industrial organization, consumer demand, labor economics, and public finance. This
prestigious journal is very technical in nature. Many articles emphasize
the quantitative methodology employed rather than the economic relationships that are discussed. Methods include input-output analysis, hedonic
approaches, state space methods, logit models, and many other statistical and econometric estimating methodologies. The authors are predominantly academic economists associated with American universities. Some
are research economists with government agencies or private research
institutes. The Review's British counterpart is Oxford Bulletin of
Economics and Statistics which limits itself to applied economics.
    The Review of Economics and Statistics is more voluminous than most.
A typical issue contains fifteen regular articles plus about ten shorter
articles in a "Notes" section. Many articles include an appendix. A
brief abstract preceeds each article.

408.   The Review of Income and Wealth. DATE FOUNDED: 1947. TITLE
CHANGES: Income and Wealth (1947-1965). FREQUENCY: q. PRICE: $46/yr.
PUBLISHER: International Association for Research in Income and Wealth,
Box 1962 Yale Station, New Haven, Connecticut 06520. EDITOR: Richard
Ruggles. ILLUSTRATIONS. INDEX. CIRCULATION: 1,500. MANUSCRIPT SELECTION:
Editor and Editorial Board. SPECIAL ISSUES. INDEXED/ABSTRACTED: InEcA,
IntBibE, JEL, PAIS. DATABASES: ECONLIT, PAIS INT. TARGET AUDIENCE: AC,
SP. SAMPLE COPIES: Libraries.

The Review of Income and Wealth is the journal of an international
research association interested in "the definition and measurement of
national income and wealth, the development of systems of economic and
social accounting, and their use for economic policy, international
comparisons, and other economic analysis." The Review, which reflects
that interest, is a scholarly journal containing research articles on
topics such as the underground economy, income inequality, the value of
household work, the treatment of health expenditures in national income
accounts, the accuracy of index numbers, the distribution of wealth in
different countries, the measurement of the public sector, productivity
in different countries, how to estimate a country's capital stock, and
the compilation of input-output tables for a specific country. Articles
are technical in nature as they are primarily aimed at specialists in
national accounting. Mathematical and statistical methodologies are
widely employed. Most articles have substantial amounts of empirical
content. The authors are economic researchers associated with univer-

sities, government agencies, or international research institutes. Most are American, European (both West and East), or Canadian.

A typical issue contains from four to six articles plus one to three notes, comments, and replies. A brief abstract preceeds each regular article. Occasionally a special issue is published such as a recent one on "Purchasing Power parities."

409.   Review of Industrial Organization. DATE FOUNDED: 1984. FREQUENCY: q. PRICE: $40/yr. institutions, $25/yr. personal. PUBLISHER: M&S Publishers, Little Rock, Arkansas 72204. EDITOR: Stanley E. Boyle. ILLUSTRATIONS. MANUSCRIPT SELECTION: Editor and Board of Editors. TARGET AUDIENCE: AC, SP. SAMPLE COPIES: Libraries and Individuals.

Review of Industrial Organization is a new journal which supersedes Industrial Organization Review, published since 1973 but suspended after 1980. As did its predecessor, RIO focuses on the applied microeconomic problems studied by industrial organization economists; specifically the structure, conduct, and performance of industrial markets. It offers more empirical articles than does Antitrust Bulletin but less theoretical ones than appear in the Journal of Industrial Economics or the International Journal of Industrial Organization. Favorite topics include market and aggregate concentration, entry, merger, vertical integration, and price discrimination. RIO also focuses on public policy responses such as merger guidelines, and antitrust measures to combat price fixing, predation, and monopolization. Articles are scholarly and make use of standard economic methodologies including diagrams, statistics, and econometrics. Most authors are academic economists at universities in the United States.

The first issue of RIO contained six articles, each about ten pages in length. This did not deviate greatly from the format of IOR.

410.   Review of Marketing and Agricultural Economics. DATE FOUNDED: 1937. FREQUENCY: 3/yr. PRICE: Free. PUBLISHER: Department of Agriculture, Division of Marketing and Economic Services, P.O. Box K220, Haymarket,, N.S.W. 2000, Australia. EDITORS: G.R. Griffith, D.W. Briggs. ILLUSTRATIONS. INDEX. CIRCULATION: 1,600. MANUSCRIPT SELECTION: Editors and Referees. BOOK REVIEWS. INDEXED/ABSTRACTED: InEcA, JEL, WAERSA. DATABASES: CAB AB, ECONLIT. TARGET AUDIENCE: AC, SP. SAMPLE COPIES: Libraries and Individuals.

The Review of Marketing and Agricultural Economics is a government publication issued by the Australian province of New South Wales. It provides "informed analysis of economic matters of significance to the Australian rural sector." The articles generally are of three distinct types -- discussion of theoretical concepts in economics, use of empirical evidence in confirmation of a theoretical concept, and descriptive articles conveying information. Examples of articles in the first category are "Cost Functions and the Regression Fallacy" and "Welfare Analysis of Price Stabilization." Examples of articles in the second category are "Input-Output Analysis in Australia" and "Elasticity of Demand for Wine and Beer." Examples of articles in the last category are "Australian Dairy Farming in the 1970's" and "Rural Land Use." The articles are scholarly in nature and some of them employ quantitative techniques. The majority of authors are economists with Australian universities or government agencies. A few contributions are made by economists from American universities, British universities, or international organizations such as the World Bank. The Review of Marketing and Agricultural Economics is more scholarly than the Quarterly Review of the Rural Economy which is entirely devoted to providing current information on Australian agriculture.

Each issue contains from three to six articles ranging in length from twelve to twenty-five pages each. Most issues include three signed book reviews.

411.   Review of Radical Political Economics. DATE FOUNDED: 1969. FREQUENCY: q. PRICE: $50/yr. institutions, $35/yr. personal. PUBLISHER: Union for Radical Political Economics, 41 Union Square West, New York, New York 10003. EDITOR: Bill James. ILLUSTRATIONS. INDEX. ADVERTISEMENTS. CIRCULATION: 2,500. MANUSCRIPT SELECTION: Editorial Board. MICROFORMS: UMI. REPRINTS: Publisher. BOOK REVIEWS. SPECIAL ISSUES. INDEXED/ABSTRACTED: InEcA, IntBibE, JEL, PAIS, WAERSA. DATABASES: CAB AB, ECONLIT, PAIS INT. TARGET AUDIENCE: AC. SAMPLE COPIES: Libraries.

The Review of Radical Political Economics is published by "an interdisciplinary educational foundation founded in 1968 by a group of socialist intellectuals and activists." It disseminates "radical political economic theory and applied analysis." Emphasis is on "a continuing critique of the capitalist system and of all forms of oppression and on the construction of progressive social policy." Topics discussed in recent issues include Marxist theory, capitalist development, women as a reserve army of labor, Chinese population policies, Lenin's theory of imperialism, work incentives, economic surplus and surplus value, and sex segregation in the U.S. labor force. Articles are written in a narrative style. Most are non-technical although a few have mathematical appendices. The typical article includes many footnotes and a long list of references. Few have any empirical content. The authors are predominantly academic economists at American universities. A few are sociologists or philosophers and some are associated with European and Australian universities. The Review provides the same general viewpoint as Journal of Australian Political Economy and Studies in Political Economy: a Socialist Review.

A typical issue contains five or six articles, two or three notes and comments, and from four to six in-depth signed book reviews. Some issues also include an essay in a "Pedagogy" section or one or more essays in a "Review Articles" section. Special issues based on topical themes appear from time to time. Topics covered have been energy, health, racism, contemporary imperialism, and the political economy of women.

412.   Review of Regional Economics and Business. DATE FOUNDED: 1976. FREQUENCY: 2/yr. PRICE: $4/yr. PUBLISHER: The University of Oklahoma, Center for Economic and Management Research, College of Business Administration, 307 West Brooks, Room 4, Norman, Oklahoma 73019. EDITOR: James. E. Hibdon. ILLUSTRATIONS. CIRCULATION: 900. MANUSCRIPT SELECTION: Editor and Editorial Review Board. INDEXED/ABSTRACTED: PAIS. DATABASES: PAIS INT. TARGET AUDIENCE: AC, GP, SP.

The Review of Regional Economics and Business is more scholarly than the average business school publication. While its stated purpose is to "provide a format for an exchange of ideas, opinions, experience, and research on economics and business topics of special interest to Oklahoma and the Southwest," it publishes primarily research articles, about half of which have much wider appeal than the State and Region. Many articles are technical in nature and use quantitative methodologies in addition to providing data in tables and charts. It covers virtually all areas of economics and business administration. Topics discussed in recent issues include the regional distribution of federal funds, the demand for natural gas, price followership, the soft drink industry, zoning, hospital costs, international oil prices, unemployment in the Southwest and geographic diversification of business. This journal contains the type of regionally oriented articles found in the University of Rhode Island's New England Journal of Business and Economics plus the more general ones found in the University of Nebraska's Quarterly Journal of Business and Economics. The authors are predominantly academics in departments of economics or business administration. The majority are from the Southwest, but universities in other parts of the U.S. and in Canada and England are also represented.

A typical issue is from thirty to fifty pages long and contains from four to six articles.

413.   The Review of Regional Studies. DATE FOUNDED: 1971. FREQUENCY: 3/yr. PRICE: $15/yr. institutions, $10/yr. personal. PUBLISHER: Southern Regional Science Association and University of Alabama in Birmingham, School of Business, Birmingham, Alabama 35294. EDITOR: James C. Hite. ILLUSTRATIONS. INDEX. ADVERTISEMENTS. CIRCULATION: 500. MANUSCRIPT SELECTION: Editor and Editorial Board. INDEXED/ABSTRACTED: WAERSA. DATABASES: CAB AB. TARGET AUDIENCE: AC, SP. SAMPLE COPIES: Libraries and Individuals.

The Review of Regional Studies is a publication of a regional professional association of economists, geographers, urban planners, and management experts. The Review focuses on papers that combine scholarly interest with regional and urban planning concerns. Articles offer analyses of such concerns with an intent to facilitate public decision at all levels of government. Recent issues have dealt with topics such as relocation decisions by central city manufacturers, regional perspectives on the underground economy, energy prospects for the Southeast, migration decisions, and taxation for pollution control. The articles vary in their treatment of these subjects from purely descriptive to econometric model building. Many use empirical evidence obtained from U.S. Census Data or surveys. The authors are government researchers or academics associated with U.S. universities. A large number are from the Southeast.

A typical issue contains seven articles from ten to twenty pages each. Currently there exists a three year lag in publication schedule which the editors are attempting to shorten.

414.   Review of Research in Futures Markets. DATE FOUNDED: 1982. FREQUENCY: 3/yr. PRICE: $60/yr. PUBLISHER: Chicago Board of Trade, LaSalle at Jackson, Chicago, Illinois 60604. EDITOR: Lloyd Besant. ILLUSTRATIONS. MANUSCRIPT SELECTION: Editors. TARGET AUDIENCE: AC, SP.

The Review of Research in Futures Markets has recently developed out of
the numerous seminars sponsored over the past decade by the Chicago
Board of Trade. It supersedes seminar proceedings such as International
Futures Trading Seminar Proceedings, Industry Research Seminar Proceedings, and Research on Speculation Seminar Report. This scholarly journal
publishes technical articles reporting on research concerning futures
markets. It contains proceedings of Chicago Board of Trade seminars,
specially invited research studies, and selected research papers that
have been funded by the Chicago Board of Trade Foundation. Specific
topics discussed in early issues of the Review include interest rate
futures, agricultural commodity futures, London commodity options,
pricing efficiency of grain futures markets, portfolio strategies using
options and futures, the relation of futures and spot prices, the
history of futures markets, trade practices of specific futures markets,
the regulation of futures markets, and the commercial use of options.
Articles vary greatly as to their nature and type. Some are highly
technical and make use of sophisticated quantitative methodologies while
others are descriptive and expository in style. The majority of authors
are academics associated with departments of finance, economics, or
agricultural economics at American universities. Others are futures
industry professionals and government officials. The only other futures
market journal, The Journal of Futures Markets, has a somewhat broader
scope in that it deals with the performance and contributions of
organized futures markets to society.

A typical issue of the Review includes four to six articles. Each
article is followed by one or two commentaries by other experts plus a
brief discussion between the author and seminar participants.

415.   Review of Social Economy. DATE FOUNDED: 1944. FREQUENCY: 3/yr.
PRICE: $30/yr. institutions, $20/yr. personal. PUBLISHER: Association
for Social Economics, Department of Economics, Marquette University,
Milwaukee, Wisconsin 53233. EDITOR: William R. Waters. INDEX. ADVERTISE-
MENTS. CIRCULATION: 1,300. MANUSCRIPT SELECTION: Editor and Referees.
MICROFORMS: UMI. BOOK REVIEWS. SPECIAL ISSUES. INDEXED/ABSTRACTED: BPIA,
CathI, HistAb, InEcA, JEL, PAIS, WAERSA. DATABASES: CAB AB, ECONLIT,
HISTAB, MC, PAIS INT. TARGET AUDIENCE: AC, SP. SAMPLE COPIES: Libraries
and Individuals.

The Review of Social Economy publishes articles by and for "social
economists". It is claimed by some that social economics is an alternative to the individualistic, rational maximizing thrust of mainstream
economics. The Review focuses on ethics, social welfare and political
economy. Closely tied to several American Catholic universities, the
Association for Social Economics and its Review are embued with Catholic
social doctrine. Some articles are written in a narrative style while
others present a model and empirical results. Articles in recent issues
deal with topics such as corporate social responsibility, rationality in
economics, financing social security, economic democracy, urban residential segregation, solar energy use, Scandinavian social economics,
cooperatives, and the question of whether Karl Marx was a social
economist. The authors are predominantly American academic economists.

Most issues contain five or six articles, one or two notes in a
"Communications" section, four to eight signed book reviews, a list of
books received, and the minutes and financial reports of the Association. The December issue has a special theme such as "The Social

Economics of John Maurice Clark", "The Solidarist Economics of Goetz A. Briefs", or "Ethics and Economics: Retrospect and Prospect."

Revue Canadienne d'Economie Rurale. see Canadian Journal of Agricultural Economics/Revue Canadienne d'Economie Rurale.

Revue Canadienne d'Economique. see Canadian Journal of Economics/Revue Canadienne d'Economique.

La Revue Canadienne des Sciences Regionales. see Canadian Journal of Regional Science/La Revue Canadienne des Sciences Regionales.

416.   Rivista Internazionale Di Scienze Economiche E. Commerciali/ International Review of Economics and Business. DATE FOUNDED: 1954. FREQUENCY: m. PRICE: $50/yr. PUBLISHER: Casa Editrice Dott, Antonio Milani, Via Jappelli 5, Padua, Italy. EDITOR: Aldo Montesano. ILLUSTRA- TIONS. INDEX. ADVERTISEMENTS. CIRCULATION: 8,000. MANUSCRIPT SELECTION: Editor and Editorial Board. BOOK REVIEWS. SPECIAL ISSUES. INDEXED/ ABSTRACTED: InEcA, JEL, PAIS, WAERSA. DATABASES: CAB AB, ECONLIT, PAIS INT. TARGET AUDIENCE: AC, SP. SAMPLE COPIES: Libraries.

Rivista Internazionale Di Scienze Economiche E Commerciali/International Review of Economics and Business is a multilingual journal published under the auspices of the Universita Commerciale Luigi Bocconi in Milano, Italy. About sixty percent of the articles are in English; most of the rest in Italian with an occasional one in French or German. The journal publishes a great variety of articles, both in type and subject area. Some are highly technical papers that stress the quantitative methodology employed while others are descriptive in nature. The majority incorporate some economic theory and offer some empirical results. The journal accepts articles in every field of economics as well as in some business areas. These include the history of economic thought, socialist and Marxist economics, economic development, price theory, income analysis, environmental economics, political economy, labor economics, public finance, industrial organization, and account- ing. The authors are predominantly American and Italian academic economists. Some other European, Canadian, Indian, and Australian academics also contribute.

Rivista publishes close to 100 articles each year. A brief English language abstract precedes every article. An Italian summary follows all English language articles. Most issues include one to five Italian language signed book reviews and a lengthy list of books received. Occasionally a special issue, such as a recent one on the economic affects of tourism, is published.

417.   Scandinavian Economic History Review. DATE FOUNDED: 1953. MERGER: Economy and History (1981). FREQUENCY: 3/yr. PRICE: NOK 175/yr. PUBLISHER: Scandinavian Society for Economic and Social History and Historical Geography, Norges Handelshoyskole, Helleveien 30, 5035, Bergen-Sandviken, Norway. EDITOR: Trygve Solhaug. ILLUSTRATIONS. INDEX. CIRCULATION: 800. MANUSCRIPT SELECTION: Editors. REPRINTS: Editor. BOOK

REVIEWS. SPECIAL ISSUES. INDEXED/ABSTRACTED: HistAb, IntBibE. DATABASES:
HISTAB. TARGET AUDIENCE: AC, SP.

The <u>Scandinavian Economic History Review</u> is a scholarly journal that
deals with "the Scandinavian historical experience within the field of
economic and social development in four separate countries or states."
Topics discussed in recent issues include wealth distribution in Finland
in 1800, regional economic development in Sweden from 1550 to 1914,
industrial financing in Denmark from 1840 to 1914, Icelandic fisheries
in the nineteenth century, emigration from Denmark to the U.S. from 1870
to 1913, investment in Finland from 1860 to 1979, early history of
banking in Sweden, women's role and work in Danish urban society of the
fourteenth to sixteenth centuries, and the methodologies employed in
historical national accounts. Articles typically include data in the
form of tables and charts but quantitative economic history methodologies are not employed. The authors are academics and researchers in
the fields of economics, history and anthropology. While the authors are
always named, information concerning discipline or affiliation is
supplied for only about half of them.
  Each issue contains either two or three regular articles of various
lengths. A review article is included in some issues. An average of six
in-depth signed book reviews appear in an issue.

418.   The Scandinavian Journal of Economics. DATE FOUNDED: 1899. TITLE
CHANGES: <u>Ekonomisk Tidskrift</u> (1899-1964). <u>Swedish Journal of Economics</u>
(1965-1975). FREQUENCY: q. PRICE: SEK 400/yr. institutions, SEK 250/yr.
personal. PUBLISHER: University of Stockholm, Department of Economics,
S-106 91 Stockholm, Sweden. EDITOR: Seppo Honkapohja. ILLUSTRATIONS.
INDEX. ADVERTISEMENTS. CIRCULATION: 1,200. MANUSCRIPT SELECTION: Editor
and Referees. REPRINTS: Authors. BOOK REVIEWS. SPECIAL ISSUES. INDEXED/
ABSTRACTED: InEcA, IntBibE, JEL, PAIS. DATABASES: ECONLIT, PAIS INT.
TARGET AUDIENCE: AC, SP. SAMPLE COPIES: Libraries and Individuals.

The <u>Scandinavian Journal of Economics</u> is a scholarly publication which
encourages research by economists in the Scandinavian countries. This
journal publishes articles in both theoretical and empirical economics.
Empirical articles utilize data from the Scandinavian countries.
Theoretical articles in recent issues deal with topics such as income
distribution theory, industry equilibrium, and the effect of taxation on
the real cost of capital. Articles in recent issues that offer empirical
studies focus on topics such as investment risks in Norwegian industries, price behavior in grocery retailing in Oslo, and union growth in
Denmark. All of the articles employ advanced quantitative methodologies.
The preponderance of authors are academics from the Scandinavian
countries.
  A typical issue includes from four to six full length articles. Some
issues contain a few notes and comments or a signed book review. A
regular feature of this journal is "The Nobel Memorial Prize in Economics" section which includes the official announcement of the Royal
Swedish Academy of Sciences, an article about the recipient's contributions to economics, and a bibliography of the recipient's publications.
An annual special issue is devoted to "a topic of current interest in
economics and features contributions by both Scandinavian and non-
Scandinavian authors."

419.   Scottish Journal of Political Economy. DATE FOUNDED: 1954.
FREQUENCY: 3/yr. PRICE: $55/yr. PUBLISHER: Longman Group Ltd, 6th Floor,
Westgate House, The High, Harlow, Essex CM20 INE, England. EDITOR: L.C.
Hunter. ILLUSTRATIONS. INDEX. ADVERTISEMENTS. CIRCULATION: 900. MANU-
SCRIPT SELECTION: Editor and Referees. REPRINTS: Publisher. BOOK
REVIEWS. SPECIAL ISSUES. INDEXED/ABSTRACTED: BritHumI, InEcA, IntBibE,
JEL, KeyEcS, WorkRelAbstr. DATABASES: ECONAB, ECONLIT. TARGET AUDIENCE:
AC, SP. SAMPLE COPIES: Libraries and Individuals.

The Scottish Journal of Political Economy is associated with the
Scottish Economic Society. It concentrates on publishing articles in
applied economics and economic policy pertaining to the United Kingdom
and especially Scotland. Articles are scholarly and usually quite
technical in nature. Many present models and almost all have strong
empirical content. Quantitative analysis is employed. Topics discussed
in recent issues include the projection of energy demand in the U.K.,
alternative modes of commuter transportation in a Scottish city,
employment discrimination, the long-run Phillips curve, income redistribution through taxes and transfers in the U.K., money flows to
regions in the U.K., economic factors and mortality in Scotland,
profitability of U.K. manufacturing firms according to urban versus
rural location, and regional policy incentives in the Scottish elec-
tronics industry. The authors are predominantly English or Scottish
academic economists. A few are associated with U.K. research institutes
or consulting firms.
   A typical issue contains five full-length articles plus one or two
shorter ones in a "Notes and Communications" section. Each issue
includes a lengthy review article of from three to five books on a
particular theme. The annual Scottish Economic Society Lecture is
published in the November issue.

420.   The Seoul National University Economic Review. DATE FOUNDED:
1967. FREQUENCY: a. PRICE: Free. PUBLISHER: Seoul National University,
The Institute of Economic Research, Seoul, 151, South Korea. ILLUSTRA-
TIONS. SPECIAL ISSUES. INDEXED/ABSTRACTED: WAERSA. DATABASES: CAB AB.
TARGET AUDIENCE: AC, SP. SAMPLE COPIES: Libraries and Individuals.

The Seoul National University Economic Review is an English language
serial published in Korea. It contains three different types of articles
-- theoretical works, empirical tests of economic theories, and pragmatic studies of economic development in Korea. Articles presenting
economic theories have included topics such as the relationship between
interest rates and expected inflation, imperfect capital markets, and
rational expectations equilibria. Articles combining theory with
empirical testing have included topics such as job search theory as
applied to American youth, the random walk hypothesis as applied to the
New York, Tokyo, and Seoul stock markets, and housing demand in Korea.
Articles discussing economic development in Korea include topics such as
rural industrialization, agricultural technological research, and
utilization of feedgrains. The articles are scholarly in style and most
of them are highly technical in content. Most of the authors are Korean
economists, some of whom are faculty members at Seoul National University and some of whom are affiliated with American universities.
   A typical issue includes four or five full-length articles. A special
issue in commemoration of the 30th Anniversary of Seoul National

University offered sixteen papers written by distinguished scholars from the international community.

421.   The Singapore Economic Review. DATE FOUNDED: 1956. TITLE CHANGES: The Malayan Economic Review (1956-1982). FREQUENCY: 2/yr. PRICE: $15/yr. PUBLISHER: Economic Society of Singapore c/o Department of Economics and Statistics, National University of Singapore, Kent Ridge, 0511, Singapore. EDITOR: Lim Chong-Yah. CIRCULATION: 500. MANUSCRIPT SELECTION: Editorial Board and Referees. BOOK REVIEWS. INDEXED/ABSTRACTED: PAIS. DATABASES: PAIS INT. TARGET AUDIENCE: AC, SP.

The Singapore Economic Review publishes articles dealing with economic issues and problems of countries in the Pacific Basin. While it empha- sizes economic development of Malaysia and Singapore, the Review also presents studies relating to the Philippines, Australia, and India. Recent issues included articles on Malaysian agricultural commodity protection, the financing of small-scale Malaysian manufacturers, income distribution in Malaysia, and the impact of tourism in Singapore. Some articles offer discussions on economic development issues that are not related to a specific country. These may involve the role of multi- national corporations in less developed countries, revenue instability in less developed countries, and evaluation of international joint venture projects. Most of the articles are presented in a scholarly style. Many are technical and employ advanced quantitative method- ologies. The authors are predominantly academics representing a wide spectrum of universities in the Pacific Basin. An occasional contribu- tion is made by an economist from the U.K.
    A typical issue contains six articles of fifteen to twenty pages each. Each issue includes three or four in-depth signed book reviews.

422.   Social and Economic Studies. DATE FOUNDED: 1953. FREQUENCY: q. PRICE: $15/yr. PUBLISHER: University of the West Indies, Institute of Social and Economic Research, Mona, Kingston 7, Jamaica. EDITOR: Vaughan Lewis. ADVERTISEMENTS. CIRCULATION: 2,000. MANUSCRIPT SELECTION: Editor. MICROFORMS: UMI. REPRINTS: UMI. BOOK REVIEWS. SPECIAL ISSUES. INDEXED/ ABSTRACTED: InEcA, JEL, KeyEcS, PAIS, SocAb, SSI, WAERSA. DATABASES: CAB AB, ECONAB, ECONLIT, PAIS INT, SOCAB, SSI. TARGET AUDIENCE: AC, SP.

Social and Economic Studies serves primarily as a forum for publication of studies undertaken at the Institute. Studies focus on social and economic problems of Jamaica and other Caribbean countries. Some articles that are sociological in nature deal with topics such as migration processes, prejudice attitudes towards ethnic groups, the relationship between population growth and health care level, and the relationship between social class and success in academic performance. Most articles deal with a variety of economic problems. Representative titles include "Exchange Rate Policy in Jamaica: A Critical Assessment", "Elasticity of Substitution and Employment Generating Capacity of A Bauxite Firm in Guyana," and "Pricing Policy in the Distributive Sector in Barbados." The level of technical treatment varies from none to the utilization of mathematical methodology. Most of the authors are faculty members at the University of the West Indies. Occasional contributions are made by economists from Canada, the U.S., and the U.K.

A typical issue includes from four to eight full-length articles. Some issues have a "Notes and Comments" section which features two or three shorter articles. Signed book reviews appear in most issues. "Special Issues" on specific topics are published frequently. Examples of recent topics include "Regional Monetary Studies", "Public Sector Issues in the Commonwealth Carribean", and "Rural Financial Markets."

423.   Social and Labour Bulletin. DATE FOUNDED: 1974. FREQUENCY: q. PRICE: $26/yr. PUBLISHER: International Labour Office, CH-1211 Geneva 22, Switzerland. EDITOR: H. Sarfati. INDEX. ADVERTISEMENTS. MANUSCRIPT SELECTION: Editor. INDEXED/ABSTRACTED: WorkRelAbstr. TARGET AUDIENCE: GP, SP.

Social and Labour Bulletin is published on behalf of the 150 member International Labor Organization (ILO), an agency associated with the United Nations. This publication reports on many aspects of international labor concerns such as social and economic policies, effects of new technology, labor relations, personnel management, trade unions, collective agreements, wages, working conditions, employment, occupational safety and health, social security, equal opportunity, migrant workers, multinational enterprises, and education. The articles, which are non-technical and journalistic in style present information on recent developments in these areas. All of them are re-printed or excerpted from original sources such as newspaper articles, government documents, news releases, and reports from ILO offices. Only occasionally is the author's name given. Social and Labour Bulletin deals with the same subject matter as ILO Information but is more comprehensive in coverage.
    Each issue contains from 150 to 200 brief articles. Many of them have been translated into English. The articles contain references to earlier Bulletin articles that deal with the same topic. Bibliographic citations of the original sources are included for all articles. The articles are arranged by subject, and within each subject, by country.

424.   Social Security Bulletin. DATE FOUNDED: 1938. FREQUENCY: m. PRICE: $23/yr. PUBLISHER: Social Security Administration, 1875 Connecticut Ave., N.W., Washington, D.C. 20009. EDITOR: Marilyn Thomas. MANUSCRIPT SELECTION: Editor. MICROFORMS: MIM, UMI. REPRINTS: UMI. SPECIAL ISSUES. INDEXED/ABSTRACTED: BPI, InEcA, JEL, PAIS, Pred, WorkRelAbstr. DATABASES: ECONLIT, PAIS INT, PF. TARGET AUDIENCE: AC, GP, SP.

The Social Security Bulletin is a government publication that deals with all aspects of the U.S. Social Security System. Occasionally, an article deals with social security systems of other countries. Recent issues have featured articles on topics such as the economic effects of social security, income changes after retirement, benefits for short-term sickness, the supplemental security income program (SSI), financial status of the Social Security program, low-income energy assistance, and new provisions of legislation affecting social security programs. Most of the articles are not technical but include large amounts of data. The authors are staff members of the Social Security Administration. The Social Security Bulletin concentrates on the U.S. system while the International Social Security Review provides information on social security systems in many countries. The latter contains far less statistical data.

A typical issue includes two articles. Most of the issue is devoted to statistical tables providing data on monthly government expenditures for retirement, disability, survivors, health care, public assistance, unemployment, and supplemental benefits. Each issue has a short "Social Security in Review" section and a "Notes and Brief Reports" section. An annual statistical supplement provides detailed data on benefits paid and number of beneficiaries in each of the separate programs that make up the total system.

425.   Socio-Economic Planning Sciences. DATE FOUNDED: 1967. FREQUENCY: 6/yr. PRICE: $130/yr. institutions, $45/yr. personal. PUBLISHER: Pergamon Press, Fairview Park, Elmsford, New York, 10523. EDITOR: Sumner N. Lurne. ILLUSTRATIONS. INDEX. ADVERTISEMENTS. CIRCULATION: 1,700. MANUSCRIPT SELECTION: Editor. MICROFORMS: Publisher. SPECIAL ISSUES. INDEXED/ABSTRACTED: BPIA, IntBibE, PAIS, WAERSA. DATABASES: CAB AB, MC, PAIS INT. TARGET AUDIENCE: AC, SP.

Socio-Economic Planning Sciences is an interdisciplinary journal encompassing the areas of economics, geography, engineering, sociology, public administration, and regional planning. This publication emphasizes a systems analysis approach to problems in these areas. Some articles offer a theoretical analysis of a planning problem and others provide an analysis of an actual situation. Examples of the former type include articles on location theory, capacity expansion planning, break-even analysis, and resource allocation in complex hierarchies. Examples of the latter type include articles on nursing home costs in Nebraska, economic costs of the Three-Mile Island accident, displaced households in Saskatoon, and cost-benefit analysis of Medicaid services in New York State. The articles are scholarly and highly technical. A majority of the authors are from the U.S. and are either academics or researchers with government agencies. Some contributions are from academics in Canada, Israel, India, Nigeria, and other countries.

A typical issue includes eight to ten articles ranging in length from eight to fifteen pages each. Occasionally, a special issue is devoted to a specific topic under the direction of a guest editor.

426.   The South African Journal of Economics/Die Suid-Afrikaanse Tydskrif Vir Ekonomie. DATE FOUNDED: 1932. FREQUENCY: q. PRICE: R30/yr. PUBLISHER: The Economic Society of South Africa, P.O. Box 31213, 2017 Braamfontein, Johannesburg, South Africa. EDITOR: D.J.J. Botha. ILLUS-TRATIONS. INDEX. ADVERTISEMENTS. CIRCULATION: 1,700. MANUSCRIPT SELEC-TION: Editors and Referees. BOOK REVIEWS. SPECIAL ISSUES. INDEXED/ABSTRACTED: InEcA, IntBibE, JEL, KeyEcS, PAIS, WAERSA, WorkRelAbstr. DATABASES: CAB AB, ECONAB, ECONLIT, PAIS INT. TARGET AUDIENCE: AC, SP. SAMPLE COPIES: Libraries.

The South African Journal of Economics/Die Suid-Afrikaanse Tydskrif Vir Ekonomie publishes economics articles "in all its fields and aspects, especially as relating to South Africa and her neighbours". In recent issues, articles have appeared in the fields of economic history, industrial organization, monetary theory, economic education, international trade, macro-economic analysis, consumer behavior, economic development, and the analysis of financial markets. About half relate to the South African economy; either analyzing a portion of the South African economy such as the gold mining industry, coal mining industry, and education or using South African data to test extant economic theory such as the St. Louis equation, the structure-conduct-performance paradigm, and the Heckscher-Ohlin model. Some articles are expository in nature, but most are technical papers that make use of modern quantitative methodologies. The authors are predominantly South African academic economists. Occasionally economists from other countries such as the U.S., England, the Netherlands, and Turkey make contributions.

A typical issue contains from five to seven articles plus some shorter notes, comments and replies. Special issues are published such as the recent "Keynes Centenary Issue", seven articles dealing with the contributions of J.M. Keynes and the "Jubilee Issue", six articles marking the Fiftieth anniversary of The South African Journal of Economics.

427.   South Dakota Business Review. DATE FOUNDED: 1942. FREQUENCY: q. PRICE: Free. PUBLISHER: University of South Dakota, Business Research Bureau, School of Business, Vermillion, South Dakota 57069. EDITOR: Jerry W. Johnson. ILLUSTRATIONS. ADVERTISEMENTS. CIRCULATION: 2,800. MANUSCRIPT SELECTION: Editor. INDEXED/ABSTRACTED: BPIA. DATABASES: MC. TARGET AUDIENCE: GP. SAMPLE COPIES: Libraries and Individuals.

The South Dakota Business Review is a fairly typical business school publication aimed primarily at South Dakota's business community. It concentrates on the economic and business trends in the state. In this respect it resembles the Pennsylvania Business Survey, Montana Business Quarterly, and Arizona Business, among others. Articles are nontechnical, almost never employ mathematical or statistical methodologies, but usually include a substantial amount of data in tables and charts. Topics covered in recent issues include financing education in South Dakota, the dual economies of the State, personal income in South Dakota, tax exporting and importing, futures markets, South Dakota's water development districts, the supply and demand for nurses in South Dakota, South Dakota's international developments, interest rates and home prices, and change in the banking industry. The articles are written by Bureau staff and by professors in the departments of economics, finance, marketing, or accounting at the University of South Dakota.

Each issue contains an article, "Trend of Business", which provides a brief statement on the national economy and an in-depth look at the economy of South Dakota. Most issues include two or three additional articles. Regular features are forecasts projected by the South Dakota Labor Market Model and annual "Perspectives" from the previous year and "Outlook" for the new year.

428.   Southern Economic Journal. DATE FOUNDED: 1933. FREQUENCY: q. PRICE: $40/yr. PUBLISHER: University of North Carolina at Chapel Hill, Hanes Hall 019A, Chapel Hill, North Carolina 27514. EDITOR: Vincent J. Tarascio. ILLUSTRATIONS. INDEX. ADVERTISEMENTS. CIRCULATION: 3,800. MANUSCRIPT SELECTION: Editor and Referees. MICROFORMS: MIM, UMI. REPRINTS: Authors. BOOK REVIEWS. INDEXED/ABSTRACTED: BPI, BPIA, InEcA, IntBibE, JEL, PAIS, SSI, WAERSA, WorkRelAbst. DATABASES: CAB AB,

ECONLIT, MC, PAIS INT, SSI. TARGET AUDIENCE: AC, SP. SAMPLE COPIES: Libraries.

The Southern Economic Journal is the publication of the Southern Economic Association. It is a scholarly journal that publishes research articles in virtually all fields of economics. During the past few years more articles have appeared in microeconomics than in macroeconomics. Many of the articles in applied price theory are in the area of industrial organization. Other areas in which a large number of articles appear include international trade, monetary theory, and labor economics. Most articles are technical in nature. Many are theoretical while others have strong empirical content. A large number of articles present a formal model, economic analysis, and the results from testing the model. Such articles make use of sophisticated mathematical and statistical methodologies. Occasionally non-quantitative articles appear such as those on the history of economic thought and conference addresses by noted economists, including the Presidential Address at the Southern Economic Association. Most authors are academic economists at American universities. Some are researchers with government agencies or private research institutions. A few authors are associated with Canadian or Asian universities. This journal is comparable in level of scholarship to Economic Inquiry published by the Western Economic Association.

A typical issue contains between fifteen and twenty full-length articles plus from five to ten shorter articles, comments and replies in a "Communications" section. A "Book Reviews" section offers approximately twenty-five signed one page reviews and a "Books Received" section lists a large number of new titles.

429.   Southern Economist. DATE FOUNDED: 1962. FREQUENCY: sm. PRICE: $45/yr. institutions, $40/yr. personal. PUBLISHER: Southern Economist, Ltd., 106-108 Infantry Road, Saleh Ahmed Bldg., Bangalore 560001, India. EDITOR: K.N. Subrahmanya. ILLUSTRATIONS. ADVERTISEMENTS. CIRCULATION: 8,000. MANUSCRIPT SELECTION: Editor. BOOK REVIEWS. SPECIAL ISSUES. INDEXED/ABSTRACTED: WAERSA. DATABASES: CAB AB. TARGET AUDIENCE: AC, GP. SAMPLE COPIES: Libraries and Individuals (send $1 for postage).

Southern Economist is one of the few independent economic journals published in India. It does not reflect the viewpoint of any lobby or pressure group. It focuses on economic problems of the Indian economy but occasionally publishes general articles on economic development. Topics pertaining to India that have been the subject of articles in recent issues include income inequality, economic planning, modernization of rural industries, farm management, capital goods imports, the balance of payments, public enterprise, inflation, banking, productivity, joint ventures, alternative tax programs, power production, foreign trade, tourism, and the progress and problems of such industries as chemicals, sugar cane, natural rubber and cashew nuts. Most articles are sufficiently non-technical for non-economists to understand. They are expository in style and do not employ mathematical or statistical methodologies. Most do, however, contain empirical content and present tables of data. Articles are descriptive and policy oriented. The authors are predominantly Indian academic economists. Occasionally Indian business managers and economists with a private or government institute or agency will make a contribution. The Southern Economist is comparable in technical level to Artha-Vikas, but provides a national rather than a regional focus.

Most issues contain from six to eight fairly brief signed articles plus many even shorter unsigned ones in sections called "Current Topics", "Glass House Gossip", "Banking World", "Public Sector", and "Company Notes". Each issue also includes an average of two editorials and two signed book reviews. About one-quarter of the issues are special issues, either concentrating on a specific region of India, or a national topic such as the Indian budget, banking, productivity, foreign trade, or tourism.

430.   Southern Journal of Agricultural Economics. DATE FOUNDED: 1969. FREQUENCY: 2/yr. PRICE: $15/yr. institutions, $10/yr. personal. PUBLISHER: Southern Agricultural Economics Association, c/o N.R. Martin Jr., Department of Agricultural Economics and Rural Sociology, Auburn University, Auburn, Alabama, 36849. EDITOR: Neil R. Martin Jr. ILLUSTRATIONS. CIRCULATION: 950. MANUSCRIPT SELECTION: Editors and Editorial Council. MICROFORMS: UMI. REPRINTS: UMI. INDEXED/ABSTRACTED: InEcA, JEL, WAERSA. DATABASES: CAB AB, ECONLIT. TARGET AUDIENCE: AC, SP.

The Southern Journal of Agricultural Economics is the publication of a leading regional agricultural economics association. It is a scholarly journal that publishes articles in "methodology and applications in business, extension, research and teaching phases of agricultural economics", especially as they pertain to the southern region of the United States. Regional topics discussed in recent issues include cost estimation for Tennessee livestock auction markets, cotton integrated pest management strategies, Florida tomato market order restrictions, and production, price, and risk factors in channel catfish farming. The majority of articles do not have a regional context. These may deal with agricultural issues and problems that affect the whole U.S. and beyond such as the impact of federal fiscal-monetary policy on farm structure, entry into farming, and the interaction of Japanese rice and wheat policy. Others emphasize methodology such as the use of tobit models, spline functions and logit models, as well as how to adopt microcomputer technology for teaching and research. Most articles are technical in nature and employ quantitative methodologies. The authors are predominantly American academic agricultural economists. This publication and the Western Journal of Agricultural Economics are similar in their use of quantitative methodologies and their mix of regional and national concerns.

A typical issue contains twenty-five articles plus a few notes, comments and replies. Some issues include invited papers each of which is followed by a discussant's brief comments. Each article begins with an abstract and a list of keywords. In 1984 SJAE announced its intention to add a section of microcomputer software articles in future issues. These will present "an overview of the software in sufficient detail to provide a recognized body of literature and to assist the readership in discovery of areas of interest in microcomputer software."

431.   Southwest Journal of Business and Economics. DATE FOUNDED: 1964. TITLE CHANGES: El Paso Economic Review (1964-1979), Southwest Business & Economics Review (1979-1983). FREQUENCY: q. PRICE: $10/yr. PUBLISHER: University of Texas at El Paso, Bureau of Business and Economic Re-

search, 202 Bell Hall, El Paso, Texas 79968. EDITOR: Glenn Palmore.
ILLUSTRATIONS. INDEX. CIRCULATION: 1,000. MANUSCRIPT SELECTION: Editor
and Review Board. INDEXED/ABSTRACTED: PAIS. DATABASES: PAIS INT. TARGET
AUDIENCE: AC, GP, SP. SAMPLE COPIES: Libraries.

The Southwest Journal of Business and Economics has recently been
upgraded "in order to attract articles from the faculty of nationally
and internationally recognized institutions." Before 1984 it included a
mix of subjects of interest to business men and women in the Southwest
United States and Mexico as well as subjects interesting to a general
academic readership. The areas of greatest interest have been and will
continue to be "economic development, regional and urban economics,
business policy, management (behavioral, quantitative, and human
capital) financial, accounting, and marketing analysis." The majority of
articles are technical in nature, but seldom use very sophisticated
mathematics or statistics. This journal has resembled business school
journals such as Arkansas Business and Economic Review and Illinois
Business Review, but is now aspiring to be more like Akron Business and
Economic Review or even the Quarterly Journal of Business and Economics.
The authors are predominantly academics in business or economics
departments. The percentage teaching at the University of Texas at El
Paso is decreasing.
    A typical issue contains four or five articles averaging ten pages in
length. An abstract is provided for each article.

432.   The Southwestern Review of Management and Economics. DATE
FOUNDED: 1981. FREQUENCY: q. PRICE: $27/yr. institutions, $15/yr.
personal. PUBLISHER: University of New Mexico, Bureau of Business and
Economic Research, Alburquerque, New Mexico 87131. EDITORS: Roger D.
Norton, William S. Peters. ILLUSTRATIONS. MANUSCRIPT SELECTION: Editors
and Editorial Advisory Board. BOOK REVIEWS. INDEXED/ABSTRACTED: PAIS.
DATABASES: PAIS INT. TARGET AUDIENCE: AC, GP, SP. SAMPLE COPIES:
Libraries.

The Southwestern Review of Management and Economics features articles
"in economics and management and in related fields such as applied
technology, law, demography, political science and other social sciences." It publishes research on issues of special interest in the
southwestern United States and Mexico. In its first few issues it
concentrated on such topics as water issues in the Southwest, air
quality in the Southwest, technology and industrial development,
demographic change and community development in the Southwest, imple-
menting solar energy concepts, governmental issues in the Southwest, and
economic forecasts for various southwestern states. Other topics covered
included the U.S. - Mexican labor market, problems of Spanish and
Mexican land grants in the Southwest, and the relationship between
energy prices and irrigation patterns in U.S. argiculture. Articles are
scholarly but not very technical in nature. They stress interpretation
of research results and discussion of policy implications. The authors
are predominantly academics in departments of economics, management,
agricultural economics, or political science. Many are associated with
research institutes, the majority in the Southwestern United States.
This journal is more scholarly than are the publications offered by most
regionally oriented university business and economic research bureaus.

A typical issue contains eight articles, each about ten to fifteen pages in length. Most issues have about half the articles deal with different aspects of a common topic. An English and Spanish abstract accompanies each article. An issue typically includes two signed book reviews. Because of a variety of difficulties early volumes of this journal have not always been published on a regular quarterly basis.

433.   Soviet and Eastern European Foreign Trade. DATE FOUNDED: 1965. TITLE CHANGES: American Review of Soviet and Eastern European Foreign Trade (1965-1966). FREQUENCY: q. PRICE: $178.50/yr. institutions, $46.20/yr. personal. PUBLISHER: Myron E. Sharpe, Inc., 80 Business Park Drive, Armonk, New York 10504. EDITORS: Josef Brada, Marvin Jackson. ILLUSTRATIONS. INDEX. ADVERTISEMENTS. MANUSCRIPT SELECTION: Editors. INDEXED/ABSTRACTED: KeyEcS, PAIS. DATABASES: ECONAB, PAIS INT. TARGET AUDIENCE: AC, SP. SAMPLE COPIES: Libraries and Individuals.

Soviet and Eastern European Foreign Trade "contains unabridged transla- tions of articles from Soviet and Eastern European academic sources, primarily scholarly journals and collections of articles published in book form." It is aimed at readers who are "professionally concerned" and therefore the articles are selected according to whether they "provide information on the institutions and policies connected with foreign trade and international finance of the Soviet Union and the Eastern European countries or illustrate the outcome of such policies" and whether they "accurately reflect the state of scholarly and policy opinion regarding an important trade-related issue in the Soviet Union or Eastern Europe." The usual editorial criterion of whether a paper makes an important scientific contribution is not used. Before 1984, each issue contained articles from different countries on different topics. Beginning in 1984 each issue consists of articles from different countries and offering different viewpoints on a common topic. Examples of topics include Council for Mutual Economic Assistance (CMEA) integra- tion, foreign trade planning and reform, CMEA trade with developing countries, CMEA prices and terms of trade, and cooperation in science and technology. Articles vary greatly in style and nature; some are quite technical while others are merely descriptive. Authors' home countries, but not always their affiliations, are provided. Most are associated with a government agency or an academic institution.
    Issues contain from one to six articles of varying lengths. The bibliographic citation of the original source and the name of the translator is provided.

434.   Soviet Studies. DATE FOUNDED: 1949. FREQUENCY: q. PRICE: $55/yr. PUBLISHER: Longman Group Ltd., Longman House, Burnt Mill, Harlow, Essex CM20 1NE, England. EDITOR: R.A. Clarke. ILLUSTRATIONS. INDEX. ADVERTISE- MENTS. CIRCULATION: 1,550. MANUSCRIPT SELECTION: Editorial Board. MICROFORMS: UMI. REPRINTS: Johnson. BOOK REVIEWS. INDEXED/ABSTRACTED: BritHumI, HumI, IntBibE, KeyEcS, PAIS, WAERSA. DATABASES: CAB AB, ECONAB, PAIS INT. TARGET AUDIENCE: AC, SP. SAMPLE COPIES: Libraries.

Soviet Studies, subtitled a Quarterly Journal on the USSR and Eastern Europe, is published for the University of Glasgow. It is a scholarly journal that publishes articles in economics, political science and sociology. Economics topics discussed in recent issues include the

Polish economy under the 1981-1983 martial law, shortages in the Hungarian car market, investment patterns of Soviet industry renovation, income distribution in the USSR, the economics of nuclear power in the USSR, the regulation of Poland's labor supply, and labor productivity in Soviet industry. Other articles are socio-economic or political-economic in nature. Examples of such topics discussed in recent issues are the economic problems of the Soviet health service, the economics of soviet arms transfers to third world countries, and the Marxist-Leninism affect on economic policy governing natural resource pricing in the Soviet Union and East Germany. The articles are non-technical as neither formal models nor modern quantitative methodologies are employed. They are, however, well documented, often in areas where this is not easy to achieve. The authors are predominantly British, American, and Canadian academic researchers; often from prestigious universities. Occasionally, authors are from other countries such as Israel, Scotland, Australia, Hungary, and China. Soviet Studies offers the same subject coverage as Jahrbuch der Wirtschaft Osteuropas.

A typical issue contains from six to eight articles, from one to three notes or comments, and from ten to fifteen signed book reviews. Some issues also include a list of Soviet statistical abstracts or a report of a recently held conference.

435.   Studies in Political Economy: a Socialist Review. DATE FOUNDED: 1979. FREQUENCY: 3/yr. PRICE: C$26/yr. institutions, C$16/yr. personal. PUBLISHER: Studies in Political Economy: a Socialist Review, Box 4729, Station E, Ottawa, Ontario K1S 5H9, Canada. EDITOR: Rianne Mahon. INDEX. ADVERTISEMENTS. CIRCULATION: 1,000. MANUSCRIPT SELECTION: Editor and Referees. INDEXED/ABSTRACTED: PAIS. DATABASES: PAIS INT. TARGET AUDIENCE: AC, SP.

Studies in Political Economy: A Socialist Review receives financial assistance from the Social Sciences and Humanities Research Council of Canada, Studies in the Political Economy of Canada, and Carleton University. SPE publishes "interdisciplinary analyses on Canadian, international and theoretical questions in political economy." Articles present a Marxist-Socialist analysis of both current and historical developments in economics and politics. Representative titles include "The Political Economy of Joseph Schumpeter", "Political Ironies in the World Economy," "The Soviet Black Market," "Appropriating Workers' Knowledge: Quality Control Circles at a General Motors Plant", and "Concentration and Centralization of Capital in Agriculture." The articles are scholarly in style with extensive footnotes and documented data. Quantitative methodology is not employed. The authors are predominantly academics at Canadian universities. An occasional contribution by a European academic is included. SPE provides much the same viewpoint as Review of Radical Political Economics and Journal of Australian Political Economy.

Each issue includes five articles ranging in length from twenty to thirty-five pages each. Some issues include a short comment and a reply on a previously published paper.

Die Suid-Afrikaanse Tydskrif Vir Ekonomie. see The South African Journal of Economics/Die Suid-Afrikaanse Tydskrif Vir Ekonomie.

436.   **Survey Of Business.** DATE FOUNDED: 1965. TITLE CHANGES: Tennessee
Survey of Business (1965-1975). FREQUENCY: q. PRICE: Free. PUBLISHER:
The University of Tennessee, Center for Business and Economic Research,
College of Business Administraiton, Suite 100, Glocker Hall, Knoxville,
Tennessee 37996. EDITOR: David A. Hake. ILLUSTRATIONS. ADVERTISEMENTS.
MANUSCRIPT SELECTION: Consulting Editors. REPRINTS: Publisher. INDEXED/
ABSTRACTED: PAIS. DATABASES: PAIS INT. TARGET AUDIENCE: GP. SAMPLE
COPIES: Libraries and Individuals.

Survey of Business is one of the many business school publications that
is aimed at a regional business community readership. What makes it
different from its counterparts published by South Carolina, Arizona
State, Arkansas, South Dakota, and Mississippi among others, is that
each issue is entirely devoted to a single topic. The topic may focus on
a strictly Tennessee issue or it may be of more general interest. Some
recent issues that concentrated on Tennessee dealt with "Alternatives
for Tax Restructure in Tennessee", "Employment Trends in Tennessee", and
"Technology in Tennessee". Of more general interest were issues that
dealt with "Industrial Organization and Antiturst Policy", "Quality
Managment", "Deregulation", and "Management Accounting". Most articles
are non-technical and do not employ quantitative methodologies. They
are, however, more scholarly than the average business school publication. The authors are predominantly academics at the University of
Tennessee. A few are academics at other universities and the remainder
are state and federal government researchers or business executives.
    Issues contain from four to eight articles. The Winter issue is
entirely devoted to the economic outlook for the state of Tennessee and
the nation.

437.   **Survey of Current Business.** DATE FOUNDED: 1921. FREQUENCY: m.
PRICE: $30/yr. PUBLISHER: U.S. Department of Commerce, Bureau of
Economic Analysis, Washington, D.C. 20230. EDITOR: Carol S. Carson.
ILLUSTRATIONS. INDEX. CIRCULATION: 14,000. MANUSCRIPT SELECTION:
Editors. MICROFORMS: MIM, UMI. SPECIAL ISSUES. INDEXED/ABSTRACTED: ASI,
InEcA, IntBibE, IUSGovPer, JEL, KeyEcS, Pred. DATABASES: ECONAB,
ECONLIT, PF. TARGET AUDIENCE: AC, GP, SP.

The Survey of Current Business is among the most used and important
government publications in the field of economics. True to its title, it
provides data and analysis on the current condition of U.S. business and
the U.S. economy. It, together with its weekly supplement, Weekly
Business Statistics, is the best source for current data on the U.S.
national income and product accounts. Articles discuss the general
business situation in the U.S. as well as many specific subject areas
that contribute to the economic well being of the U.S. Examples of such
topics are federal budget developments, U.S. investment in other
countries, capital expenditures by foreign affiliates of U.S. firms, the
automobile industry, foreign investment in the U.S., cyclical adjustment
of the federal budget and federal debt, state and local government
fiscal positions, regional and state wages and salaries, federal
personal income taxes, and macroeconomic effects of price shocks.
Articles are written by professional research economists in the Bureau
of Economic Analysis, U.S. Department of Commerce. Articles vary in the
amount of technical material that they include, but all contain data
presented in tables and charts.

Each issue begins with a seven to ten page report on "the Business Situation." This is followed by tables of data and an average of three articles. In the center of each issue are thirty-five pages of tables providing "Current Business Statistics".

438.   Swedish Economy. DATE FOUNDED: 1960. FREQUENCY: 3/yr. PRICE: $10/yr. PUBLISHER: National Institute of Economic Research/Konjunktur-institutet, Stockholm, Sweden. ILLUSTRATIONS. INDEX. CIRCULATION: 900. TARGET AUDIENCE: AC, GP, SP.

Swedish Economy is the English translation of the Swedish publication, Konjunkturlaget. It is published under the auspices of the Ministry of Economic Affairs in Stockholm. It provides detailed information and analysis of the current condition of the Swedish economy. It contains no articles by individual authors as do regular journals, but instead provides, in chapter form, narrative, tables and charts, and a diary of important economic events that took place in Sweden during a recent period. No credit for authorship is given, but it is clear that the material is written by competent professional economists. The material is presented in a straight-forward and non-technical style and can be understood by non-economists. A voluminous amount of data in the form of tables and charts is included, but no quantitative methodologies are employed.

Each issue begins with a chapter that provides a general summary of the economic situation and economic development. This is followed by more detailed chapters on the international situation, foreign trade, production, the labor market, household finances, investments, indus-trial profits, costs and prices, the public sector, and credit markets. An economic diary and approximately thirty pages of tables and charts are found at the end of each issue. The material in the January issue is taken from the Preliminary National Budget and the material in the April issue is from the Revised National Budget.

439.   Thames Papers in Political Economy. DATE FOUNDED: 1974. FRE-QUENCY: 3/yr. PRICE: Free. PUBLISHER: Thames Polytechnic, School of Social Sciences, Economics Division, Wellington Street, London SE18 6PF, England and North East London Polytechnic, Faculty of Business, Depart-ment of Applied Economics, Longbridge Road, Dagenham, Essex RM8 2AS, England. EDITORS: Philip Arestis, Thanos Skouras. MANUSCRIPT SELECTION: Editors. TARGET AUDIENCE: AC, SP. SAMPLE COPIES: Libraries and Indi-viduals.

Thames Papers in Political Economy is published jointly by two Poly-technic institutions in England. The editorial aims of this publication are "to stimulate public discussion of practical issues in political economy" and "to bring to the notice of a wider audience controversial questions in economic theory." The Papers cover all areas of economics but emphasize discussions of economic theory. Examples of papers dealing with economic theory include "An Essay on Keynes and General Equilibrium Theory," "Unpacking the Post Keynesian Black Box: Wages, Bank Lending and the Money Supply", and "General Thought - Schemes and the Econ-omist". Examples of papers dealing with "practical issues" include "Crisis and Reform of the International Monetary System", "The Rise of Monetarism as a Social Doctrine," and "The Macrodynamics of the U.S. and

U.K. Economies through Two Post-Keynesian Models." The Papers are
scholarly and provide extensive references. Some are expository in style
and others incorporate econometric models. The majority of authors are
British academics but many contributions are made by economists from the
U.S., India, Austria, Australia, and Canada.

Each of the three Papers issued per year contains just one article.
The length ranges from thirteen to fifty-three pages.

440.   Transport Reviews. DATE FOUNDED: 1981. FREQUENCY: q. PRICE:
$86/yr. PUBLISHER: Taylor & Francis Ltd, 4 John Street, London WCIN 2ET,
England. EDITOR: S.M.A. Banister. ILLUSTRATIONS. INDEX. MANUSCRIPT
SELECTION: Editor and Referees. REPRINTS: Authors. BOOK REVIEWS. TARGET
AUDIENCE: AC, SP.

Transport Reviews is a relatively new journal that deals with all modes
of transport for "policy makers, transport practitioners, research
workers and post-graduate students." It presents "problems of interest
to many countries (transnational)" and is written "for people not
necessarily expert in the discipline of the writer (transdisciplinary)."
Articles present a variety of aspects of transportation problems. Recent
ones that offer an economic evaluation deal with topics such as subsidi-
zation of public transport, road pricing of urban traffic; comparison of
trucking regulation in Canada, the U.K., and the U.S., and changes in
cargo shipping technology. The articles are scholarly empirical research
studies. The level of technical treatment varies. The authors have
backgrounds in engineering, economics, urban studies, or geography. Some
are academics while others are government officials with transportation
agencies or researchers at private institutes. Transport Reviews is more
international in scope and presents more articles on broad policy issues
than Transportaion Journal that concentrates on the U.S. transporation
industry. It is most similiar in subject area and level of treatment to
Transportation Quarterly.

A typical issue includes four or five full-length articles. Each
article is summarized in French, German, and Spanish. A unique feature
is "Editorial Suggestions for Further Reading" at the end of each
article. Most issues have one or two signed book reviews.

441.   Transportation Journal. DATE FOUNDED: 1961. FREQUENCY: q. PRICE:
$25/yr. PUBLISHER: American Society of Transporation and Logistics, 1816
Norris Place, Louisville, Kentucky 40205. EDITOR: John C. Spychalski.
ILLUSTRATIONS. INDEX. CIRCULATION: 3,500. MANUSCRIPT SELECTION: Editor
and Editorial Board. MICROFORMS: UMI. REPRINTS: Authors, UMI. BOOK
REVIEWS. INDEXED/ABSTRACTED: BPI, PAIS. DATABASES: PAIS INT. TARGET
AUDIENCE: AC, SP.

Transportation Journal is the publication of a professional association
of individuals interested in transportation. It publishes "original
articles in the fields of economics, industrial and carrier management,
physical distribution, general business, regulation, public policy,
education and other relevant subjects." Recent issues have included
articles dealing with market performance of domestic airlines, improving
productivity, labor/management relations, commuter airlines, federal
mass transit policy, bus deregulation, and railroad costing models. The
emphasis of these articles is on the U.S. transportation industry but

occasionally articles deal with other countries such as Canada and the
U.K. The articles are well-researched and scholarly. Some employ
quantitative analyses and some are expository in style. The authors are
academics from departments of economics, finance, management, or
transportation; government officials with transportation agencies; or
executives with accounting firms. This journal focuses on problems of
the U.S. transportation industry while Transport Reviews has a broad
international scope and is more concerned with the social implications
of transportation problems.

A typical issue includes five to seven full-length articles and two
or three signed book reviews.

442.   Transportation Quarterly. DATE FOUNDED: 1947. TITLE CHANGES:
Traffic Quarterly (1947-1981). FREQUENCY: q. PRICE: Free. PUBLISHER: Eno
Foundation for Transportation, Box 2055, Westport, Connecticut 06880.
EDITOR: Wilbur S. Smith. ILLUSTRATIONS. INDEX. CIRCULATION: 5,000.
MANUSCRIPT SELECTION: Editor. MICROFORMS: UMI. REPRINTS: Publisher.
INDEXED/ABSTRACTED: EI, PAIS. DATABASES: COMPENDEX. PAIS INT. TARGET
AUDIENCE: AC, GP, SP.

Transportation Quarterly is published by a private foundation which was
established "to improve transportation in all its aspects" and to
distribute "information pertaining to transportation planning, design,
operation, and regulation." This journal covers all aspects of transportation, including the moving of both people and goods. The main focus
is on the U.S. situation but problems of other countries are discussed
also. Articles emphasizing the economic aspects of transportation
include topics such as cost-based highway financing, overnight air
express services, labor costs of public transit, revenue sources of
public transit, government assistance to railways, and state gasoline
taxes. Most of the articles are descriptive in nature with charts,
graphs, and tables of data. A few do use more technical quantitative
techniques. The majority of authors are professors of engineering, urban
planning, geography, and economics at American universities. Occasional
contributions from academics in other countries are included. Of the
several journals in the transporation field, Transportation Quarterly
most resembles Transport Reviews in coverage and level of treatment. It
is less quantitative and includes more articles on other countries than
does Transportation Journal.

Each issue includes ten full-length articles and an editorial. The
April issue summarizes discussions held at the annual Foundation
conference.

443.   Transportation Research. DATE FOUNDED: 1967. FREQUENCY: m.
PRICE: $240/yr. institutions, $90/yr. personal. PUBLISHER: Pergamon
Press, Inc., Maxwell House, Fairview Park, Elmsford, New York 10523.
EDITOR: Frank A. Haight. ILLUSTRATIONS. INDEX. ADVERTISEMENTS. CIRCULA-
TION: 1,600. MANUSCRIPT SELECTION: Editor and Referees. MICROFORMS:
Publisher, UMI. REPRINTS: Authors. BOOK REVIEWS. SPECIAL ISSUES.
INDEXED/ABSTRACTED: BPIA. DATABASES: MC. TARGET AUDIENCE: AC, SP.

Transportation Research is published in two parts which appear in
alternate months. Part A is "General" and Part B is "Methodological".
Both parts contain papers of "general interest in all passenger and

freight transportation modes..." The journal is both interdisciplinary and international in scope. It includes papers in the subject fields of transportation engineering, traffic engineering, urban and regional planning, decision making, technological innovations, environmental studies, public policy, and economics. Recent issues have included economics articles that deal with topics such as gasoline rationing, allocation, and price controls; local transit taxes; cheating in the taxi market; cost structure of urban bus transportation; and checkpoint dial-a-ride systems. The articles are scholarly. All those in Part B make use of mathematical modeling techniques. Those in Part A are less technical and frequently expository in style. The authors are of many different nationalities and have a variety of educational and professional backgrounds. Engineers, economists, and geographers are represented. Most are associated with universities, but some authors are with government agencies or private research institutes. Transportation Research is a more technical journal than Transport Reviews, Transportaton Journal, or Transportation Quarterly.

A typical issue of either Part A or Part B contains six or seven full-length papers. Part A includes a "Bibliographic Section" that contains two signed full-length reviews, brief notices of recent publications, abstracts of doctoral dissertations, and bibliographic listings of new books. Occasionally Part A is devoted to a single theme such as the 1984 issues on "Public Policy" and "Technology Development."

Travailleur Canadien. see Canadian Labour/Travailleur Canadien.

Tydskrif vir Studies in Ekonomie en Ekonometric. see Journal for Studies in Economics and Econometrics/Tydskrif vir Studies in Ekonomie en Ekonometrie.

444.   Urban Studies. DATE FOUNDED: 1964. FREQUENCY: q. PRICE: $50/yr. PUBLISHER: Longman Group Ltd., Westgate House, The High, Harlow, Essex CM20 1NE, England. EDITORS: W.F. Lever, W.J. Money. ILLUSTRATIONS. INDEX. ADVERTISEMENTS. CIRCULATION: 1,850. MANUSCRIPT SELECTION: Editors and Referees. MICROFORMS: UMI. REPRINTS: UMI. BOOK REVIEWS. INDEXED/ ABSTRACTED: InEcA, IntBibE, JEL, PAIS, SSI, WAERSA. DATABASES: CAB AB, ECONLIT, PAIS INT, SSI. TARGET AUDIENCE: AC, SP. SAMPLE COPIES: Libraries.

Urban Studies aims to "provide an international forum of social and economic contributions to the fields of urban and regional planning." This scholarly journal is associated with the University of Glasgow. Besides an international editorial board it also has an American editorial board whose chairman receives manuscripts from U.S. authors. While Urban Studies publishes both empirical and theoretical papers on an international scope, its main focus is on empirical research. Recent issues have included articles on topics such as Third World urbanization, spatial structure of metropolitan areas, industrial migration, spatial variation in unemployment, air pollution, and population dispersal policies. The bulk of empirical evidence is gathered in the U.K., the U.S., and Australia, but studies conducted in Morocco, Sweden, Brazil, and other countries appear also. The scholarly level of the articles is high. Both descriptive essays and quantitative analyses are

published. The authors are academics from the U.K., the U.S., Australia,
and other countries or researchers with government agencies in those
same countries.

A typical issue has five full-length articles and three to six
shorter notes and comments. An extensive book review section includes as
many as fifteen signed reviews as well as four or five short annotations. The journal offers an annual Urban Studies Fellowship to assist a
visiting scholar in conducting research at the Center for Urban and
Regional Research at the University of Glasgow.

445.   **Utah Economic and Business Review.** DATE FOUNDED: 1941. FRE-
QUENCY: 9/yr. PRICE: Free. PUBLISHER: University of Utah, Graduate
School of Business, Bureau of Economic and Business Research, Salt Lake
City, Utah 84112. EDITOR: R. Thayne Robson. ILLUSTRATIONS. CIRCULATION:
3,500. MANUSCRIPT SELECTION: Editor. INDEXED/ABSTRACTED: PAIS. DATA-
BASES: PAIS INT. TARGET AUDIENCE: GP. SAMPLE COPIES: Libraries and
Individuals.

Utah Economic and Business Review is a business school publication which
concentrates almost entirely on "important changes in Utah's economy."
In this respect it resembles several other business school publications
such as South Dakota Business Review, Pennsylvania Business Survey, and
Georgia Business and Economic Conditions. Topics covered in recent
issues include the medical supply and biomedical research industries in
Utah, the economic impact of high Great Lake levels, population estimates for the State, personal income in Utah counties, how Utah's
Standard Needs Budget affects public assistance, the contribution of
skiing to Utah's economy, the impact of natural resource development on
small businesses in Utah, public employment in the State, and apartment
construction activity in Utah. Articles typically include many tables of
data, but are non-technical and devoid of quantitative methodologies.
The authors are all "in-house" research economists or analysts.

Each issue contains one article from five to fifteen pages in length.
The remainder of the issue is devoted to Utah business statistics. The
Review is published each month except for dual issues in April-May,
July-August and September-October.

446.   **The Wall Street Review of Books.** DATE FOUNDED: 1973. FREQUENCY:
q. PRICE: $34/yr. institutions, $21/yr. personal. PUBLISHER: Redgrave
Publishing Company, 380 Adams Street, Bedford Hills, New York 10507.
EDITOR: David O. Whitten. INDEX. CIRCULATION: 500. MANUSCRIPT SELECTION:
Editor and Board of Contributing Editors. MICROFORMS: UMI. REPRINTS:
UMI. INDEXED/ABSTRACTED: BRI, CBRC. TARGET AUDIENCE: AC, SP. SAMPLE
COPIES: Libraries.

The Wall Street Review of Books is a publication entirely devoted to
reviewing books in economics and business. The editor and contributing
editors aim at including books that are scholarly and deal with a
subject matter of considerable interest to professors of business and
economics as well as professional practitioners. More economics books
than business books are reviewed. Every area of economics and business
is covered. Reviewers are predominantly academics associated with
departments of economics and business administration at American
universities. Occasionally, political scientists and historians write

reviews. A few Canadian and Australian academics make contributions. Some reviews are written by the Editor and by fourteen contributing editors. This publication is substantially different from Economic Selection and Economic Books: Current Selections. The latter two provide large numbers of annotations while The Wall Street Review of Books contains a relatively small number of in-depth book reviews.

A typical issue contains about twenty book reviews, most from three to five pages in length. Some are outlines such as a recent review that spanned twenty-four pages. Reviews that cover several books are usually from six to twelve pages long. A brief biographical statement about the reviewer follows each review. Some issues have an "Editor's Bookshelf" section, listing new books and a "Commentary" section featuring authors' replies.

447.   Waseda Economic Papers. DATE FOUNDED: 1962. FREQUENCY: a. PRICE: Free. PUBLISHER: Waseda University, Graduate School of Economics, Tokyo, Japan. EDITORS: Tomiju Masuda, Junzaburo Yasuda, Tadao Horie. MANUSCRIPT SELECTION: Editors. TARGET AUDIENCE: AC, SP. SAMPLE COPIES: Libraries and Individuals.

Waseda Economic Papers is an English language serial published in Japan. It covers a broad range of topics in economics. Some articles are in the area of economic history such as the recent ones analyzing the apprenticeship system in England in the early part of the twentieth century and explaining the growth of the French economy after the Second World War. Other articles offer critiques of Marxian economics such as the recent ones discussing the contradictions in Marx's Labor-Value Theory, transformation of money into capital, and prophesies of Marx and Lenin. International economic development is a third subject area which is covered in several papers. The level of treatment varies from expository to quantitative. The authors are predominantly Japanese but their affiliations are not provided except for those who are named as editors of this publication. One can assume that all the authors are faculty members at Waseda University. This publication is like other publications of Japanese universities such as Hokudai Economic Papers, KSU Economic And Business Review, and Kansai University Review of Economics and Business in that they serve as a vehicle for publishing papers by members of their own faculty.

A typical issue has two or three papers from twenty to thirty pages each in length.

448.   Western Journal of Agricultural Economics. DATE FOUNDED: 1976. FREQUENCY: 2/yr. PRICE: $15/yr. institutions, $10/yr. personal. PUBLISHER: Western Agricultural Economics Association, Department of Agricultural Economics, University of Nebraska, Lincoln, Nebraska 68588. EDITORS: Darrell L. Hueth, Richard S. Johnston. ILLUSTRATIONS. CIRCULATION: 950. MANUSCRIPT SELECTION: Editors and Referees. REPRINTS: Authors. INDEXED/ABSTRACTED: AGRICOLA, WAERSA. DATABASES: AGRICOLA, CAB AB. TARGET AUDIENCE: AC, SP. SAMPLE COPIES: Libraries.

The Western Journal of Agricultural Economics supersedes Western Agricultural Economics Association Proceedings. Articles deal with "the economics of agriculture, natural resources, human resources, or rural and community development." The journal accepts articles that are "theoretical, methodological, and empirical contributions in Extension, research, or the teaching phases of agricultural economics." Preference is given to articles dealing with "Problems and issues of concern in the Western and Great Plains regions of the U.S. and Canada." Topics in recent issues include the barley futures market, the food stamp program, the estimation of risk preferences, the Canadian beef cattle industry, estimation of nonlinear demand systems, pricing in the U.S.-Japan softwood trade, small-scale fuel alcohol production, forecasting alfalfa hay prices, and the optimal stocking of rangeland for livestock production. Most articles in this scholarly journal are technical in nature and make use of modern mathematical, statistical, and econometric methodologies. The authors are predominantly American and Canadian academic agricultural economists or economic researchers with the U.S. Department of Agriculture. This publication and the Southern Journal of Agricultural Economics are similar in their use of quantitative methodologies and their mix of regional and national concerns.

The length and the number of articles in an issue vary greatly; ten articles in one issue and twenty-seven in another. In addition to the regular articles, the December issue includes from four to six "Proceedings" articles taken from the WAEA annual meeting held in July.

449.   The World Economy. DATE FOUNDED: 1977. FREQUENCY: q. PRICE: $89.50/yr. institutions, $44.20/yr. personal. PUBLISHER: Basil Blackwell Publisher, Ltd., 108 Cowley Road, Oxford OX4 1JF, England. EDITORS: Peter Oppenheimer, Ingo Walter. ILLUSTRATIONS. INDEX. ADVERTISEMENTS. CIRCULATION: 1,400. MANUSCRIPT SELECTION: Editors and Editorial Board. BOOK REVIEWS. INDEXED/ABSTRACTED: IntBibE, PAIS, WAERSA. DATABASES: CAB AB, PAIS INT. TARGET AUDIENCE: AC, GP, SP. SAMPLE COPIES: Libraries.

The World Economy subtitled "a Quarterly Journal on International Economics Affairs" is the publication of the Trade Policy Research Centre in London, England. It focuses on national and international policies that have important effects on international trade. Topics addressed in recent issues include the role of the trade ombudsman in Japan, developing country exports, China's foreign investment policy, the world information economy, economic problems of the European Community, industrial policies, Euro-Japanese trade relations, international maritime transport, and how to strengthen the international trade and financial systems. Most articles are non-technical and expository in nature. Tables of data are sometimes provided, but no quantitative methodologies are employed. Most of the authors are economists who are associated with universities, research institutes, government agencies, international organizations, and consulting firms. The majority are European, American, and Japanese. A few are high level government officials or very well known academic economists.

Each issue includes about six articles of varying lengths. A "Matters of Opinion" section includes short notes on current issues, short comments on previously published articles, and short remarks on studies published by the Centre. Book reviews are offered in two parts: 1) "Additions to the Bookshelf", a reviewer's discussion of a number of books on a particular theme and 2) "Book Reviews", several brief signed reviews.

450.   **World Development**. DATE FOUNDED: 1973. FREQUENCY: m. PRICE: $260/yr. institutions, $75/yr. personal. PUBLISHER: Pergamon Press Inc., Maxwell House, Fairview Park, Elmsford, New York 10523. EDITOR: Anne Gordon Drabek. INDEX. ADVERTISEMENTS. CIRCULATION: 1,600. MANUSCRIPT SELECTION: Editor and Referees. MICROFORMS: MIM, UMI. REPRINTS: UMI. SPECIAL ISSUES. INDEXED/ABSTRACTED: BPIA, KeyEcS, SSI. DATABASES: ECONAB, MC, SSI. TARGET AUDIENCE: AC, SP.

World Development, which incorporated New Commonwealth, is a scholarly journal that encompasses a wide range of subjects related to the economic development of the Third World. Articles present discussions on topics such as poverty; relations between rich and poor countries; direct foreign investment; shortages of food, energy, and raw materials; world inflation; relations between developing countries; the European Economic Community; the international monetary system; the emergence of the People's Republic of China; the ascendancy of Japan; and the effect of technology transfer. Most of the studies are based on empirical research but some theoretical analyses or conceptual discussions are included. The level of treatment ranges from descriptive to mathematical. Many articles use data prepared by the World Bank. The majority of authors are professors at American universities but contributions are made by academics from many nations. The Journal of Developing Areas examines the same subject area as World Development but takes a broader and more inter-disciplinary approach.

A typical issue has six or seven articles ranging in length from ten to twenty-five pages. Each year, one or two special issues are devoted to a single topic under the direction of guest editors. Two recent special issues focus on "The Impact of World Recession on Children" and "Exports of Technology by Newly-Industrializing Countries."

Yearbook of East-European Economics. see Jahrbuch der Wirtschaft Osteuropas/Yearbook of East-European Economics.

English-Language
Indexes and Abstracts
in the Field of Economics

Business Periodicals Index. DATE FOUNDED: 1959. FREQUENCY: 11/yr.
PRICE: Varies-$75/yr. minimum. PUBLISHER: H. W. Wilson Company, 950
University Avenue, Bronx, New York 10452. EDITOR: Bettie Jane Third.
MANUSCRIPT SELECTION: Editors.

The Business Periodicals Index covers business periodicals published in
the English language. BPI is published monthly, except for August, with
three quarterly cumulations and one annual cumulation each year. The
periodicals are selected from recommendations made by the Reference and
Adult Services Division of the American Library Association as well as
subscriber preferences. BPI's subject coverage includes accounting,
banking, economics, finance and investments, industrial relations,
international business, management and personnel administration, public
utilities, regulation of industry, and specific businesses and industries.
　　　The main body of BPI consists of a subject index of bibliographic
citations. The subject terms are arranged alphabetically and frequently
have one or more subheadings. There are both "see" references guiding
the user to the form of subject heading used and "see also" references
guiding the user to related subject terms. A book review index appears
after the subject index. The front matter includes explanatory notes,
abbreviations of periodicals indexed, and a list of titles of periodicals indexed together with publishers' addresses and subscription
prices.

Business Publications Index and Abstracts. DATE FOUNDED: 1983.
FREQUENCY: m. Publisher: Gale Research Company, Book Tower, Detroit,
Michigan 48226. DATABASES: MC.

Business Publications Index and Abstracts is the printed version of the
"Management Contents" online database. It is published monthly in two
parts, one containing subject and author indexes of bibliographic
citations and one containing abstracts of articles and books. The
monthly subject and author indexes are cumulated month-by-month through
each quarter. Annual cumulations of subject and author indexes as well
as of abstracts are published. BPIA covers business literature in such
areas as general management, accounting, finance, marketing, production,
and personnel management. It aims to provide timely access to the

literature by indexing and abstracting source materials within ten-twelve weeks of receipt of the materials.

The main body of the subject/author citations volume consists of a subject index of bibliographic citations. Subject terms frequently have subheadings. There are cross references to related subject terms and alternate subject terms. Each citation displays an abstract number. A substantial author index follows the subject index. The abstracts volume consists of 50-300 word summaries arranged in numerical order. Both volumes include a list of publications indexed and abstracted and a guide to using the specific volume.

Index of Economic Articles in Journals and Collective Volumes. DATE FOUNDED: 1969. MERGER: Index of Economic Journals (1961-1967) and Index of Economic Articles in Collective Volumes (1969-1972). FREQUENCY: a. PRICE: $50/yr. PUBLISHER: American Economic Association, 1313 21st Avenue South, Nashville, Tennessee 37212. EDITOR: Moses Abramovitz. MANUSCRIPT SELECTION: Editors. DATABASES: ECONLIT.

The Index of Economic Articles in Journals and Collective Volumes is prepared in association with the Journal of Economic Literature. The Index includes the same journals and collective volumes covered in JEL. Articles are arranged in a more detailed classification system in the Index than in JEL but JEL offers more timely access to the economics literature. The Index is currently providing access to articles published five years previously. Its scope includes articles having economic content that would be helpful to professional economists. The majority of articles are in English but a few appear in other languages with English summaries.

International Bibliography of Economics. DATE FOUNDED: 1952. FREQUENCY: a. PRICE: $108/yr. PUBLISHER: Tavistock Publications Ltd., 11 New Fetter Lane, London EC4P 4EE, England. EDITOR: Jean Meyriat. CIRCULATION: 2,000.

The International Bibliography of Economics is one of four annual volumes of the International Bibliography of the Social Sciences. The Bibliography is prepared by the International Committee for Social Science Information and Documentation with the financial support of UNESCO. It covers all field of economics and includes publications from all countries and in all languages. Approximately half the citations are to articles published in English.

The main body of the Bibliography consists of entries arranged in a classification system. Each entry provides a full bibliographic citation and is assigned a number for identification. In addition, there is an author index and two subject indexes, one in English and one in French. All three indexes refer to the numerical identification number of each entry. The front matter includes prefaces in both English and French, a list of periodicals consulted, and the classification scheme in both English and French. The classification scheme uses an alphanumeric designation of each subject term. The scheme can be expanded to five digits within each letter designation.

Journal of Economic Literature. DATE FOUNDED: 1969. FREQUENCY: q.
PRICE: $100/yr. institutions, includes subscription to American Economic
Review, $49/yr. personal, includes membership to AEA and subscription to
American Economic Review. PUBLISHER: American Economic Association, 1313
21st Avenue South, Suite 809, Nashville, Tennessee 37212. EDITOR: Moses
Abramovitz. ILLUSTRATIONS. INDEX. ADVERTISEMENTS. CIRCULATION: 26,000.
MANUSCRIPT SELECTION: Editor and Board of Editors. MICROFORMS: MIM, UMI.
BOOK REVIEWS. INDEXED/ABSTRACTED: BPIA, InEcA, IntBibE, JEL, KeyEcS.
PAIS, SSI, WAERSA. DATABASES: CAB AB, ECONAB, ECONLIT, MC, PAIS INT,
SSI. TARGET AUDIENCE: AC, SP. SAMPLE COPIES: Libraries.

The Journal of Economic Literature is both a journal of articles and
book reviews and a reference work providing subject access to the major
literature of economics. Its scope covers all areas of applied and
theoretical economics. Articles do not report on the research of the
author, but are review articles covering the literature concerning some
problem or issue in economics. In most instances a reader can learn
about the most important research and ideas that the profession has to
date on a particular topic.
A typical issue contains from two to four review articles, each
thirty or forty pages in length. Some issues have a "Communications"
section with one or two brief comments and/or replies regarding previously published articles. Each issue also contains an extensive book
review section which includes from thirty to fifty one-to-two page
signed reviews separated according to subject category. An annotated
listing of hundreds of new books, arranged according to a classification
system, provide further coverage of the monographic literature in the
field. The periodical literature is covered by publishing the table of
contents of a large number of current economics periodicals. These
contents listings are arranged alphabetically by periodical title. This
section is followed by a subject index to periodical articles. Bibliographic citations are arranged according to a three digit classification
system. This system is displayed just before the index. A smaller
section provides selected abstracts of articles cited in the index.
These abstracts are provided by the author of each article. The final
section offers an author index to all articles cited in the subject
index.

Key to Economic Science and Managerial Sciences. DATE FOUNDED:
1953. TITLE CHANGEs: Economic Abstracts (1953-1975) Key to Economic
Science (1976-1977). FREQUENCY: sm. PRICE: Dfl 168/yr. PUBLISHER:
Martinus Nijhoff Publishers, c/o Kluwer Academic Publishers Group
Distribution Center, P.O. Box 322, 3300 AH Dordrecht, The Netherlands.
DATABASES: ECONAB.

Key to Economic Science and Managerial Sciences offers a selection from
the abstracts published in Economic Titles/Abstracts. The latter covers
the world literature on economics, finance, trade, industry, foreign
aid, management, marketing, and labor. Both indexes are compiled by the
Library and Documentation Center of the Netherlands Foreign Trade
Agency.
The Key is a twenty to thirty page publication which is issued
semi-monthly. There is an annual author and subject index. The
abstracts are arranged numerically according to the abstract number. The
abstract includes the complete bibliographic citation plus a summary of

the source material. Abstracts are primarily in English, with some in
French, German, or Dutch. Readers may obtain photocopies of articles
from the compiling agency for a modest fee.

Predicasts F&S Index United States. DATE FOUNDED: 1960. TITLE
CHANGES: Funk and Scott Index of Corporations and Industries (1960-
1967), F&S Index of Corporations and Industries. (1968-1978). FREQUENCY:
m. PRICE: $600/yr. PUBLISHER: Predicasts, Inc., 11001 Cedar Avenue,
Cleveland, Ohio 44106. EDITOR: George Cratcha. DATABASES: PF.

Predicasts F&S Index United States covers business news about American
and foreign companies in the U.S. This information is derived from
financial publications, newspapers, trade magazines, and special
reports. It contains information "on corporte acquisitions and mergers,
new products, technological developments, and social and political
factors affecting business." Predicasts, Inc. also publishes companion
volumes--a European Index and an International Index--which provide the
same information about the rest of the world.
    The Index is published monthly, with quarterly and annual cumula-
tions. Each Index consists of two main sections. Section One reports
on new products, sales, business investment, government regulation, and
related data. Entries are arranged by a numerical system based on the
Standard Industrial Classification (SIC) codes. Each numerical code is
further subdivided by subject headings. Section Two reports on merger
and acquisition data, sales and profits, analyses of companies by
securities firms, and other financial data. Entries are arranged
alphabetically by company name with a subdivision by subject headings.
Other sections include a guide for users, a list of industry groups
arranged by SIC code, a list of publications indexed, and an alphabetical listing of products and industries with their corresponding SIC
codes.

Public Affairs Information Service Bulletin. DATE FOUNDED: 1915.
FREQUENCY: Sm. PRICE: $225/yr. PUBLISHER: Public Affairs Information
Service, Inc. 11 West 40th Street, New York, New York 10018. EDITOR:
Lawrence J. Woods. MANUSCRIPT SELECTION: Editors. DATABASES: PAIS INT.

The Public Affairs Information Service Bulletin is published by a
non-profit association of libraries. It is associated with the New York
Public Library and uses the resources found in the Economic and Public
Affairs Division of the NYPL. The PAIS Bulletin emphasizes public
affairs information likely to be useful to "legislators, administrators,
the business and financial community, policy researchers and students".
Highly technical writings, employing concepts or terminology accessible
only to specialists are normally not indexed. The PAIS Bulletin's scope
includes business, economics, finance, political science, public
administration, international law and relations, sociology and demography. It offers a subject index of books, government publications,
and periodical articles in the English language.
    The PAIS Bulletin is issued semimonthly with three quarterly
cumulations and an annual cumulation with an author index. The main
body of the index consists of bibliographic citations arranged by
subject entries. There are frequent cross references to alternate
subject terms and related subjects. The front matter includes a user's

guide to the PAIS Bulletin, a key to bibliographical symbols and abbreviations, a key to periodical references, and a directory of publishers and organizations. The annual cumulation includes a listing of both personal and corporate authors in a separate section.

Social Sciences Index. DATE FOUNDED: 1975. FREQUENCY: q. PRICE: Varies-$60/yr. minimum. PUBLISHER: H. W. Wilson Company, 950 University Avenue, Bronx, New York 10452. EDITOR: Joseph Bloomfield. MANUSCRIPT SELECTION: Editor. DATABASES: SSI.

The Social Sciences Index supercedes the International Index (1907-1965) and the Social Sciences & Humanities Index (1966-1974). Its scope includes English language periodicals in the fields of "anthropology, economics, environmental sciences, geography, law and criminology, planning and public administration, political science, psychology, social aspects of medicine, sociology and related subjects." The Index offers author and subject entries to periodical articles as well as "an author listing of citations to book reviews." The selection of periodicals for indexing is based upon recommendations from the American Library Association's Reference and Adult Services Division and subscriber preferences.

Social Sciences Index is issued quarterly and in an annual cumulation. The main body of the Index consists of a combined author and subject listing of bibliographic citations. There are frequent cross references to alternate subject terms or forms of entry. There is a substantial listing of book reviews arranged alphabetically by author. The front matter includes abbreviations of periodicals indexed; a list of the name, address, and subscription price of periodicals indexed; a list of general abbreviations; and a sample entry with explanations for the user.

Work Related Abstracts. DATE FOUNDED: 1950. TITLE CHANGES: Labor Personnel Index (1950-1958). Employment Relations Abstracts (1959-1972). FREQUENCY: m. PRICE: $360/yr. PUBLISHER: Information Coordinators, Inc. 1435-37 Randolph Street, Detroit, Michigan 48226. EDITOR: Sonja Hempseed. CIRCULATION: 500.

Work Related Abstracts provides an index to periodical articles in the fields of labor-management relations, personnel management, labor markets, government policies and legislation, labor and industrial history, labor unions, and related areas.

The main body of this index consists of brief abstracts arranged into twenty broad subject fields. Each field has a letter designation, and within each letter the abstracts are arranged numerically. A detailed author and subject index, cumulated monthly follows the abstracts section and provides the letter and number designation of the appropriate abstract. As many as six subject headings may be assigned to an abstract, so there are multiple access points to each article. Other sections include a guide for the user, a listing of the twenty broad subject sections, a list of standard abbreviations, a list of geographic abbreviations, periodicals included in WRA, periodical abbreviations, a list of labor organizations, and labor organization abbreviations. A biennial list of geographical and subject headings with "see" and "see also" cross references is issued in a separate volume.

World Agricultural Economics and Rural Sociology Abstracts. DATE FOUNDED: 1959. FREQUENCY: m. PRICE: ₺ 162/yr. PUBLISHER: Commonwealth Bureau of Agricultural Economics, Dartington House, Little Clarendon Street, Oxford OX1 2HH, U.K. EDITOR: M.A. Bellamy. CIRCULATION: 1,550. DATABASES: CAB AB.

World Agricultural Economics and Rural Sociology Abstracts provides an index to the world literature in agricultural economics. This broad subject field includes agricultural policy, prices, marketing, international trade, finance, economiecs of production, cooperatives and collectives, and rural sociology.

The main body of WAERSA consists of abstracts arranged in a classification schedule. The schedule includes ten broad subject fields, each of which is further subdivided into narrower subject fields. Within the narrower subject fields, the abstracts are arranged numerically by abstract number. An author index and detailed subject index follow the abstract section. The front matter includes the classification schedule, a guide to abbreviations, abbreviations of libraries holding the publication abstracted, a guide to readers, and explanations of sample entries. Cumulative author and subject indexes to the abstracts are published at the end of the year. Recent volumes have not included a list of publications abstracted.

Geographical Index

Number cited refers to entry number in body of book. Country refers to place of publication.

Index of Publishers

Number cited refers to entry number in body of book.

Classified Title Index

GENERAL ECONOMICS

254. Journal of Contemporary Studies
255. Journal of Cultural Economics
289. Journal of Law and Economics
446. The Wall Street Review of Books

GENERAL ECONOMICS THEORY

133. The Economic Studies Quarterly
220. International Journal of Game Theory
260. Journal of Economic Behavior and Organization
261. Journal of Economic Dynamics and Control
268. Journal of Economic Theory,
269. Journal of Economics and Business
290. Journal of Macroeconomics
291. Journal of Mathematical Economics
329. Lloyds Bank Review
339. Mathematical Social Sciences
343. Metroeconomica
369. Oeconomica Polona
396. The Rand Journal of Economics
406. The Review of Economic Studies
410. Review of Marketing and Agricultural Economics
418. The Scandinavian Journal of Economics

HISTORY OF THOUGHT, METHODOLOGY

114. Economic Forum
139. Economy and Society
191. History of Political Economy

ECONOMIC HISTORY

010. African Economic History
036. Australian Economic History Review
058. Business History
059. Business History Review
116. The Economic History Review
150. Explorations in Economic History
199. The Indian Economic and Social History Review
224. International Labor and Working Class History
263. Journal of Economic History
272. The Journal of European Economic History
295. The Journal of Peasant Studies
417. Scandinavian Economic History Review

ECONOMIC SYSTEMS

002. Abstracts of Bulgarian Scientific Literature, Economics
      and Law
004. The ACES Bulletin
073. Capital and Class
096. Eastern European Economics
136. Economics of Planning
223. International Journal of Social Economics
238. Journal of Australian Political Economy
250. Journal of Comparative Economics

411. Review of Radical Political Economics
415. Review of Social Economy
435. Studies in Political Economy: a Socialist Review

ECONOMIC EDUCATION

262. Journal of Economic Education

ECONOMIC GROWTH; DEVELOPMENT; PLANNING: FLUCTUATIONS

006. Acta Oeconomica
009. Africa Development/Afrique et Developpement.
038. Australian Economic Review
040. Bangkok Bank Monthly Review
042. Bank of England Quarterly Bulletin
044. Bank of Japan Monthly Economic Review
061. Business Mexico
064. Cambridge Economic Policy Review
090. Development and Change
091. Development Digest
107. Economic Bulletin
111. Economic Development and Cultural Change
127. Economic Policy Issues
131. Economic Review
155. Federal Reserve Bank of Boston. New England Economic Review
195. IDS Bulletin
201. The Indian Economic Review
256. The Journal of Developing Areas
257. Journal of Development Economics
258. The Journal of Development Studies
267. Journal of Economic Studies
296. Journal of Philippine Development
352. National Institute Economic Review
369. Oeconomica Polona
404. Review of Business
421. The Singapore Economic Review
450. World Development

ECONOMIC GROWTH, DEVELOPMENT, AND PLANNING THEORY AND POLICY

092. Development Policy Review
093. Development Research Digest
162. Federal Reserve Bank of Minneapolis Quarterly Review

ECONOMIC DEVELOPMENT STUDIES

030. Artha Vijnana
031. Artha-Vikas
032. Asian Economic Review
033. Asian Economies
037. Australian Economics Papers
041. The Bangladesh Development Studies
043. Bank of Israel Economic Review
045. Bank of Korea Quarterly Economic Review
046. Bank of Montreal Business Review
053. Bulletin of Indonesian Economic Studies

ECONOMIC FLUCTUATIONS, FORECASTING, AND INFLATION

ECONOMIC STATISTICS

ECONOMETRIC, STATISTICAL, AND MATHEMATICAL METHODS AND MODELS

ECONOMIC AND SOCIAL STATISTICS

154. Federal Reserve Bank of Boston. New England Economic
     Indicators
168. Federal Reserve Bank of St. Louis Monetary Trends
169. Federal Reserve Bank of St. Louis National Economic Trends
171. Federal Reserve Bulletin
177. Foreign Agricultural Trade of the United States.
211. Industry of Free China
218. International Economic Conditions
391. Quarterly Economic Reviews
408. The Review of Income and Wealth
437. Survey of Current Business

MONETARY AND FISCAL THEORY AND INSTITUTIONS

007. The AEI Economist
074. Carnegie-Rochester Conference Series on Public Policy
163. Federal Reserve Bank of New York Quarterly Review
166. Federal Reserve Bank of San Francisco Economic Review
167. Federal Reserve Bank of San Francisco Weekly Letter
290. Journal of Macroeconomics

DOMESTIC MONETARY AND FINANCIAL THEORY AND INSTITUTIONS

001. ABA Banking Journal
152. Federal Home Loan Bank Board Journal
156. Federal Reserve Bank of Chicago Economic Perspectives
157. Federal Reserve Bank of Cleveland Economic Commentary
158. Federal Reserve Bank of Cleveland Economic Review
159. Federal Reserve Bank of Dallas Economic Review
160. Federal Reserve Bank of Kansas City Economic Review
164. Federal Reserve Bank of Philadelphia Business Review
165. Federal Reserve Bank of Richmond Economic Review
170. Federal Reserve Bank of St. Louis Review
171. Federal Reserve Bulletin
174. The Financial Review
239. Journal of Bank Research
240. Journal of Banking and Finance
273. The Journal of Finance
274. Journal of Financial and Quantitative Analysis
275. Journal of Financial Economics
276. The Journal of Financial Research
293. Journal of Monetary Economics
294. Journal of Money, Credit and Banking

DOMESTIC FISCAL POLICY AND PUBLIC FINANCE

215. Institute of Public Affairs Review
235. Journal of Accounting and Economics
353. National Tax Journal
386. Public Choice
387. Public Finance/ Finances Publiques
388. Public Finance Quarterly

INTERNATIONAL ECONOMICS

042. Bank of England Quarterly Bulletin

TRADE RELATIONS, COMMERCIAL POLICY, ECONOMIC INTEGRATION

BALANCE OF PAYMENTS, INTERNATIONAL FINANCE

ADMINISTRATION; BUSINESS FINANCE; MARKETING; ACCOUNTING

206. Indiana Business Review
229. The Israel Economist
242. Journal of Business
245. Journal of Business Finance and Accounting
247. Journal of Business Research
269. Journal of Economics and Business
311. Kansai University Review of Economics and Business
316. Kobe Economic and Business Review
317. KSU Economic and Business Review
328. Liiketaloudellinen Aikakauskirja/The Finnish Journal of
     Business Economics
344. The Mid-Atlantic Journal of Business
345. Mid-South Business Journal
346. Mississippi Business Review
371. The Oriental Economist
385. Process Economics International
392. Quarterly Journal of Business and Economics
394. The Quarterly Review of Economics and Business
404. Review of Business
405. Review of Business and Economic Research
412. Review of Regional Economics and Business
416. Rivista Internazionale Di Scienze Economiche E Commerciali
431. Southwest Journal of Business and Economics
437. Survey of Current Business

ADMINISTRATION

086. Decision Sciences
188. Harvard Business Review
189. Harvard Business School Bulletin
297. Journal of Policy Modeling
332. Management Science
333. Managerial and Decision Economics
441. Transportation Journal

BUSINESS FINANCE AND INVESTMENT

044. Bank of Japan Monthly Economic Review
045. Bank of Korea Quarterly Economic Review
151. Far Eastern Economic Review
174. The Financial Review
273. The Journal of Finance
274. Journal of Financial and Quantitative Analysis
275. Journal of Financial Economics
276. The Journal of Financial Research
278. The Journal of Futures Markets
303. The Journal of Risk and Insurance
342. MERI's Monthly Circular: Survey of Economic Conditions in
     Japan
350. Multinational Business
414. Review of Research in Futures Markets

ACCOUNTING

235. Journal of Accounting and Economics

INDUSTRIAL ORGANIZATION; TECHNOLOGICAL CHANGE; INDUSTRY STUDIES

212. Information Economics and Policy
221. International Journal of Industrial Organization
281. The Journal of Industrial Economics
385. Process Economics International

INDUSTRIAL ORGANIZATION AND PUBLIC POLICY

015. American Business Law Journal
022. The Antitrust Bulletin
023. Antitrust Law and Economics Review
289. Journal of Law and Economics
302. Journal of Reprints for Antitrust Law and Economics
307. Journal of Transport Economics and Policy
330. The Logistics and Transportation Review
341. Mergers and Acquisitions
386. Public Choice
389. Public Utilities Fortnightly
396. The Rand Journal of Economics
409. Review of Industrial Organization
440. Transport Reviews
441. Transportation Journal
442. Transportation Quarterly
443. Transportation Research

INDUSTRIAL STUDIES

233. Japanese Finance and Industry

AGRICULTURE; NATURAL RESOURCES

019. American Journal of Agricultural Economics
364. Northeastern Journal of Agricultural and Resource Economics

AGRICULTURE

011. Agricultural Economics Research
012. Agricultural Outlook
039. Australian Journal of Agricultural Economics
067. Canadian Farm Economics
068. Canadian Journal of Agricultural Economics/Revue Canadienne
     d'Economie Rurale
126. Economic Planning
148. European Review of Agricultural Economics
175. Food Policy
176. Food Research Institute Studies
177. Foreign Agricultural Trade of the United States
178. Foreign Agriculture
202. Indian Journal of Agricultural Economics
236. Journal of Agricultural Economics
237. Journal of Agricultural Economics and Development
351. National Food Review
363. North Central Journal of Agricultural Economics
395. Quarterly Review of the Rural Economy
410. Review of Marketing and Agricultural Economics

LABOR MARKETS, PUBLIC POLICY

015. American Business Law Journal

TRADE UNIONS, COLLECTIVE BARGAINING, LABOR-MANAGEMENT RELATIONS

025. The Arbitration Journal
121. Economic Notes
320. Labor History
322. Labor Notes
325. Labour History

DEMOGRAPHIC ECONOMICS

016. American Demographics
087. Demography
088. Demography India
283. Journal of Institute of Economic Research
382. Population and Development Review
383. Population Studies

WELFARE PROGRAMS; CONSUMER ECONOMICS; URBAN AND REGIONAL ECONOMICS

021. The Annals of Regional Science
055. Business and Society
082. Council on Economic Priorities Newsletter
187. Growth And Change; A Journal of Public, Urban, and Regional
      Policy
254. Journal of Contemporary Studies
397. Regional Science and Urban Economics
399. Regional Studies
425. Socio-Economic Planning Sciences

WELFARE PROGRAMS

213. Inquiry
228. International Social Security Review
279. Journal of Health Economics
300. Journal of Public Economics
306. The Journal of the Institute for Socioeconomic Studies
351. National Food Review
403. The Review of Black Political Economy
415. Review of Social Economy
424. Social Security Bulletin

CONSUMER ECONOMICS

112. Economic Education Bulletin
251. The Journal of Consumer Affairs
252. Journal of Consumer Policy
253. Journal of Consumer Research
266. Journal of Economic Psychology

URBAN ECONOMICS

026. AREUEA Journal

305. Journal of the American Planning Association
308. Journal of Urban Economics
443. Transportation Research
444. Urban Studies

REGIONAL ECONOMICS

014. Alaska Review of Social and Economic Conditions
027. Arizona Business
028. Arizona Review
029. Arkansas Business and Economic Review
054. Business and Economic Review
070. Canadian Journal of Regional Science/La Revue Canadienne des
      Sciences Regionales
079. Colorado Business Review
102. Economic Analysis and Policy
109. Economic Bulletin for Europe
115. Economic Geography
129. Economic Report
153. Federal Reserve Bank of Atlanta Economic Review
154. Federal Reserve Bank of Boston. New England Economic
      Indicators
159. Federal Reserve Bank of Dallas Economic Review
161. Federal Reserve Bank of Kansas City Financial Letter
183. Georgia Business and Economic Conditions
196. Illinois Business Review
206. Indiana Business Review
227. International Regional Science Review
301. Journal of Regional Science
314. Kentucky Economy: Review and Perspective
331. Louisiana Business Review
347. Montana Business Quarterly
357. Nevada Review of Business and Economics
358. The New England Journal of Business and Economics
365. Northern California Review of Business and Economics
378. Pennsylvania Business Survey
398. Regional Science Perspectives
412. Review of Regional Economics and Business
413. The Review of Regional Studies
427. South Dakota Business Review
431. Southwest Journal of Business and Economics
432. The Southwestern Review of Management and Economics
436. Survey of Business
445. Utah Economic and Business Review

About the Compilers

BEATRICE SICHEL is a librarian at Western Michigan University.
WERNER SICHEL is an economist at Western Michigan University.